M000279384

BRADY'S BOOK OF
FIXED STARS

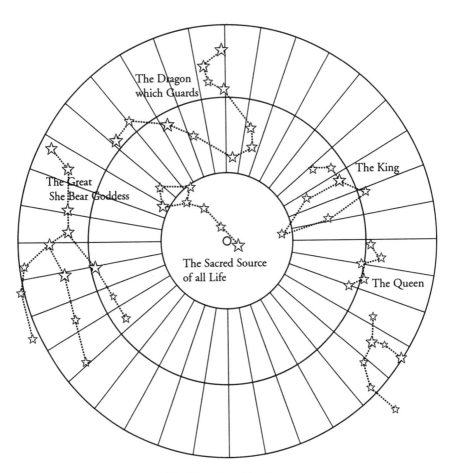

The Dragon
which Guards

The Great
She Bear Goddess

The King

The Sacred Source
of all Life

The Queen

The First Rose Window

BRADY'S BOOK OF
FIXED STARS

BERNADETTE BRADY

SAMUEL WEISER, INC.

York Beach, Maine

First published in 1998 by
Samuel Weiser, Inc.
Box 612
York Beach, ME 03910–0612

Library of Congress Cataloging-in-Publication Data

Brady, Bernadette
    [Book of fixed stars]
    Brady's book of fixed stars / Bernadette Brady.
        p.   cm.
    Includes bibliographical references and index.
    1. Astrology.   I. Title.
    BF1708.1.B66   1998
    133.5—dc21   97–51492
                                                CIP

ISBN 0–87728–886–0   (hardcover)
ISBN 1–57863–105–X   (paper)

MV

Typeset in 11 point Garamond
Cover art by Ray Rue

Printed in the United States of America

04 03 02 01 00 99 98
10 9 8 7 6 5 4 3 2 1

The paper used in this publication meets the minimum requirements
of the American National Standard for Permanence of Paper for
Printed Library Materials Z39.48–1984.

To Darrelyn

CONTENTS

CHARTS

FIGURES

PARAN MAPS

STAR MAPS

ACKNOWLEDGMENTS

My thanks go to my long-time friend, Gillian Helfgott, who introduced me to the world of fixed stars and filled me with raw enthusiasm for the subject. Many years later she made her home, deep in the rain forest of New South Wales, available for me to begin the journey of this book.

In my search through ancient literature two lights shone through the dust of time. These are the works of Aratus in the fourth century B.C.E., and some seven hundred years later, the work of an author whose name is lost to us, known simply as Anonymous of 379. These two authors showed me the pathway to travel.

No astrologer works alone, and during the many years of developing this material and writing this book, the South Australian community of astrologers (students and colleagues) have provided me with valuable, untiring, patient, and continual support.

Part 1

IN THE BEGINNING

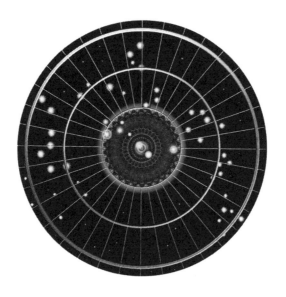

INTRODUCTION

TO UNDERSTAND THE IMPORTANCE OF fixed stars and constellations in astrology, one must return to the dawn of time and the original role that stars played in human lives.

Before time was conceived by the human mind, all was considered perfect. The world was seen as hanging by a thread from the great, immortal, never-setting point, the North Pole Star. Seasons came and seasons went and nothing changed. This was the Golden Age, the age of perfection, the age of the immortal goddess, when the cosmos and all that was divine was regarded as perfect and in complete harmony. The polestar, with the heavens rotating around it every night, was seen as a great mill churning out gold and wealth, the source of all life and all order, the point of stillness around which all other things moved.[1] Aeons later the Greeks called this point the *Omphaloessa*, coming from the word *omphalos* meaning the center of things. In Latin this is translated as *umbilicus* from which we gain the word *umbilical*. The pole was the Earth's umbilical cord and all power, all strength, and all divinity came from this point. The Babylonians called it the "Mother Bond of Heaven." This connection from the point of stillness to the Earth was seen in some cultures as a pole or axis, a shaft around which the golden millstone turned. Other cultures considered it to be a Cosmic Tree,[2] the Tree of Life of the Garden of Eden,[3] or a measuring rod.

Ancient societies structured themselves around the omphalos in an attempt to mirror on Earth the immortal life of the heavens, the goddess, and the Mother of the World. Since all power was believed to come from the pole, the Cosmic Center, it therefore followed that the power, authority, and wisdom to rule could be achieved by occupying the physical center of the tribe or group. Thus the center position belonged to the king, queen, or chief. This leader sat on a particular rock or stood beside a particular tree and claimed the power of the celestial pole by holding a staff or rod that symbolized the pole or shaft of the sacred mill. Later, this pole became the Royal or Holy Scepter, as well as the Sacred Sword of the Celts. This philosophy of divine power that came from the center was echoed at all levels of human society, from the very physical seat of government or throne to the central fireplace in every home.

The Celts called their centers *Thing* or *Ting*,[4] a word still present in many place names throughout the United Kingdom—Thingwall near Liverpool, Ting-

---

[1] G. de Santillana and Hertha von Dechend, *Hamlet's Mill* (Boston: Nonpareil Books, 1977), p. 3.
[2] John Mitchell, *At the Center of the World* (London: Thames & Hudson, 1994), p. 24.
[3] De Santillana and von Dechend, *Hamlet's Mill*, p. 223.
[4] Mitchell, *At the Center of the World*, p. 24.

ley near Leeds, and Tingrith in Bedfordshire, to name just a few—indicating that these places were considered to be the center of government and law of those areas. This word is also used in Icelandic societies whose system of central government was called the *Al-thing*. We use the phrase "the center of government" when referring to capital cities, only now we no longer place these capitals in the physical center of our countries. Ancient societies, however, believed that from such a position they held the divine power to rule the country, province, tribal grounds, farm, or household. Thus the center of tribal lands was always marked with rocks or standing stones. These stones, later symbolized by a flagpole, were protected in battle at all cost, for the center was the heart of the tribe and soul of the people. Indeed, one of the many prehistoric sites which reflect this is Stonehenge, placed equidistant from Land's End in Cornwall, Holyhead in Wales, and the northeast extremity of the Norfolk coast, indicating that it was an omphalos for the Celtic Druidic world and therefore a point of power and authority.[5]

Plato, in his quest for the perfect human society, expressed this omphalic philosophy in his *Laws*, Book 5, where he designed what he considered to be the perfect society and city, a city where all humans would live in perfect harmony and order. This city was designed in such a way that all roads, buildings, and the like moved out from the center. Like ancient cultures before him, he believed that when society was in tune with the immortal center, the world would return to the Golden Age; that to return to such omphalic tenets would re-create human life in perfect order.

This obsession with the omphalos of a culture or its people and its representation through all levels of society remains deep inside our collective psyche. We still seek the center of our countries, just like our ancient ancestors, but without knowing or understanding our motives. In 1988, when Australia celebrated 200 years of white settlement, one of the projects undertaken was to find the center of the country. It took many months of work, but the point was found: a place in the Northern Territory at Latitude 25°36'36.4" South and Longitude 134°21'17.3" East. A flagpole, an exact replica of the flagpole on Parliament House in Canberra, the Australian center of government, was erected on this desert site. Here are instinctual omphalic behavior patterns emerging in modern humans, as they attempt, for reasons they themselves do not understand, to transmit the source of power of the country, its center, to its seat of government. In the United States, at a point in Lebanon, Kansas, Latitude 39°50' North and Longitude 98°35' West, stands a stone monument from which a flagpole flies the Stars and Stripes.[6] This is the geographical center of the USA (not including Alaska and Hawaii). There are many such sites in many countries. In the UK this

---

[5] Mitchell, *At the Center of the World*, p. 41.
[6] Mitchell, *At the Center of the World*, p. 30.

site is guarded and marked by an oak tree, the Midland Oak at Lillington, near Leamington Spa, Warwickshire. This tree died just after the Second World War and was then replaced by an oak sapling from the original stock.[7] The Cosmic Tree, instead of a flagpole.

This external seeking is a reflex based on earlier tendencies and is now most commonly seen or recognized in personal, internal spiritual journeys where we seek the center of our own minds. Plato was not in error in his beliefs, for we do try to find our own centers in order to become whole. In the deep folds of our mind we still consider centeredness as stillness, centeredness as sacred, centeredness as enlightenment or the Golden Age. We do not seek the edge of our minds, like explorers in space moving away from planet Earth or Columbus crossing the great ocean. In personal journeys, we seek the center. Our concepts of immortality, enlightenment, and the individual's spiritual journey have been born from this omphalic beginning, this pole-centered heaven where all things moved around the sacred point of stillness. This was the first great impact that the constellations, the fixed stars, and the night sky had on the human mind: a primary philosophy that is so unconscious in the collective that it is generally unnamed and unrecognized, yet so strong it has formed the very foundation of our minds.

So, in this early human world where the polar regions, the central point of stillness of the starry sky, were duplicated physically in human life and in the human mind, the Earth was considered the plane between four gateways to the otherworld or afterlife. These four gateways were the points of the solar year, the two equinoxes and the two solstices,[8] which were held by the four mutable signs: Sagittarius and Gemini, the equinox points; Virgo and Pisces, the solstice points.

The Sun moved along a golden road which we now know as the Milky Way and eventually settled onto the ecliptic, spending half the year in Gemini to Sagittarius, above the Earth giving light and warmth, and the other half in Sagittarius to Gemini, below the Earth in the great ocean, giving way to a period of cold and dark. In modern terminology, these were the two periods of northern or southern declination, respectively. The afterlife began with a journey on the Milky Way, the road or path which dipped below the ocean toward the other pole, the South Pole.

This perfect world was created and given life by the goddess at the sacred pole and maintained in its seasonal rhythm by the god who rose with the Sun on the morning of the spring equinox. This god rode the chariot or boat of the Sun and gave humanity the seasons and thereby the ring of life. Each year was measured by his rising. He was mythically connected to the goddess at the pole, and

---

[7] Mitchell, *At the Center of the World,* p. 123.
[8] De Santillana and von Dechend, *Hamlet's Mill,* pp. 62–3.

the two ruled the world in complete harmony. The Egyptians called him Horus/Osiris[9]; he is known today as the constellation Orion.

However, as the effects of precession slowly broke this union of balance and harmony between god and goddess, society believed that the world was coming undone and that a great crisis had occurred. The Greeks said that Zeus angrily banged the tabletop of the heavens, tilting the table, and talked of Zeus battling the Titans to overthrow the world order. The Celts said that Arthur pulled the Sacred Sword from the stone like his earlier counterpart, the nine-year-old hero, Kara Par, of Turkey, who was able to lift and extract the central copper rod from the Earth's navel or mill.[10] The Egyptians claimed that Osiris's brother, Set, attacked and killed him. In Christian mythology a snake (Draco) appeared in the Tree of Life at the center of the Garden of Eden (the pole). Whatever the story, and there are many, the Golden Mill fell to earth, landed in the oceans of the sky, and created a whirlpool. Until this moment, the world had been pinned at the polestar, keeping this great axis in place.[11] In the crisis, this axis was knocked from its groove. The pole shifted focus to another star and the world became undone.

The whirlpool created by the falling mill is talked about in many myths, from the myth of Gilgamesh, to the world of the magical fish of the Celts, where one is lost in the world of water in order to gain wisdom, to the Greek myth of Hephaestus being cast from Olympus into the ocean.[12] The whirlpool was located at the tip of the constellation Orion, at the point occupied by the fixed star Rigel, the foot of Orion, the point which "slipped" into the great starry ocean. The "whirlpool" was and still is the intersection of the ecliptic with the equator. The effect of precession is that constellations seem to slip slowly against the seasons, so stars that rise with the spring equinox in one period of time will, over thousands of years, appear to slip southward. Visually, then, Orion slowly sank into the sea. Less and less of him appeared from one equinox to another. He had been ripped away from the union with Ursa Minor, separated from the immortal mother goddess and subjected to the whirlpool of the ecliptic where he underwent death and eventual rebirth. The whirlpool and its ceaseless churning cycle began to swallow all the gods, the zodiac, one after another. Precession had begun.

Time began in human consciousness when we realized that the equator and the ecliptic were separate. One solar journey was no longer like the others before it, and there was a larger cycle where immortal gods died, slipped into the sea,

---

[9] Gertrude and James Jobes, *Outer Space: Myths, Name Meanings, Calendars* (New York: Scarecrow Press, 1964), p. 219.

[10] De Santillana and von Dechend, *Hamlet's Mill*, p. 235.

[11] De Santillana and von Dechend, *Hamlet's Mill*, p. 141.

[12] Pierre Grimal, *The Dictionary of Classical Mythology*, trans. A. R. Maxwell-Hyslop (Oxford, England: Blackwell Reference, 1986), p. 191.

traveled on a boat, and then moved into the underworld. Gods could now die. History had started and the Golden Age had ended. The Greeks tell us that the goddess Virgo, in distress at the end of the Golden Age, left humankind forever and returned to the heavens.[13] This is the mythic story of the historical demise of the constellation Virgo from her place in the summer solstice.

At such times of transition from one world order to the next, symbolized and heralded by one constellation entering the whirlpool and slipping into southern declinations, another taking its place on the spring equinox, the old world order is said to be "flooded."[14] This was reflected in all the many diverse stories of great floods and deluges. The Greeks told the story of Deucalion, who seems to be a classical version of the biblical Noah. In Babylon it was the story of Utnapishtim, another Noah-like figure dealing with a great flood caused by the anger of Ea, the god of the waters. The native Hawaiians also talk of a flood called *Kai-a-ka-hina-li'I*, translated as "Sea that made the chiefs fall down."[15] In reality, these "floods" are mythology's record of prehistorical cosmic floods.

The Bible (Isa. 14:12) also tells us that Lucifer is cast out by God and falls to hell. Lucifer is the Lord of Light and is identified by some with Venus, as an evening star, and with Castor, the alpha star of Gemini. This constellation, along with Orion, slipped into the waters of the underworld. So Lucifer appeared to be cast into hell but was actually cast into the whirlpool. In the same way, Adam and Eve were cast out from the Garden of Eden when the devil, Draco, appeared in the Tree of Life in the center of the Garden, the North Pole. This was the end of the Golden Era: Paradise Lost.

Religions which contained the concepts of life, death, and rebirth emerged in the human psyche to embody the evidence of our eyes.[16] The pole, the female divine goddess, was still immortal since she never set, but now the axis was tilted and male divine gods were subject to a cycle of life, death, and rebirth. In Egyptian mythology, Osiris died (Gemini/Orion having slipped from the equinox) to become the ruler of the underworld, passing his throne to his son Horus (Taurus as the new equinox sign).[17] Horus, when he, too, slipped into the sea, passed his throne to Amen-Ra, a god known by the Egyptians as "King of the Gods." This signified Aries coming to the equinox. The emerging Greek culture gave this title of "King of the Gods" to Zeus, their Aries god. Two thousand years later when Zeus sensed the end of his time, he desperately needed to create an heir. This he

---

[13] A. W. and G. R. Mair (trans.), *Callimachus, Lycophron, Aratus* (Cambridge: Harvard University Press, 1989), p. 215.

[14] De Santillana and von Dechend, *Hamlet's Mill,* p. 59.

[15] J. F. Bierlein, *Parallel Myths* (New York: Ballantine, 1994), p. 127.

[16] Jane B. Sellers, *The Death of the Gods in Ancient Egypt* (London: Penguin, 1992), p. 123.

[17] Sellers, *The Death of the Gods in Ancient Egypt,* p. 123.

did via the human Semele. Thus was Dionysus born, the new god of a new world order, with Pisces ruling the equinox point. Dionysus, like the gods before him, also needs to have an heir. Indeed in our time Pisces is nearly totally submerged in the whirlpool and Dionysus (Christ) has left not an heir, but only the vague promise of a Second Coming.

Thus our ancient instincts tell our modern minds that the world is out of balance. Science, which took us away from the sky and its philosophies of centeredness, now embraces the Big Bang theory, in which all things start from a common source or center, time and space not existing until that hypothetical explosion.[18] Science has come full circle. Once pulling us away from the concept of a cycle and connectedness, it now turns toward finding its great central tenet, the logical extension of the Big Bang Theory, the Unified Field Theory in which all things will be one.

The recognition of precession acted like a seed in the collective mind, an unanswered question of "why" and "how," which pushed us into the world of science and logic. From this point on we questioned our world, and as a result began to lose our innocence and naiveté. We started to move away from the Mother's cradle and the safety of the circumpolar life. Cycles were devalued and the goddess and the cyclic, biological lives of women became less significant. Yet before we lost sight of this nightly centeredness, the pole, our mind had been created in its image, created from the apparent order of circumpolar life. And so, like migrating birds, we are driven till the end of time to strive towards perfect centeredness. It was the first drum beat we heard as we became humans and it still beats, maybe not the loudest but definitely with the greatest vibration.

In the words of Giorgio de Santillana and Hertha von Dechend, astrologers are those who have "speculated on the traditional systems of the world, and made use of whatever there was of astronomy, geography, mythology, holy text of laws of time and change, to build up an ambitious system."[19] As astrologers we should therefore extrapolate and learn from these world myths, scientific facts, and observations of the human psyche, and begin to conclude that the starry sky—with its constellations and fixed stars—could possibly be the very model for the formation of the human mind. And if we did reach that type of conclusion, then we would be inclined to reinstate fixed stars into our planet-driven astrology, making them a central tenet rather than a discarded fragment at the bottom of a psychological melting pot. We could put the "astro" back into astrology. In a way, each human mind can be viewed as a starry sky centered around the sacred pole of one's own center, one's own point of stillness.

---

[18] Stephen W. Hawking, *A Brief History of Time* (New York: Bantam, 1988), p. 9.
[19] De Santillana and von Dechend, *Hamlet's Mill*, p. 228.

But the impact of the heavens as the model for the formation of the human mind goes beyond the polar regions. For the whole starry sky was a canvas on which ancient people painted their myths, stories, oral history, and religion, while at the same time providing a model for their tribal structures. People watched and named the bright stars from the North Pole to as far south as one could see, and on this canvas myths could live forever. The starry sky became a great picture book unraveling its stories every night as people sat around their fires. These stories of the sky were carried by migration waves from one culture to another, so that by the beginning of time, the time of the great mythological loss of perfection which was the dawn of history, the sky was filled with many stories shared by many cultures whose origins had already been lost in the delicate fabric of oral history.

The night sky was a great cosmic book which fulfilled a need for these people. It was the original cathedral, or temple, a holder or a visual display of their morals, religion, and lifestyle. It showed them their place in the cosmos and gave surety to them in an uncertain world. It was the abode of the divine. Aeons later, Christians mimicked this sky full of stories by building great cathedrals, with their vaulted, lofty arches filled with colored glass to represent the Christian myths. Cathedrals were the books of the people, containing the stories of their myths and religion, and the rose window in every cathedral symbolized the sacred celestial pole, its holiness indicated by its prestigious placement. Instead of stars there was stained glass.

THE BACKGROUND TO THE ASTROLOGICAL DECLINE OF FIXED STARS

As soon as precession was recognized, it acted as a catalyst on the human mind. The puzzle of it teased the human mind into awareness, logic, numbers, maths, and eventually science. This puzzle that longed to be solved concerned the nature and rate of movement of precession. By the time of Ptolemy (100–173 C.E., approximately) the question was still largely unanswered and so attracted a great deal of his attention.

Ptolemy was primarily an astronomer. He was really more interested in the mathematics of the sky than its symbolic meaning. His main logistical problem was that two sets of data were required to answer the question on precession: the accurate position of stars for one period in time; and the position of the same list of stars, measured for a later period. By comparing the two lists and knowing the time period between the two, the rate of precession could be found.

The method of locating a star in the sky, in use by the early astronomers before Ptolemy, was to note the date and time of lunar cycles, along with the Moon's degree of longitude and latitude, then to mark its orientation to a star. This was a cumbersome method which the following excerpt from Ptolemy's *Almagest* describes:

> Again, Timnicharis says he observed in Alexandria that in the year 36 of the First Callippic Period exactly at the beginning of the tenth hour, the moon appeared to overtake with its northern arc the northern star of those in the Scorpion's forehead. And this date is the year 454 of Navonassar, Egyptian wise Phaophi 16–17, 3 seasonal hours after midnight and 3 2/5 equatorian hours, because the sun was 26° within the Archer, but 3 1/6 hours with respect to regular solar days. At that hour the true position of the Moon's centre was 31 1/4° from the autumn equinox and 1 1/3° north of the ecliptic.[20]

Ptolemy proceeded to repeat the situation, found the position of a particular lunation for his current date, and then calculated the star's movement. But it was tedious and not all that accurate, so Ptolemy decided to develop a better system of recording the position of stars. His logic was that if he could clearly lay down a technique for measuring stars and use that technique for measuring "as many stars as we could up to those of the sixth magnitude,"[21] then he could produce a list of stars that could be used by future generations of astronomers to check his estimates of the rate of precession.

His method was simple. He first developed an instrument which would enable him to make the measurements needed. He found the poles of the ecliptic and then he projected every star onto the ecliptic via the lines of longitude from these poles. The point where the projected star cut the ecliptic was carefully measured, as well as the star's latitude north or south of the ecliptic. He measured 1022 stars and published this list in his *Almagest.*

It was an ingenious system. It meant that the position of a star could be accurately and simply recorded. It could be reproduced in years to come so that any change in the ecliptical position of the star could be easily noted. It was a huge advancement for astronomers and placed Ptolemy among the giants of astronomy. However, it seems to have altered the way in which astrology worked with fixed stars. Until that time the evidence suggests that the predominant method for working with stars in astrology was via their risings, culminations, and set-

---

[20] Claudius Ptolemy, *The Almagest* (Chicago: Britannica, Great Books of the World, 1985), p. 232.
[21] *The Almagest*, p. 233.

tings.[22] However, within several hundred years, astrologers had taken Ptolemy's convenient list of stars with their ecliptical degrees and were applying it to their trade, forsaking the more tedious, older methodologies. Ptolemy had developed the list as an astronomer, for astronomical needs. He was, after all, an astronomer, and the book where he published this listing was not his book on astrology, *Tetrabiblos*, but his great astronomical work, *The Almagest*. Later astrologers, however, swayed by the eminence of his name, chose to use Ptolemy's star list of ecliptical projected degrees as the preferred methodology for working with fixed stars astrologically.

This was a slow transition, for in 379 C.E., "The Treatise on Bright Fixed Stars," written by an unknown author,[23] talks of using stars which are close to the ecliptic in the above fashion but uses stars that are away from the ecliptic to work with the "pivot points"[24] of the chart. This is known today as working in parans.

The projected ecliptical degrees (called PED in this text) of Ptolemy were based on the poles of the ecliptic. His list of 1022 stars and their PED were then precessed through the ages, with each generation of astrologers adding the current rate of precession to find the current ecliptical position of any star in their time. Ptolemy's star catalog was used in this manner for well over a thousand years until the time of Ulugh Beg (1394–1449), a Mongolian-Turkish ruler and astronomer who developed the Fahkri sextant, and that of Regiomontanus (1436–1476). These two astronomers re-plotted all of Ptolemy's star catalog, which laid the foundation for Albrecht Dürer (1471–1528) to produce star maps based on the poles of the equator (rather than in the manner of Ptolemy who based his measurements on the poles of the ecliptic.[25] (See figure 1, p. 12). Using this new method of projection, each of the 1022 stars of Ptolemy's list was given a new ecliptical position. The astrologers at the time of Ulugh Beg and Regiomontanus seemed to accept this change in the position of the fixed stars without question. Since that day, astrologers and astronomers alike have used the poles of the equator rather than that of the ecliptic for all such projections.[26] So, first the astrological world accepted Ptolemy's astronomical work, which in turn

---

[22] According to the writings of Ptolemy and those of Anonymous of 379.

[23] Anonymous of 379. See *The Treatise on the Bright Fixed Stars*, trans. Robert Schmidt (Berkeley Springs, WV: Golden Hind Press, 1994), p. 379.

[24] Ascendant, Descendant, MC, and IC.

[25] Tomas J. Filsinger, *Manual Notes and Tables for the Map of the Universe* (Berkeley: Celestial Arts, 1988), p. 2.

[26] For astrologers who prefer to work with the system of projected degrees for fixed stars, I have included in Appendix E a list of 176 stars with the 2,000 C.E. position given for Ptolemy's method of projection, versus the method used currently by astrologers. Astrologers may find it interesting to work in the original projection system rather than the one devised by later astronomers.

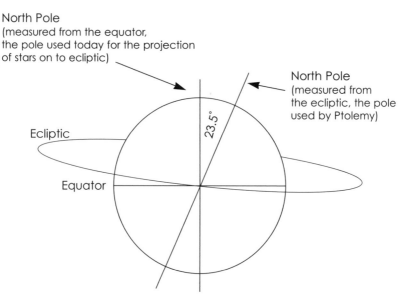

North Pole
(measured from the equator,
the pole used today for the projection
of stars on to ecliptic)

North Pole
(measured from
the ecliptic, the pole
used by Ptolemy)

Ecliptic

23.5°

Equator

Figure 1. The poles of the ecliptic versus the poles of the equator.

led to the decline in the use of the older system of parans. And if that was a valid step to take, then we have to question why the astrological community accepted the work done by Ulugh Beg, for it changed the ecliptical position of every fixed star recorded by Ptolemy.

If an astrologer works with a star's projected ecliptical degree, when a star is in the same degree as the Ascendant for a particular chart, it bears no visual connection to the actual location of the star. The star may have risen hours earlier or may not be due to rise for some hours to come.

In figure 2 (p. 13) the shaded area is the plane of the horizon. The figure shows the star Hamal, the alpha star of Aries, rising on the horizon. If you look at the ecliptical degree on the Ascendant at the time that Hamal is rising, it is 24° Pisces. So, for that particular location, Hamal will always rise with 24° Pisces. However, if you can imagine a line drawn from one celestial pole to the other,[27] (the dashed line in the figure), and have that line pass through Hamal, it will cut the ecliptic at 5° Taurus. So Hamal's PED would be 5° Taurus. Now if we say that Hamal's PED is 5° Taurus and accept that as the position for Hamal, we could, by mistake, actually imply that the star is physically at 5° Taurus, when in truth this is just a mathematical concept. For when 5° Taurus eventually does rise

---

[27] The modern method of projection and now the only pole used for such projections.

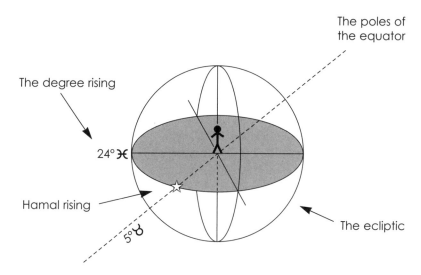

Figure 2. The possible position of a star when its projected degree is rising.

at that location, Hamal, which co-rises with 24° Pisces, would have long since left the horizon and be quite high in the sky.

Thus, although Hamal may be projected back to 5° Taurus, it also has another ecliptical position which is based on the degree in which it co-rises. This new position varies from latitude to latitude and in this example links Hamal with 24° Pisces. This question of what degree a star co-rises at is an example of the older method of parans.

PTOLEMY'S OTHER CONTRIBUTION
TO THE HISTORY OF FIXED STARS IN ASTROLOGY

Ptolemy is also renowned for linking the energy of each fixed star to a combination of planetary energies. He published this work in the *Tetrabiblos*, chapter 9, where he makes such statements as: "The stars in the head of Aries possess an influence similar in its effect to that of Mars and Saturn."[28] It is important to think about what Ptolemy was trying to achieve by linking each star to a combination of planets. In the *Timaeus*, Plato talks of the creator, the Demiurge, making the human soul in the same manner as the Soul of the Universe, and that the number of these souls is the number of the fixed stars. Based on this, the "wandering stars," or planets, were singled out as the time keepers, and it was thought that

---

[28] *Ptolemy's Tetrabiblos,* J. M. Ashmand, trans. (London: Foulsham, 1917), p. 24.

the souls moved from fixed stars to the wanderers, their power thereby translated into the souls of men.[29]

Thus Ptolemy, who would have been familiar with the work of Plato, would have felt it was proper and correct to translate the mythological impact and meaning of every fixed star into a planetary combination. The purpose here was not to ignore the fixed stars mythologically but to seek their possible planetary power, hinted at by Plato. However, as time passed, it seems that these planetary meanings took center stage, with astrologers losing or forgetting the once great stories, morals, and life lessons woven around each star. So the combination of all these factors—the use of projected ecliptical degrees for the stars, their later modification by Ulugh Beg and Regiomontanus, and the loss of many of their original meanings by their reduction to planetary expressions—has meant that fixed stars have lost their central place of importance in astrology.

As astrologers abandoned the constellations, no longer observing and taking note of their rising and setting, the images and stories preserved in the starry sky disintegrated. The sky was left open to astronomers who, having no love for the shape of the heavens, proceeded to place their world on the skies and to carve ancient and beautiful constellations into smaller groups to suit their purpose. The Great She-Bear goddess protector of all life, the celestial north pole, became the Big Dipper. Orion, god on the equator, became a saucepan or a tea pot. Argo, the great ship of the south originally used by the Egyptian pharaohs for their journeys to the underworld, became a broken wreck drifting around the South Pole. The starry sky, the *very model* for the formation of the individual human psyche and the collective's theology, was eventually discarded even by the people who sought to study humans and events via their relationship to the cosmos. Astrology seems to have lost contact with that which is the very central tenet of our art.

---

[29] De Santillana and von Dechend, *Hamlet's Mill,* p. 307.

PARANS: THE FOUNDATIONS

IN RECONSTRUCTING THE WAY IN WHICH the sky and stars were possibly used in astrology, we cannot simply search out the original stories and meanings and apply modern techniques to their use. The first important step is to understand the original methodologies that were used by our ancient predecessors.

As already mentioned, the mathematical system used by the ancient star gazers is what is called parans. It is a simple concept. Imagine that you have a 360° clear view of the horizon and let it be a starry night. If you look eastward you will see stars rising. They will be rising on half the circle of the horizon, not just due east. As you watch a star that is rising northeast of you, there may be, at the same time, another star in the southeast also rising. The two stars rising simultaneously are said to have a paran relationship (see figure 3, below), aspected by the horizon line which is the straight line that joins the stars together. Similarly, a star may be rising as a star is setting. These two stars are also in paran relationship.

So if you are watching the Moon rise and just as the Moon cuts the horizon[30] you notice that a bright star in the southeast is also rising, then the Moon is said to be in paran with that star. They are connected by the horizon line. The same situation could occur with a bright star setting in the northwest. The Moon would still be in paran to that star. See figure 4 (p. 16).

The important point is that the full circle of the horizon is used, not just the eastern and western points of the ecliptic. Stonehenge in England is a monu-

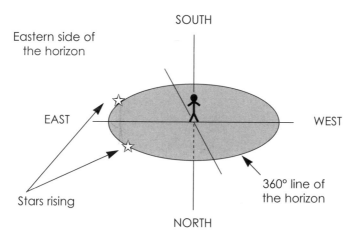

Figure 3. Two stars on the eastern horizon at the same time.

---

[30] This would be known as apparent rising.

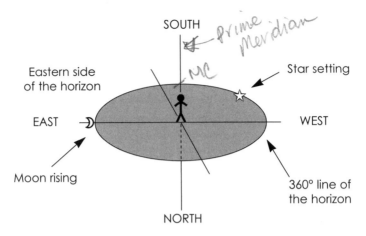

Figure 4. Moon rising as star sets.

ment that supports the use of the full circle of the horizon. If the stars on or near the ecliptic were the only ones used and the rest of the sky was ignored, then Stonehenge would have been two parallel cross beams of stone rather than the full circle that it is. The existence of this structure, in other words, means that the pre-Druidic people of England were working with parans.

Another very obvious feature of the sky is the culmination point. If you face either south or north and imagine a line passing directly overhead cutting the sky in two, you will be imagining what is called the prime meridian. Where this line cuts the ecliptic is the current MC, or Midheaven. Stars anywhere along this line are culminating, reaching the top of their rising arc, and are about to start traveling down toward the western horizon. In figure 5 (p. 17), stars A and B are both culminating but star B is at a higher altitude than A.

The culminating point adds another possible paran placement. You may notice the Moon culminating just as a bright star is setting or rising. If this were the case, then the Moon would be in paran to this star. See figure 6 (p. 17). Similarly, it may be that a star to the north of you is culminating as a star in the southeast is rising. These two stars would be in paran.

There are four points where parans can occur:

- The rising side of the horizon circle
- The setting side of the horizon circle
- The upper part on the prime meridian, or "culminating"
- The part opposite this below the horizon, or "on the nadir"

If a star or a planet is on any of these four points at the same time as a star or a planet is on the same point or any of the other three points, then those two planets or stars are in paran.

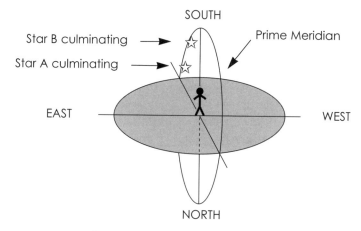

Figure 5. Two stars culminating.

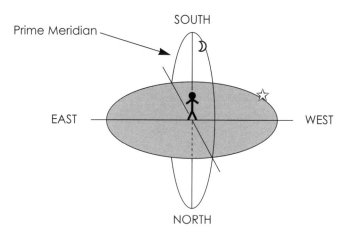

Figure 6. Moon culminating while a star is setting.

THE LOCATION OF THE OBSERVER

For a particular location, the same stars will be in paran with each other.[31] However, as the latitude changes, so the circle of the horizon line changes its orientation to the stars. So a star at one latitude might rise at the same time as Venus, but at another latitude, on the same day, the star may have already risen or still be below the horizon when Venus rises.

---

[31] Precession does affect this as it alters the declination of a star so that, over a thousand years, stars that were once in paran will most likely no longer have this relationship at that particular location.

For example, using Castor, the alpha star of Gemini, one of the Twins, if an observer is at a latitude of 40° North, Castor will be seen to rise when the rising degree on the Ascendant is 10° Cancer (see figure 7). For that particular location, then, every time that 10° Cancer is on the Ascendant, Castor will be rising. If a birth chart for that location had Venus at 10° Cancer, then Castor and Venus would be in paran, both rising together. Venus would be on the ecliptic and Castor would be further along the horizon to the north.

However, if on the same day Venus was still at 10° Cancer but the observer had moved to 20° North, then Castor would be rising as the degree on the Ascendant was 17° Cancer. Therefore, Venus would have risen approximately thirty minutes earlier than Castor and the two would not be in paran. See figure 8.

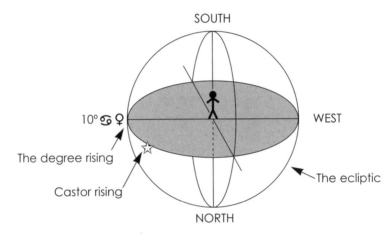

Figure 7. Castor rising at a latitude of 40° North.

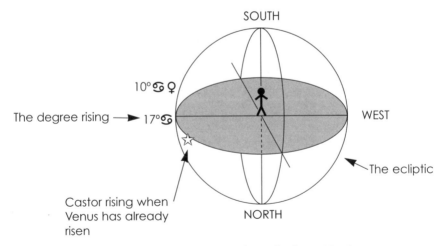

Figure 8. Castor rising at a latitude of 20° North.

The situation would develop further that same day if Venus was still at 10° Cancer, and the observer was now at latitude 30° South, for Castor would be rising when the Ascendant was 29° Cancer and Venus would have risen over an hour earlier. See figure 9, below.

Thus, in terms of a birth chart, a person born at a latitude of 40° North would have a Venus-Castor paran connection, whereas those born at the other two latitudes would not. Parans are very location specific.

Now, Castor is actually located in the heavens very close to the ecliptic—as it belongs to the zodiac constellation of Gemini. However, even with this star there is a range of 20° in co-rising with Cancer from 40° North to 30° South. If we increased this range of latitude to cover Scotland south to Tasmania, then the differences are even greater. Castor will co-rise with 6° Cancer in Scotland but will not rise until 20° Leo in Tasmania.

The further a star is from the ecliptic, the greater will be this range. But even with stars of the zodiac signs, as is the case with Castor, this range is well beyond even the most generous of orbs. It is this very location-sensitive situation that motivated the earlier astrologers to move away from the use of parans.

Parans' sensitivity to location makes it necessary to create graphs of co-rising/-setting degrees for each star plotted against latitude.[32] These graphs or "maps," are given in this book with all the major stars. The maps show the changes of rising and setting ecliptical degrees against latitude.

Figure 10 (p. 20) is the paran map for Castor. The vertical axes are the degrees of the ecliptic with the left side being degrees of longitude and the right side zodiacal degrees. The horizontal axis is the latitude of birth of the observer.

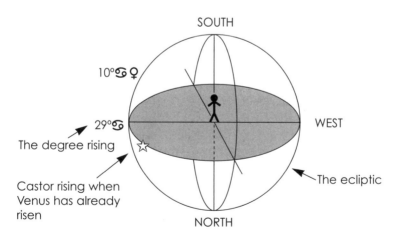

Figure 9. Castor rising at a latitude of 30° South.

---

[32] Shifts in longitude along the same parallel of latitude do not affect parans.

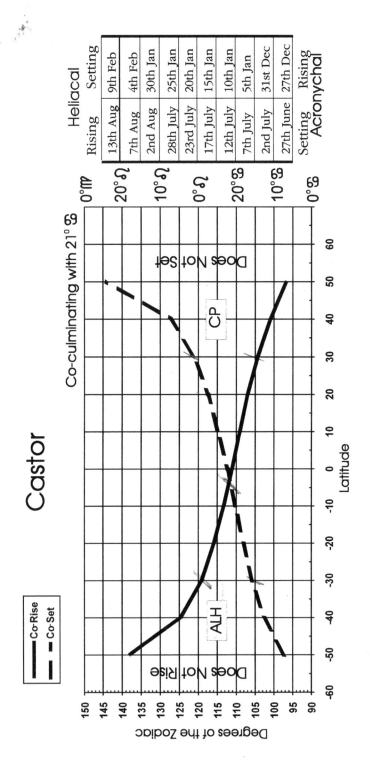

Heliacal		Acronychal	
Rising	Setting	Setting	Rising
13th Aug	9th Feb		
7th Aug	4th Feb		
2nd Aug	30th Jan		
28th July	25th Jan		
23rd July	20th Jan		
17th July	15th Jan		
12th July	10th Jan		
7th July	5th Jan		
2nd July	31st Dec		
27th June	27th Dec		

Figure 10. Paran map of Castor.

Negative latitudes are south and positive latitudes are north. (The tables of dates labeled Heliacal, Acronychal, and so on, are discussed in the section on Star Phases.) There are two curving lines on the map: the dashed line is the degree on the ecliptic at which the star will be co-setting, and the solid line is the degree at which the star will be co-rising.

We can check the earlier example for Castor by looking at 40° North. Move up until the solid line is cut. You will notice that the right hand side of the vertical axis reads 10° Cancer. If you now look at 20° North the solid line is cut at just around 17° Cancer. Moving to 30° South (–30), you will notice that the solid line is cut at around 29° Cancer.

The map also shows that the degree on the ecliptic with which Castor co-rises is not necessarily the degree with which it will co-set. Look again at 40° North, with Castor's co-rising degree at 10° Cancer. If you now look up to the dashed line, it shows that Castor will co-set with about 7° Leo. Similarly, for the latitude of 30° South Castor is co-rising with 29° Cancer but will co-set with about 16° Cancer. This difference in rising and setting degrees is because the star is not on the ecliptic and thus transcribes a different arc in the sky to the sun.

On the top of each map is the degree with which the star will co-culminate. This is not affected by latitude changes, so no matter where you were born, if you have a planet at 21° Cancer you will have that planet co-culminating with Castor. Or if you have a planet at 21° Capricorn, then the planet will be on the Nadir as Castor culminates.

Each map covers a range of latitude from 60° North to 60° South, unless a star is no longer rising or setting. When this is the case, the map is marked accordingly, as is the case for Castor at latitudes higher than 50° North or South.

CHECKING A NATAL CHART
FOR A PARAN RELATIONSHIP TO A FIXED STAR

Continue with the example of Castor. If you were born at 30° North, you would find that Castor co-rises with 14° Cancer and co-sets with 2° Leo; it culminates at 21° Cancer and is therefore on the nadir at 21° Capricorn. If, in your natal chart, you have any planet around any of these four points, then that natal planet has a paran relationship to Castor. The mythology symbolized by Castor will be married to that natal planet in your chart and will be seeking expression in the journey of your life.

An important point to keep in mind is that the maps are most accurate if your natal planet is exactly on the ecliptic, that is to say, 0° of celestial latitude. Most planets do not stray too far from the ecliptic but Pluto can have quite a large celestial latitude. Any celestial latitude held by the natal planet will alter the exact degree that is rising or setting. Thus the maps are a guide only, for the most accurate method of working with parans is to acquire a computer program which will produce the information for you. Since 1986, mainstream astrological software has been available to produce paran printouts for fixed stars.[33]

At this stage one could be tempted to move straight into finding the paran relationship in a chart and working with the fixed star myths. However, astro-archaeology, like any other archaeological dig, is best done with patience and thoroughness.

USING ONLY VISIBLE STARS

If an observer is standing directly underneath the North Celestial Pole, the heavens will appear to rotate around the point directly overhead. So at the North Pole stars will not rise or set but simply travel around the rim of the horizon. See figure 11.

As the observer travels southward, the celestial pole seems to drop in the sky and stars that were out of sight on the southern side of the horizon now come into view. At a latitude of 50° North, the North Celestial Pole will be at an angle of 50⁰ to the observer, as shown in figure 12 (p. 23).

A lot more stars in the south are now going to be visible to the observer, and some stars that never set when closer to the pole now do so. The further

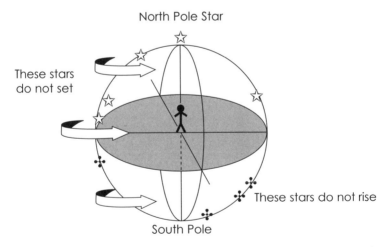

North Pole Star

These stars
do not set

These stars do not rise

South Pole

Figure 11. Diurnal movement of stars at the North Pole.

---

[33] I have used Solar Fire for Windows. Esoteric Technologies, Adelaide, Australia, 1996.

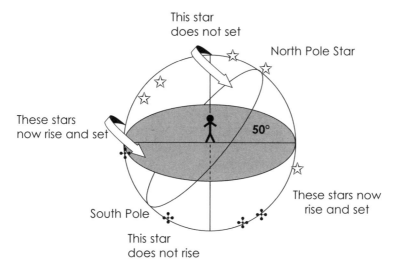

Figure 12. Diurnal movement of stars at latitude 50° North.

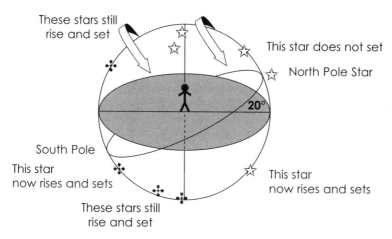

Figure 13. Diurnal movement of stars at latitude 20° North.

south the observer travels, the more southern stars will be seen, but to the north, stars that never set begin to dip below the horizon for just a short time. The further south the observer goes, the longer these northern stars stay below the horizon. See figure 13 (above).

By the time the observer reaches the equator, the North Celestial Pole, which was overhead at the beginning of this journey, is now sitting on the northern horizon, while the first glimpses of the South Celestial Pole are appearing on the southern horizon (see figure 14, p. 24).

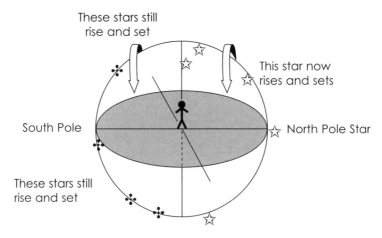

Figure 14. Diurnal movement of stars at the equator.

As the observer travels south from this point, the South Celestial Pole climbs higher and higher in the sky, its angle, to the observer, always equal to the degree of latitude of the observer. Northern hemisphere stars disappear while the southern sky is revealed (see figure 15, p. 25).

Therefore, at any given location, there will be some stars that never rise above the horizon and some stars that never set.[34] For example, there is a great and beautiful star called Canopus. It is in one of the rudders of the Argo, the huge ship that sails around the South Pole. Canopus was recognized by Ptolemy and other writers as one of the important stars. Yet in locations where it was not visible, it was not used. In *The Treatise on the Bright Fixed Stars* we read:

> For this reason, we set out the differences and actions of the bright and notable stars, excepting only Canopus, since it is quite southerly and almost does not appear in these parts, as my inquiry is being conducted in the zone through Rome.[35]

(Canopus in modern times is visible from latitudes south of 35° North and from 35° South it never sets.) This then, is a very important point: for a particular location or birth place, if a star is not able to rise and therefore will never be visible, it should not be used in the birth chart. To aid in this exercise, Appendix B is a

---

[34] This precise combination for a particular location is affected by precession. The ancients could see more of the southern sky from their locations than is visible now; indeed, the Southern Cross was last seen in Jerusalem around the time of the Crucifixion. But from one lifetime to the next, the effects are quite minimal.

[35] Anonymous of 379, *The Treatise on the Bright Fixed Stars*, p. 10.

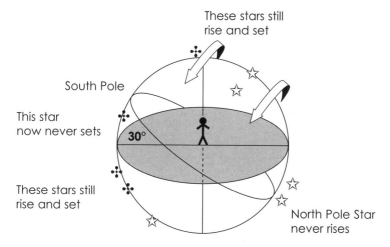

Figure 15. Diurnal movement of stars at latitude 30° South.

listing of all major stars in relationship to their rising or setting per latitude of observation. Also, after every star's paran map, you will find its effective range of latitudes. If the birth place is within the range given, then the star is going to be seen to rise and set on the line of the horizon, or never set.

Therefore, in reconstructing these methods the following points need to be taken into account:

- Stars that rise and set on the horizon (appearing on any of the four angles: rising, culminating, setting, or on the Nadir)
- Stars that never set are always in a phase of curtailed passage—see example of Toliman in figure 16, (p. 26)
- Stars that never rise (not used at all)

All of this information can be found by using the paran maps of each star. The following, figure 16, is the map for Toliman, Alpha Centaurus, which has a declination of 60° 49' South.

If you are at 30° South in latitude, this star will never set. It will transcribe a circle around the South Pole but will never touch the horizon line. Within that circle it will rise, culminate, set, and be on the Nadir of its own circle. If it is at one of those positions at the time when a planet is on one of the angles—rising, setting, culminating, or at the Nadir—then the planet and Toliman have a paran relationship. These stars that "rise" or "set" in their own circle around the pole, have an expression which is far more black and white than at latitudes where they can actually touch the horizon. Their pattern of motion is called *curtailed passage* and it is discussed in the section on Star Phases.

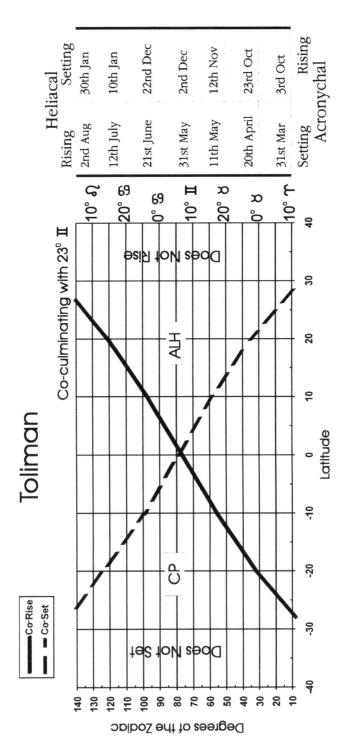

Figure 16. Paran map of Toliman.

Thus, in reconstructing the original techniques for working with fixed stars, one needs to first know how to work with parans, and then, secondly, fine tune this technique by using stars that were visible from the natal location, using them according to how they interacted with the angles.

Having established this method of working with and sorting the fixed stars, the next point to consider is the natal points or planets that form the relationships with fixed stars.

PLANETS AND ORBS

SINCE THE ANCIENT ASTROLOGICAL USE of fixed stars was a visually based system, for individual natal work one should only work with the planets that are visible and not the recently discovered planets of Uranus, Neptune, and Pluto. This also makes sense in terms of the generational nature of the outer planets. For example, if in London a particular star was rising with Neptune, or on any of the other angles, then that would be the case for all people born at that location while Neptune was at a particular degree. Since Neptune can stress a degree for over eighteen months, this would mean that all people born in London for a particular year would have Neptune linked with that star. Yet we can expand this group even more, for a star's co-rising and co-setting is not affected by terrestrial longitude. So the star would be linked not just to London births but to every other person born at the same latitude as London, right around the globe. There will always be some individuals whose Neptune will represent the collective and therefore their outer planets may well be linked to an interesting fixed star. But this is the exception and definitely not the rule.

The same visual rule applies to the Moon's Nodes. The early astrologers were well aware of the Nodes, yet they do not seem to be included in the writings on fixed stars. The Nodes are not a visual point. You do not enthusiastically point to the east on a summer's night and say, "Oh look! The Node is rising." So use the Nodes with caution, for they may or may not be sensitive to fixed stars on an angle.

ORBS AND YOUR HAND

Like every other area of astrology, the question of orbs also needs some consideration. Working in this visual system, the orbs can be measured using your hand. The distance of one degree in the sky is the width of one of your fingers held out at arm's length in front of your eye. It does not matter how thick or thin your finger is; the length of your arm helps to compensate for this variation. If you then hold your closed fist up to the sky, it will be covering a distance of around four degrees. If you then extend your little finger and your thumb as far as you can with your fist still clenched, that distance is about fifteen degrees. To summarize:

- One finger = 1°
- Closed fist = 4°
- Extended fist = 15°

If you use an orb of 1° to decide if a star and a planet are both on an angle, then this is a finger width either side of the angle. This is actually quite a large visual distance in the sky. The orb used for all the examples after major stars is half a finger, 30' of arc.

USING THE WHOLE DAY

When parans are being used, the whole twenty-four hours of a day is scanned. A person may be born with no planets on any of the four angles. However, some time after the birth a planet will rise. When that planet rises, check to see if any stars are on any other angle at that time. Follow this procedure for the full rotation of the chart. Indeed, the birth time is only required to see if any stars were on angles at the precise moment of birth. Examine a chart, in other words, for its *potential* to have a planet on an angle at the same time as a star. It does not matter if, at the actual time of birth, the chart's angles are not occupied.

This necessity of working with the full twenty-four hours of the day can cause problems when working with the Moon, for, by the time one advances the Moon on the date of birth through its rising position, its culminating position, its setting position, and then its nadir, it will have moved about 12° forward in the zodiac. Be sure to take this into account.

DECIDING WHAT STARS TO USE

DECIDING WHAT STARS TO USE IS A personal choice. If you are using a list of about 50 stars with an orb of only 30' of arc, you will get an average of 10 to 15 stars interacting with the chart. This list of star contacts can be reduced to 8 or 10 by eliminating those stars that are not visible from the birth location. If we expand this to an orb of 1° and use 250 stars, the number of contacts can measure in the hundreds. Clearly, not all of these stars will have meaning in your life. So the first aim with any fixed star work is to find the most important interactions of the most important stars.

Without doubt some fixed stars are more important than others. Some stars have caught the imagination of many cultures, either for their brilliance or for their location at key points in the solar year. They are Stars among the stars. Some of these high profile stars are a joy to find in a chart, while others will always prove more difficult in their expression. The following is a short description of what I believe are absolutely essential stars.

THE FOUR ROYAL STARS OF PERSIA: EARLY CARDINAL POINTS

- *Aldebaran*, in Taurus. Considered by Anonymous of 379 to be the greatest star of them all. Linked with integrity and honesty.
- *Antares*, in Scorpius. Linked with obsession; intense, and probing.
- *Formalhaut*, in Piscis Australis. Related to ideals and dreams.
- *Regulus*, in Leo. Linked with success without revenge.

All of these four stars are quite special. Each one brings its own unique type of life journey and lessons. Each one gives power and promises success, but only if you can deal with the particular hurdles that will be placed in front of you. Each star represents a specific type of human dilemma or weakness. The presence of any of these four stars in your chart will add a considerable amount of mythology to your life's journey.

THE STARS OF ORION

- *Rigel* (located in Orion's foot). Linked with giving knowledge to or teaching others.

- *Betelgeuse* (in the right armpit or shoulder). Indicates victory, success, achievement.
- *Bellatrix* (in the left shoulder). Indicates success by facing one's shadow.

These are not the only stars in Orion but these three stars radiate achievement. Indeed, it is my own opinion that Betelgeuse is the most auspicious star of all, for the fulfillment it offers seems to be totally uncomplicated by trials and hassles. The presence of one of these stars will be of great benefit if you are striving to achieve something at any level of your life.

OTHER KEY STARS

- *Sirius*, in Canis Major. The brightest star and known as the Dog Star. Gives brilliance.
- *Spica*, in Virgo. Indicates a great gift.
- *Canopus*, in Carina, part of the rudder of the great ship Argo. Augurs pathfinding.

These are probably the most important stars of the sky. There are others that clamor to be on the list, and indeed after working with the stars for a while, you may create your own short list. But if your chart has any of these stars active via the concept of parans, then your life will be entwined with some of the most ancient and profound myths of the human race.

A LIST OF THE MOST DIFFICULT STARS

Early twentieth-century astrology gave the fixed stars meanings connected with hellfire and destruction. These meanings, I believe, are simply not true and are at times quite strange. However, some stars present lessons to charts that are definitely more difficult than others. The following list, not in order of difficulty, is just a guide; the meanings of the stars are given in more detail in the sections about their own constellations.

- *Facies*, in Sagittarius. Pure combative energy.
- *Capulus*, in Perseus's sword. Primitive, male, sexual energy; penetrating and ruthless.
- *Algol*, in Perseus's hand. Primitive, female, sexual energy; passionate, intense, and also hysterical in the true sense of the word.

- *Menkar*, in Cetus. The unconscious becoming conscious. The sudden emergence of deep unconscious issues.
- *Zosma*, in Leo. Part of the triangle of victim, saviour, or perpetrator.

None of these stars are evil and they can exist in the charts of wonderful people. But each one has its own wounds or worries that will either be owned and worked on or projected onto another, who then seems to embody the worst side of the star's energy.

THE FOUR ANGLES AND THE FIXED STARS

IN WORKING WITH PARANS, THE ANGLES are the four gateways that stars have into your chart. If a star does not touch one of the angles of a place or person's chart (not visible), it was believed in ancient times that the star could not influence that place or person's chart. This point is expanded in part 4 in the section on star phases.

The four angles—the Ascendant, MC, Descendant, and the Nadir—were seen long ago as four great pillars which held up the ceiling of the moving heavens. These were/are the channels by which the fixed stars translate their energy down to the earth. These points are the connections, the bridge, between us and the stars. Like modern astrological aspects, each particular angle combined its meaning with any star it encountered. However, the angles were connected to the timing of the expression and the intensity of the star energy, rather than altering and grading the expression, as is the case with modern aspect work.

The following guidelines are based primarily on the work of Anonymous of 379 and on what I have found to be the modern expression. Future research may bring the modern empirical expression closer to or further from the ancient opinions.

RISING ON THE LINE OF THE HORIZON

According to Anonymous of 379,[36] if a star is rising and a planet is on the same or another angle, the expression of the star's energy manifests throughout a person's life and is considered to be in its strongest position. The star's impact on your life, via the planet in paran, is the greatest it can express.

However, it would seem that the most notable feature of a star in the rising position, linked to a planet on any angle, is that its energy appears to peak early. The energy may well be manifested through the whole life but it seems to be very strong when the person is young. There is not the slow, steady climb to success or any other life expression.

An example of this is Laurence Olivier, born May 22, 1907. Olivier had his Venus culminating as Murzims rose. In his natal chart, Olivier did not have Venus on his MC. However, during the course of the day of his birth, when Venus culminated Murzims rose. See Chart 1 (p. 34) and figure 17 (p. 34). Murzims is a star that rises just before the Dog Star Sirius, and was called "The Announcer." It is an extroverted star, concerned with being seen and speaking out. Thus, this extroverted, speaking-out star, whose mission or role is to "announce," to make known, is connected to Olivier's Venus.

---

[36] Anonymous of 379, *Treatise on the Bright Fixed Stars*, p. 1.

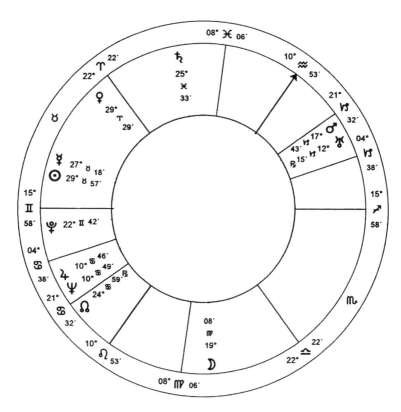

Chart 1. Natal chart for Laurence Olivier. Born May 22, 1907; 05:00 GMT; Dorking, Surrey, England; 51N14 000W20. Geocentric, Tropical, Placidus Houses, True Node. Data from Blackwell. Source: The Oliviers by F. Barker, cited in "AQ" for June, July, August, 1956.

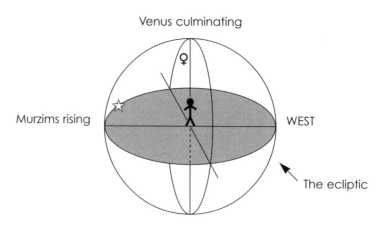

Figure 17. Laurence Olivier's Venus culminating as Murzims rises. Configuration for May 22, 1907 at Dorking, UK, 51N14, 0W20.

Laurence Olivier started his acting career at age 9, and by the time he was 19 he was a successful, recognized actor. Here we can see both the early expression of the star in his life, as well as the career in acting through the Venus/ MC. The important point is that the energy of announcing, being seen, speaking out is "expressed" through the parans of Venus on the MC at a very early age, not after he had slaved for years to build a name and then finally get a break in his 20s or 30s or 50s.

CULMINATING

According to Anonymous of 379,[37] if a star culminates and a planet is on the same or another angle, the expression of the star's energy manifests at an early age, continues through a person's life and gives him or her success in their city of birth.[38] This seems very much like the rising point. One finds in working with this angle, however, that when a star is culminating, its expression is focused on the position held in the community, the career, or social standing. Thus the star's energy gains expression in one's life in the middle years, even while ambition or drive was established from quite a young age.

Laurence Olivier also had Mercury culminating as Alcyone reached its culmination. Here we have a fixed star coming to the same angle at the same time as a natal planet. This tends to give very strong outcomes. Alcyone is the alpha star of the Pleiades and as such is discussed later. The Pleiades are linked to mysticism but also to power, life, and death. Olivier did not want to work in mediocre plays or films. He was a Shakespearian specialist, recognized in his prime as a genius for his ability to give the words of the great bard the power and mystery they deserved. Laurence Olivier used his voice and oratory skills in his career (culminating), and the magic and charisma of that voice had as its source the very essence of the power of the Pleiades, Alcyone.

SETTING ON THE HORIZON LINE

According to the author Anonymous of 379, if a star is setting and a planet is on the same or another angle, the expression of the star's energy manifests in middle age and in a foreign country.

This statement seems to be holding true in modern work. For example, Charles Dickens, the great Victorian novelist, had Alhena setting at the same time as his Jupiter was setting. Alhena is in the heel of Pollux, one of the Twins of

---

[37] Anonymous of 379, *Treatise on the Bright Fixed Stars*, p. 1.
[38] What is implied here is a form of fixed star Astro*Carto*Graphy.

Gemini. The presence of Alhena in a chart implies that the person has a mission to go forth with an objective. Dickens gained success from an early age onward, but it was his works in the latter years of his life, in which he described the social injustice of Victorian England, which were most important to him. Indeed, social reform became the major driving force of his life in his later years.

Alhena did not cause Dickens to focus on issues of social justice. However, its presence in his chart, particularly sharing an angle with a natal planet, indicates that he would have a mission, a cause. Alhena is the wounded heel. Dickens suffered hard labor in a children's factory in his childhood, so in his later life and in keeping with the meaning of Jupiter, he strove to heal this wound by teaching others through his writing.

NADIR

Anonymous of 379 also said that if a star is on the Nadir and a planet is on the same or another angle, the expression of the star's energy manifests in old age "and their deaths are widely noted and much recognised."[39]

The Nadir is a great resource, for it represents what lies underneath the surface. Natal planets in this position may take many years before they are expressed, and similarly a star on this point is very strong but hidden, like an underground spring, not immediately apparent but once discovered a real treasure.

Dickens's Jupiter also reached the Nadir at the same time as Betelgeuse reached its Nadir. Betelgeuse is the right shoulder of Orion and augurs success more than almost any other star in the sky. It shows honor and greatness. Linked with his Jupiter and on the Nadir, this implies that Dickens was able to gain much fame which lived on after his death.

TO BE BORN WITH A STAR ON AN ANGLE

The strongest position for a star is when it occupies one of the angles at the time of birth. In this situation the energy of the star is focused on that point and functions from the day of birth to the day of death and sometimes even long after.

Pablo Picasso and Galileo Galilei were both born at the moment Sirius was rising. Sirius is the brightest star in the sky and is connected to great deeds, the mundane becoming sacred. It can burn if it is not used and its presence on the

---

[39] Anonymous of 379, *Treatise on the Bright Fixed Stars*, p. 2.

Ascendant at birth is a huge indication that one is going to be asked to do great things. A person may fail in this endeavour but if he or she is brave enough to stride forward and go through the pain and turbulence implied by Sirius, then success is assured. For to be born with such a star rising, or on any of the other angles, implies that desired actions can have far-reaching consequences.

THE EFFECT OF STARS ON NATAL PLANETS

ONCE YOU HAVE FOUND THE STAR AND delineated the meaning of the angle that is focusing the star into the chart, the next part of the formula is the meaning of the natal planet or luminary which is sharing the pivotal position with the star. The author Anonymous of 379 places great emphasis on the Moon, indicating that this is the most important natal point in working with fixed stars. However, this lunar emphasis does not seem to be supported by practical results. All of the visible planets and the luminaries seem equally sensitive to contact with a star, with the Sun being the most sensitive but only because a star to the Sun will be expressed through one's identity and sense of self and therefore more obvious to the astrologer's eye. Whether future work will reveal the greater importance of the Moon remains to be seen.

The following can be used as a guide to how the planets and luminaries are affected by fixed stars. You can also use your own knowledge of luminaries and planets.

THE SUN

If the Sun is affected, then your personal identity, the sense of who you are, the conscious idea of what your life is about, is altered and becomes linked with the meaning and mythology of the star. This, however, is not an unhappy marriage but rather an unconscious union. If your Sun was linked to Capulus, you would identify yourself with forceful action, being strongly focused. However, if your Sun was linked with Wega, you would define yourself either as a person with a magnetic type of personality or one who was very gullible.

Abraham Lincoln had his Sun rising as Aldebaran, one of the great royal stars of Persia, was in the Nadir. Aldebaran represents a ruler or person who is driven to function with strong integrity or a noble cause. Being on the Nadir implies that he will be remembered in this light.

We see the two sides of Algol, the great star of female passion and intensity or ruthlessness, in the case of Adolf Hitler, who had his Sun on the Nadir as Algol was setting. He is remembered (Nadir) for the ruthless events (Algol) in the later part of his life (setting). However—to demonstrate the beneficent effects of Algol—Jules Verne, the father of science fiction, and writer of short stories and novels such as *Around the World in Eighty Days, Journey to the Center of the Earth* and *Twenty Thousand Leagues Under the Sea*, also had Algol rising with his Sun. The star rising showed that this star's passion and intensity was connected to Verne's massive outpouring of creative work.

THE MOON

The Moon is like the Sun in fixed star work. It is another form of identity: how you feel, what you seek or find in your life. If the Moon is affected, then it alters what you believe in, what your ideals are, what you are passionate about. A Moon linked with Formalhaut will be passionate about the arts or metaphysical subjects. Rather than who you are, it speaks of what pleases you, what nurtures you, what you therefore consciously or unconsciously seek and draw into your life.

Jules Verne was born on a day when the Moon set as Altair rose. Altair is the alpha star of Aquila the Eagle. Altair is the flight of the Eagle, to go higher and in a bolder fashion than anybody has before, to soar to unexplored great heights. Linked to his Moon via the Ascendant, this implies that as a young boy Jules Verne quested for adventure, for new places. As he became older, he found an outlet for all of this in his writing. He did not travel physically to these places but rather, moon-motivated, he traveled to them emotionally.

Here are some instances of the Moon connected with Facies, a star from the constellation Sagittarius. Facies is in the face of the Archer and represents war as a concept in the human way of life. It has no mercy and is ruthless in its aggression and its attitudes. Linked to the Moon it implies a person who loves the combative way of life, loves the military and may even be sadistically inclined. Adolf Hitler had Facies culminating as his Moon culminated (manifesting itself in his career). Another example is Jim Jones, the leader in the Jamestown massacre. He had Facies rising (strong all through his life) as his Moon culminated. And to show Facies in another light, Margaret Thatcher, long-standing right wing Prime Minister of the UK, whose finest hour was the Falklands War, had Facies setting (in the latter part of her life) as her Moon was on her Nadir.

The Moon is also how we receive nurturing, and if connected to a rising star, then that star's energy will give a description of your view of your mother, or what your mother taught or instilled in you, because the star is most active in the early part of your life. For example, a client with Algol rising as the Moon was on the Descendant, once described her mother as a monster. Prince Charles has Murzims rising as his Moon culminates. Murzims is the star in the paws of the dog of Canis Major. It is called the Announcer, and its meaning is to speak out or to have something to say. This star indicates that Charles sees his mother as someone who speaks out or has a message to announce. In adulthood this influenced his own actions as well as the type of woman to whom he would be drawn. He married the shy, young Diana, only to find that she was also a person who spoke out; she was a person with something to say to the world.

MERCURY

Mercury in fixed star work is about ideas and intellect. It may affect the way you speak or it may emphasize all things Mercurial in your life. If you have Capulus, the star of aggressive male energy, linked to your Mercury, you are a very direct speaker, freely speaking your mind for better or worse. However, if Mercury is connected to Rigel, the star of the educator and teacher, then you may well be an educator, wanting to impart knowledge.

A lovely example of the connection of Mercury with a star is Lewis Carroll, the man who gave us the character of Alice in Wonderland. When he was born, Mercury set as Formalhaut, one of the great stars of Persia from the constellation Piscis Australis, was culminating. Formalhaut is linked to romance and poetic ability. Thus, Carroll's highly imaginative, idealistic, romantic, fantasy writing. The connection to Mercury via the MC indicates that this imaginative expression in his speech or writing will form part of his career or become part of his social status.

On the other side of this coin there is a star called Wega or Vega, the alpha star of the constellation Lyra, the Harp of Orpheus, which covers everything it touches in enchanting charisma. On the day that Hitler was born, Mercury set as Wega rose. This is an indication of a most charismatic and spell-creating orator. The star does not describe the way he will use his charismatic skills, merely that he has them focused on his Mercury.

VENUS

Venus in fixed star work seems to be strongly connected to the arts as well as to ideas about harmony and relating. Thus, it can affect your private life, friendships, and alliances, as well as push you into some form of creative expression. If you had Venus connected to Capulus, for example, you would have little concern for harmony, balance, or social skills, whereas if you had Venus connected to Diadem, a star of female sacrifice, you may be very self-sacrificing in personal relationships.

Elizabeth Taylor, with her many marriages and turbulent private life, was born on the day that Venus set as Procyon culminated. Procyon is the alpha star of Canis Minor. Procyon comes before "the shining one," Sirius, and relates to rash actions that do not last. Linked to her Venus and connected to the MC, one of the ways she is known in the world is for her many failed marriages.

Another example of Venus, but this time in the arts, is Leonardo da Vinci, whose Venus was setting while the alpha star of the Pleiades, Alcyone, was setting. This is the same star that Laurence Olivier had linked to his Mercury, but with Leonardo its mysterious energy is focused on Venus, manifesting in many of his works and drawings and most of all in the faint smile and mystery of the Mona Lisa.

MARS

When Mars is linked to a fixed star, motivation, sexual energy, aggression, or drive are colored by the mythology and process of the star. Mars repersents your ability to focus energy and move it toward an emotional or physical goal without consideration of others. A star like Alcyone with Mars could result in idealism without drive, or a person who is strongly focused on higher ideals or the mysteries of physical or spiritual life. Immanuel Kant had Mars setting as Alcyone was on the Nadir. His life work was in the field of philosophy. In contrast to Kant's Mars, Joan of Arc's Mars was rising as Antares was on the Nadir. Antares is the heart of the Scorpion and indicates great passions, transformations, warriorship. And Joan of Arc, of course, was burnt to death by the English for her part in leading the French nation to victory against the English.

JUPITER

Stars linked to Jupiter will be emphasized in their expression, as well as affecting the way you learn and expand your world. You may see the big picture and rush toward it or see the big picture and run away from it. When Regulus, one of the Royal Stars of Persia which promises success as long as revenge is avoided, is with Jupiter it can be a very powerful combination, suggesting great success or a great struggle to avoid revenge. Jupiter is a magnifier: it takes the energy of the star and expresses it to the world in a magnified form.

A most vivid example of this is Adolf Hitler. He had Facies rising at the same time as his Jupiter: Facies, the essence of war and combat, is magnified by its contact with Jupiter. On a brighter note, Wolfgang Amadeus Mozart had Spica and Jupiter culminating together. Spica, the alpha star of Virgo, is the gift of genius. Linked to the MC of Mozart, it indicates that we will know his work and know him as a genius—a clear instance of Jupiter magnifying the star it touched.

SATURN

A star linked with Saturn has a lasting effect. It relates to what you build with your life or what you leave behind after death. It will express itself in issues of leadership and may even be projected onto the father or authority figures. Saturn linked with Castor, for example, describes a leading writer or communicator who leaves behind a body of work or ideas. John Lennon[40] had Castor on his Nadir as his Saturn rose. Once again, we see the impact of the Nadir in how Lennon's recognition continued after death as his music and songs gained greater acclaim.

In contrast Oliver Cromwell—the man who led the English civil war, overthrew the monarchy, and became Lord Protector of England—had Saturn on the Nadir as Procyon rose. Procyon was the star connected to Venus in Elizabeth Taylor's chart: to rise quickly but not to last—which her marriages didn't. After Cromwell's death, his body of work was destroyed and the monarchy returned to power.

---

[40] John Lennon's time of birth is in question, but in this method any change of time would not alter the paran relationships in his chart.

SUMMARY: HOW TO WORK
WITH PARANS AND FIXED STARS

In summary, then, keep all of the following points in mind when working with fixed stars:

1. Work with the stars that can be seen from the place of birth. The star must be so situated as to rise and set at the latitude of birth. If it can only culminate at that latitude, then be aware that the star will always be of curtailed passage, which is explained in the section on Star Phases.
2. Start with a short list of stars. By starting with the great stars you will not miss anything really important and it will be easier for you to get used to the names and the meanings. It is better to have a short list of stars that have a known effect than a long, confusing list of stars that you do not know.
3. Use small orbs, about half the width of your finger, or 30' of arc. Any more than that and your calculations will get cluttered with too many, unnecessary stars.
4. Take note of all the stars in a chart. Once you start to understand the stars, you will notice that it takes more than the presence of one malefic star to turn a person into a monster. It is the combination of stars which is important.
5. The angles indicate when in a person's life the star's energy will manifest. The Ascendant indicates an early influence, continuing throughout life; the culmination point or MC relates to the middle years of life and is connected to worldly status; the Descendant indicates the later years of life; and the Nadir represents one's life work, the end of life and one's reputation after death.
6. Only work with the visible planets. Outer planets are significant for generations and even in mundane work, but for natal chart work limit yourself to working with the two luminaries and the planets out to Saturn. The Nodes are not used with fixed star work, so explore them but recognize that there is no historical basis for their use.
7. The planet will show the area of life being affected by the star. Once the star is active in a chart it will affect a particular planet and so will influence the area of life ruled by that planet.
8. Stars on an angle. Make a note of any star that is on any of the four angles at the time of birth. That is to say, a person may be born at the moment a star is rising, setting, culminating or on the nadir. If this is the case, then such a star will be strong throughout the entire life.

Part 2

THE CONSTELLATIONS

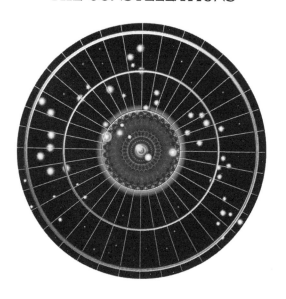

.

THE CANVAS IN THE SKY

THE CONSTELLATIONS REPRESENT STORIES captured in the sky, cave paintings perfectly preserved for the use of generation after generation of humans. In the beginning these stories were seen as particular themes taking up whole sections of the sky, rather than as isolated images with isolated stories. Some of these sweeping themes were recorded in the work of Aratus, an early astronomer believed to be the first person to record the positions of the constellations, in his book *Phaenomena*, written around the year 275 B.C.E. In this work he grouped some of the constellations into themes such as the Water and the Royal Family.

If we, as astrologers, are ever to reconstruct the sky to understand the canvas of the sky, the vaulted ceiling of the earliest temple or first cathedral, then it is important that we start viewing the sky not as isolated objects but as a whole. Thus, although the constellations in this part of the book are listed alphabetically, their relationships to each other have been included.

After the description of each constellation, there is a list of its important stars with a summary of the opinions of Claudius Ptolemy (c. 140 C.E.), Vivian E. Robson (1923), Reinhold Ebertin and Georg Hoffmann (1971), and lastly, Joseph E. Rigor (1979)—these representing the major astrological literature available on fixed stars. Each star is then put into a modern framework based on its history and myths. The star's astronomical data is given (explained in Appendix A) and, if it is not circumpolar, a paran map is provided.

ANDROMEDA, THE PRINCESS

Placed just south of Draco and the two Bears, the constellation of Andromeda is one member of a royal family, which consists of Cepheus the king, Cassiopeia the queen, Andromeda the daughter or princess, and Perseus the prince (see Star Map 1, p. 48). Situated beside the divine and worshiped Pole area, this grouping depicts the shape of human society.

In his *Phaenomena*, Aratus refers to this royal family: "Nor all unnamed shall rest the hapless family of Iasid Cepheus."[1]

As daughter of Cepheus and Cassiopeia, Andromeda lends herself to many meanings. The Greeks saw this constellation as the figure of a princess chained to a rock, about to be eaten by the sea monster Cetus the Whale.[2] However, she was

---

[1] A. W. and G. R. Mair (trans.), *Callimachus, Lycophron, Aratus* (Cambridge: Harvard University Press, 1989), p. 221.

[2] Adrian Room, *Dictionary of Astronomical Names* (New York: Routledge, 1988), p. 57.

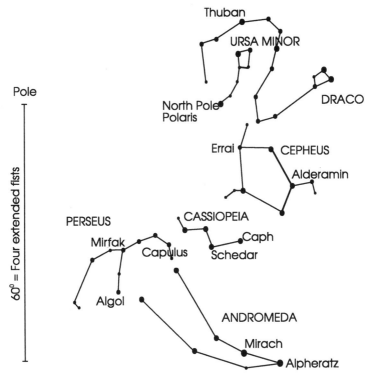

Star Map 1. The Royal Family.

saved from the jaws of death by the hero, Perseus, holding the head of Medusa. Perseus then fell in love with Andromeda and married her. The medieval Christians considered Perseus to be David holding Goliath's head[3] and did not link him with the figure of Andromeda. However, a Japanese myth talks of Kushinada-hime, the rice goddess who is rescued by the sea lord from the jaws of an eight-headed monster[4]; after the rescue the young couple marry. These different tales of princesses who need to be rescued, leading to marriage or fertility, occur throughout many myths and fairy tales.

Andromeda's alpha star is Alpheratz, which is both the navel of Pegasus and the neck or head of Andromeda. In Greek mythology, Pegasus the winged horse was born after his mother's head had been severed—his mother being Medusa, the

---

[3] Richard Hinckley Allen, *Star Names: Their Lore and Meaning* (New York: Dover, 1963), p. 331.

[4] Gertrude and James Jobes, *Outer Space: Myths, Name Meanings, Calendars* (New York: Scarecrow Press, 1964), p. 111.

so-called Gorgon slain by Perseus.[5] So these two constellations, Perseus and Andromeda, are both connected with stories about horses and heads, slayings and rescues.

If, however, we take another view of these constellations, we could see the Princess Andromeda as the Gorgon Medusa. The constellations of Perseus and Andromeda could be seen as the scene of Perseus slaying Medusa with Perseus holding her head as her decapitated body gives birth to Pegasus, the flying horse, the constellation emerging out of Andromeda's neck. Indeed this myth would actually fit the celestial components far better.

There is yet another way that this group of stars may be considered. Andromeda is a princess, daughter of the king and queen of the sky. She is therefore part of the sky stories showing the natural balance of the human tribe or civilization. She is the young, fertile virgin, the marriageable daughter waiting for suitors. She is in a passive, surrendering position, showing her readiness. Her legs are apart. However, this symbol of willing receptiveness of the fertile virgin ready to take a suitor, ready to receive, could have been altered by the Greeks to a symbol of a chained, helpless, powerless, and dependent position, a woman weak and needing the masculine to free her—at the time the collective stripped power from women. She probably received her chains at the same time as her mother, the queen, was chained to her throne, indicating the loss of female sovereignty.

Perseus can be seen in the Greek mold as the conquering hero saving the damsel in distress, with his raised sword holding his prize of Medusa's head. Or we can see him as part of this natural balance: Andromeda's suitor, young, masculine, full of male energy, symbolized by his raised sword like a huge phallus. He holds in his hand the head of an animal or the head of an enemy as his offering, his hunting prize or the symbol of his courage, his ability to protect or show off his hunting skill. Maybe he is not only saving Andromeda, but courting her. The presence of Pegasus, the sacred horse, could be her dowry or her power, for in the times of the matrilineal civilization all horses were ruled by the goddess. Andromeda and Perseus, the princess and the prince, the young woman and the young man. Courtship. Two constellations or stories in the sky showing human society, customs, and the natural balance of life and order.

STARS OF ANDROMEDA

The brightest star in Andromeda is Alpheratz, located in the neck. The other stars, in descending order of magnitude, are: Mirach, her left hip; Almach, her left foot; and Adhil, the train of her dress.

---

[5] Pierre Grimal, *The Dictionary of Classical Mythology*, trans. A. R. Maxwell-Hyslop (Cambridge: Blackwell Reference, 1986), p. 349.

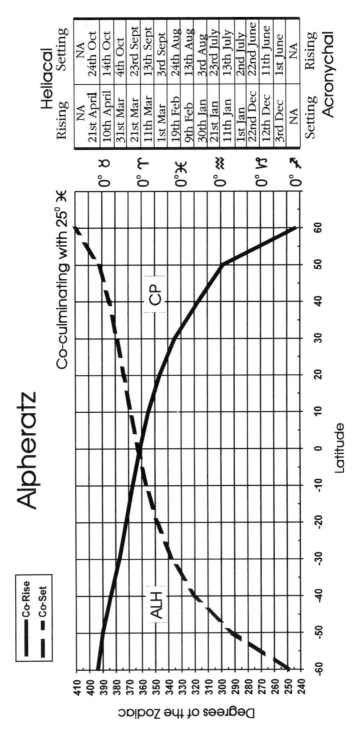

Alpheratz

	Heliacal	
	Rising	Setting
0° ♉	NA	NA
	21st April	24th Oct
	10th April	14th Oct
0° ♈	31st Mar	4th Oct
	21st Mar	23rd Sept
	11th Mar	13th Sept
0° ♓	1st Mar	3rd Sept
	19th Feb	24th Aug
	9th Feb	13th Aug
0° ≈	30th Jan	3rd Aug
	21st Jan	23rd July
	11th Jan	13th July
0° ♑	1st Jan	2nd July
	22nd Dec	22nd June
0°	12th Dec	11th June
	3rd Dec	1st June
0° ♐	NA	NA
	Setting	Rising
	Acronychal	

Co-culminating with 25° ♓

CP

ALH

Co-Rise
Co-Set

Latitude

Degrees of the Zodiac

Paran Map 1. Alpheratz.

ALPHERATZ

(Alpha Andromeda. Magnitude 2.2. RA 00:08:09". Declination 29N03' 50". PED = 13° Aries 37'.) See Paran Map 1, page 50. *An example of how to read the map:* If you were born in Devonport, UK at a latitude of 50° North, then the star rose at about 0° Aquarius. If you have a planet at either 0° Aquarius or Leo then that planet rose or set with the star. The star also set at 0° Taurus. Therefore, if you have a planet at 0° Taurus or Scorpio, it would have set or risen as the star set. The star culminates at 25° Pisces, so if you have a planet at either 25° Pisces or Aries, then it culminated or was on the Nadir as the star culminated.

At this latitude of 50° North the star has a phase of curtailed passage. This period will be from about July 23 (reading the date from the right-hand column of the date next to 0° Aquarius) to about October 24 every year (reading the date from the right-hand column of the date next to 0° Taurus), and is the true or cosmic heliacal rising star about January 21 (reading the date for the rising line at 50° North in the "heliacal rising" column).

Alpheratz can be used on all four points for charts between latitudes of 60° South and 60° North. South of that the star never rises and north of that the star never sets, and therefore has permanent curtailed passage.

EARLIER OPINIONS

Ptolemy links this star to Venus. Robson (1984) links the star to independence and a love of freedom, based, it would seem, more on the star's connection with the sacred horse than with the princess. Ebertin (1971) calls it *Sirrah* and says that it is connected to being popular. Rigor (1978) links it with the princess imagery and associates the star with wealth, honor, cheerfulness, and love of life.

ALPHERATZ, THE CONCEPT

It seems, however, that Alpheratz is not at home in Andromeda and has no connection to the symbolism of this constellation. Gertude and James Jobes point out that ". . . this star formerly was part of Pegasus, whence it was transferred to the Woman's Hair, and inspired someone to give it the strange title Umbilicus Andromedae."[6]

If Alpheratz is placed back in the constellation Pegasus where it used to reside, it can be linked to freedom, love of movement, speed, and the sheer joy of the wind in one's hair. In this capacity, one can understand its presence in the chart of Alfred Dreyfus, the nineteenth-century French army officer who was falsely accused of treason and sent to the infamous penal colony of Devil's Island. Dreyfus had Jupiter rising as Alpheratz was culminating, and thus the middle

---

[6] Jobes, *Outer Space*, p. 300.

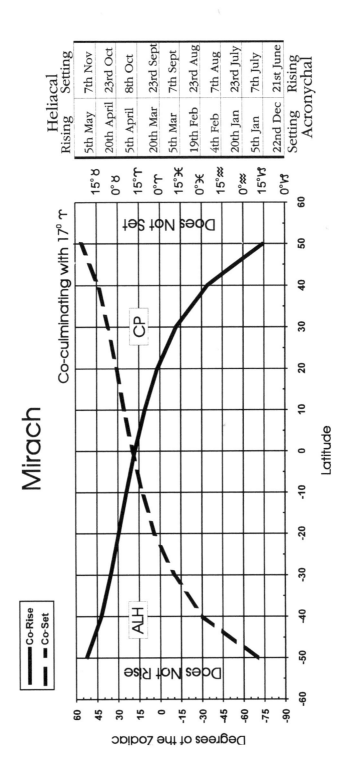

Heliacal			
Rising		Setting	
5th May		7th Nov	
20th April		23rd Oct	15° ♉
5th April		8th Oct	0° ♉
20th Mar		23rd Sept	15° ♈
5th Mar		7th Sept	0° ♈
19th Feb		23rd Aug	15° ♓
4th Feb		7th Aug	0° ♓
20th Jan		23rd July	15° ♒
5th Jan		7th July	0° ♒
22nd Dec		21st June	15° ♑
Setting		Rising	0° ♑
		Acronychal	

Mirach

Co-culminating with 17° ♈

Does Not Set

CP

ALH

Does Not Rise

Co-Rise
Co-Set

Degrees of the Zodiac

Latitude

Paran Map 2. Mirach.

years of his life were symbolized by his fight for freedom in a battle that grew into a major political issue, until he eventually gained his acquittal and release twelve years later. The star is also present in the chart of John Glenn, the first US astronaut to orbit the Earth. It culminated as his Mars rose, linking the love of speed and freedom of movement to his motivation and focus. It is also found in the chart of Henry VIII, who wanted freedom from the laws of the Catholic Church. Alpheratz culminated as his natal Mercury rose, indicating that he wanted the freedom at a legal or intellectual level.

ALPHERATZ IN THE NATAL CHART

If Alpheratz is in your chart, then the freedom to move and the ability to act became a feature of the planet which is influenced. For example, linked to Mercury it will indicate freedom of thinking, new ideas, or headstrong stubbornness; if linked to your Mars, it may well indicate strong motivation or willfulness.

ALPHERATZ AS THE HELIACAL RISING STAR AT BIRTH

Alpheratz is one of Ptolemy's stars, so can confidently be used as both the cosmic and the apparent heliacal rising star. If Alpheratz has claimed the Sun on the day you were born, then you will carry the hallmarks of this star. Your greatest talent will be your ability to take action and this strength is one of your natural talents, along with your love of independence. James Dean, the gifted young actor who killed himself in a car accident because of his love of speed, was born on the heliacal rising of Alpheratz. So was Jules Verne, father of science fiction, author of *Journey to the Moon*, and Galileo Galilei, the sixteenth-century astronomer, father of modern physics, who was the first to point a telescope at the stars.

MIRACH

(Beta Andromeda. Magnitude 2.4. RA 01:09:28.5". Declination 35N35' 38". PED = 29° Aries 42'.) See Paran Map 2, page 52. *An example of how to read the map:* If you were born at a latitude of 30° South, then the star rose at about 5° Taurus. If you have a planet at either 5° Taurus or Scorpio, then that planet rose or set with the star. The star also set at 20° Pisces. Therefore, if you have a planet at 20° Pisces or Virgo, it would have set or risen as the star set. The star culminates at 17° Aries, so if you have a planet at either 17° Aries or Libra, then it culminated or was on the Nadir as the star culminated.

At this latitude of 30° South the star has a phase of "arising and lying hidden." This period is from about March 10 (reading the date from the left-hand column of the date box next to 20° Pisces) to April 25 every year (reading the date from the left-hand column of the date box next to 5° Taurus), and is the true or cosmic heliacal rising star about April 25 (reading the date for the rising line at 30° South in the "heliacal rising" column).

Mirach can be used on all four points for charts between latitudes of 54° South and 54° North. South of that the star never rises and north of that the star never sets and therefore has permanent curtailed passage.

EARLIER OPINIONS

Ptolemy links the star to Venus. Robson connects it to happiness in marriage, being kind, forgiveness, and great devotion. Ebertin talks of happiness, artistic ability, and mediumship. Rigor includes all of the points of Robson and then adds secrecy, bad habits and stubbornness.

MIRACH: THE CONCEPT

If Mirach truly is the main star of Andromeda, allowing Alpheratz to be part of Pegasus, then this is the star that should show the concepts of the young fertile virgin—receptivity, feminine power, intuition, the arts, and so on.

Immanuel Kant, the German philosopher who believed in the possibility of a perfect society, with a world federation of republican states[7] which would benefit the welfare of every individual, had this star culminating with the Moon on the day he was born. The idealism of these views for the welfare of the human race shows us flickers of the influence of Mirach. Leonardo da Vinci had Mirach linked with his Mercury, which culminated with Mirach on the day of his birth and resulted in his great art. Fred Astaire had Mirach culminating with his Venus and here the harmony and rhythm of the star was expressed in dancing.

There are many other examples but all of them seem to have the common theme of seeking the harmonious way. Mirach seems to embody Andromeda far better than Alpheratz.

MIRACH IN THE NATAL CHART

The themes of this star are receptivity and fertility. If present in your chart it implies that you are open to ideas, willing to be receptive. Some people may mistake this as naivete or innocence but Mirach is not naive, for she can make use of that which she receives. She is fertile. Her skills are the ability to listen and think and to use this input in a most creative way.

---

[7] Lewis White Beck, ed. *Immanuel Kant Selections* (New York: Macmillan, 1988).

MIRACH AS THE HELIACAL RISING STAR AT BIRTH

Mirach is not on Ptolemy's list of stars to be used as the heliacal rising star at birth, so can only be used as the cosmic rising star of the day. If it is in such a position in your chart, you will be very receptive, open to ideas. This could imply a certain naivete but, on the other hand, it could also give you creative talents with art and color or the ability to bring out the best in others.

AQUILA, THE EAGLE

THIS CONSTELLATION IS PART OF A GROUP
in the northern sky which consists of three birds: the eagle, Aquila; the swan,
Cygnus; a third renamed in modern times, Lyra; and the arrow, Sagitta. See Star
Map 2 (below). These three birds were known to the Greeks as the Stymphalian
Birds, killed by Hercules as his sixth labor.[8] The Arrow in the sky is said to be-
long to Hercules.

Aratus called Aquila the storm bird,[9] for in the northern hemisphere it rises
in winter, bringing with it the bad weather and storms of that season. The constellation has been recognized as a bird for the last 3,500 years and the Greeks incorporated it into their mythology by naming it the Eagle, whose form Zeus

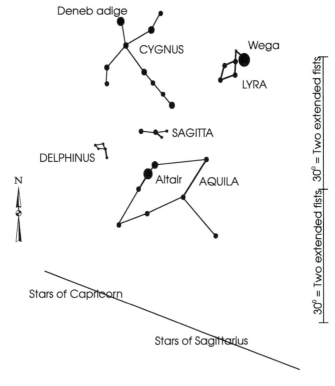

Star Map 2. Three Birds and an Arrow.

[8] Allen, *Star Names*, p. 350.
[9] Mair, *Callimachus, Lycophron, Aratus*, p. 231.
[10] H. A. Guerber, *The Myths of Greece and Rome* (London: Harrap, 1991), p. 27.

assumed to swoop down and kidnap Ganymede.[10] Zeus fell in love with the handsome youth and took him as his personal cupbearer. The myth continues with Ganymede being granted immortality and placed in the sky as the archetypal cupbearer of the constellation Aquarius.[11] Another version of the latter story is that Emperor Hadrian's life was extended by the willing sacrifice of the youth Antinous. An eagle lifted the youth to heaven and placed him there as Aquarius.[12]

The eagle has always been associated with fire, lightning, and sun gods, so that the Greeks claiming this eagle as a form of Zeus, god of thunder and lightning, is in keeping with its mythology. It was a Roman custom to release eagles over the funeral pyres of emperors, for they believed the eagle would carry the soul of the warrior to the land of the immortals. The eagle was also the instrument for calling fire down from heaven to consume sacrifices made on the altar. Having passed through the sacrificial fire, the victims were borne away by the eagle or rose to heaven in the form of an eagle.[13]

This symbolism is reflected in the Old Testament with the fires sent down by Yahweh to consume the son of Abraham. Because of its connection with fire, the eagle was often confused with the phoenix.[14] The eagle was the royal bird of Rome and a symbol of male sovereignty. A modern country that has adopted this as its emblem is the USA, which has shown over the years its ability to bring down fire from the sky as an act of war probably more powerfully than any other country.

STARS OF AQUILA

The brightest star is Altair, with the other named stars in descending order of magnitude being: Alshain, the head of Ganymede; Tarazed, the body of the eagle; and Deneb, the eagle's tail.

ALTAIR

(Alpha Aquila. Magnitude 0.9. RA 14:54:51.6". Declination 8N51'31". PED = 1° Aquarius 04'.) See Paran Map 3, page 58. *An example of how to read the map:* If you were born in Rome, Italy at a latitude of 42° North, then the star rose at

---

[11] Jobes, *Outer Space*, p. 116.
[12] Jobes, *Outer Space*, p. 117.
[13] Barbara Walker, *The Woman's Encyclopedia of Myths and Secrets* (San Francisco: HarperSanFrancisco, 1983), p. 262.
[14] Walker, *The Woman's Encyclopedia of Myths and Secrets*, p. 262.

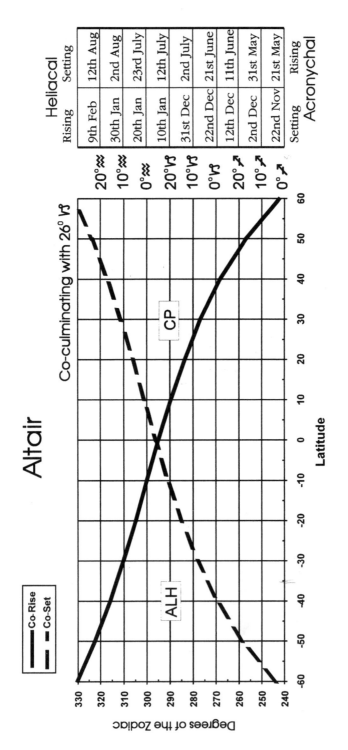

Altair

Co-culminating with 26° ♑

Heliacal	
Rising	Setting
9th Feb	12th Aug	20° ♒
30th Jan	2nd Aug	10° ♒
20th Jan	23rd July	0° ♒
10th Jan	12th July	20° ♑
31st Dec	2nd July	10° ♑
22nd Dec	21st June	0° ♑
12th Dec	11th June	20° ♐
2nd Dec	31st May	10° ♐
22nd Nov	21st May	0° ♐
Setting	Rising
Acronychal	

Paran Map 3. Altair.

about 25° Sagittarius. If you have a planet at either 25° Sagittarius or Gemini, then that planet rose or set with the star. The star also set at 18° Aquarius. Therefore, if you have a planet at 18° Aquarius or Leo, it would have set or risen as the star set. The star culminates at 26° Capricorn, so if you have a planet at either 26° Capricorn or Cancer, then it culminated or was on the Nadir as the star culminated.

At this latitude of 42° North the star has a phase of curtailed passage. This period will be from about June 15 (reading the date from the right-hand column of the date box next to 25° Sagittarius) to August 10 every year (reading the right-hand column of the date box next to 18° Aquarius), and is the true or cosmic heliacal rising star about December 17 (reading the date for the rising line at 42° North in the "heliacal rising" column).

Altair can be used on all four points for charts between latitudes of 81° South and 81° North. South of that the star never rises and north of that the star never sets and therefore has permanent curtailed passage.

EARLIER OPINIONS

Ptolemy said the stars of Aquila, including Altair, resembled Mars and Jupiter. Robson talks of the ability to rise in life, bold and courageous, but that the person so influenced can be guilty of bloodshed and in danger from reptiles. Ebertin agrees with Robson's emphasis on success and courage. Rigor does not mention the star.

ALTAIR: THE CONCEPT

A star of boldness and action, but one that is also connected to human relationships and caring, Altair's daring was shown in the chart of Leonardo da Vinci, who had Altair rising as his Saturn culminated. Such a combination indicates his willingness to think and explore new areas and new frontiers, a drive that was present all through his life. In contrast to Leonardo is John Lennon, whose Sun was connected to Altair, for the star rose as the Sun culminated on the day he was born. In Lennon's case, we see Altair's forceful drive to explore gaining expression in Lennon's musical protest for human rights and peace, making him a leader in his own right. Jules Verne's life is another expression of the star. On the day he was born the Moon set as Altair culminated. Altair's connection to his Moon affected his passions and beliefs. Verne's science fiction books all demonstrate the boldness and courage of the eagle, linked in his case to the less action-oriented Moon.

ALTAIR IN THE NATAL CHART

Altair's presence in your chart adds boldness and determination, the ability to achieve through risk-taking or through dogged determination. This masculine star of action and strength, however, uses this quest for action not just for itself, but also for others.

ALTAIR AS THE HELIACAL STAR RISING AT BIRTH

One of the stars on Ptolemy's list, it can therefore be used as both the cosmic and apparent heliacal rising star. This is an important placement of this star. Swiftness and boldness of action will be a part of your sense of self. This could lead to rashness or determination, or the ability to soar to places others have not been. An interesting example of Altair is Johannes Kepler, born on the apparent heliacal rising of this star. His mathematical ability could be attributed to Scheat (in the constellation Pegasus) rising with his Mercury, but his determination to solve the riddle of the orbits of the planets was the focal influence of Altair.

ARA, THE ALTAR

ARATUS WROTE IN HIS *PHAENOMENA*: "Below the fiery sting of the dread monster, Scorpion, and near the South is hung the Altar. Brief is the space thou wilt behold it above the horizon."[15] Ara is located between 50 and 60 degrees of southern declination and in current times is only visible south of latitude 40° North (see Star Map 7, p. 98). Seen as an altar in many forms, it has been considered the altar of Dionysus, an incense pan, as well as a hearth. Its main importance in classical times was its heliacal rising dates for weather forecasting.

Aratus writes: "But that Altar even beyond aught else hath ancient Night, weeping the woe of men, set to be a mighty sign of storm at sea. . . . I bid thee pray, when in the open sea, that that constellation wrapt in clouds appear not amidst the others in the heavens."[16]

This is the altar that Chiron, as the constellation The Centaur, approaches carrying his offering of the wolf, Lupus, to make a sacrifice.

STARS OF ARA

There are no astrologically significant stars in this constellation, but the whole constellation may well be worth considering in weather prediction, given the strength of Aratus's warnings. One needs to recognize, however, that as a particular star or constellation is always visible in the same season from one year to the next, it could gain the reputation of being a storm-causing constellation simply because it rises in the stormy season.

Nevertheless, Aratus's warnings do seem valid. On Christmas morning, 1974, in Darwin, Australia (12° S 28') the Neptune-Mars conjunction at 10° Sagittarius rose at that latitude with Antares, the alpha star of Scorpio, known as the Heart of the Scorpion. This is a difficult enough combination but over on the southern horizon Ara also rose. This heralded the arrival of Cyclone Tracey, which was the worst storm in Australian history.

---

[15] Mair, *Callimachus, Lycophron, Aratus*, p. 239.
[16] Mair, *Callimachus, Lycophron, Aratus*, p. 239.

ARGO, THE SHIP
(CARINA, THE KEEL; PUPPIS, THE STERN; VELA, THE SAILS; PYXIS, THE COMPASS)

IN OLDEN TIMES, FAR TO THE SOUTH under the hidden part of the sky, were the lands of mystery, the lands of sorcerers and magic, where the laws of nature could be bent and changed. Humans have always needed a Land Far Away. To the Vikings it was countries like Ireland, on the edge of Europe across wild seas, which embodied this archetype. In later times it became the Spice Islands of the West Indies. Later still it was Australia, the southern continent filled with animals that were so strange the Old World considered them a hoax. In this century first it was the Moon, followed rapidly by deep space and the cosmos. The human collective dreams of Far Away Places where the world is quite different. A wonderland, a place of science fiction before it becomes scientific fact. Such dreaming is a basic human trait. It is in our genes. It is the very thing that drives us onward. The Argo, to the Egyptians and later the Greeks, was the constellation that represented the ship which could be used to undertake these journeys.

Lying entirely in the southern hemisphere and over 75° in length, Argo has now been divided into four separate constellations—effectively asterisms, for ease of reference (see Star Map 3, p. 63). The four new constellations are Carina the Keel, Puppis the Stern, Vela the Sails and Pyxis the Compass, called in ancient maps the Mast. Many other subdivisions have been made over the centuries, the Mast and the Nautical Box to name but two, none of which are now recognized.

At northern latitudes this southern ship rises and lies close to the horizon as it travels from east to west, looking like a ship sailing the ocean far to the south. In ancient times this group of stars was seen as a great ship capable of going anywhere and sailing to lands unknown. Its oldest known expression is the vessel used by Osiris and Isis after the great Deluge which covered the earth[17] (see figure 18, p. 63). The Greeks claimed this great southern ship as the Argo,[18] the mythical vessel that was the first great ocean-going boat, built and used by Jason with fifty followers to set sail, "where no one has gone before," and find the Golden Fleece. To the Hindus this is the vessel that Vishnu, in fish form, towed to safety during the Hindu version of one of the great floods. To the Christians this was Noah's Ark.[19] Whatever the constellation is named, it represents a great vessel that enables its occupants to travel to places otherwise unreachable.

---

[17] Allen, *Star Names*, p. 66.
[18] Allen, *Star Names*, p. 65.
[19] Jobes, *Outer Space*, p. 120.

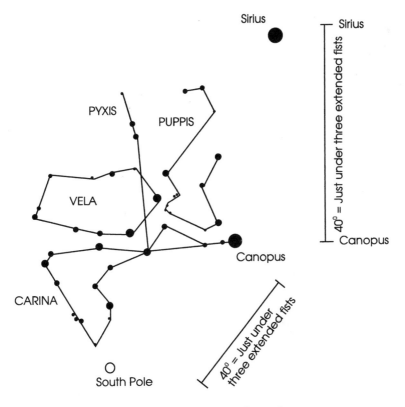

Star Map 3. The Great Southern Ship Argo.

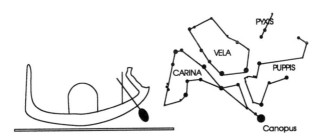

Figure 18. Egyptian hieroglyphic of the boat of the underworld, and the constellation Argo.

Since we have become disconnected from the sky, the need for this ship in our psyche is now filled by the spaceships of NASA and, in the world of film and television, great spaceships that sail the never-ending oceans of space. To us the Argo is now the *Enterprise* of Star Trek fame, or the Apollo missions of NASA.

Canopus

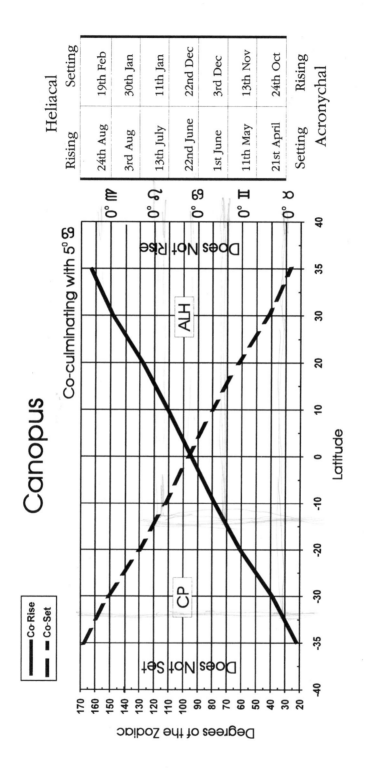

Heliacal	
Rising	Setting
24th Aug	19th Feb
3rd Aug	30th Jan
13th July	11th Jan
22nd June	22nd Dec
1st June	3rd Dec
11th May	13th Nov
21st April	24th Oct
Setting	Rising
Acronychal	

Paran Map 4. Canopus.

But more than just a ship, this constellation represents the very essence of human desire for adventure and exploration, be it with our minds for personal growth, or via the heavens for the growth of collective knowledge. To break apart such a sea-going or space-going vessel makes a massive statement to the human psyche, akin to breaking up the *Enterprise* or the shocking explosion of the *Challenger* in recent times. Hence astrologers should resist breaking up The Argo into smaller constellations. For The Argo is the symbol of our quests for new knowledge and our deep desire as a species to expand our world.

STARS OF THE ARGO

The brightest star is Canopus, in the Keel. Other named stars, in descending order of magnitude, are: Miaplacidus, also in the keel; Muhnithain, a triple star group in Vela, the sails; and Al Suhail, also in the sails.

CANOPUS

(Alpha Carina (Alpha Argo). Magnitude –0.9. RA 06:23:49.8". Declination 57S07'14". PED = 14° Cancer 16'.) See Paran Map 4, page 64. *An example of how to read the map:* If you were born in Madras, India, at a latitude of 13° North, then the star rose at about 25° Cancer. If you have a planet at either 25° Cancer or Capricorn, then that planet rose or set with the star. The star also set at 13° Gemini. Therefore, if you have a planet at 13° Gemini or Sagittarius, it would have set or risen as the star set. The star culminates at 5° Cancer, so if you have a planet at either 5° Cancer or Capricorn, then it culminated or was on the Nadir as the star culminated.

At this latitude of 13° North the star has a phase of arising and lying hidden. This period will be from about June 3 (reading the date from the left-hand column of the date box next to 13° Gemini) to July 18 every year (reading the left-hand column of the date box next to 25° Cancer) and is the true or cosmic heliacal rising star about July 18 (reading the date for the rising line at 13° North in the "heliacal rising" column).

Canopus can be used on all four points for charts between latitudes of 37° South and 37° North. North of that the star never rises and south of that the star never sets and therefore has permanent curtailed passage.

EARLIER OPINIONS

Ptolemy said that the star resembles Saturn and Jupiter. Robson says that the star gives piety, conservatism, and can turn evil into good. Ebertin talks simply of a love of travel. Rigor says that the star can give domestic problems.

CANOPUS, THE CONCEPT

This is one of the great stars of the sky, and the above dry, dusty words about "conservatism" and "domestic problems" are a mockery of it. Canopus derives its name from the chief pilot of the fleet of Menelaus who died on his return from the Trojan war.[20] However, the Egyptians knew of the great navigator long before the Greeks claimed the Egyptian vessel as the Argo and said that, after this ancient pilot's death, he became the navigator of the ship used to carry the dead to the afterlife.[21] Other cultures gave it other names: The Arabs at different times called it The Bright One; another name was The Wise One; and the Persians called the star *Al-Anwar i Suhaili,* the Light (or Wisdom) of Canopus. Canopus was also worshipped in the deserts as a form of god and was known as the Star of Egypt.[22] In about 6,000 B.C.E. it was the heliacal rising star for the autumn equinox and a series of temples were built in Egypt in alignment with these risings.[23] Modern people see this star now being claimed by NASA, as they use this ancient location point as a navigational aid for spacecraft.

The Arabs used Canopus like a South Pole star, using it to navigate across the sea of the deserts and often called it Heart of the South. Being such a bright star, it was considered the South Pole star by many cultures. It was also called the Heavy-Weighing Canopus, a name which tells us the importance of this star. For Canopus was considered the weight at the end of the plumb line used to define the poles. As the plumb line got knocked off course, the plumb weight at the end of the string logically started to move. This was the ancient explanation of the effects of precession on Canopus, the supposed Point of Stillness in the south.[24]

Many cultures, including the mythology of some Native American tribes, saw this South Pole star moving northward and delineated this as the timing of the end of the world. So Canopus became linked with the concept of time. This gained greater support by the Greeks, who considered that in the battle between the Olympians and the Titans, Cronos (Saturn) was cast from his chariot into the river Eridanus in a parallel story to Apollo and Phaethon.[25] Where Cronos fell was the star Canopus and from there he became a type of Lord of the Underworld, receiver of all souls, moving in his slow path to announce the end of the world by eventually conjoining the North Pole star. The Pawnee Indians put it: "Now the South Star, the Spirit Star, or Star of Death comes higher and higher

---

[20] Allen, *Star Names,* p. 68.

[21] G. de Santillana and Hertha von Dechend, *Hamlet's Mill* (Boston: Nonpareil Books, 1977), p. 283.

[22] Jobes, *Outer Space,* p. 311.

[23] Norman J. Lockyer, *The Dawn of Astronomy* (Kila, MT: Kessinger, 1992), p. 312.

[24] De Santillana and von Dechend, *Hamlet's Mill,* p. 73.

[25] De Santillana and von Dechend, *Hamlet's Mill,* p. 265.

in the heavens, and nearer and nearer to the North Star, and when the time for the end of life draws nigh, the Death Star will approach so close to the North Star that it will capture the star . . ."[26]

So there is considerable mythological argument to include Canopus in the constellation Eridanus, as it becomes the great receiver of souls. However, maybe it is possible for Canopus to be a most unusual star and contained in both: in Eridanus, thereby becoming a moving South Pole point of stillness ticking away the minutes of creation, defining the end of the world; and at the same time the pilot or navigator of the Argo, representing our insatiable need to explore as much as possible before Canopus turns out the lights on the human race.

If you live south of latitude 37° North, go outside and look at Canopus, and think about how the more ancient levels of your mind view this amazing star: great navigator and spirit guide, the death star and father of time, the South Pole and a sacred point of stillness.

Pablo Picasso was born at a latitude of 36N45 and had Venus rising as Canopus was culminating. Canopus was above the horizon for only a few hours, describing a tiny arc on the southern horizon, and at the time Venus rose, Canopus was sitting at the top of that arc. Pablo Picasso was a path-forger in the world of art. His different styles in art became known as Protocubism, Cubism, and Cubist Sculpture, and his greatness lay in his many-changing and cutting-edge styles. Canopus-Venus did not make him the great artist he was, but once he embarked upon such a life style, it ensured that his style, good or bad, would be different, setting new dimensions to the world of art.

Mao Tse-Tung was born at a latitude of 27N 52 where Canopus can rise and set. His Sun was linked to Canopus. When his Sun culminated, Canopus was on the Nadir. Here we see Mao Tse-Tung's very sense of identity married to the concepts of Canopus: the leader, the pathfinder for the Chinese people and culture, and eventually the darker side of Canopus as the dark father, the one who eventually consumes his children in a Saturnian theme. Fidel Castro was born with his Mars culminating as Canopus rose and he chose to lead his people in a martial, military way.

CANOPUS IN THE NATAL CHART

Canopus is a powerful star and, as long as you are born south of 37° North, it can influence you toward skills of leadership, new directions, or as a pathfinder who could destroy what is created. This is a complex star similar to a Royal Star, for it relates to success but the nemesis of one strongly influenced by it is that of needing too much control.

---

[26] H. B. Alexander, "North American Mythology," in *Mythology of all Races*, vol. 10. Boston, 1916, p. 116.

CANOPUS AS THE HELIACAL RISING STAR AT BIRTH

On Ptolemy's list of stars Canopus is certainly bright enough to herald the dawn and may be used as the apparent as well as the cosmic rising star. In such a position in your chart, then, it would talk about the potential for great leadership or the finding of new pathways or the breaking of new ground. At the same time it would bring with it the internal struggle to dominate and control which could damage the very work that you are trying to achieve.

AURIGA, THE CHARIOTEER

ONE OF THE GREAT STEPS FORWARD FOR the human race was the beginning of cultivation and the domestication of plants and animals. The importance of this process is represented in the constellations in the sky by the next cluster out from the North Pole. These are the constellations of Pegasus, the Winged Horse, Equuleus the Little Horse and Auriga the Charioteer, all of them involved with horses.

The Charioteer is the harnesser of the Horse. Different cultures used different images for this constellation, varying from a man holding a whip and reins to a man riding in a chariot with a goat supported on his left shoulder.[27] It is generally believed that this image originated in the Euphrates and that it was a well established sky figure millennia ago.[28] Jobes talks of the crippled Hephaestus being the maker of the chariot and the rider being his deformed son, Attica, whose feet and legs were coils of snakes. He was placed in the chariot to hide his snake-feet.[29] The constellation also has links from early times to a shepherd watching over his flocks and from this connection, in biblical times, it was seen as Christ the Good Shepherd.[30]

Auriga, with its asterism[31] of a she-goat nursing two kids, seemed to cause some problems for early writers, as the nursing imagery was not in keeping with the image of the mighty charioteer racing across the heavens (see Star Map 4, p. 70). One solution to the problem was to suggest that the asterism was the goat that suckled Zeus and was therefore sacred and placed in the heavens in thanks for her services.[32] They do not even try to explain the two kids. In another attempt they placed the horn of Cornucopia in the arms of the charioteer saying that the infant Zeus broke off its tip and it is the tip of this horn that the charioteer carries.[33]

However, because it contained the brightest star in the constellation, Capella, this asterism could not be ignored. Capella was adored and deified by both the Egyptians and the Greeks. In Egypt, temples were aligned to its rising and setting in about 5,200 B.C.E.;[34] and later in Greece it seemed to have been the orientation point of a temple at Eleusis dedicated to the Moon goddess, Diana.[35] Indeed, Capella is a goddess star and is one of the faces of the goddess.

---

[27] Allen, *Star Names*, p. 83.
[28] Allen, *Star Names*, p. 84.
[29] Jobes, *Outer Space*, p. 126.
[30] Jobes, *Outer Space*, p. 126.
[31] An *asterism* is a constellation within a constellation.
[32] Allen, *Star Names*, p. 87.
[33] Allen, *Star Names*, p. 87.
[34] Lockyer, *The Dawn of Astronomy*, p. 312.
[35] Allen, *Star Names*, p. 88.

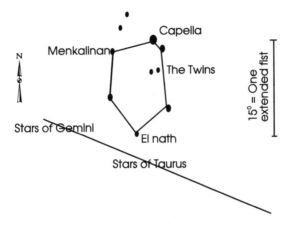

Star Map 4. The Charioteer.

However, if one considers the imagery of the nursing goat held in the left arm of the charioteer and leaning over his shoulder, plus the strong historical female association to Capella by Egypt, and later by Greece, and also the myth of Attica being the user of the chariot because his legs were snakes, it is obvious that what the charioteer carries is a feminine, nurturing object. Whether it is a she-goat suckling two kids or whether it is the tip of the horn of Cornucopia, it is a symbol of the nurturing, feminine breast.

With this in mind it is interesting to peel back the layers of mythology to that place that sits on the borderline between oral and written myths. Here one can find fragments of stories concerning women, chariots, and twins. The Celts were the race of people who, if they did not invent the chariot, certainly developed it as a major part of their society. In Celtic mythology there is a story about Arianhrod, the goddess of the star-wheel, the wheel or chariot in the sky, giving birth to twins.[36] And the story about Macha, the great Celtic horse goddess,[37] similarly associates feminine symbolism with the chariot motif.

Macha appeared one night at the door of a humble man's house. He recognized her for who she was, and she said she would live with him as his wife provided he did not reveal her identity to anyone. This arrangement worked well, and Macha would often run for miles just for the thrill and the pleasure of the speed of her feet and the freedom of the air against her face. Macha eventually fell pregnant to her mortal husband who was delighted at the thought of fathering a child by a goddess. Time passed . . .

---

[36] R. J. Stewart, *Celtic Gods, Celtic Goddesses* (London: Blandford, 1990), p. 85.

[37] There are many references to Macha but the following story can be read in full in Moyra Caldecott, *Women in Celtic Myth* (Rochester, VT: Destiny Books, 1992), p. 127.

In those days a man's worth was measured by the speed of his chariot. The king therefore needed to have the fastest horses in the kingdom. One day the warriors fell to bragging and Macha's husband boasted that his wife, on foot, could outrace the king's chariot. Outrage broke out and he was ordered to bring Macha to the king so she could race his horses. The pregnant Macha was taken to the king. She pleaded compassion, saying it was near her time to give birth and asked that the race be delayed. However, her pleading was ignored, an act considered by mythologists to symbolize the demarcation line between the matrilineal and the patriarchal in Celtic society. For by not respecting her condition, the king was performing an act against the sacredness of the goddess. She was ordered to race. So, heavy with child, Macha raced the king's chariots and, being the goddess of all horses, won the race but with great pain and difficulty. At the end of the race her water broke and there in front of the warriors, she gave birth to twins. These twins could be seen to symbolize the split that had now occurred between men and women. In her anger at the lack of respect shown by the warriors she cursed the men of Ulster, causing them to experience the pain of childbirth every time they were challenged in mortal battle. No one knows what happened to Macha's twins, but Macha's land is still honored in Ireland today, and the effect of her curse is a living memorial in the history of Ulster and Northern Ireland.

Great and powerful stories do not exist as isolated events. There would have been other such stories but unfortunately the mythology of the goddess was not written down. We see, however, from this one particular story that has survived, that there is a mythological basis for considering this stellar charioteer to be the symbol of a horse goddess, demonstrating her fertility by carrying her children. Instead of the nipples of a she-goat draped over the man's chest, placing them in the correct alignment for a woman's breast, it may be far simpler to let this figure be a Macha symbol. These types of questions can never have final answers but they are worth considering.

STARS OF AURIGA

The brightest star is Capella and the other stars, in descending order of magnitude, are: Menkalinan, the shoulder; El Nath, the heel; Maaz and Duo Haedi, the twins. The star El Nath is also assigned in modern day to the constellation Taurus, although traditionally it is considered to be the charioteer's heel.

CAPELLA

(Alpha Auriga. Magnitude 0.3. RA 05:16:18". Declination 45N59'22". PED = 21° Gemini 10'.) See Paran Map 5, page 72. *An example of how to read the*

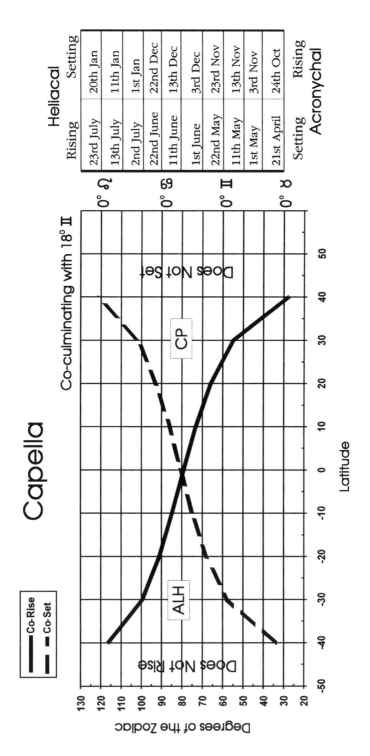

Capella

Co-culminating with 18° Ⅱ

Heliacal	
Rising	Setting
23rd July	20th Jan
13th July	11th Jan
2nd July	1st Jan
22nd June	22nd Dec
11th June	13th Dec
1st June	3rd Dec
22nd May	23rd Nov
11th May	13th Nov
1st May	3rd Nov
21st April	24th Oct
Setting	Rising
Acronychal	

Ω 0°
69 0°
Ⅱ 0°
ö 0°

Co-Rise
Co-Set

Does Not Set

CP

ALH

Does Not Rise

Degrees of the Zodiac

Latitude

-50 -40 -30 -20 -10 0 10 20 30 40 50

20 30 40 50 60 70 80 90 100 110 120 130

Paran Map 5. Capella.

map: If you were born in Miami, USA at a latitude of 26° North, then the star rose at about 0° Gemini. If you have a planet at either 0° Gemini or Sagittarius, then that planet rose or set with the star. The star also set at 9° Cancer. Therefore, if you have a planet at 9° Cancer or Capricorn, it would have set or risen as the star set. The star culminates at 18° Gemini, so if you have a planet at either 18° Gemini or Sagittarius, then it culminated or was on the Nadir as the star culminated.

At this latitude of 26° North the star has a phase of curtailed passage. This period will be from about November 23 (reading the date from the right-hand column of the date next to 0° Gemini) to about December 30 every year (reading the date from the right-hand column of the date next to 9° Cancer), and is the true or cosmic heliacal rising star about May 20 (reading the date for the rising line at 26° North in the "heliacal rising" column).

Capella can be used on all four points for charts between latitudes of 43° South and 43° North. South of that the star never rises and north of that the star never sets and therefore has permanent curtailed passage.

EARLIER OPINIONS

Ptolemy said that the bright stars resemble Mars and Mercury. Robson connects the star to honors and wealth, renowned public position, and a love of learning. Ebertin links the star to inquisitiveness and curiosity and indicates that this star can make a person "odd." Rigor agrees with Robson and adds ambition, as well as a tendency to become envious and have many problems.

CAPELLA: THE CONCEPT

Capella in most charts lends a nurturing but free-spirited flavor. It is similar to the concept of the fertile goddess, but she is of the horse and therefore embodies action and movement. Probably one of the clearest expressions of Capella in a person's life is the story of Amelia Earhart. On the day that Amelia Earhart was born, Venus culminated at the same time as Capella. The culmination point implies that this is how a person is seen by the world. Amelia Earhart achieved feats of speed and travel that stunned the world of aviation. The determination she must have shown in order to get the backing for her ideas, as a woman in the 1930s, must have been immense. She set aviation speed records for crossing the Atlantic and after this flight wrote a book called *For the Fun of It*. She also set speed records flying from Mexico City to New York City. The plane was the modern day chariot and Amelia Earhart, with her Venus connected with Capella, was seen as a woman breaking the speed records. Nor did she lose her feminine persona to her aviation. Like Macha, she could cover distances faster than any other person alive or dead. Her love was speed and the freedom of flight. These were the things she valued. Amelia was almost an embodiment of the archetype of Macha.

On a totally different note the chart that is given to the comic strip character Superman, based on the time of his creation, has Capella rising with Mars. So right from his "birth" this character is associated with speed and flight. John Glenn, whose chart is connected to Alpheratz (love of freedom and movement), the navel of Pegasus in the constellation of Andromeda, has Saturn culminating with Capella. These two stars in his chart are strong indicators that his life will be connected in some way with the concepts of speed, freedom and/or flight.

CAPELLA IN THE NATAL CHART

If you have Capella in paran with one of your planets you will express freedom and independence in a nonaggressive way. There will be a need for freedom that will be expressed in the area of your life indicated by the planet that is involved with Capella. In relationships, for example, if connected to Venus; in thinking, if connected to Mercury; and so on.

CAPELLA AS THE HELIACAL RISING STAR AT BIRTH

Capella is one of the most beautiful stars in the sky and her apparent heliacal rising was a cause for celebration and also ritual. To be born on such a day, either on the apparent or cosmic rising, is to be linked with the Macha-like problems of a love of freedom versus the desire for domestication; the need for a partner and desire for a family, struggling against the need for freedom with no commitments. These are the two themes such a person will be juggling. The lesson is to blend the two, rather than denying or hiding one side of the story.

BOOTES, THE HUNTER WHO NOW FARMS

BOOTES IS A MEMBER OF THE SERIES OF
constellations which begin at the Pole with the sacred stars of Draco and Ursa
Major and Minor, and radiate outward in a pattern mirrored by the components
of civilized village society (see Star Map 5, p. 76). This constellation is a symbol
of the domestic or civilized human.

Bootes, the hunter, herdsman and farmer, has been known by the same
name for over 3,000 years,[38] although at first this name was applied to just the
alpha star, Arcturus. He symbolizes the important transition from the Paleolithic
hunter-gatherer to the Neolithic cultivator and the domesticator of animals.
Many stories were woven around his starry image—a plowman driving his oxen,
for example, plowing the fields of the sky.[39] Later, the Athenians saw him as the
leader of his people who, having fallen on difficult times, invented the plow,
which he used to ease his labors, and thereby became one of the great benefactors
of humankind.[40] Bootes may well have acted as a reminder, a piece of starry
history, long before any words were written, of the transition from the hunter-
gather to the cultivator.

However, the Greeks in their drive to name and claim everything in the
heavens, saw Bootes as the son of Zeus and Callista, a wood nymph. Zeus was
said to have raped Callista, and when she discovered that she was pregnant, Zeus
turned her into a bear so that Artemis would not harm her. Eventually she gave
birth to a son who grew up to be a strong hunter. Many years passed, and one
day in the woods she saw her grown son. In joy she went to hug him, forgetting
that she was a bear. Her son, thinking he was being attacked by a bear, raised his
spear to kill his mother. In order to prevent the unthinkable and unforgivable
crime of matricide, Zeus quickly placed both of them in the heavens: Callista as
Ursa Major or Minor, and her son as Bootes. The Greeks pictured him hunting
the bears of the Pole.[41]

Bootes stands in the sky holding weapons and farming tools, while in front
of him he guides two hunting dogs, once part of this constellation but now separated from their farmer, hunter, and master. The dogs are the constellation Canes
Venatici and are named Asterion and Chara. The alpha star of Bootes is Arcturus,
probably one of the first stars ever named,[42] since it appears in all literature on the
sky. It was used in the agricultural calendar, as its acronychal and heliacal risings

---

[38] Allen, *Star Names*, p. 92.
[39] Room, *Dictonary of Astronomical Names*, p. 65.
[40] Jobes, *Outer Space*, p. 128.
[41] Guerber, *The Myths of Greece and Rome*, p. 35.
[42] Jobes, *Outer Space*, p. 306.

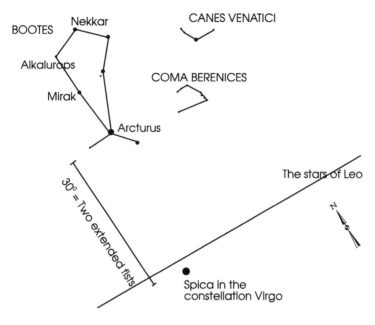

Star Map 5. Bootes with his dogs.

once corresponded to the important dates in the farming year. The concept of cultivator is captured by the great Greek poet Hesiod (c. 800 B.C.E.), who wrote:

When in the rosy morn Arcturus shines,
Then pluck the clusters from the parent vines.[43]

STARS OF BOOTES

The brightest star is Arcturus, on the knee of the herdsman. Some other named stars, in descending order of magnitude, are: Nekkar, his head; Mirak, his waistcloth; and Alkalurops, the tip of his spear.

ARCTURUS

(Alpha Bootes. Magnitude 0.3. RA 14:15:25.2". Declination 19N12'47". PED = 23° Libra 32'.) See Paran Map 6, page 77. *An example of how to read the map:* If you were born in Hobart, Australia, at a latitude of 43° South, then the star

---

[43] Allen, *Star Names*, p. 95.

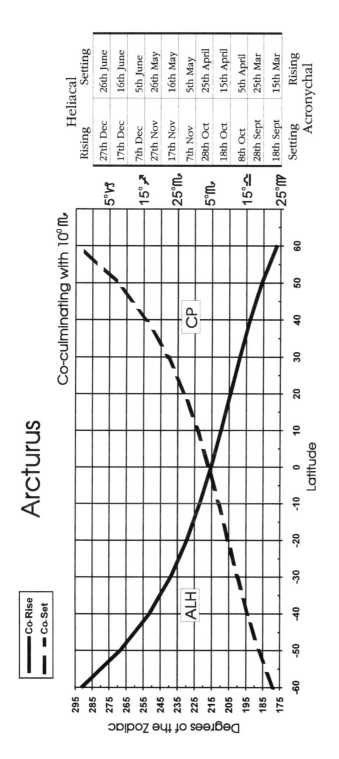

Heliacal			Acronychal	
Rising	Setting		Setting	Rising
27th Dec	26th June	5°♑		
17th Dec	16th June	15°♐		
7th Dec	5th June	25°♏		
27th Nov	26th May			
17th Nov	16th May			
7th Nov	5th May	5°♏		
28th Oct	25th April			
18th Oct	15th April	15°♎		
8th Oct	5th April			
28th Sept	25th Mar			
18th Sept	15th Mar	25°♍		

Paran Map 6. Arcturus.

rose at about 29° Capricorn. If you have a planet at either 29° Capricorn or Cancer, then that planet rose or set with the star. The star also set at 10° Libra. Therefore, if you have a planet at 10° Libra or Aries, it would have set or risen as the star set. The star culminates at 10° Scorpio, so if you have a planet at either 10° Scorpio or Taurus then it culminated or was on the Nadir as the star culminated.

At this latitude of 43° South the star has a phase of arising and lying hidden. This period is from about October 3 (reading the date from the left-hand column of the date box next to 10° Libra) to December 7every year (reading the date from the left-hand column of the date box next to 29° Capricorn), and is the true or cosmic heliacal rising star about December 7 (reading the date from for the rising line at 43° South in the "heliacal rising" column).

Arcturus can be used on all four points for charts between latitudes of 70° South and 70° North. South of that the star never rises and north of that the star never sets and therefore has permanent curtailed passage.

EARLIER OPINIONS

Ptolemy says that, because of its red color, Arcturus is like Mars and Jupiter. Robson claims it gives riches and honors, as well as prosperity through journeys.[44] Ebertin suggests it can make the native belligerent and quarrelsome and, at the same time, give the person a get-ahead enterprising spirit. Rigor agrees about the honor and riches, and also relates success in the arts to the influence of Arcturus.

ARCTURUS: THE CONCEPT

Arcturus is a sentry who guards or patrols the border between the circumpolar and equatorial regions.[45] He is the one who bridges the lands between the hunter-gatherer nomad and the herder-cultivator-plowman villager. Thus Arcturus embodies the symbolism of guarding, learning, teaching, leading—leading and protecting people as they embrace a new life style. One who can lead the way, one who has the vision or the spirit to take the first step. It shows itself quite strongly in this way in the chart of Mao Tse-Tung. On the day of his birth, Mars set with Arcturus, linking his motivating energy to a desire to create a new life. With this drive he strove to move China from a feudal system to a communist republic. Adolf Hitler, whose chart was also linked to Algol in the constellation Perseus, also had connections to Arcturus, which rose as his Jupiter was on the Nadir. This demonstrates the influence of Arcturus magnified by Jupiter, the

---

[44] This is an interesting statement, as shipping insurance would increase dramatically once Arcturus was visible in the night sky, for it was considered very unfortunate for the sailor.

[45] Jobes, *Outer Space*, p. 305.

ability to lead and protect people as they enter a new lifestyle, linked with the passion and potential ruthlessness of Algol.

A totally different example is the chart of Mary Shelley, the English novelist who wrote *Frankenstein*. She had three contacts with Arcturus: she was born at the moment it was setting, and that day Arcturus rose with Venus and culminated as the Moon rose. Mary Shelley was a very different figure from Mao Tse-Tung, but she did create a new pathway in literature, for *Frankenstein*, a novel she wrote when she was only twenty, created a whole new genre of writing.

ARCTURUS IN THE NATAL CHART

A strong Arcturus in your chart will indicate that you are a pathfinder, a person who needs to create a better way of life or a new way of doing something, not just for yourself but for others as well. There will also be a strong sense of leading others involved with this new path or new idea.

ARCTURUS AS THE HELIACAL RISING STAR AT BIRTH

This is one of Ptolemy's stars, so it can be used as both the apparent as well as the cosmic rising star. When it is linked to the Sun it will indicate leadership qualities and the ability to explore or move forward into new fields. You will be known as a person with these abilities, either in your local community or on a global level. The other stars in your chart will indicate the manner in which you use these skills.

CANIS MAJOR, THE DOG

NOT FAR FROM THE STERN OF THE ARGO lie two dogs, a large one lying in the south, Canis Major, and a smaller dog, Canis Minor, sitting above it on the equator (see Star Map 6, below). These are the dogs of Orion, chasing a hare, Lepus, and harassing the mighty bull of Taurus.

Aratus refers to Canis Major as one of Orion's hunting dogs, sitting up in a begging position but with a watchful eye on the nearby hare.[46] But this dog was in the sky long before Aratus recorded it in the fourth century B.C.E. The dog was one of the first animals that human beings domesticated, thousands of years before the written word, and was worshiped universally as a guardian, usually guarding the dead or taking the dead souls back to their mother, the goddess. In early times, dogs in myth only accompanied the goddess and guarded the gates of death.[47] The Egyptians called this guard or judge of the dead Anubis, who became their god of mummification.[48] In Christian mythology, he seems to have been represented by Saint Peter at the pearly gates of heaven, playing the same role as the dog—guarding, and sometimes judging who could pass through.

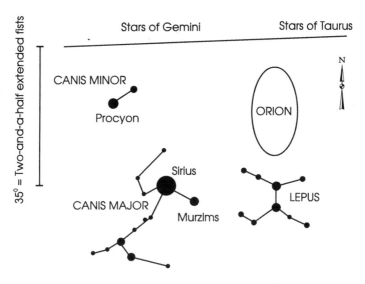

Star Map 6. Two Dogs and a Hare.

[46] Mair, *Callimachus, Lycophron, Aratus*, p. 233.
[47] Walker, *The Woman's Encyclopedia of Myths and Secrets*, p. 240.
[48] Walker, *The Woman's Encyclopedia of Myths and Secrets*, p. 241.

This image of the dog guarding the doorway to another world is an easy extension of the domestic dog guarding its owner's door. In Celtic cultures, the death of a faithful hound meant it was buried underneath the door steps so it could continue to guard the home. It is from this tradition that we have the custom of carrying the bride across the threshold so the spirit guardians would think of her as a resident rather than an intruder.[49]

Canis Major has been called by many names over its long history, and in earlier writings it is not clear whether writers are talking about the constellation or its alpha star, Sirius. In the days before the fall of Troy it was called The Dog of the Sun,[50] for it was thought to hold Sirius, the brightest star in the sky, in its mouth.

STARS OF CANIS MAJOR

The brightest star is Sirius, and the other named stars, in descending order of magnitude, are: Murzims, in the paw, also known as The Announcer; Wezen, in the chest; and Aludra, in the tail.

SIRIUS

(Alpha Canis Major. Magnitude −1.43. RA 06:44:55". Declination 16S42'25". PED = 13° Cancer 24'.) See Paran Map 7, page 82. *An example of how to read the map:* If you were born in Melbourne, Australia, at a latitude of 37° South, then the star rose at about 10° Gemini. If you have a planet at either 10° Gemini or Sagittarius, then that planet rose or set with the star. The star also set at 9° Leo. Therefore, if you have a planet at 9° Leo or Aquarius, it would have set or risen as the star set. The star culminates at 14° Cancer so if you have a planet at either 14° Cancer or Capricorn, then it culminated or was on the Nadir as the star culminated.

At this latitude of 37° South the star has a phase of curtailed passage. This period will be from about December 3 (reading the date from the right-hand column of the date box next to 10° Gemini) to January 29 every year (reading the right-hand column of the date box next to 9° Leo), and is the true or cosmic heliacal rising star about June 1 (reading the date for the rising line at 37° South in the "heliacal rising" column).

Sirius can be used on all four points for charts between latitudes of 73° South and 73° North. North of that the star never rises and south of that the star never sets and therefore has permanent curtailed passage.

---

[49] Walker, *The Woman's Encyclopedia of Myths and Secrets*, p. 242.
[50] Jobes, *Outer Space*, p. 136.

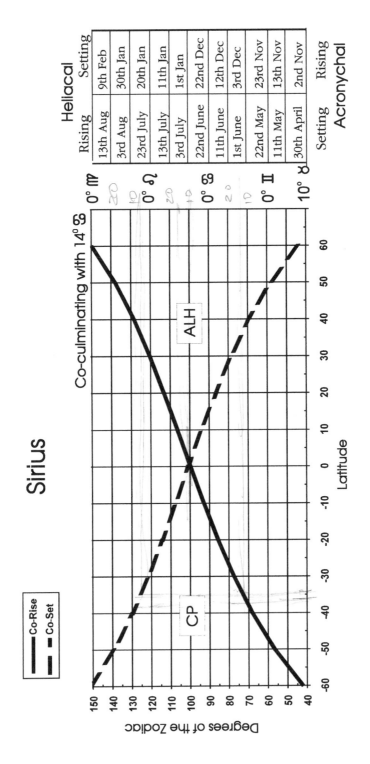

Sirius

Co-culminating with 14° ♋

	Heliacal	
Rising		Setting
13th Aug		9th Feb
3rd Aug		30th Jan
23rd July		20th Jan
13th July		11th Jan
3rd July		1st Jan
22nd June		22nd Dec
11th June		12th Dec
1st June		3rd Dec
22nd May		23rd Nov
11th May		13th Nov
30th April		2nd Nov
Setting		Rising
	Acronychal	

0° ♍
0° ♌
0° ♋
0° ♊
10° ♉

ALH

CP

Co-Rise
Co-Set

Degrees of the Zodiac

Latitude

Paran Map 7. Sirius.

EARLIER OPINIONS

Ptolemy states that Sirius is like Jupiter with a touch of Mars. Robson mentions fame and honor, as well as faithfulness and guardians. Ebertin agrees with Robson and adds that a person influenced by Sirius is in danger of pushing things forward too fast. Rigor agrees with Ebertin and adds that such a person loves power.

SIRIUS: THE CONCEPT

Sirius is one of the great stars of the sky and, with its magnitude of -1.43, it is the brightest star in the heavens apart from our Sun. The Egyptians called it The Shining One or The Scorcher.[51] The heat from Sirius was thought to cause rabies or madness in dogs, and its risings and settings were so regularly recorded it formed the foundation of the Egyptian calendar. It was worshiped as early as 3,285 B.C.E., the dog symbol being a predominant feature in hieroglyphics.[52] It was linked to the life-giving rising of the Nile and in that capacity it was also called the Nile Star.[53] The Egyptians called it Sirius Isis,[54] (see figure 19, below). By a quirk of the Julian calendar, it did not appear to be affected by precession over thousands of years,[55] for its precessional movement was in perfect timing with the error of the calendar—thus Sirius always rose on the same calendar date. The Egyptian year opened with the heliacal rising of Sirius which, from about 5,000 B.C.E. to around the time of Christ, occurred every fourth year, on July 19 and 20 in the Julian calendar. Thus it appeared that only goddesses were not subject to precession, for they were the points of stillness, or what we know as the

Figure 19. Egyptian hieroglyph for the Isis Knot or the Blood of Isis.

---

[51] Jobes, *Outer Space*, p. 368.
[52] Jobes, *Outer Space*, p. 364.
[53] Allen, *Star Names*, p. 124.
[54] Lockyer, *Dawn of Astronomy*, p. 196.
[55] Lockyer, *Dawn of Astronomy*, p. 252.

Pole Star. However, the Egyptian priests knew of her seasonal movement; to maintain her immortality and her secret they adjusted the calendar to totally match her heliacal rising.[56] The eventual abandonment of this calendar after thousands of years, and its replacement by the Alexandrine year in 23 B.C.E.,[57] shifted this star's heliacal rising calendar date, thereby subjecting the star to the effects of precession. And so for the first and only time, it was thought that a goddess had "died."

De Santillana and von Dechend in their book, *Hamlet's Mill,* discuss the wide range of myths which are announcements that a god or goddess has died. They talk of the lament, "The great Pan is dead," that was heard floating down the Aegean during the reign of Tiberius, and how this Pan was not the Greek or Roman god, but a far more ancient Egyptian figure of some 15,000 years in age. They suggest that this Egyptian Pan was indeed the star Sirius and the goddess Isis, and that the fall of this star symbolized the death of this ancient god[58] who was linked to Isis and thus Sirius through the goddess connection with the dog. There is also the lament to Tammuz, an Egyptian grain god allegedly called out on the night between July 19 and 20, the exact night which used to be the heliacal rising of Sirius before the new calendar was instated. Sirius did not rise before the Sun on that day and, therefore, the unthinkable had happened: a goddess had been affected by precession and slipped into the whirlpool. A death had occurred, not gradually, as in the case of Osiris over several thousands of years, but in one night. For in that night, 5,000 years of precession was applied to Sirius. Thus, with the change of calendar, a divine being was struck down or fell, which de Santillana and von Dechend suggest was also the time that oracles began to fail.

All this is very interesting to astrologers as it suggests the end of an era or an age where the world of interconnectedness and cycles, the foundation stones of oracles and astrology, was center stage, and now they would be put to one side for the sake of the development of logic and science. This leads one to speculate that it may be the death of another goddess, or the birth of one, that will mark the reemergence of cycles and their importance into mainstream thought.

The goddess Isis was the wife of Osiris (constellation Orion), the great god who was the first to be swallowed by precession into the whirlpool. In mythology he is killed and his body dismembered. Isis in mourning traveled through the land and found all the pieces of his body and, binding them together, she breathed life back into him. He lived long enough to impregnate her with their

---

[56] The pharaohs would only be crowned by the priest after they had sworn a holy oath to maintain this Sirius-based calendar. To adopt a more accurate calendar meant that Isis would lose her power as an immortal goddess.

[57] Lockyer, *Dawn of Astronomy,* p. 281.

[58] De Santillana and von Dechend, *Hamlet's Mill,* p. 286.

son Horus (Aldebaran in the constellation of Taurus), who later became heir to the throne.[59]

Sirius, therefore, when present in a chart by paran, is a marker of great deeds. It indicates that the mundane may become sacred, that the small action of the individual has a large effect on the collective. The individual, however, may be sacrificed to this collective expression, or may gain fame and glory. It is a blast of energy that can burn your fingers or help you achieve levels that seem impossible. The Isis/Sirius mythology includes one of the earliest episodes of a woman building a fire which will burn away mortal flesh,[60] which is echoed by the Greeks in the story of Thetis and Achilles,[61] as well as in its darker expression in the story of Althea and Meleager,[62] where Althea kills her son by burning a stick which fate has decreed indicates his length of life. Sirius can bring immortality to its bearer, but the price may be the burning away of the mortal flesh.

One of the most striking examples of Sirius was its heliacal rising with Pluto in early August, 1945, which occurred at latitudes 32° to 35° North. In this period two Japanese cities at that latitude, Hiroshima and Nagasaki, experienced nuclear attacks. Thousands had their flesh burnt away, and yet they have been immortalized, as these cities are now sacred places dedicated to the removal of nuclear weapons from the earth.

Abraham Lincoln was born on the day that Sirius culminated as his Venus set. Although the Venus content is not clear, Lincoln is a typical Sirius figure. He strove to achieve a dream, the freedom of all people, and indeed he succeeded at that goal only to lose his life. He is now seen as one of the great immortal figures of American history.

Princess Diana was also born with Sirius culminating with her Sun. I had always thought this showed that she came to world attention in the middle of her life, but now, after her tragic death and the consequent world mourning, we can see how, in the middle of her life, her death has made her memory "immortal" and sacred.

SIRIUS IN THE NATAL CHART

This very strong star indicates that you may, by your effort, gain far more than what is expected—the mundane becoming sacred. Hence a small action becomes a symbol for the collective, a sense of ritual in daily life. Sirius, in some ways, is not an easy star with which to work, as it demands expression somehow in your life—and the huge success it can bring may "burn" you.

---

[59] J. F. Bierlein, *Parallel Myths* (New York: Ballantine, 1994), p. 212.
[60] Bierlein, *Parallel Myths*, p. 214.
[61] Liz Greene, *The Astrology of Fate* (York Beach, ME: Samuel Weiser, 1984), p. 201.
[62] Thomas Bulfinch, *Myths of Greece and Rome* (New York: Penguin, 1979), p. 163.

SIRIUS AS THE HELIACAL RISING STAR AT BIRTH

Obviously this star can be used as both the apparent and the cosmic rising star. If you were an Egyptian child born on this day, you would have been sacred and special and your life may well have been devoted to the service of Isis. This is a strong position of a very strong star, and although this star is clear and of honest intent, its energy is so strong it can be difficult to handle. Fundamentally, your actions could have a profound effect far beyond what you expect, so choose them with care and if situations escalate, do not try and stop them; rather, try and direct them to a positive outcome.

MURZIMS (MIRZAM)

(Beta Canis Major. Magnitude 1.9. RA 20:25:16.3". Declination 17S57'04". PED = 6° Cancer 29'.) See Paran Map 8, page 87. *An example of how to read the map:* If you were born in New Orleans, USA, at a latitude of 30° North then the star rose at about 27° Cancer. If you have a planet at either 27° Cancer or Capricorn, then that planet rose or set with the star. The star also set at 13° Gemini. Therefore, if you have a planet at 13° Gemini or Sagittarius, it would have set or risen as the star set. The star culminates at 6° Cancer so if you have a planet at either 6° Cancer or Capricorn, then it culminated or was on the Nadir as the star culminated.

At this latitude of 30° North the star has a phase of arising and lying hidden. This period will be from about June 4 (reading the date from the left-hand column of the date box next to 13° Gemini) to July 20 every year (reading the left-hand column of the date box next to 27° Cancer and is the true or cosmic heliacal rising star about July 20 (reading the date for the rising line at 30° North in the "heliacal rising" column).

Murzims can be used on all four points for charts between latitudes of 72° South and 72° North. North of that the star never rises and south of that the star never sets and therefore has permanent curtailed passage.

EARLIER OPINIONS

Ptolemy links the stars of Canis Major to Jupiter and Mars. Robson, Ebertin, and Rigor do not refer to this star.

MURZIMS: THE CONCEPT

Murzims was called The Announcer because it rose before Sirius.[63] This star seems to embody the symbolism of the dog: just like a dog its nature is to announce, to make noise, to speak out. The person influenced by Murzims often

---

[63] Jobes, *Outer Space*, p. 334.

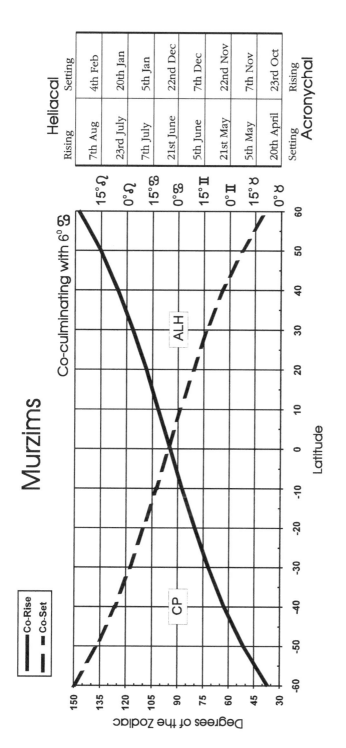

Paran Map 8. Murzims.

seems to carry a message or to have something important to say. Albert Einstein had Murzims culminating as both his Mercury and Saturn set. He conceived of the theory of relativity when he was only 17 years old, and he admitted at the end of his life that he had spent his whole life explaining it to others. Another person with a message to announce was Edward VIII, of England (1894–1972), who had Mars rising as Murzims was on the Nadir. A star on the Nadir is one which will indicate the summary one's life, and indeed we remember Edward VIII as the monarch who announced that he would give up the throne of England "for the sake of the woman that I love."

MURZIMS IN THE NATAL CHART

Unlike Sirius, this is not a star of great importance. It will, however, carry this "Announcer" energy into the life of the person influenced by it. On the personal level, this can mean that you have something to say or are involved in groups; or on a public level, you may have a desire to speak out or to make an announcement to the world.

MURZIMS AS THE HELIACAL RISING STAR AT BIRTH

Murzims is not included on Ptolemy's list, so it can only be used as the cosmic rising star. If it holds this position in your chart, then you will identify yourself with information, talking, or the carrying of some type of message.

CANIS MINOR, THE LESSER DOG

ABOVE CANIS MAJOR ON THE EQUATOR IS
a much smaller "dog" (see Star Map 6, p. 80). Thought of as Orion's second
hound, it has also been called The Puppy.[64] It rises before Canis Major and, like
the star Murzims, the beta star of Canis Major, its main claim to fame is the fact
that it heralds the arrival of Sirius.

STARS OF CANIS MINOR

The brightest star is Procyon; the other named star is Gomeisa.

PROCYON

(Alpha Canis Minor. Magnitude 0.5. RA 07:39:1.5". Declination 05N14'18".
PED = 25° Cancer 06'.) See Paran Map 9, page 90. *An example of how to read the
map:* If you were born in Athens, Greece, at a latitude of 39° North then the star
rose at about 3° Leo. If you have a planet at either 3° Leo or Aquarius, then that
planet rose or set with the star. The star also set at 9° Cancer. Therefore, if you have
a planet at 9° Cancer or Capricorn, it would have set or risen as the star set. The star
culminates at 25° Cancer so if you have a planet at either 25° Cancer or Capricorn,
then it culminated or was on the Nadir as the star culminated.

At this latitude of 39° North the star has a phase of arising and lying hidden. This period will be from about July 1 (reading the date from the left-hand
column of the date box next to 9° Cancer) to July 25 every year (reading the left-hand column of the date box next to 3° Leo), and is the true or cosmic heliacal
rising star about July 25 (reading the date for the rising line at 39° North in the
"heliacal rising" column).

Procyon can be used on all four points for charts at any latitudes, except at
the extremes of the poles.

EARLIER OPINIONS

Ptolemy likens the star to Mercury, with a hint of Mars. Robson relates it to violent actions, disasters, danger of dog bites, and misfortunes in general. Ebertin
talks of a hot temper—being hasty, jealous, and pig-headed—but does add that
the individual will still be able to put together successful plans. Rigor, however,
links Procyon to fortune and fame, with the warning that one can fall quickly
from such lofty heights.

---

[64] Allen, *Star Names*, p. 132.

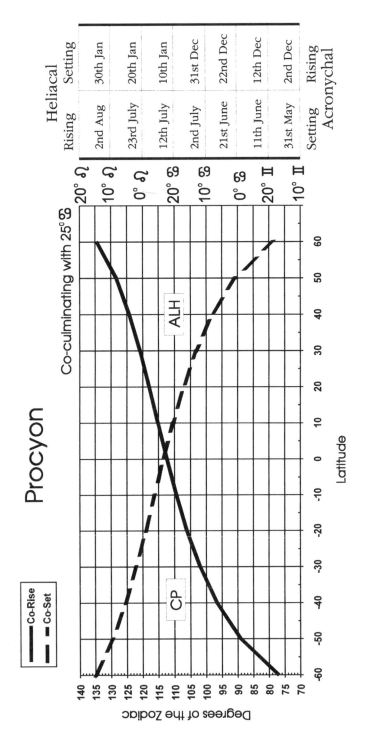

Heliacal			Setting	Rising
	Rising	Setting		
20° ♌	2nd Aug	30th Jan		
10° ♌	23rd July	20th Jan		
0° ♌	12th July	10th Jan		
20° ♋	2nd July	31st Dec		
10° ♋	21st June	22nd Dec		
0° ♋	11th June	12th Dec		
20° ♊	31st May	2nd Dec		
10° ♊			Setting	Rising
				Acronychal

Procyon

Co-culminating with 25° ♋

ALH

CP

Co-Rise
Co-Set

Degrees of the Zodiac

Latitude

Paran Map 9. Procyon.

PROCYON: THE CONCEPT

The actor James Dean is a simple example of influence of this star: a young actor who shoots to fame and then is killed in a car accident. Dean was born on the day that Procyon set as the Moon culminated. Oliver Cromwell also had Procyon involved with his chart. As his Saturn was at the Nadir, or IC, of his chart, Procyon rose. He enjoyed fame all his life and was buried in Westminster Abbey along with the kings and queens of England. Within three years of his death, his republic had fallen and the people had brought back the monarchy. His body was removed from Westminster and he was hung as a traitor with his head put on a pole and mounted above Westminster Hall.

PROCYON IN THE NATAL CHART

Procyon comes before The Shining One, Sirius, and so can indicate a quick rise but with no real substance. If this star is in your chart, depending on how it affects your chart, you will experience early gains upon which you should capitalize quickly, rather than expecting these gains to last forever.

PROCYON AS THE HELIACAL RISING STAR AT BIRTH

Procyon is able to be both the apparent as well as the cosmic rising star, since it is cited by Ptolemy. This may prove to be a difficult star to have linked to your Sun, not because the star itself has any negative energy but because it can be out of phase with modern thought. Modern life teaches us that one has to work hard and long for one's success, which comes over time. However, with Procyon in this position in your chart, you would always need to be harvesting your gains and moving on to the next thing. It encourages short, quick success rather than long, hard, slow, Saturnian success—which, in this case, will lead to losses.

CANES VENATICI, BOOTES' HUNTING DOGS

THE TWO DOGS HELD BY BOOTES ARE originally part of that constellation. They were made into their own constellation in 1690. It is considered that they do not contain any stars of astrological note. Robson, however, does associate the love of hunting with the stars in this constellation. The northern dog is called Asterion, or Starry, and the southern dog, which contains the two brightest stars, is called Chara and, according to Allen, is said to be dear to her master's heart. The Chinese named the three stars in the head of Asterion "the three Honorary Guardians of the Heir Apparent." This implies that these three stars, originally part of the constellation Bootes, not only had the customary dog's role of guardianship, but that they were guarding something as precious as an heir apparent.

The alpha star is known as Cor Caroli. In 1725 this was turned into an asterism by Edmond Halley as the "Heart of Charles I" in honor of that executed king. It is interesting to note that this star is featured in Prince Charles' chart. His Neptune, a planet that is usually not used unless the individual represents the collective, culminates with Cor Caroli, which implies that, although he is the heir apparent, there may possibly be some loss or confusion (Neptune) around the succession.

CASSIOPEIA, THE QUEEN

CASSIOPEIA IS THE WIFE OF CEPHEUS. The Greeks claimed she was even more beautiful than the Nereids.[65] In punishment for Cassiopeia's crime of vanity, she was chained to her chair and set in the sky to orbit around the Pole for eternity. This symbol in the sky was a reminder to women of their powerless state. This same theme of the restraint of powerful women is repeated by Zeus, in his torture of Hera. When he failed to believe that Hephaestus was her parthenogenous child, he imprisoned her in a mechanical chair with arms that folded against the sitter.[66]

But Cassiopeia is an ancient constellation like the rest of her family of circumpolar stars (see Star Map 1, p. 48). The Arabs called these stars The Lady in a Chair,[67] although earlier writings talk of them as The Hand Stained with Henna, i.e., the red hand.[68] The Christians called her Mary Magdalene and at other times Deborah.[69] The Egyptians placed the shape of this constellation, as well as the rest of the celestial royal family, on their seals. It would seem, therefore, that the major theme of this group of stars is one of female sovereignty, initially placed next to the king in balance but thrown into a state of punishment when that balance was lost.

STARS OF CASSIOPEIA

The brightest star is Schedar, the left breast of the queen. Other named stars, in descending order of magnitude, are: Caph, the corner of the chair; Tsih, the queen's girdle; Ruchbah, the Knee; and Marfak, the elbow.

SCHEDAR

(Alpha Cassiopeia. Magnitude variable 2.2 to 2.8. RA 0:40:15.7". Declination 56N30'33". PED = 7° Taurus 05'.) See Paran Map 10, page 94. *An example of how to read the map:* If you were born in Darwin, Australia at a latitude of 12° South then the star rose at about 28° Aries. If you have a planet at either 28° Aries or Libra then that planet rose or set with the star. The star also set at 18°

---

[65] The Nereids were similar to the fairies, nymphs, and mermaids of Northern European mythology.

[66] Robert Graves, *The Greek Myths*, vol. 1 (London: Penguin, 1960), p. 51.

[67] Allen, *Star Names*, p. 143.

[68] Allen, *Star Names*, p. 144.

[69] Allen, *Star Names*, p. 145.

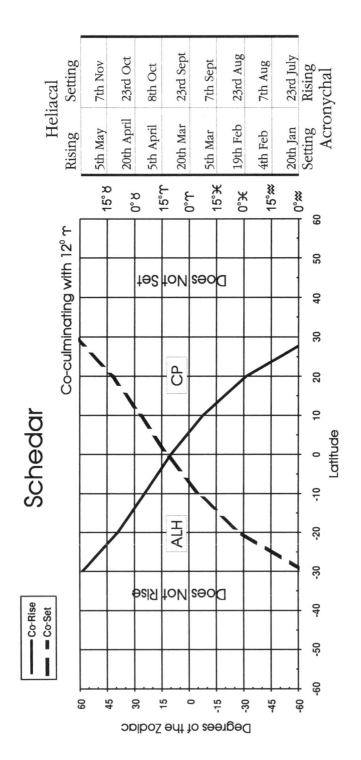

Param Map 10. Schedar.

Pisces. Therefore, if you have a planet at 18° Pisces or Virgo, then it would have set or risen as the star set. The star culminates at 12° Aries, so if you have a planet at either 12° Aries or Libra, then it culminated or was on the Nadir as the star culminated.

At this latitude of 12° South the star has a phase of arising and lying hidden. This period is from about March 8 (reading the date from the left-hand column of the date box next to 18° Pisces) to April 16 every year (reading the date from the left-hand column of the date box next to 28° Aries), and is the true or cosmic heliacal rising star about April 16 (reading the date from the rising line at 12° South in the "heliacal rising" column).

Schedar can be used on all four points for charts between latitudes of 33° South and 33° North. South of that the star never rises and north of that the star never sets and therefore has permanent curtailed passage.

EARLIER OPINIONS

Ptolemy states that the stars of Cassiopeia are like Saturn and Venus. Robson does not mention Schedar but talks of those influenced by the constellation as commanding respect. Ebertin warns that too much good living can lead to difficulties, and even hints at a certain amount of demonic power attached to the star. Rigor also mentions demonic power and sorrows in love, but, on the other hand, fame through the help of superiors. It would seem that the symbol of female sovereignty has undergone difficult times in the last several thousand years.

SCHEDAR: THE CONCEPT

If we take away the chains, the punishment, and the loss of dignity, what is left is the potential to command respect. The stars of this constellation could well embody the archetypal concept of the queen: a natural ability to command respect, endowed with wisdom, embodying a leadership style based on the feminine model that incorporates intuition and mysticism—just as the masculine model emphasizes strength and focus.

General George Patton's life is an interesting example of the influence of Schedar. On the day he was born, the Moon set as Schedar culminated, linking his emotions to this celestial queen. Patton's emotional conviction that he was always right and his deep belief in reincarnation and mysticism is typical of this star's influence. In contrast to this military figure, Margaret Thatcher was born on the day that Mars was on the Nadir as Schedar was culminating. So in the middle period of her life she took on the persona of a queen in her role as the British prime minister. Another case from Britain is that of Princess Diana, who was born with her Jupiter setting as Schedar was culminating. This hardly needs an explanation, but it is interesting to note firstly that, as it is her Jupiter that was connected with the star, the influence of the star was magnified; and secondly, since the star was culminating she was not born with this apparent sovereignty but rather manifested it in the middle or adult period of her life. Margaret Thatcher's command was through politics; Princess Diana's was through marriage.

SCHEDAR IN THE NATAL CHART

This star symbolizes a strong woman who demands dignity and rules by the power of her respectability and honor. If she is in your chart, you can rely on your desire to always function with propriety, to treat others as you would like to be treated, to know that your dignity is the source of your power.

SCHEDAR AS THE HELIACAL RISING STAR AT BIRTH

Schedar is limited by its declination from taking on the role of the heliacal star. However, if it is focused this way in your chart, then recognize that you have great strength in maintaining your honor and decency and that, under stress, these will prevail. Your sense of identity is linked to your morals and ethics, so respect them.

CENTAURUS, THE CENTAUR

CENTAURUS THE CENTAUR, LUPUS THE Wolf, and Ara the Altar are a group of three constellations entangled in a story of worship and devotion (see Star Map 7, p. 98). Aratus called this constellation "The Centaur,"[70] as the Greeks perceived this constellation this way (in contrast to Sagittarius who was seen primarily as an archer). The Centaur is a large constellation covering an area between 30 and 60 degrees of southern declination and is said to be holding Lupus, the Wolf, in his outstretched hand. He was thought, by both the Greeks and the Arabs, to be making his way to Ara, the Altar, to make a sacrifice.[71] To that end he is often shown carrying a water canteen for the necessary libation.

He was identified with either Chiron or Pholos,[72] both famous centaurs in Greek mythology. The stories of Chiron and Pholos are intertwined. Hercules, while hunting a boar, was offered the hospitality of the centaur Pholos. Hercules asked for some of the wine that Pholos had in jars. However, Pholos refused, explaining that the wine was not his to give as it belonged to all the centaurs as collective property. Hercules, in a show of roughness and bad manners, broke open a jar and proceeded to drink his fill. The wild centaurs smelled the wine and became so excited they rushed to the cave of Pholos. By this time Hercules had consumed a little too much wine and mistook the excitement of the centaurs as an attack. In the succeeding fight he accidentally wounded his old tutor Chiron. The wound was a mortal wound and condemned Chiron to eternal pain, since he was immortal and could not die. As Pholos removed the arrow from Chiron's leg, he grazed himself with the tip and thus was also wounded. Pholos was not immortal, so he could die. And Chiron later gave his immortality to the Titan Prometheus, so that he, too, could die.[73]

Legend has it that Chiron[74] was placed in the sky, some say as Sagittarius, others as the Centaur. However, the two constellations are quite different: Sagittarius is a fighting figure with a drawn bow, known as the Archer; The Centaur is a religious figure about to perform a libation and sacrifice at the altar. Given the choice between the two, The Centaur seems to represent the gentle Chiron more accurately. Indeed, in Greek myth Zeus tried to place Chiron in the place of

---

[70] Mair, *Callimachus, Lycophron, Aratus*, p. 241.

[71] Mair, *Callimachus, Lycophron, Aratus*, p. 241.

[72] Allen, *Star Names*, p. 148–149.

[73] Allen, *Star Names*, p. 149.

[74] This is the same mythological creature that has recently been assigned to the burnt out comet called Chiron, but one should be aware that Zeus had already placed him in the sky as this constellation.

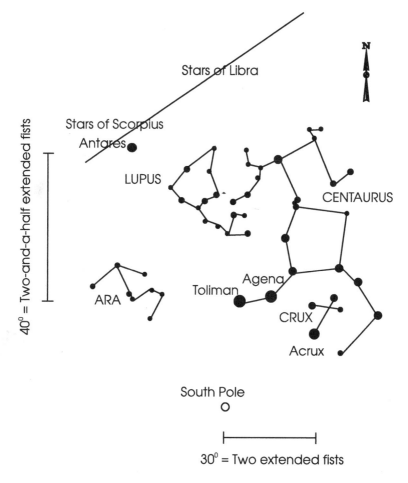

Star Map 7. Centaurus, Lupus, and Ara.

Sagittarius but failed due to the ferocity of the Archer, and was forced to place Chiron deep in the southern sky.[75]

The constellation Centaurus, then, symbolizes a gifted teacher and healer, with a deep wound that becomes the personal catalyst to self-awareness.

STARS OF THE CENTAUR

The brightest star is Toliman, meaning "Hereafter," also known as Rigil Kentaurus, the Centaur's foot, or more commonly, Alpha Centaurus. Other named stars,

---

[75] Jobes, *Outer Space*, p. 146.

in descending order of magnitude, are: Agena, the horse's belly, also called Hadar; and Chort, on the left shoulder.

Toliman and Agena are a pair of bright stars close together and are believed by Australian aborigines to be two brothers hurling spears at an animal.[76] Both stars form a line that points to the Southern Cross and are seen as a pair, like the twins Castor and Pollux of Greek and Roman mythology. Being a set of paired stars they will, I believe, take on the expression of one single concept or theme but display this theme through two lenses, one which is light and bright and the other more shadowy.

TOLIMAN

(Alpha Centaurus. Magnitude 0.1. RA 14:39:14.5". Declination 60S49'. PED = 28° Scorpio 51'.) See Paran Map 11, page 100. *An example of how to read the map:* If you were born in New York, at a latitude of 41° North, then the star would not rise at any time in the year. Therefore, because it would never be visible, you would not consider it in working with your natal chart and fixed stars.

Toliman can be used on all four points for charts between latitudes of 29° South and 29° North. North of that the star never rises and south of that the star never sets and therefore has permanent curtailed passage.

EARLIER OPINIONS

Ptolemy says that the bright stars in the horse part of the Centaur are of the nature of Venus and Jupiter. Robson calls the star Bungula and says that it bestows friends and honor. Ebertin also calls the star Bungula and indicates that it causes problems in relating to women. Rigor agrees with Robson and adds that the star gives a fatalistic attitude.

AGENA

(Beta Centaurus. Magnitude 0.9. RA 17:39:44.5". Declination 60S21'04". PED = 23° Scorpio 06'.) See Paran Map 12, page 101. *An example of how to read the map:* If you were born in Invercargill, New Zealand, at a latitude of 47° South, then the star would be permanently in a curtailed passage phase, always visible but never touching the horizon. You would only consider the star in your chart if it was culminating at the same degree as one of your planets. Agena culminates at 14° Gemini so if you have a planet at either 14° Gemini or Sagittarius, then it culminated or was on the Nadir as the star culminated.

Agena can be used on all four points for charts between latitudes of 29° South and 29° North. North of that the star never rises and South of that the star never sets and therefore has permanent curtailed passage.

---

[76] Jobes, *Outer Space*, p. 147.

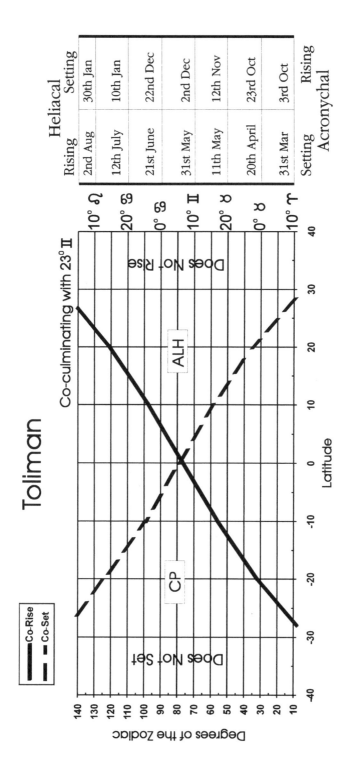

Heliacal		
Rising	Setting	
2nd Aug	30th Jan	♌ 10°
12th July	10th Jan	♋ 20°
21st June	22nd Dec	♋ 0°
31st May	2nd Dec	♊ 10°
11th May	12th Nov	♉ 20°
20th April	23rd Oct	♉ 0°
31st Mar	3rd Oct	♈ 10°
Setting	Rising	
Acronychal		

Toliman

Co-culminating with 23° ♊

Co-Rise
Co-Set

Does Not Rise

ALH

CP

Does Not Set

Latitude

Degrees of the Zodiac

Paran Map 11. Toliman.

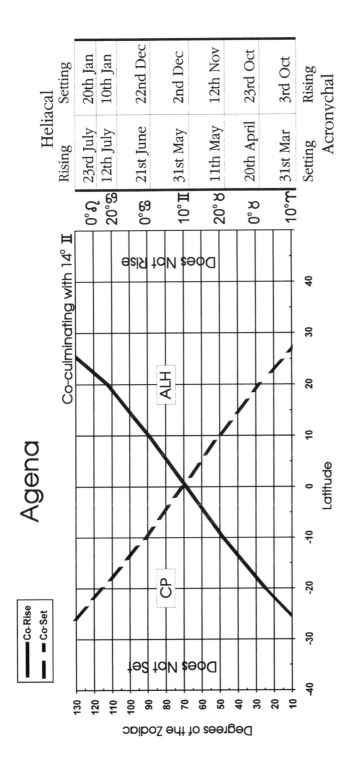

Agena

Legend:
— Co-Rise
- - - Co-Set

Co-culminating with 14° ♊

Does Not Rise

ALH

CP

Does Not Set

Latitude: -40, -30, -20, -10, 0, 10, 20, 30, 40

Degrees of the Zodiac: 10, 20, 30, 40, 50, 60, 70, 80, 90, 100, 110, 120, 130

Heliacal

	Rising	Setting
0° ♌	23rd July	20th Jan
20° ♋	12th July	10th Jan
0° ♋	21st June	22nd Dec
10° ♊	31st May	2nd Dec
20° ♉	11th May	12th Nov
0° ♉	20th April	23rd Oct
10° ♈	31st Mar	3rd Oct
	Setting	Rising

Acronychal

Paran Map 12. Agena.

EARLIER OPINIONS

As previously mentioned, Ptolemy says that the bright stars in the horse part of the Centaur are of the nature of Venus and Jupiter. Robson relates them to friendships and good health. Ebertin says that the stars may be beneficent but will generally cause a pronounced sensuality, as well as gossip and scandal. Rigor agrees with Robson.

TOLIMAN AND AGENA: THE CONCEPT

Both these stars potentially have limited use in astrology because, in a large number of births, the stars are either not visible or can never set. In cases where they are used, it's important to remember that this Centaur is going to the Altar to make a sacrifice. Chiron is a healer and a teacher but he carries his wound. Toliman's being situated on the foot of the great tutor, like Rigel on the foot of Orion, could well imply that this star's meaning is connected to matters of learning and education that expand the person's worldview. Agena, being the partner star, could well be concerned with the sacrifices required for growth to occur.

Due to the southern declination of these two stars it is difficult to research them. However, they were both present in the chart of Mao Tse-Tung, who was born at a latitude of 27° 52' North, so both stars would have been visible above the horizon for a short time. On the day of Mao Tse-Tung's birth Agena was setting as Mars was culminating, and Toliman was setting as the Moon set. Toliman's link to the Moon shows that Mao was at first loved by the Chinese people (Toliman taking the role of the caring healer, the one who brings healing because he loves or cares). Agena, however, the more shadowy part, the wound of Chiron, is linked to a culminating Mars, indicating the force used to achieve his aims.

TOLIMAN AND AGENA IN NATAL CHARTS

Great care should be taken to only use these stars in charts south of 29° North. When present in such a chart, the person will be concerned with some cause or issue that needs to be corrected or healed, either privately or collectively.

TOLIMAN AND AGENA AS THE HELIACAL RISING STAR AT BIRTH

Back in the 1960s in my home state of South Australia, we elected to power as premier, leader of the state government, a man named Don Dunston. He was born in Suva Fiji at 18° South on the morning that Agena was the heliacal rising star for that latitude. He came to power and dramatically altered the state's future. He legalized homosexuality, making South Australia one of the first places in the world to pass this law, and changed many old-fashioned conventions. He was eventually forced from power through failing health and deep personal crisis. In many ways he symbolized the essence of Agena.

CEPHEUS, THE KING

CEPHEUS IS A MEMBER OF THE ROYAL family that moves around the North Pole (see Star Map 1, p. 48). It is a very ancient constellation, whose origins were long lost before any myths were recorded. Aratus, along with the general belief of the day, considered him to be of Euphratean origin. He filled the role of "the King" in many cultures. The Chinese allocated that place in the sky to the Inner Throne of the Five Emperors; the medieval Christians called him King Solomon;[77] and the Chaldeans saw him as son of Belos,[78] a key figure in their creation mythology. The interesting thing is that, although it is a very faint constellation, it persisted in importance as an image of male sovereignty. Cepheus occupied the Pole Star position between 21,000 and 23,000 years ago, and more than likely gained its kingly role in that period. It will not return to that predominant role until around 7,500 C.E.

STARS OF CEPHEUS

The brightest star is Alderamin on the right shoulder, with other named stars in descending order of magnitude being: Alfirk, in the king's side; and Errai, marking the left knee.

ALDERAMIN

(Alpha Cepheus. Magnitude 2.6. RA 21:17: 23". Declination 62N22' 24". PED = 12° Aries 05'.) No paran map is required for this star. Alderamin culminates at 16° Aquarius.

Alderamin can only be used on all four points for charts between latitudes of 27° South and 27° North. South of that the star never rises and north of that the star can only be used as it culminates.

EARLIER OPINIONS

Ptolemy stated that the stars of this constellation were like Jupiter and Saturn. Robson does not mention the star but refers to the constellation and links it to death by hanging, decapitation, crucifixion, or impalement. Ebertin does not deal with the stars of Cepheus. Rigor also refrains from comment.

---

[77] Jobes, *Outer Space*, p. 149.
[78] Allen, *Star Names*, p. 155.

ALDERAMIN: THE CONCEPT

Apart from Robson's warnings, the other authors have left the King, once guardian of the Pole, very much alone. One is tempted to think that this is not the time for this constellation, and possibly it will grow in importance as the Bears fade and come to its glory in 7,500 C.E., when it once again will occupy the Pole position. If meaning were to be given to these stars, they would relate to the concept of the successful king, raised to the heavens as an example for others to see and learn.

This star, therefore, could well talk of a different role model for male sovereignty. At the moment the model, as a collective statement, is one of aggression. At best it is simply out of step with planet Earth and the laws of nature and is thereby a destructive influence. However, Alderamin could represent a balanced male energy in harmony with the feminine and the Earth but focused and concentrated, in contrast to the more passive, intuitive energy of the feminine.

A wonderful example of this model of male sovereignty is Nelson Mandela, the South African activist against apartheid, who spent many years as a political prisoner and who, on his release, was the only man respected and loved enough by the different factions to become the first prime minister of a united South Africa. He was born at a latitude where this star skimmed the horizon before dropping out of sight, but his Mercury was at its Nadir as Alderamin culminated low on the line of the horizon. What he believed in, the power of his words and of his writing, is a demonstration of this gentler meaning of Alderamin: gentle male sovereignty.

ALDERAMIN IN THE NATAL CHART

If this star is predominant in your chart, your skills are to be strongly focused but not aggressive. The greatest benefits and success will come by gentle determination rather than dramatic action.

ALDERAMIN AS THE HELIACAL RISING STAR AT BIRTH

Because of the star's high declination, it was never used in the position of heliacal rising star. For the large majority charts, it can be used only in culmination, and therefore will never be linked to the Sun.

CETUS, THE WHALE

OVER 50° IN LENGTH IN MODERN MAPS, Cetus reaches from the Urn of Aquarius to the edge of the constellation Eridanus, the River, crossing the equator on its way (see Star Map 8, below).

According to the Greeks, Cetus is the sea monster who was sent to devour Andromeda. Perseus, however, saved her by using the severed head of Medusa which turned the sea monster to stone.[79] But the stories of this whale in the sky seem to predate the Greek version. It has had various forms but it is always some aquatic beast that blows water from a blowhole. Cetus has been illustrated at times with a dog's head and forelegs and with a mermaid-like tail. It would seem that this creature is more like the freshwater mythic creature the Loch Ness monster than a marine whale, in that it represents an unknown beast from the depths rather than what we know as a gentle giant of the sea. Aratus referred to the constellation as "the hateful Monster Cetus,"[80] and Jobes refers to it as representing a monster "that rises from the dark nether sea with a ravenous appetite for humans."[81] Christian mythology saw this as the whale that swallowed Jonah, whereas the Arabs broke it into three separate constellations: the Hand, the Ostrich, and the Necklace.[82]

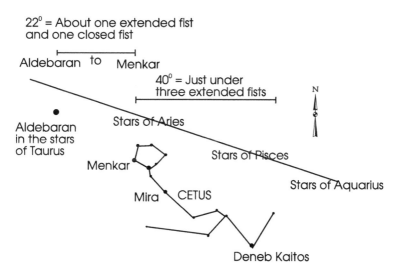

Star Map 8. Cetus, the Whale.

[79] Room, *Dictionary of Astronomical Names*, p. 73.
[80] Mair, *Callimachus, Lycophron, Aratus*, p. 235.
[81] Jobes, *Outer Space*, p. 149.
[82] Allen, *Star Names*, p. 162.

STARS OF CETUS

The brightest star is Menkar, the nose or jaw of the whale. Other named stars in descending order of magnitude are: Deneb Kaitos, the tail; Baten el Kaitos, on its chest; Deneb Kaitos Schemali, the tip of the tail; and Mira, in the neck, and called "wonderful" by astronomers since it was the first variable star discovered.[83]

MENKAR

(Alpha Cetus. Magnitude 2.8. RA 03:02:1.6". Declination 4N4'15". PED = 13° Taurus 37'.) See Paran Map 13, page 107. *An example of how to read the map:* If you were born in Indianapolis, USA, at a latitude of 40° North, then the star rose at about 9° Taurus. If you have a planet at either 9° Taurus or Scorpio, then that planet rose or set with the star. The star also set at 2° Gemini. Therefore, if you have a planet at 2° Gemini or Sagittarius, then it would have set or risen as the star set. The star culminates at 20° Taurus, so if you have a planet at either 20° Taurus or Scorpio, then it culminated or was on the Nadir as the star culminated.

At this latitude of 40° North the star has a phase of arising and lying hidden. This period will be from about April 30 (reading the date from the left-hand column of the date box next to 9° Taurus) to May 23 every year (reading the left-hand column of the date box next to 2° Gemini), and is the true or cosmic heliacal rising star about May 23 (reading the date for the rising line at 40° North in the "heliacal rising" column).

Menkar can be used on all four points for charts of all latitudes except for the extremities of the Poles.

EARLIER OPINIONS

Ptolemy compares the stars of Cetus to Saturn. Robson relates it to disease, disgrace, and ruin. Ebertin places the star in the neck of the Whale and then talks of it causing sore throats, quoting the medical history of Elsbeth Ebertin as his main source. Rigor basically agrees with Robson.

MENKAR: THE CONCEPT

One needs to move away from our modern view of the whale, renowned for its gentleness, to understand that this constellation represents a human-eating monster. The unpleasant meaning of this star is justified if we think of this whale in the sky as representing the human unconscious or the collective unconscious which, like a beast from the deep, can erupt with moments of great collective in-

---

[83] A variable star is a star that varies in its magnitude.

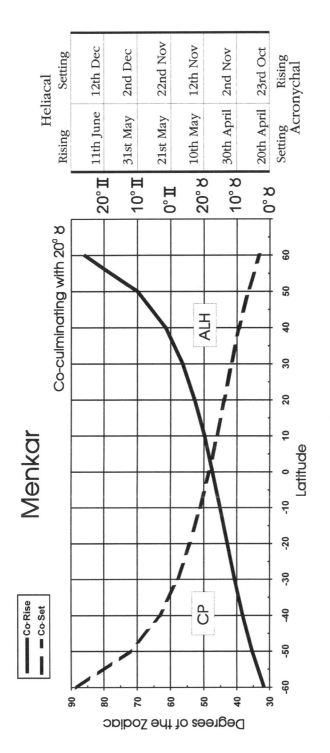

Menkar

Co-culminating with 20° ♉

| | ALH | |
| CP | | |

Degrees of the Zodiac

Latitude

— Co-Rise
- - Co-Set

	Heliacal	
	Rising	Setting
20° ♊	11th June	12th Dec
10° ♊	31st May	2nd Dec
0° ♊	21st May	22nd Nov
20° ♉	10th May	12th Nov
10° ♉	30th April	2nd Nov
0° ♉	20th April	23rd Oct
	Setting Acronychal	Rising

Paran Map 13. Menkar.

sight, or bring chaos and mayhem. For such an unconscious beast would, and indeed has, in both the collective history and the lives of individuals, emerged suddenly and appeared to be huge, unstoppable, and destructive.

Because Cetus is symbolic of these unconscious forces in the human collective, physically out of sight in the depths of the human ocean, its placement in a chart can be difficult. Adolf Hitler had his Mars culminating with Menkar on the day he was born; Mao Tse-Tung had Menkar culminating as his Venus was setting; and Benito Mussolini had Menkar on the Nadir as Jupiter culminated. However, the collective unconscious is not always evil or dark. Sigmund Freud had his Sun culminating with Menkar. His life work was to discover and chart the human unconscious.

Although astrological writings would have Menkar remembered as a permanent curse on the human race, it is, in fact, a living process rather than a few empty keywords.

MENKAR IN THE NATAL CHART

If Menkar is present in your chart, you will be open to the human collective at the point or planet being affected. The sea of the collective can be a stormy one in which to sail, so a great deal would depend on the presence of other fixed stars in your chart. The positive use would manifest as the ability to achieve something for the collective; the negative use, on the other hand, could be that you are the victim of the collective. However, by recognizing your sensitivity to the collective, you can work with your dreams or other spontaneous images to gain greater understanding of this connection.

MENKAR AS THE HELIACAL RISING STAR AT BIRTH

Too faint to herald the dawn, Menkar can only be used when it is the cosmic rising star, such a position implying that you have a very deep connection to the collective, giving you the gift of creating something on behalf of it or, negatively, becoming a victim to seemingly random collective acts. Anastasia of Russia, the daughter of the murdered czar who, some say, survived the massacre of her family only to flee and then spend her life trying to prove her identity, was born at the cosmic rising of Menkar.

COMA BERENICES, BERENICE'S HAIR

THERE ARE TWO CROWNS AND ONE HEAD
of hair represented in the constellations and all are connected to women in some way. Two are in the northern hemisphere, Coma Berenices and Corona Borealis, the Northern Crown, and the third, Corona Australis, lies in the south.

Coma Berenices was once the tuft of the lion's tail in Leo. It was first alluded to as Ariadne's Hair or Ariadne's Crown by Eratosthenes.[84] The Greeks placed a date of 243 B.C.E. on the naming of the constellation, and, according to their history, the hair belonged to a woman called Berenice.[85] Coma Berenice is situated between Bootes and his dogs and is shown on Star Map 5 (p. 76).

The Greek story was that Berenice, sister-wife of Ptolemy III, was awaiting her husband's return from war and prayed to Aphrodite (Venus) daily for his safety. One day it came to her that if she could sacrifice something of great importance, then this would ensure her husband's safe return. Her sacrifice was her hair, traditionally amber in color. This may seem a small sacrifice in the twentieth century but a woman's hair in that period was a sign of her status and to have short hair was a form of disgrace. Some cultures still punish women by shaving their heads. So she cut off her hair and offered it to Aphrodite. However, the hair disappeared from the altar and some said that it had been stolen, while others said that Aphrodite, so moved by the sacrifice, took the tress of hair and placed it in the heavens.[86]

This story was probably based on the custom of lovers giving locks of their hair to the god Hippolytus before marriage, as this was thought to strengthen the union between god and goddess and thus the young couple.[87] The Egyptians believed that locks of a wife's hair were protection in the afterlife for the husband, so women buried their husbands with locks of their hair in the tomb. A woman's hair, if she loved you, was the most sacred form of talisman that could be carried.[88]

Isis restored life to Osiris by the use of her hair. She then protected their divine child Horus by draping her hair over him. Hair was the source of strength for the goddess and if she was a goddess of death or a goddess of the underworld, her hair would stand out above her head as a sign of her power and strength; or, in the case of Medusa, her hair would stand out as a head of snakes. The shaven-headed woman had no power or magic and so Christian nuns and Jewish wives

---

[84] Allen, *Star Names*, p. 168.
[85] Allen, *Star Names*, p. 168.
[86] Jobes, *Outer Space*, p. 152.
[87] Walker, *The Woman's Encyclopedia of Myths and Secrets*, p. 367.
[88] Walker, *The Woman's Encyclopedia of Myths and Secrets*, p. 367.

had to shave their heads.[89] In the most austere Jewish communities, in fact, women are still expected to give up their feminine power by shaving their heads and wearing wigs in public—a practice still followed in orthodox communities here in Australia.

So Berenice's offering to her husband was a sacred action: the surrendering of her power in order to save and protect his life. There may not have ever been a real Berenice, but a woman's hair is still part of our starry sky and in that sense is an important constellation for all women.

STARS OF COMA BERENICES

This is a very faint constellation with the brightest star being the only star with a proper name. It is called Diadem.

DIADEM

(Alpha Coma Berenices. Magnitude 4.3. RA 13:09:43.3". Declination 17N33'33". PED = 8° Libra 15'.) See Paran Map 14, page 111. *An example of how to read the map:* If you were born in Wellington, New Zealand at a latitude of 41° South, then the star rose at about 24° Scorpio. If you have a planet at either 24° Scorpio or Taurus, then that planet rose or set with the star. The star also set at 1° Libra. Therefore, if you have a planet at 1° Libra or Aries, it would have set or risen as the star set. The star culminates at 19° Libra, so if you have a planet at either 19° Libra or Aries, then it culminated or was on the Nadir as the star culminated.

At this latitude of 41° South the star has a phase of arising and lying hidden. This period will be from about September 23 (reading the date from the left-hand column of the date box next to 1° Libra) to November 14 every year (reading the left-hand column of the date box next to 24° Scorpio) and is the true or cosmic heliacal rising star about November 14 (reading the date for the rising line at 41° South in the "heliacal rising" column).

Diadem can be used on all four points for charts between latitudes of 72° South and 72° North. South of that the star never rises and north of that the star never sets and therefore has permanent curtailed passage.

---

[89] Walker, *The Woman's Encyclopedia of Myths and Secrets*, p. 368.

Diadem

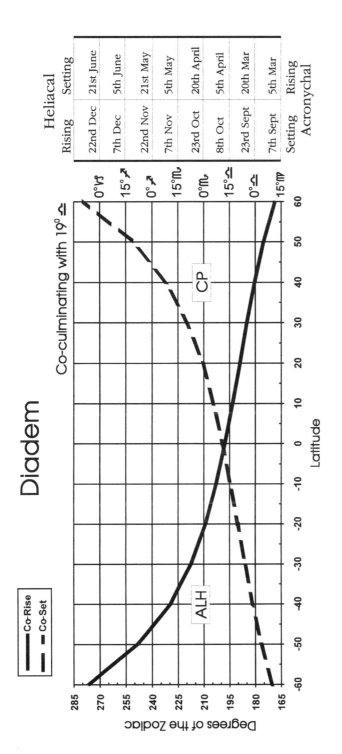

Heliacal		
Rising	Setting	
22nd Dec	21st June	
7th Dec	5th June	
22nd Nov	21st May	
7th Nov	5th May	
23rd Oct	20th April	
8th Oct	5th April	
23rd Sept	20th Mar	
7th Sept	5th Mar	
Setting	Rising	
Acronychal		

Co-culminating with 19° ♎

Paran Map 14. Diadem.

EARLIER OPINIONS

Ptolemy does not refer to Coma Berenices, even though astrologers used it in his day. Robson does not list Diadem, but says that its constellation has an influence of charm, possibly leading to an idle life. Robson also quotes Lilly as saying that these stars cause blindness and baldness. Ebertin does not mention them. Rigor also has no comments.

DIADEM: THE CONCEPT

Diadem takes it name, of course, from that symbol of royalty worn on the head, a small crown. Diadem the constellation seems to be about feminine strength. George Eliot was born on the day that Saturn set as this star rose. Saturn in fixed star work has to do with what is built with one's life. Diadem is rising in Eliot's chart, so its influence was felt from an early stage of her life onward. George Eliot was one of the great nineteenth-century English writers, encouraged to write by the man she loved, George Lewes. Lewes was a married man separated from his wife, but could not divorce, so George Eliot lived with him and considered their long and happy relationship a marriage. This was in the 1850s. Throughout their relationship, Lewes supported her writing and hid any negative reviews of her work from her. However, after his death she decided to stop writing for the sake of her love for Lewes. In a sense her writing was her "hair," for it gave her the strength and the courage to fly in the face of English society in 1850, living unmarried with a married man and using a man's name to publish her work. And upon the death of her lover, like an Egyptian wife, she buried her hair with her husband. Berenice's Hair did not make her a writer. It gave her the strength to dare to be one.

A different figure from George Eliot is Christopher Reeve, the actor who was known for his role as Superman before a tragic riding accident resulted in his becoming a quadriplegic. He was born with Diadem setting as his Jupiter rose. Jupiter always magnifies any star it touches and with Diadem setting it implies this star expressing itself toward the later part of Reeve's life. Throughout his working life as an actor, Reeve quietly went about trying to make the life of the poor and the homeless a little easier. But it is only since his accident he has become a symbol of strength and caring for those who need help.

This star does not seek glory or personal fame. It belongs to the quiet workers, the people who slave for years helping or working for the benefit of a group but never seeking personal recognition or fame. And at times the sacrifice that it asks may seem beyond the person's ability to give. Thus, by its very nature, it tends to not be represented in the charts of the famous.

DIADEM IN THE NATAL CHART

Strongly placed in a chart, Diadem can suggest a self-sacrificing person who is motivated by the love for another. In that sacrifice the person can find great strength and dignity.

DIADEM AS THE HELIACAL RISING STAR AT BIRTH

Because it is so faint, this star was never used as the apparent rising star. However, if it was the cosmic rising star on the day you were born, then this story of lovers, hair, and quiet, gentle sacrifice will be a part of your life's journey.

CORONA AUSTRALIS, THE SOUTHERN CROWN

THIS CONSTELLATION IS ONE OF THE original forty-eight constellations recognized by Ptolemy; he called it the Southern Wreath. It has also been called the Corona Sagittarii, associated with the centaur of Sagittarius; and the Bunch of Arrows, which were said to be radiating from the hand of Sagittarius.[90] There are no notable stars in the constellation, although Ptolemy says that the stars are of the nature of Saturn and Jupiter. See Star Map 24 (p. 293).

---

[90] Jobes, *Outer Space*, p. 154.

CORONA BOREALIS, THE NORTHERN CROWN

CALLED BY MANY NAMES, THE EARLY Greeks called it a Wreath[91] as well as Ariadnaea Corona, Ariadne's Tiara, and sometimes even the Coiled Hair of Ariadne.[92] The imagery of this crown has been predominantly that of a woman's headpiece, a crown or garland of flowers. The Greeks saw it as the wedding garland of flowers given to Ariadne by Venus to celebrate her marriage to Dionysus after she was deserted by Theseus.[93] The constellation was also known by the Persians as The Broken Platter, for the circle of stars is incomplete. This sense of its being broken lead to another name, The Pauper's Bowl. However, most cultures have seen it as a type of crown, and Christian mythology linked it to the Crown of Thorns worn by Christ.[94]

As a wedding garland of flowers or Crown of Thorns, the constellation suggests a crown which is a gift, wanted or not wanted. It is situated between Hercules and Bootes, and is displayed on the star map for Hercules (Star Map 11, p. 143).

STARS OF CORONA BOREALIS

The brightest and only named star is Alphecca.

ALPHECCA

(Alpha Corona Borealis. Magnitude 2.3. RA 15:34:27.8". Declination 26N44'11". PED = 11° Scorpio 35'.) See Paran Map 15, page 116. *An example of how to read the map:* If you were born in Paris, at a latitude of 49° North, then the star rose at about 13° Libra. If you have a planet at either 13° Libra or Aries, then that planet rose or set with the star. The star also set at 25° Capricorn. Therefore, if you have a planet at 25° Capricorn or Cancer, it would have set or risen as the star set. The star culminates at 26° Scorpio, so if you have a planet at either 26° Scorpio or Taurus, then it culminated or was on the Nadir as the star culminated.

At this latitude of 49° North the star has a phase of curtailed passage. This period will be from about April 3 (reading the date from the right-hand column of the date box next to 13° Libra) to July 17 every year (reading the right-hand column of the date box next to 25° Capricorn), and is the true or cosmic heliacal

---

[91] Room, *Dictionary of Astronomical Names*, p. 76.
[92] Allen, *Star Names*, p. 174.
[93] Jobes, *Outer Space*, p. 155.
[94] Jobes, *Outer Space*, p. 156.

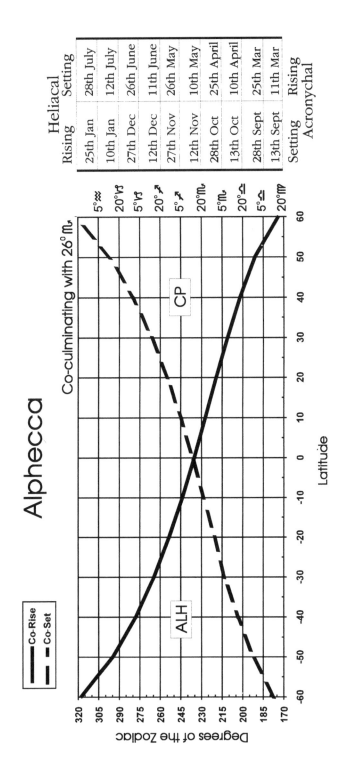

Heliacal	
Rising	Setting
25th Jan	28th July
10th Jan	12th July
27th Dec	26th June
12th Dec	11th June
27th Nov	26th May
12th Nov	10th May
28th Oct	25th April
13th Oct	10th April
28th Sept	25th Mar
13th Sept	11th Mar
Setting	Rising
Acronychal	

Alphecca

Co-culminating with 26° ♏

CP

ALH

Co-Rise
Co-Set

Latitude

Degrees of the Zodiac

Paran Map 15. Alphecca.

rising star about October 5 (reading the date for the rising line at 49° North in the "heliacal rising" column).

Alphecca can be used on all four points for charts between latitudes of 63° South and 63° North. South of that the star never rises and north of that the star never sets, and therefore has permanent curtailed passage.

EARLIER OPINIONS

Ptolemy says that the stars in this constellation are of the nature of Venus and Mercury. Robson talks of it bestowing honor and artistic ability. Ebertin does not mention the star. Rigor expands on Robson's statements and talks of occult ability which can assist in healing the sick, adding that those influenced by Alphecca can get into backbiting situations.

ALPHECCA: THE CONCEPT

If Alphecca is going to be used in a chart interpretation, then its meaning would have to incorporate the symbolism of a woman's crown: quiet achievements. Its influence indicates advancement, but not necessarily through one's own efforts. An interesting example of Alphecca is in the chart of Princess Diana. Alphecca was culminating as her Venus was on the Nadir. She was given a crown and some would say that it is a crown of thorns. However, Alphecca's culminating presence shows that she will be known as a woman with this gift. Medieval astrologers believed that people could rise above their fated place in life, but that this could only happen through great pain and/or chaos, which seems to have been the case with Princess Diana.

Another woman who was given a crown and then experienced tragedy was Grace Kelly, the American actress who became one of the royals of Monaco. Grace Kelly had Alphecca linked with her Mars, for they both culminated at the same time on the day of her birth. Grace Kelly obtained a crown but, like Diana, had difficulties dealing with the change of lifestyle and was eventually killed in a car accident in the prime of her life. Alphecca bestows a gift of moving forward through society, but at a price.

A third example is the chart of Saint Joan of Arc, the French peasant girl who, through the power of her heavenly visions, rose to lead the French army to victory in order for the dauphin to be crowned. She was later captured by the British and at the age of 19 years was burnt at the stake. On the day she was born Alphecca rose as her Sun was on the Nadir. The star rising implies that it will express itself in the early part of life, which was indeed what happened. Jeanne was a very powerful person in the French court, second only to the dauphin. But as in the other examples, there was a price on the crown of Alphecca.

ALPHECCA IN THE NATAL CHART

Alphecca's presence in a chart can relate to the person being offered a change in their social status or community standing. This advancement is not one gained through hard work but rather through love or luck. This gift or possible advancement should be considered very carefully, as the star implies that the person may have to go through a dark or heavy period as a result.

ALPHECCA AS THE HELIACAL RISING STAR AT BIRTH

As one of Ptolemy's stars, it can be used as the heliacal rising star, either cosmic or apparent. This gift of Alphecca will be an integral part of the life journey for one whose Sun is linked to it. However, that person should be aware that the acceptance of this gift is the acceptance of the potential sorrows with which it seems to be associated.

CORVUS, THE CROW

THIS CROW (ALSO KNOWN AS A RAVEN) has been associated with the Hydra and the Cup for at least several thousand years, and is mentioned by Aratus: "Midway on its coil from (Hydra) is set the Crater and at the tip the figure of a Raven that seems to peck at the coil."[95] The Raven stands on the back of the Hydra, and legend has it that the Hydra stops the Raven from drinking from the Cup in punishment for failing to fulfil a duty given to it by Apollo.[96] (See Star Map 12 [p. 101], for the constellation of Corvus on the back of the Hydra.) The Greeks also saw the Raven as Apollo in his prophetic function, for he used that form in the battle between the Olympians and the Titans.[97] In the Celtic tradition, the raven was sacred and foretold of death or disaster. Most cultures see the bird as prophetic, usually in the form of an omen.[98] However, later Christian scholars combined the stars of the Raven and the Cup to form the Ark of the Covenant.[99]

STARS OF CORVUS

Ptolemy says that the stars of the Raven are like Mars and Saturn but the brightest star, Al Chiba, has a magnitude of only 4.3 and does not seem to be of astrological significance.

---

[95] Mair, *Callimachus, Lycophron, Aratus*, p. 243.
[96] Allen, *Star Names*, p. 180.
[97] Jobes, *Outer Space*, p. 158.
[98] Stewart, *Celtic Gods, Celtic Goddesses*, p. 80.
[99] Allen, *Star Names*, p. 183.

THE CRATER, THE CUP

THE CUP SITS ON THE BACK OF THE HYDRA
(see Star Map 12, p. 101), who guards it from ever-thirsty Corvus the Raven.
This was long considered the constellation *Hydra et Corvus et Crater* but modern
cataloging has broken it into its three asterisms.

The Babylonians saw this Cup as the cup used by Ishtar for brewing fertility,[100] and the only reference made by the Egyptians to this constellation is on a
vase that reads:

> Wise ancients knew when the Crater rose to sight
> Nile's fertile deluge had attained its height.[101]

The Greeks considered it the cup in which Icarus, who had been taught by
Dionysus (Bacchus) the secret of wine-making, stored his fermented beverage,
and related it also to the prophetic well of Apollo.[102] In this sense the constellation of the Cup represented for many cultures the concept of the Sacred or Holy
Cup, be it the Goblet or Well of Apollo, the skull as a prophetic drinking vessel
of the Celts, the Cauldron of Bran, the Holy Grail of Christian mythology or the
Lamp of Aladdin. It is the "Cup" with all its symbolism, the vessel that holds life
and is therefore mystical. It is appropriate that the Cup is on the back of the
Hydra, for the serpent was the most ancient symbol of the goddess and the cup
became her only remaining symbol once the Hydra had been associated with the
serpent of the Garden of Eden.

STARS OF THE CRATER

There are no bright stars in this constellation. However, the alpha star is named
Alkes.

ALKES

(Alpha Crater. Magnitude 4.1. RA 10:57:20.2". Declination 18S01'56". PED =
23° Virgo 00'.) See Paran Map 16, page 121. *An example of how to read the map:*
If you were born in Bangkok, Thailand, at a latitude of 14° North, then the star
rose at about 19° Virgo. If you have a planet at either 19° Virgo or Pisces, then
that planet rose or set with the star. The star also set at 7° Virgo. Therefore, if you

---

[100] Jobes, *Outer Space*, p. 160.
[101] Jobes, *Outer Space*, p. 160.
[102] Jobes, *Outer Space*, p. 161.

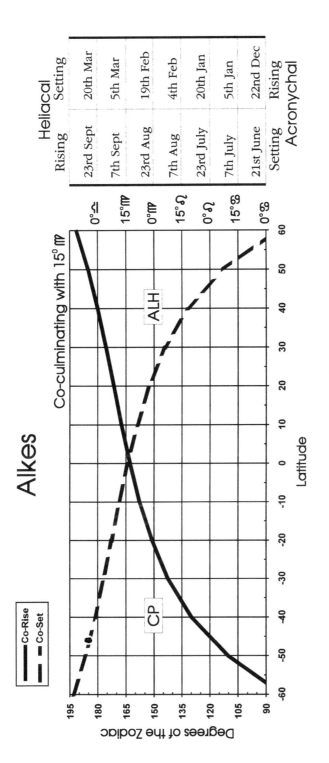

Paran Map 16. Alkes.

have a planet at 7° Virgo or Pisces, it would have set or risen as the star set. The star culminates at 15° Virgo, so if you have a planet at either 15° Virgo or Pisces, then it culminated or was on the Nadir as the star culminated.

At this latitude of 14° North the star has a phase of arising and lying hidden. This period will be from about August 28 (reading the date from the left-hand column of the date box next to 7° Virgo) to September 12 every year (reading the left-hand column of the date box next to 19° Virgo), and is the true or cosmic heliacal rising star about September 12 (reading the date for the rising line at 14° North in the "heliacal rising" column).

Alkes can be used on all four points for charts between latitudes of 71° South and 71° North. North of that the star never rises and south of that the star never sets and therefore has permanent curtailed passage.

EARLIER OPINIONS

Ptolemy ascribes a Venus-nature to the stars in this constellation, along with some Mercurial qualities. Robson goes into quite a long description of a kind, generous person with good mental abilities, but who experiences much disorder and sudden, unexpected events. Ebertin and Rigor do not list the star.

ALKES: THE CONCEPT

This is a gentle star. It is linked to spiritual, mystical, and prophetic natures, to people who carry something symbolically precious for others. In working with this star, the group that showed the most contacts with Alkes were Roman Catholic popes. Most popes of the last few hundred years have had this star linked to their charts via paran, an interesting expression of the chalice and of carrying something for others, for a Catholic pope is considered to be a living vessel for Christ. Another interesting example is Prince Charles. He has Alkes rising as his Sun culminates, so his whole life is involved with the star. He also sees himself as a holder of something special. This is not an arrogant statement, for he is Lord of the Isles and sees himself as the carrier of this Scottish energy. He is also heir to the British throne and will one day be the head of the Church of England. He carries something for others. He is a vessel.

ALKES IN THE NATAL CHART

You will be very group oriented, feeling deeply connected to the group for which you are a receptacle or vessel. You may also have strong religious or spiritual views.

ALKES AS THE HELIACAL RISING STAR AT BIRTH

Too faint to herald the dawn, Alkes can only be used in the position of cosmic rising. If you were born on this day, then your life will be dedicated to carrying something precious for others, be it your ideas, your creativity or your very genetics.

CRUX, THE CROSS

KNOWN AS THE SOUTHERN CROSS, THIS IS the smallest constellation in the sky, yet still clearly visible and located at about 60° of southern declination (see Star Map 7, p. 98). Originally part of the Centaur, the Crux was not officially named until the seventeenth century. However, well before Christ there are references made to this grouping of stars by Hindu astronomers who saw these stars in the form of a cross. Due to precession, Crux was once visible at quite high northern latitudes, and Allen points out that the last time it would have been visible on the horizon in Jerusalem would have been about the time of Christ's crucifixion.[103]

It is interesting to note that the North Pole is surrounded by one of the most ancient figures of the goddess, a bear, while the South Pole has as its pointer another, but more modern, religious symbol, the cross.

STARS OF CRUX

Acrux, at the bottom of the cross, is the brightest star, with the only other named star, Mimosa, at one end of the cross bar.

ACRUX

(Alpha Crux. Magnitude 1.6. RA 12:26:17.4". Declination 63S04'24". PED = 11° Scorpio 11'.) See Paran Map 17, page 124. *An example of how to read the map:* If you were born in Port Moresby, Papua New Guinea, at a latitude of 9° South, then the star rose at about 22° Aries. If you have a planet at either 22° Aries or Libra, then that planet rose or set with the star. The star also set at 10° Gemini. Therefore, if you have a planet at 10° Gemini or Sagittarius, it would have set or risen as the star set. The star culminates at 23° Taurus, so if you have a planet at either 23° Taurus or Scorpio, then it culminated or was on the Nadir as the star culminated.

At this latitude of 9° South the star has a phase of curtailed passage. This period will be from about October 18 (reading the date from the right-hand column of the date box next to 22° Aries) to December 2 every year (reading the right-hand column of the date box next to 10° Gemini), and is the true or cosmic heliacal rising star about April 12 (reading the date for the rising line at 9° South in the "heliacal rising" column).

---

[103] Allen, *Star Names*, p. 185.

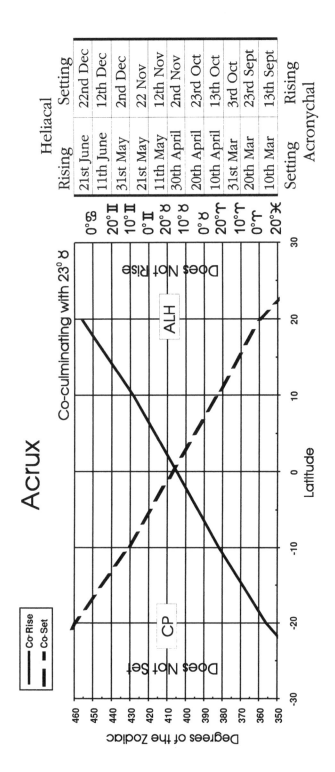

Heliacal			
Rising	Setting		
21st June	22nd Dec	0° ♋	
11th June	12th Dec	20° ♊	
31st May	2nd Dec	10° ♊	
21st May	22 Nov	0° ♉	
11th May	12th Nov	20° ♉	
30th April	2nd Nov	10° ♉	
20th April	23rd Oct	0° ♉	
10th April	13th Oct	20° ♈	
31st Mar	3rd Oct	10° ♈	
20th Mar	23rd Sept	0° ♈	
10th Mar	13th Sept	20° ♓	
Setting	Rising		
Acronychal			

Acrux

Co-culminating with 23° ♉

Does Not Rise

ALH

Does Not Set

CP

Co-Rise
Co-Set

Degrees of the Zodiac

Latitude

Paran Map 17. Acrux.

Acrux can be used on all four points for charts between latitudes of 26° South and 26° North. North of that the star never rises and south of that the star never sets and therefore has permanent curtailed passage.

EARLIER OPINIONS

Ptolemy makes no reference to the star. Robson relates Acrux to intuition, a preference for occult studies and an inventive mind, and also that it is prominent in the charts of astrologers. Ebertin discusses the whole constellation and agrees with Robson. Rigor supports the above statements but adds its influence may result in one who loves to see suffering, a form of sadist.

ACRUX: THE CONCEPT

You need to be aware that this star is not visible for the majority of northern hemisphere charts, and so in using the technique of parans, it would be excluded from those charts. The Cross is probably best considered not in the light of religious symbolism but rather in an astrological way. "The cross" in astrology is the Cross of Matter,[104] its expression being to give things substance, to give them form. A cross is at the center of every chart, symbol of the soul or spirit of the individual grappling with the physical world into which it has been born. Thus this star, Acrux, is concerned with the concrete, physical world: making money, actualizing potential.

Fidel Castro, the leader of Cuba since 1959, was born with this star rising as his Sun culminated, and has become the "symbol of communist revolution in Latin America."[105] This does not imply that Acrux is connected to communism, but rather that communism is a political philosophy concerned with the equality of material wealth.

ACRUX IN THE NATAL CHART

If your chart is affected by Acrux—depending on its placement—you will seek to express yourself physically. You are a doer, an achiever, someone who wants to move and take action, a person who gets things done.

ACRUX AS THE HELIACAL RISING STAR

This is not one of Ptolemy's stars and, although it is very bright, it is not visible for the northern latitudes. However, if you were born at a latitude where this star was seen to rise and set, then it could be used as both the apparent and cosmic rising star and would be a strong indicator of your ability to bring things to fruition.

---

[104] The axis of the Ascendant/Descendant that crosses the axis of the MC/IC.

[105] *The New Encyclopedia Britannica*, vol. 2, p. 940.

CYGNUS, THE SWAN

THE CYGNUS, THE SWAN, MAY HAVE FIRST been charted on the Euphrates, for some tablets show a large stellar bird in this position.[106] It was also known as the Hen by the Egyptians,[107] and as a type of game bird by the Arabs. The Hebrews thought of it as a swan and the Christians saw it as the Cross of Calvary.[108] The Greeks knew it as the swan that was Zeus in his seduction of Leda,[109] the mother of Castor and Pollux, or as the swan who was the son of Mars.[110] Both these myths echo older, Hindu stories, for there was a universal shamanic practice of wearing swan-feather cloaks in mimicry of the gods who took the form of a swan. Krishna, from the Hindu tradition, became a swan-knight through this process, and the story of Zeus and Leda is thought to be a Greek update on the story of Krishna and "Lady," whose union created the World Egg[111] (see Star Map 2, p. 56).

The swan is a powerful image in our modern psyche. The discovery of the black swans of Western Australia threw one of the axioms of philosophy, "All swans are white," into a tail spin (pun intended). In modern times we think of the swan as a graceful, peaceful bird, but in reality it is a very hostile animal, willing to battle any bird or beast that enters its space. This natural hostility was the source of many fables and myths and, in keeping with it, the celestial Swan is seen to be in battle with Aquila the Eagle—a battle it always wins in the northern hemisphere, where it's placed after the Eagle. The swan is a strong powerful bird, related to the sun god, Krishna, strength, and aggression.

STARS OF CYGNUS

The brightest star is Deneb Adige, sometimes called Deneb, in the tail of the Swan. Other named stars, in descending order of magnitude, are: Albiero, the beak; Gienah, the wing; Azekfafage, in the tail or the foot; and Ruchba, the tip of the left wing.

---

[106] Jobes, *Outer Space*, p. 164.
[107] Allen, *Star Names*, p. 193.
[108] Allen, *Star Names*, p. 195.
[109] Room, *Dictionary of Astronomical Names*, p. 78.
[110] Allen, *Star Names*, p. 192.
[111] Walker, *The Woman's Encyclopedia of Myths and Secrets*, p. 963.

DENEB ADIGE

(Alpha Cygnus. Magnitude 1.3. RA 20:41:17". Declination 45N16'01". PED = 4° Pisces 38'.) See Paran Map 18, page 128. *An example of how to read the map:* If you were born in Perth, Australia, at a latitude of 32° South, then the star rose at about 20° Pisces. If you have a planet at either 20° Pisces or Virgo, then that planet rose or set with the star. The star also set at 15° Sagittarius. Therefore, if you have a planet at 15° Sagittarius or Gemini, it would have set or risen as the star set. The star culminates at 8° Aquarius, so if you have a planet at either 8° Aquarius or Leo, then it culminated or was on the Nadir as the star culminated.

At this latitude of 32° South the star has a phase of arising and lying hidden. This period will be from about December 7 (reading the date from the left-hand column of the date box next to 15° Sagittarius) to March 10 every year (reading the left-hand column of the date box next to 20° Pisces), and is the true or cosmic heliacal rising star about March 10 (reading the date for the rising line at 32° South in the "heliacal rising" column).

Deneb adige can be used on all four points for charts between latitudes of 44° South and 44° North. South of that the star never rises and north of that the star never sets and therefore has permanent curtailed passage.

EARLIER OPINIONS

Ptolemy states that the stars of the swan resemble Venus and Mercury. Robson links Deneb adige to success in the arts or sciences, and being quick at learning. Ebertin agrees with these statements. Rigor adds intelligence to the list of positive points.

DENIB ADIGE: THE CONCEPT

Deneb adige is a very subtle star associated with the strength and hostility of the swan, but at the same time holding within its symbolism the mystic, transcendental qualities of shamanistic legends of the creation of the World Egg. A very good example of this curious blend is Mother Teresa, the nun who worked in India with the poor, who gained world acclaim both as a very strong speaker against any form of birth control and as a living saint. Her Sun culminated as Deneb adige was rising, and Deneb adige culminated as her Moon rose. So this majestic Swan and its symbolism is connected both to how we see Mother Teresa (the Sun), and to the belief systems and feelings (the Moon) she lived by. Another example is the artist Vincent van Gogh, who had Deneb adige on the Nadir as his Mercury set. The star in such a position will express itself at the end of life or even after death, and in this case, with its connection to Mercury, it influences how Vincent communicated and thought. His wild, postimpressionist

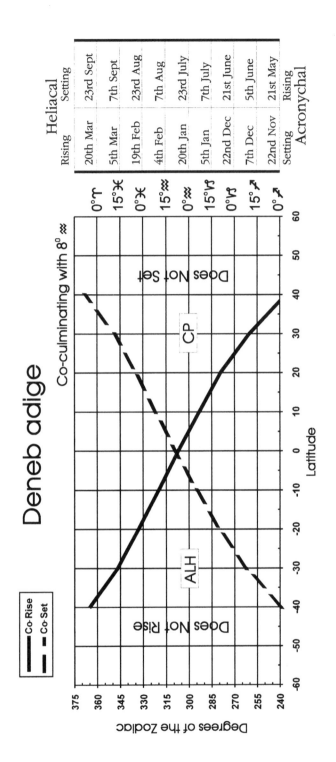

Paran Map 18. Deneb adige.

style of coloring and rapid brushstrokes, which captured the sacredness of an ordinary moment, only gained recognition after his death. Deneb adige gave to his art (Mercury) the need to explore the mystical in the everyday subjects of skies, flowers, landscapes, and people.

DENEB IN THE NATAL CHART

Deneb adige may well express itself in both the aggressive as well as the spiritual side of your life, for the star seems to have a duality about it which is equally the strong fighting bird and the swan-god, the willingness to take the hero's journey, to undertake the journey of self-awareness.

DENEB AS THE HELIACAL RISING STAR AT BIRTH

As one of Ptolemy's stars, it can be used as both the herald of the dawn and for the cosmic rising. In either position the star will be at its strongest, and the willingness to partake of the journey of life or to grow and transform to other levels of awareness will be a feature of your inner self. What you choose to do with this and how you express it will be in your hands.

DELPHINUS, THE DOLPHIN

THE DOLPHIN IS A SMALL CONSTELLATION next to Aquila the Eagle in the northern hemisphere (see Star Map 2, p. 56). It is placed in the sky in an area that Aratus called The Water. The Dolphin has maintained its present form and shape for thousands of years and there are many different stories attached to it, all with the common theme of helpfulness and playfulness. The Greeks also saw the constellation as The Sacred Fish[112] and in that light the Christians saw it as the sky emblem of the Fishes, the early symbol for Christianity.[113] In contrast to this, the Arabs saw this constellation as The Riding Camel, the ship of the desert.[114]

STARS OF DELPHINUS

The brightest star is Sualocin; another named star is Rotanev. Both are in the head of the Dolphin.

SUALOCIN

(Alpha Delphinus. Magnitude 3.9. RA 29:39:25.3". Declination 15N53'53". PED = 16° Aquarius 41'.) See Paran Map 19, page 131. *An example of how to read the map:* If you were born in Christchurch, New Zealand, at a latitude of 43° South then the star rose at about 3° Pisces. If you have a planet at either 3° Pisces or Virgo, then that planet rose or set with the star. The star also set at 28° Sagittarius. Therefore, if you have a planet at 28° Sagittarius or Gemini then it would have set or risen as the star set. The star culminates at 8° Aquarius, so if you have a planet at either 8° Aquarius or Leo, then it culminated or was on the Nadir as the star culminated.

At this latitude of 43° South the star has a phase of arising and lying hidden. This period will be from about December 20 (reading the date from the left-hand column of the date box next to 28° Sagittarius) to February 21 every year (reading the left-hand column of the date box next to 3° Pisces), and is the true or cosmic heliacal rising star about February 21 (reading the date for the rising line at 43° South in the "heliacal rising" column).

Sualocin can be used on all four points for charts between latitudes of 74° South and 74° North. South of that the star never rises and north of that the star never sets and therefore has permanent curtailed passage.

---

[112] Allen, *Star Names*, p. 199.
[113] Jobes, *Outer Space*, p. 167.
[114] Jobes, *Outer Space*, p. 167.

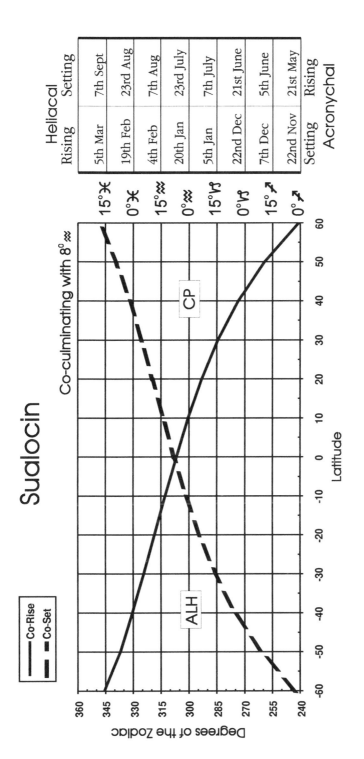

Sualocin

Co-culminating with 8° ≈

Heliacal	
Rising	Setting
5th Mar	7th Sept
19th Feb	23rd Aug
4th Feb	7th Aug
20th Jan	23rd July
5th Jan	7th July
22nd Dec	21st June
7th Dec	5th June
22nd Nov	21st May
Setting	Rising
Acronychal	

15°♓
0°♓
15°≈
0°≈
15°♑
0°♑
15°♐
0°♐

— Co-Rise
■■ Co-Set

CP

ALH

Degrees of the Zodiac

360 345 330 315 300 285 270 255 240

Latitude

-60 -50 -40 -30 -20 -10 0 10 20 30 40 50 60

Paran Map 19. Sualocin.

EARLIER OPINIONS

Ptolemy linked this star to having a natural talent, while seeing the whole constellation as being like Saturn and Mars. Robson does not list the star but talks of Delphinus as being related to a love of hunting and a cheerful nature, but one tending toward ingratitude. Ebertin does not deal with this star. Rigor also makes no mention of the star.

SUALOCIN: THE CONCEPT

There is no clear pattern that emerges when working with this star. It is present in the chart of Marilyn Monroe, setting with her Jupiter, and this may have added to her tantalizing character. Another example is in the chart of Carl Jung, who was born at the moment that Sualocin was setting. After his break with Freud he deliberately strove to allow the irrational side of his nature a free reign, in order to explore his own mind. Like a friendly dolphin of the sea, Jung is seen as a gentle guide to the depths of the human mind, in contrast to Freud and Menkar, who seemed to delight in the horrors of the sea of the mind. In addition, through its playfulness, Sualocin seems to give a certain mastery, or at least confidence of mastery, of one's environment.

SUALOCIN IN THE NATAL CHART

If Sualocin is in your chart, it will add a touch of natural talent or mastery to the planet it affects. It does not seem to be a strong star, however, so it tends to act more as a reinforcement for other indications in your chart, adding a tendency toward curiosity or mastery.

SUALOCIN AS THE HELIACAL RISING STAR AT BIRTH

Being a faint star, Sualocin is not able to be used as a herald of the dawn but it could be used with its cosmic rising. If you were born at such a time, then you would more than likely have a sense of confidence and ease with your environment.

DRACO, THE DRAGON

With vast convolutions Draco holds
Th' ecliptic axis in his scaly folds.
O'er half the skies his neck enormous rears,
And with immense meanders parts the Bears.[115]

SO WROTE AN ENGLISH NATURALIST POET
of the 18th century. Throughout the ages this constellation has been seen as a snake, a dragon, or a serpent. It was worshiped by the Babylonians as Bel the Great Dragon[116] and was referred to in Christian mythology as the serpent in the Garden of Eden. It once occupied a much larger space in the heavens, encompassing the two Bears, Ursa Major and Minor (see Star Map 9, p. 134). The Little Bear was originally known as the Dragon's wings. Half bird and half snake, this is the original mythical animal that occurred in the mythologies of all cultures. Draco's stars were the Pole stars from about 4,500 B.C.E. to about 2,000 B.C.E. Thuban, in the fifth coil of the Dragon, is the brightest star of the constellation. In 2,700 B.C.E., when it occupied the pole position, the Dragon rotated around the "unmoving point of the world" like the hands of a clock, in a reverse direction, guarding its center.

So the mighty Celestial Dragon guarded the greatest treasure of all, the pivot-point of the world. It never slept, because it never set. This was the Crocodile of the Egyptians,[117] who devoured any dead beings whose hearts were too heavy for the scale of judgment, thus stopping them from immortal life at the Pole. This is the nonsleeping, hundred-eyed dragon that the Greeks had guarding the golden apples in the Garden of Hesperides.[118] Apples were also the dragon's treasure offered to Eve in the Christian Garden of Eden. Rowan berries of eternal life were protected by its counterpart in Celtic mythology. By the time of the Arthurian legends, the dragon was seen to protect or guard material treasure of gold and jewels, and when its symbolism was in tatters with the decline of all things feminine, it was considered the perfect hunting game for knights. As the feminine has reemerged, however, the image of the dragon is no longer seen to be the fearful creature that Saint George had to kill. Draco, the Dragon, is still the guardian of both spiritual and physical treasure.

For the Dragon, even though reduced in size by modern cartographers, still coils around the unmoving point of the world, still guards the entrance to a forgotten place of immortality and creation.

---

[115] Quoted in Allen, *Star Names*, p. 202.
[116] Allen, *Star Names*, p. 203.
[117] Allen, *Star Names*, p. 205.
[118] Jobes, *Outer Space*, p. 170.

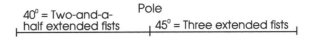

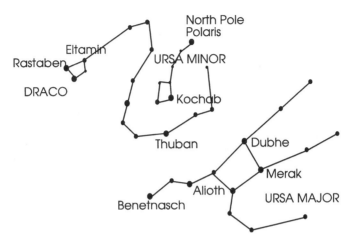

Star Map 9. The Goddess and the Dragon.

STARS OF DRACO

The brightest star is Thuban; the other stars, in descending order of magnitude, are: Rastaban and Rastaben, the Dragon's eyes; Eltamin, the dragon's head; Nodus Secundus, the second knot in its coils; Giansar; Gennam; Dsiban; and a pair of dim stars in its claws known as Al Athafar al Dhib. The many different names for some of these stars, and the fact that so many are named, indicates the importance of this circumpolar constellation.

THUBAN

(Alpha Draco. Magnitude 3.6. RA 14:04:13.2". Declination 64N24'21". PED = 6° Virgo 45'.) No paran map is required for this star. Thuban culminates at 3° Libra, and can only be used on all four points for charts between latitudes of 25° South and 25° North. South of that the star never rises and north of that the star never sets and therefore has permanent curtailed passage.

EARLIER OPINIONS

Ptolemy linked the bright stars of Draco to the expressions of Mars and Saturn. Robson omits discussing the alpha star of the Dragon but talks of Rastaban, connecting it with accidents. Ebertin does not mention Thuban either. Rigor, too, ignores Thuban but talks of Eltamin, the Dragon's head, linking it to self-destruction, but also mental ability and a preference for solitude. He considers Rastaban, but unlike Robson he connects the star to public matters that bring success but also dishonor.

THUBAN: THE CONCEPT

The predominant theme for this constellation is the guarding feminine, so another possible approach to this alpha star, Thuban, or its sisters, is to see it as one who actively guards or protects, in contrast to Ursa Major, which is linked to passive guardianship and protection.

Thuban is present in the chart of Hermann Goering, born in Rosenheim, Germany, for it culminated as his Mercury rose. He was the mind behind the raid on the art treasures from Nazi-occupied countries—thus amassing his own treasures to guard, his own personal art collection. However, this same star which appears to be the dark side of the dragon in Goering's chart, was also present in the chart of Isaac Newton. Newton was born at Woolsthorpe, England, and on the day of his birth the Moon set as Thuban culminated. Since Newton's Moon is involved he had an emotional attitude toward his acquisitions. It is interesting to note that he was a miser who jealously guarded his "treasures," his ideas and theories. He invented calculus, the new and powerful instrument that carried modern mathematics above the level of Greek geometry, but he did not publish his theories. It is thought that he was fearful of publication. Over the years he withdrew into solitude and later in life entered into bitter emotional battles over establishing his claim to calculus. The driving need to "guard" treasures, while at the same time wanting recognition for them and wanting to be publicly acclaimed as the inventor of calculus, resulted in bitter struggles. Thuban in his chart, then, indicated that he would have such difficulties.

Thuban also culminated with the Sun of Pablo Picasso, born in Malaga, Spain. Here we see a different side to the dragon. Linked with the Sun, it is part of his identity. Picasso is considered to be the greatest artist of the twentieth century and one of the most prolific artists in history. He created over twenty thousand works, each one of them having value even before his death—an instance of the Dragon's influence letting an immense treasure flow to the world. Gone are the signs of solitude, apart from Picasso's never-ending need to create; gone is the hoarding instinct. Picasso created treasures.

Thuban, then, can be about sacred matters which have degenerated into the human concept of jealously guarded physical treasure, or it can be more fruitful and yielding in its influence.

THUBAN IN THE NATAL CHART

Thuban can be used in its culminating position for most northern hemisphere births. When present in your chart, it will indicate issues around giving and sharing. You may well have a great gift but fear it will be exhausted if you use that gift. Your journey is to realize that the treasure is unlimited and to resist the nemesis of hoarding, to learn that by using the treasure even greater treasures are achieved, as was the case with Picasso.

THUBAN AS THE HELIACAL RISING STAR AT BIRTH

Because of its high declination this star was not used as the heliacal rising star at birth. However, for births in the equatorial regions Thuban can be so used, in which case it would indicate that your sense of identity is linked to the seeking, hoarding, or making of treasures, either spiritually or materially.

EQUULEUS, THE LITTLE HORSE

NEXT TO PEGASUS IS THIS LITTLE HORSE in the sky, sometimes considered a foal. The Greeks called it Celeris, the brother of Pegasus. Celeris was a gift from Mercury to Castor,[119] one of the Gemini Twins. This Little Horse was also called the First Horse simply because it rises before Pegasus (see Star Map 15, p. 178).

STARS OF EQUULEUS

Kitalpha is the brightest star of the constellation, although its magnitude is only 3.8, and it would seem that none of the stars of Equuleus have any astrological tradition. Robson refers to the constellation as connected to characteristics of friendly frivolity and a love of pleasure. These meanings have probably been derived from the concept of the playfulness of a foal, a common image associated with this constellation.

---

[119] Allen, *Star Names*, p. 213.

ERIDANUS, THE RIVER

THERE IS A RIVER THAT RUNS FROM THE feet of Cetus the sea monster or whale, through twists and turns across to the feet of Orion, and then downward towards the South Pole, finishing at about 60° South (see Star Map 10, p. 139). The Greeks believed that it emptied into the Euxine Sea near the place where the Argonauts found the Golden Fleece.[120] It is the longest constellation in the sky.

Homer saw it as the Ocean Stream that flowed around the earth, while many cultures claimed it for their own geographical rivers, such as the Rhine of Europe and the Ebro of Spain. Richard Allen points out, however, that really only the Nile could lay claim to mirroring this starry river because that river flows from north to south, as does Eridanus.[121]

The Greeks also associated this River with the tears shed by Heliades on the death of her brother, Phaethon;[122] whereas other versions of the story talk of the river already being there, his weeping sister and mother turning into poplar trees. Phaethon was the son of Apollo but had never met his father. He lived with his mother and told his friends that his father was the god Apollo. His friends jeered and mocked him, yet when the boy was born, Apollo told his mother that he would grant the boy any wish he wanted. Armed with the knowledge of his inherited promise, Phaethon set off to visit his father and prove to his friends that he was the son of Apollo. Upon finding his father, Phaethon reminded him of the paternal promise and asked that he be allowed to drive the chariot of the Sun. In this way all of his friends could see him driving his father's chariot and know that Apollo was truly his father. Apollo knew that the boy could not handle the four great stallions of his chariot and offered to let the boy ride with him in the fiery journey across the sky. Phaethon, however, insisted that he drive the chariot alone. The boy set off at dawn and it soon became obvious that he was not in control, for the vehicle careered across the sky, scorching the earth and setting fire to the sky. In order to save the earth, Zeus struck the boy out of the chariot to fall to his death. To appease Apollo, the river of tears shed by Heliades was placed in the heavens as the River.[123]

This story has far greater implications than the death of a small boy. Eridanus touches the feet of Orion as it wanders southward and in this location, close to Rigel, it is believed to be the river into which the great millstone fell, at the time of the tilting of the table, when the mill was dislodged from the North Pole. This falling, whether of a millstone or of Phaethon, caused the whirlpool

---

[120] Allen, *Star Names*, p. 215.
[121] Allen, *Star Names*, p. 216.
[122] Allen, *Star Names*, p. 216.
[123] Guerber, *The Myths of Greece and Rome*, p. 53.

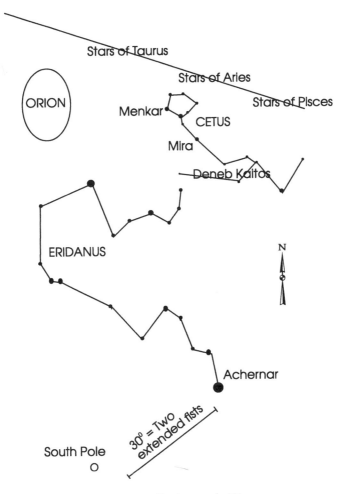

Star Map 10. Eridanus, the River.

(called *zalos*), whose effect on the world we now know as precession. Santillana and von Dechend[124] talk of this myth as a mythological history. They consider the story of Phaethon as one of the great stories of the fall of one world age and the beginning of another, the historical recording of the shift of the equinoctial colure[125] from the Milky Way, the river of life, to Eridanus—the Sun breaking out of its orbital path to finally come to rest on the ecliptic.

---

[124] De Santillana and von Dechend, *Hamlet's Mill*, p. 257.

[125] The "equinoctial colure" is the great circle that passes through the celestial poles and the equinoctial points. The solstitial colure runs through both the celestial and ecliptic poles and through the solstitial points.

Thus Eridanus took over the great mythological and theological role of the Milky Way. The next time you look at Eridanus, recognize you are looking at a living myth, as is the case with all the constellations. This is the river of life, the source of all water, the river that came to be considered the band around the center of the world once the Milky Way was abandoned by the Sun. This was the river to the otherworld, the way to a different place, the Yellow Brick Road. We also meet this river again in the constellation Argo and, in particular, in the magnificent star Canopus.

STARS OF ERIDANUS

There is only one bright star in Eridanus and that is Achernar, placed at the very end of the River in the southern hemisphere. Other named stars, in descending order of magnitude, are Cursa, Zaurac, and Azhia.

ACHERNAR

(Alpha Eridanus. Magnitude 0.6. RA 01:37:32.8". Declination 57S15'33". PED = 14° Pisces 36'.) See Paran Map 20, page 141. *An example of how to read the map:* If you were born in Hong Kong, at a latitude of 22° North, then the star rose at about 10° Gemini. If you have a planet at either 10° Gemini or Sagittarius, then that planet rose or set with the star. The star also set at 19° Pisces. Therefore, if you have a planet at 19° Pisces or Virgo, it would have set or risen as the star set. The star culminates at 26° Aries, so if you have a planet at either 26° Aries or Libra, then it culminated or was on the Nadir as the star culminated.

At this latitude of 22° North the star has a phase of arising and lying hidden. This period will be from about March 10 (reading the date from the left-hand column of the date box next to 19° Pisces) to June 1 every year (reading the left-hand column of the date box next to 10° Gemini), and is the true or cosmic heliacal rising star about June 1 (reading the date for the rising line at 22° North in the "heliacal rising" column).

Achernar can be used on all four points for charts between latitudes of 32° South and 32° North. North of that the star never rises and south of that the star never sets and therefore has permanent curtailed passage.

EARLIER OPINIONS

Ptolemy states that the stars of this constellation are like Saturn but that the last bright one has the nature of Jupiter.[126] Robson, Ebertin, and Rigor all seem to

---

[126] It is not clear if Ptolemy means the Achernar of modern times, as Achernar simply means the end of the River and this constellation has been extended since Ptolemy's day. His Achernar could have been the star we now call Acamar, magnitude 3, which is thought to have dimmed since Ptolemy recorded it with a magnitude of 1.

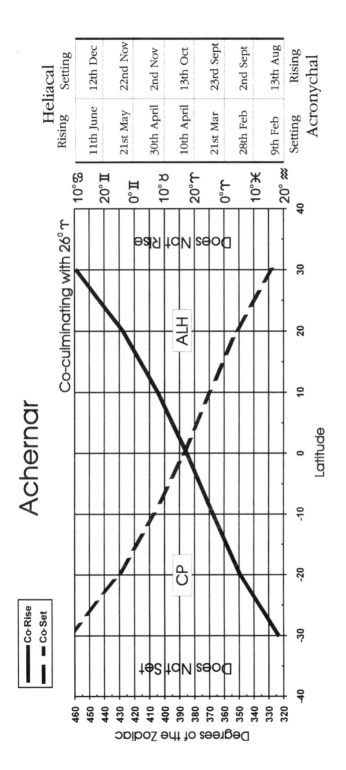

Paran Map 20. Achernar.

Heliacal	
Rising	Setting
11th June	12th Dec
21st May	22nd Nov
30th April	2nd Nov
10th April	13th Oct
21st Mar	23rd Sept
28th Feb	2nd Sept
9th Feb	13th Aug
Setting	Rising
Acronychal	

Achernar

Co-culminating with 26° ♈

Does Not Rise

ALH

CP

Does Not Set

Latitude

Degrees of the Zodiac

Co-Rise
Co-Set

10° ♋
20° ♊
0° ♊
10° ♉
20° ♈
0° ♈
10° ♓
20° ♒

(I've been in after

have confused the modern, new Achernar with the original star of Ptolemy's time, and associate it with honor and success.

ACHERNAR: THE CONCEPT

In work with southern charts of countries and events, the star seems to be more connected with natural disasters, fires, and floods, rather than with personal expression in a natal chart. In work with event charts, the presence of this star can indicate literal fire or flood. In mythological memory The River represents the result of a crisis. On April 5 to 8, 1929, in Derby, Tasmania—which is at a latitude where Achernar will not set—Tasmania experienced its worst flooding on record, with massive rain falls and a burst dam that killed fourteen people. Saturn was setting as Achernar was culminating when this happened. This one case does not justify any final conclusions, but it is interesting to note that Achernar was also involved in the chart for Cyclone Tracey, the worst cyclone to ever hit the coast of Australia, wiping out most of Darwin on Christmas day, 1974. On that day the Sun was culminating as Achernar rose, although the far more powerful stars of Antares (Scorpio), Formalhaut (Piscis Australis), and Aldebaran (Taurus) were also very much involved. I have found that Achernar tends to be involved with the charts of my Australian clients who have experienced the horrors of bushfires or flooding.

ACHERNAR IN THE NATAL CHART

The part of your life represented by the planet involved with the star will tend to be associated with crises, or will indicate where you respond best in a crisis situation. This is a turbulent star. It does not bring drama and tragedy but rather fast-occurring events, like fire and flood, with which you will need to deal quickly and efficiently.

ACHERNAR AS THE HELIACAL RISING STAR AT BIRTH

Although the modern Achernar is bright enough to be the apparent rising star, its high southern declination means that it will be limited in its use. However, if you were born at latitudes where this is possible, then coping with or experiencing crisis becomes a pattern in your life. This could make you brilliant at crisis intervention, or a person always dealing with the unexpected.

HERCULES, THE PHANTOM OR THE ONE WHO KNEELS

ARATUS REFERS TO THIS CONSTELLATION
as already ancient and forgotten:

Right there in its orbit wheels a Phantom form like to a man that strives at a task. That sign no man knows how to read clearly, nor on what task he is bent, but men simply call him On His Knees.[127]

Hercules is one of the oldest constellations and seems to have held that position, like the Bears and the Dragon, well before the beginning of time in the human mind (see Star Map 11, p. 143). Before it was associated with the solar hero, it was commonly named The Kneeler. And although its name varies through the writings of many cultures, it has always remained a human figure kneeling, with the tip of the left foot near the head of the celestial Dragon. As the matrilineal culture faded and time began to be measured, this figure took on different names. He was Gilgamesh,[128] the great solar hero who seems to be the first to encounter the

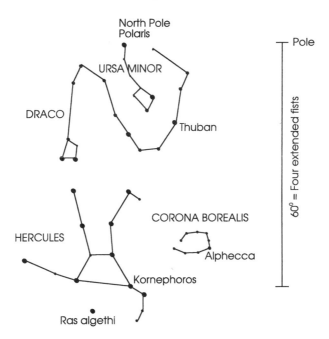

Star Map 11. Hercules, the Phantom, or the One Who Kneels.

---

[127] Mair, *Callimachus, Lycophron, Aratus,* p. 213.
[128] Jobes, *Outer Space,* p. 185.

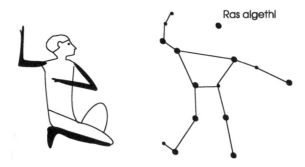

Figure 20. Hercules and the Egyptian hieroglyph for "to adore or give praise."

whirlpool and strive for immortality. The Phoenicians called him Harekhal.[129] And to the Greeks and Romans he was Hercules, the name he still carries. They focused on his left foot near the Dragon's head, showing Hercules crushing the Dragon. The reason for his kneeling is ignored. The Christian myths also strived to claim this phantom by calling him Adam, as well as Samson,[130] conveniently forgetting the kneeling position.

So who is this phantom whom the Greeks assumed to be male, orbiting around the North Pole, the sacred pivot-point? The figure is kneeling in the presence of the great She-Bear goddess and the Dragon. This figure is like the Unknown Soldier of war graves: one human to represent all humans; one human whose personal name is lost for all time.

The phantom is a constellation without a name, known only as "unknown." He or she kneels in a posture resembling the Egyptian hieroglyph for *adoration and giving service*, kneeling on one knee while holding an arm upward and bent (see figure 20, above). The phantom holds this posture perfectly in the part of the sky reserved for the sacred. Since the sky was the model for early human society, our modern kneeling "Hercules" is more than likely a human being adoring the sacred source of all life, the Pole or the goddess, shown in the ancient position of prayer rather than in the more modern Christian position, kneeling on both knees with bent head.

STARS OF HERCULES

The brightest star is Ras algethi, located in the head of the phantom. Other named stars, in descending order of magnitude, are: Kornephoros, in the shoulder; Marfak, in the elbow; and Masym, in the wrist.

---

[129] Jobes, *Outer Space*, p. 186.
[130] Jobes, *Outer Space*, p. 187.

RAS ALGETHI

(Alpha Hercules. Magnitude var. RA 17:12:22" 3. Declination 14 N 26'45". PED = 15° Sagittarius 27'.) See Paran Map 21, page 146. *An example of how to read the map:* If you were born in San Francisco, at a latitude of 38° North, then the star rose at about 23° Scorpio. If you have a planet at either 23° Scorpio or Taurus, then that planet rose or set with the star. The star also set at 17° Capricorn. Therefore, if you have a planet at 17° Capricorn or Cancer, then it would have set or risen as the star set. The star culminates at 21° Sagittarius, so if you have a planet at either 21° Sagittarius or Gemini, then it culminated or was on the Nadir as the star culminated.

At this latitude of 38° North the star has a phase of curtailed passage. This period will be from about May 17 (reading the right-hand column of the date box next to 23° Scorpio) to July 9 every year (reading the right-hand column of the date box next to 17° Capricorn), and is the true or cosmic heliacal rising star about November 17 (reading the date for the rising line at 38° North in the "heliacal rising" column).

Ras Algethi can be used on all four points for charts between latitudes of 75° South and 75° North. South of that the star never rises and north of that the star never sets and therefore has permanent curtailed passage.

EARLIER OPINIONS

Ptolemy states that the stars of Hercules are like Mercury, an interesting association for the so-called Greek solar hero. Robson does not refer to Ras Algethi. Ebertin associates it with problems with women, being popular with women, or being driven to gain power. And Rigor claims it yields great courage, boldness, power, and fame, obviously drawing on the symbolism of Hercules.

RAS ALGETHI: THE CONCEPT

If we put the Herculian imagery to one side, it is interesting to look at this star as implying the natural order of things, the natural and correct attitude of humans in awe of the gods or the goddess. In our modern life this could mean a respect for nature, a caring about the planet, a desire to have all things in their place; that is, the correct order of nature, life, and the heavens.

Martin Luther King had Venus rising as Ras Algethi was culminating. This star alone does not account for the brilliance of the man, but it starts to hint at his devotion to his cause. He devoted his life to the civil rights movement in the United States and in the end gave it his life. He saw the relationship between black and white America, and saw it as incorrect or unbalanced. Venus linked to Ras Algethi indicates the striving or deep desire for balance and order in all manner of relationships.

Ras algethi

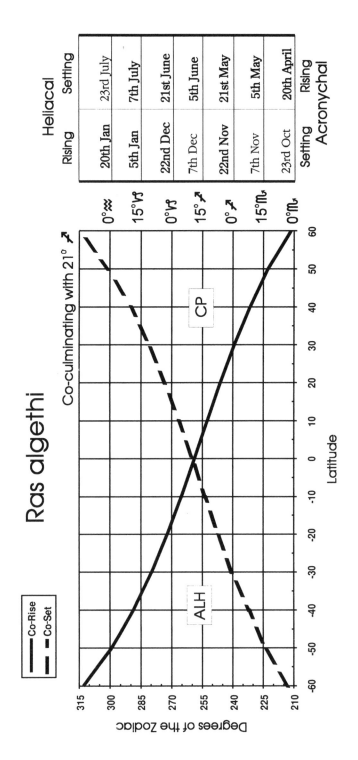

	Heliacal	
	Rising	Setting
0°≈	20th Jan	23rd July
15°♑	5th Jan	7th July
0°♑	22nd Dec	21st June
15°♐	7th Dec	5th June
0°♐	22nd Nov	21st May
15°♏	7th Nov	5th May
0°♏	23rd Oct	20th April
	Setting	Rising
	Acronychal	

Legend:
— Co-Rise
- - Co-Set

Co-culminating with 21° ♐

CP

ALH

Paran Map 21. Ras Algethi.

A different face of Ras Algethi is seen in the chart of Bhagwan Shree Raj-neesh, the guru who created the Rajneesh movement. His Sun is linked to Ras Algethi. His Sun culminated with this star, so his whole sense of identity and how he was seen by others is affected by it. Bhagwan actually has many fixed stars linked to his Sun which accounts for his solar strength. However, the inclusion of Ras Algethi among them indicates one who adores or one who is linked to the concept of "how to adore," the correct pathway to adoration. As a point of inter-est, this star is not represented in the charts of Roman Catholic popes.

RAS ALGETHI IN THE NATAL CHART

Ras Algethi will indicate, via the planet to which it is linked, a sense of order or correctness, or a seeking of this order. There is a natural need to submit to or honor something larger than yourself. This can give a sense of purpose to one's life. The shadow or lesser expression is adoration of another human, being an ar-dent admirer or follower.

RAS ALGETHI AS THE HELIACAL RISING STAR AT BIRTH

Ras Algethi is not traditionally used as the heliacal rising star at birth. However, if you were born on its cosmic rising, rising with the Sun, a strong sense of purpose would be a major part of your definition of yourself. This could imply leadership or it may express itself in your spiritual life.

HYDRA, THE SERPENT

TWO ANCIENT CONSTELLATIONS WERE
involved with snakes or serpents, Hydra and Ophiuchus. A third snake, Hydrus,
has been added in modern times. Both of the ancient serpents cut the equator
and one of them, Ophiuchus, sits more firmly on the ecliptic than Scorpio.

Hydra is the largest constellation in the sky, stretching for nearly 95° across
the heavens, from Cancer to Scorpio (see Star Map 12, p. 149). It has been
given many names, but in most cultures it has been either a snake, a serpent, or
a water snake. Aratus says of it: "Like a living creature it winds afar its coiling
form."[131] The Greeks claimed it was the creature that attacked the Argo.[132]
Hydra is also considered to be the constellation on an uranographic[133] stone
from the Euphrates area, 1,200 B.C.E., which shows it as the source of connection to the "great deep" and to the great dragon Tiamat.[134] The constellation was
also considered the wandering path of the Moon before she settled into her
orbit. Therefore, writes Allen, the Nodes of the Moon are called the Dragon's
Head and Dragon's Tail.[135]

Most cultures have a snake or serpent connected with their creation myths
in some way. In Hinduism it is Ananta the Infinite who embraced the gods and
gave them life. She was also the Kundalini energy coiled in a person's pelvis to be
released as life-giving sexual energy.[136] The Chinese myth states they are all de-
scendants of Mat Chinoi, the Serpent-goddess who received the souls of the dead
in her belly and then gave birth to new life.[137]

In the ancient Aegean world, women were worshiped with serpents, and
males could be involved if they were priests of the bull god. However, they were
subordinate to the priestess until they themselves could be called "serpent." Indeed, the word for priest meant *snake charmer.*[138] Such stories run through culture after culture, including the Old Testament creation myth of the Garden of
Eden and the serpent in the Tree of Life.[139]

---

[131] Mair, *Callimachus, Lycophron, Aratus*, p. 243.

[132] Allen, *Star Names*, p. 248.

[133] The Urartians were a group of people who lived in a mountainous region southeast of the
Black Sea from about 3,000 B.C.E. to the time they were overcome by the Armenians, toward the end of the seventh century B.C.E.

[134] Allen, *Star Names*, p. 248.

[135] Allen, *Star Names*, p. 249.

[136] Walker, *The Woman's Encyclopedia of Myths and Secrets*, p. 903.

[137] Walker, *The Woman's Encyclopedia of Myths and Secrets*, p. 903.

[138] Walker, *The Woman's Encyclopedia of Myths and Secrets*, p. 903.

[139] Allen, *Star Names*, p. 191.

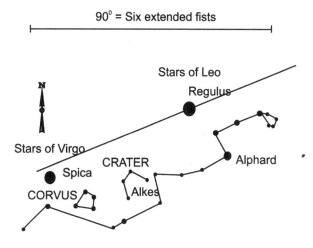

Star Map 12. Hydra the Serpent.

Hydra, then, is related to the goddess energy in one of its original forms, and has probably been so considered for tens of thousands of years. What is most interesting is that, although it is the largest of all the constellations, it has not been broken up and redistributed to other groupings, by either the Greeks or later astronomers.

STARS OF HYDRA

Hydra's brightest star is Alphard, also known as the Heart of the Serpent. Other named stars, in descending order of magnitude, are: Al Sharasif, the ribs; Al Minliar al Shuja, the Snake's nose; and the curve in the neck, Ukda.

ALPHARD

(Alpha Hydra. Magnitude 2.2. RA 09:25:7.8". Declination 8S26'27". PED = 26° Leo 35'.) See Paran Map 22, page 150. *An example of how to read the map:* If you were born in Atlanta, USA, at a latitude of 34° North, then the star rose at about 0° Virgo. If you have a planet at either 0° Virgo or Pisces, then that planet rose or set with the star. The star also set at 28° Cancer. Therefore, if you have a planet at 28° Cancer or Capricorn, it would have set or risen as the star set. The star culminates at 17° Leo, so if you have a planet at either 17° Leo or Aquarius, then it culminated or was on the Nadir as the star culminated.

At this latitude of 34° North the star has a phase of arising and lying hidden. This period will be from about July 20 (reading the date from the left-hand

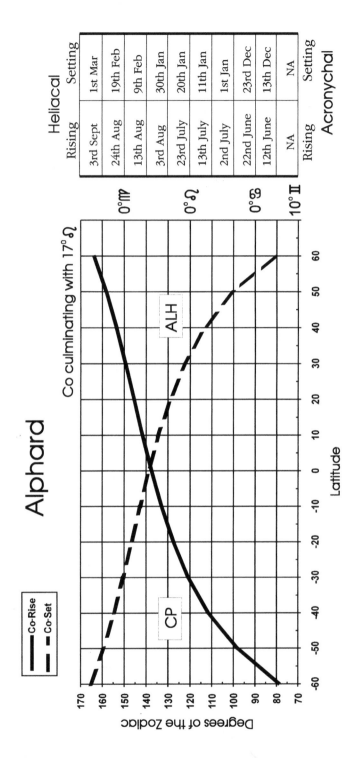

Heliacal	
Rising	Setting
3rd Sept	1st Mar
24th Aug	19th Feb
13th Aug	9th Feb
3rd Aug	30th Jan
23rd July	20th Jan
13th July	11th Jan
2nd July	1st Jan
22nd June	23rd Dec
12th June	13th Dec
NA	NA
Rising	Setting
Acronychal	

Co culminating with 17° ♌

Alphard

ALH

CP

Co-Rise
Co-Set

Degrees of the Zodiac

Latitude

Paran Map 22. Alphard.

column of the date box next to 28° Cancer) to August 24 every year (reading the left-hand column of the date box next to 0° Virgo), and is the true or cosmic heliacal rising star about August 24 (reading the date for the rising line at 34° North in the "heliacal rising" column).

Alphard can be used on all four points for charts between latitudes of 81° South and 81° North. North of that the star never rises and south of that the star never sets and therefore has permanent curtailed passage.

EARLIER OPINIONS

Ptolemy likens the bright star of this constellation to Saturn and Venus. Robson relates it to poisoning, including blood-poisoning, murder by poisoning, death by gas poisoning, poison bites, rabies, drug abuse, and the poisoning and hatred of women. He also says it gives wisdom and musical, artistic appreciation! Ebertin agrees with Robson. Rigor also agrees with Robson and then adds "revolting deeds" to the list.

ALPHARD: THE CONCEPT

Alphard is a difficult star: people who have natal contacts with Alphard, particularly Alphard-Mars, are often the perpetrators or victims of violent crimes. Thus the Heart of the Serpent manifests in violent, untamed, emotional outbursts. To think of Alphard in this purely violent way is misleading, however. William Blake, the English poet whose passion burned into his religious poetry, had Alphard rising as his Jupiter contacted his Nadir. The darkness, the passion, and the religious or mystical focus of Blake gives us an insight into a more balanced Alphard.

A writer with a very different nature is Stephen King, the famous writer of horror stories. King was born on the day that Alphard culminated with Saturn. A star linked with Saturn influences the body of work that is built up over a person's lifetime, and the culmination point suggests this star expresses itself in the prime of his life. Stephen King has built a large body of work and has become one of the world's leading horror writers. On the other side of the coin, O. J. Simpson, who was born with Algol culminating, also has Alphard setting as his Jupiter culminates. This configuration implies that toward the end of his life he would become almost a symbol (Jupiter) of Alphard.

ALPHARD IN THE NATAL CHART

The Serpent, and thus the Serpent's Heart, is only just reemerging in the human psyche, and although it is still mostly submerged in the unconscious, it can be murderous and violent when it manifests. Its preferred expression is conscious passion. Its interpretation would depend on how it was affecting a chart. If it is present in your chart, you are working with very strong feelings and will need to resist striking back in anger. A better use of the energy is to focus on a subject or a cause to which you can devote your strength and determination.

ALPHARD AS THE HELIACAL RISING STAR AT BIRTH

This is one of Ptolemy's stars, so that it can be used as both the cosmic and the apparent rising star, and if it claimed the Sun on the day you were born, you will need to be aware that your life is connected to the great Serpent. Intense, transforming, and really only now becoming conscious in the human mind, this star can be vicious. However, she also offers great wisdom to those who hold back from their desire to strike.

LEPUS, THE HARE

SITUATED NEAR THE FEET OF ORION AND next to Canis Major, there is a Hare[140] (see Star Map 6, p. 80). The constellation consists of faint stars and has been associated with many different objects over time. The Arabs saw it as a thirsty camel bending down to drink from the Milky Way.[141] The Egyptians claimed it as Osiris's boat and the Chinese called it The Shed.[142] "The Hare" has been its name since Ptolemy, and various myths have been built up around the fact that, for most locations, the Hare will be setting as the Eagle, Aquila, rises. Thus the hare runs from the eagle.

The only named star is Arneb, meaning "Whole,"[143] and there seem to be no stars of astrological significance. Ptolemy states that the stars are like Saturn and Mars. Robson states that it gives a quick wit. However, even though this constellation does not seem to contribute stars to astrology, it has contributed much to the social customs of the Western world. In Egyptian mythology there is a sacred hare whose role was to guard, or collect and deliver the sacred egg for the goddess. The egg meant life itself, and in this capacity the hare was seen as a messenger for the goddess. In modern times we have reduced this great sacred hare to the "Easter Bunny,"[144] but nonetheless he or she is still busy with the eggs of life. By a cute twist of fate, the Hare is the Acronychal rising (rising at sunset) constellation for the period of the year of the Christian Easter.

[140] Mair, *Callimachus, Lycophron, Aratus*, p. 233.
[141] Allen, *Star Names*, p. 265.
[142] Allen, *Star Names*, p. 265.
[143] Allen, *Star Names*, p. 268.
[144] John Layard, *The Lady of the Hare* (Boston: Shambhala, 1988), p. 171.

LUPUS, THE WOLF

LUPUS THE WOLF, ARA THE ALTAR, AND

Centaurus the Centaur are a group of three constellations entangled in a story of worship and devotion. The wolf is the offering taken to the altar by the centaur (see Star Map 7, p. 98).

South of the Scorpion and at the end of Hydra lies the constellation that Aratus called The Beast,[145] or simply The Wild Animal (see Star Map 7, p. 98). Other cultures called it the Leopard or the Lion. It was also known as the Star of Dead Fathers or the Beast of Death.[146]

STARS OF LUPUS

The brightest star is Men, RA 14:43', Declination 47° S24', with a magnitude of 2.6. The only other named star is Ke Kwan (Chinese).

EARLIER OPINIONS

Ptolemy says that the bright stars are partly like Saturn and partly like Mars. Robson lists characteristics which seem to have been generated by the nature of the actual animal itself, such as grasping, aggressive, and treacherous natures. Ebertin and Rigor do not mention the stars.

LUPUS: THE CONCEPT

Although there are no major stars, this constellation is worth considering if it forms a visual paran relationship with natal planets. A quirky example of its energy is displayed in the chart for Jack Nicholson. Jack Nicholson was born on the day that the stars of Lupus were the heliacal setting stars. The older he has become, the more sinister are the roles he plays, and recently he was acclaimed for his role in *Wolf*, where he plays a character who turns into a human wolf. Here is an interesting example not so much of an individual star (pun intended), but of a whole constellation connected to a person because it was the heliacal setting constellation (setting at sunrise) on the day of birth.

---

[145] Mair, *Callimachus, Lycophron, Aratus*, p. 241.

[146] Allen, *Star Names*, p. 278.

LYRA, THE HARP

DIFFERENT CULTURES HAVE CALLED THIS constellation by many names, but the common thread is the theme of a musical instrument. The Greeks thought of it as the lyre of Orpheus. This lyre was made from a tortoise shell by the infant Mercury and later given to Orpheus by Apollo.[147] Aratus called it the Little Tortoise, explaining how Hermes used the animal to create the first lyre.[148] Pliny called it the Harp Star. The Anglo-Saxons and Celts knew it as a harp and later saw it as *Talyn Arthur*, the Hero's Harp.[149] The Christians named it King David's Harp,[150] and later, totally out of step with the tradition of the constellation, identified it with the Manger of the Infant Savior.[151]

In India this grouping was also linked to the vulture, and at times in the desert of Arabia it was the Great Swooping Eagle, in contrast to the constellation of Aquila, which was the Great Flying Eagle.[152] Up to a few centuries ago it was also known as a swooping vulture which held a lyre in its beak. In this guise as a harp-carrying vulture, it was the third Stymphalian Bird[153] (see Star Map 2, p. 56).

STARS OF LYRA

The brightest star is Vega or Wega. Other named stars, in descending order of magnitude, are Sheliak and Jugum, in the strings of the instrument.

WEGA

(Alpha Lyra. Magnitude 0.1. RA 18:36:46.7". Declination 20N33'10". PED = 14° Capricorn 37'.) See Paran Map 23, page 156. *An example of how to read the map:* If you were born in Mexico City, at a latitude of 19° North, then the star rose at about 13° Sagittarius. If you have a planet at either 13° Sagittarius or Gemini, then that planet rose or set with the star. The star also set at 0° Aquarius. Therefore, if you have a planet at 0° Aquarius or Leo, it would have set or risen as the star set. The star culminates at 16° Capricorn, so if you have a

---

[147] Room, *Dictionary of Astronomical Names*, p. 107.
[148] Mair, *Callimachus, Lycophron, Aratus*, p. 229.
[149] Jobes, *Outer Space*, p. 207.
[150] Jobes, *Outer Space*, p. 206.
[151] Jobes, *Outer Space*, p. 206.
[152] Jobes, *Outer Space*, p. 206.
[153] Jobes, *Outer Space*, p. 206.

Wega

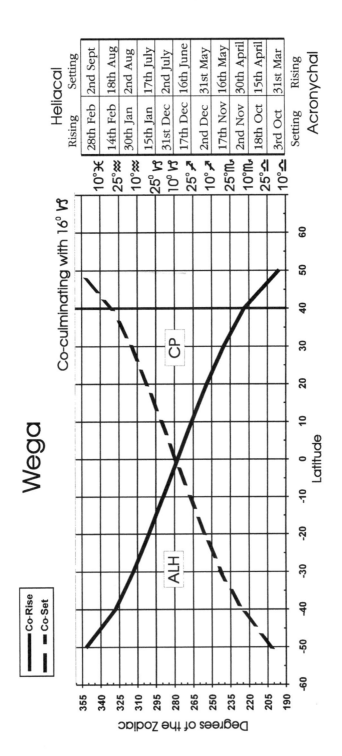

Co-culminating with 16° ♑

Heliacal		
Rising	Setting	
28th Feb	2nd Sept	10° ♓
14th Feb	18th Aug	25° ≈
30th Jan	2nd Aug	10° ≈
15th Jan	17th July	25° ♑
31st Dec	2nd July	10° ♑
17th Dec	16th June	25° ♐
2nd Dec	31st May	10° ♐
17th Nov	16th May	25° ♏
2nd Nov	30th April	10° ♏
18th Oct	15th April	25° ♎
3rd Oct	31st Mar	10° ♎
Setting	Rising	
Acronychal		

Degrees of the Zodiac

Latitude

Paran Map 23. Wega.

planet at either 16° Capricorn or Cancer, then it culminated or was on the Nadir as the star culminated.

At this latitude of 19° North the star has a phase of curtailed passage. This period will be from about June 5 (reading the date from the right-hand column of the date box next to 13° Sagittarius) to July 25 every year (reading the right-hand column of the date box next to 0° Aquarius), and is the true or cosmic heliacal rising star about December 6 (reading the date for the rising line at 19° North in the "heliacal rising" column).

Wega can be used on all four points for charts between latitudes of 51° South and 51° North. South of that the star never rises and north of that the star never sets and therefore has permanent curtailed passage.

EARLIER OPINIONS

Ptolemy states that the stars of Lyra are like Venus and Mercury. Robson declares that Wega gives hopefulness, and at the same time "makes the natives grave, sober, outwardly pretentious, and usually lascivious." Ebertin saw this star as giving artistic talents in both acting and music, possibly leading to a debauched life. Rigor ignores its influence on arts and associates it with leadership ability and social awareness.

WEGA: THE CONCEPT

Wega was the pole star around 12,000–10,000 B.C.E. and was then, it is believed, called Maat, the great Egyptian goddess who helped souls move from one life to another.[154] Her weight was only that of a feather and the soul's weight was measured against hers. If the soul was the same weight as Maat, then it could go on to an afterlife. Lockyer believed that the temple of Tyre as described by Herodotus, was aligned to the rising of Wega in about 4,000 to 3,000 B.C.E.[155] It will be the pole star again in about 11,500 C.E.

Wega is a most beautiful and bright star, and through its connection to Orpheus is linked to magic and divine spells. Those who are influenced by it are full of charisma and have been touched by the otherworld. The Greeks myth of Orpheus is about a muscian whose music could tame the wildest of animals, and that is the sense in which Wega is the star of music. The fact that it was rising when Mozart was born, a man considered by many to be the greatest composer of all times, seems a fitting and obvious statement. For music is a spell and music can be spellbinding. The Chinese saw this star as a goddess who helped a poor but noble youth buy his way out of slavery by becoming his wife and then spinning the most beautiful silk hangings that had ever been seen. They see this star

---

[154] Allen, *Star Names*, p. 286.
[155] Lockyer, *Dawn of Astronomy*, p. 161.

as representing all that is artistic, particularly in the field of fabrics.[156] Yet the power of Wega, this charismatic star full of allure and appeal, can also be seen in the chart of Adolf Hitler. On the day he was born Wega rose as his Mercury set. Here the spellbinding magic of Wega manifests in Hitler's charismatic skill as an orator. Casanova, the eighteenth-century writer, soldier, spy, and lover—who was the model for Ian Fleming's character James Bond, was born with Wega culminating as his Sun rose.

WEGA IN THE NATAL CHART

Wega's expression is going to very much depend on what other fixed stars are influencing the chart, as well as what planet it is influencing. It gives creative, mysterious skills which can be used by the artist or the criminal. It is a beautiful, magical star, much like Formalhaut, one of the Royal Stars of Persia, and will give to all it touches a charismatic quality.

WEGA AS THE HELIACAL RISING STAR AT BIRTH

Wega is one of the very important stars of the sky, available for use as both the apparent and cosmic rising star. If you are born on the day that it claims the Sun and mixes its energy with the Sun's rays, then your natal Sun, and therefore your life journey and personal mythology, are deeply connected to this star. It may give you great charisma or great artistic gifts, but your role will be to realize these gifts without deception, bringing a touch of the heavens to the earth.

---

[156] Jobes, *Outer Space*, p. 378.

OPHIUCHUS, THE SERPENT HOLDER AND SERPENS, THE SERPENT

THE STARS OF OPHIUCHUS AND SERPENS are now broken up into three constellations: Ophiuchus, the Serpent Holder; Caput Serpens; and Cauda Serpens, the latter two being sections of the serpent which are on each side of Ophiuchus (see Star Map 13, below). When Scorpio lost its claws to Libra, it also lost most of its contact with the ecliptic. Ophiuchus cuts a larger tract across the ecliptic than the modern Scorpio. The section of the zodiac traveled by the Sun from November 21 to December 16 is currently predominantly among the stars of Ophiuchus, rather than the stars of Scorpio.

Ophiuchus was known to the Greeks as Serpentarius the Healer, who was also the god Asclepius, son of Apollo.[157] He learned the healing arts from Chiron and is usually depicted as holding a stick on which a serpent is coiled. This symbol is now used as the symbol of Western medicine. Asclepius was the ship's surgeon on the Argo and became so skilled he was able to bring patients back from the dead, a practice quickly forbidden by the gods, who eventually smote him with a thunderbolt for fear that he would surpass them with his healing powers. He was placed in the heavens as Ophiuchus.[158]

Later, under Christian influence, this constellation became Saint Paul with the Maltese Viper; Moses, who held up the blazing serpent in the wilderness; and, lastly, Saint Benedict, the founder of the Benedictine monks, standing among thorns.[159]

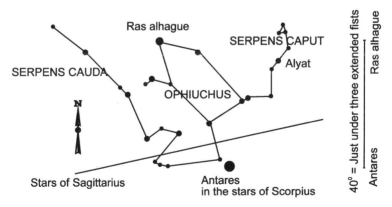

Star Map 13. Ophiuchus and the Serpent.

[157] Room, *Dictionary of Astronomical Names*, p. 123.
[158] Grimal, *Classical Mythology*, p. 63.
[159] Allen, *Star Names*, p. 299.

The serpent was seen as a healing agent because it represented prudence, rejuvenation, wisdom, and rebirth. This is the healing side of the ancient goddess, for just as she had the ability to create life, she also had the wisdom and knowledge of how it could be healed, as well as the knowledge of how it can be destroyed. Asclepius was said to have the blood of Medusa in his veins. The blood that flowed on Medusa's left side created fatal poison, while the blood that flowed on the right was beneficial.[160]

Thus Ophiuchus is connected with all aspects of healing: medicine and drugs, ranging from the alcohols produced by Benedictine monks, to the knowledge of drugs and herbs in Western and Eastern medicines. As Melanie Reinhart points out in her lectures, its position as the thirteenth ecliptical sign could well be an echo of the thirteen lunar months clashing with the established twelve solar signs.

STARS OF OPHIUCHUS AND SERPENS

The brightest star is Ras Alhague, the head of the Serpent Holder; and in the Serpent itself is Alyat, the neck of the Snake.

Ras Alhague

(Alpha Ophiuchus. Magnitude 2.1. RA 17:34:42.5". Declination 12N34'04". PED = 21° Sagittarius 45'.) See Paran Map 24, page 161. *An example of how to read the map:* If you were born in Buenos Aires, Argentina, at a latitude of 35° South, then the star rose at about 18° Capricorn. If you have a planet at either 18° Capricorn or Cancer, then that planet rose or set with the star. The star also set at 2° Sagittarius. Therefore, if you have a planet at 2° Sagittarius or Gemini, it would have set or risen as the star set. The star culminates at 25° Sagittarius, so if you have a planet at either 25° Sagittarius or Gemini, then it culminated or was on the Nadir as the star culminated.

At this latitude of 35° South the star has a phase of arising and lying hidden. This period will be from about November 22 (reading the date from the left-hand column of the date box next to 2° Sagittarius) to January 8 every year (reading the left-hand column of the date box next to 18° Capricorn), and is the true or cosmic heliacal rising star about January 8 (reading the date for the rising line at 35° South in the "heliacal rising" column).

---

[160] Grimal, *Classical Mythology,* p. 63.

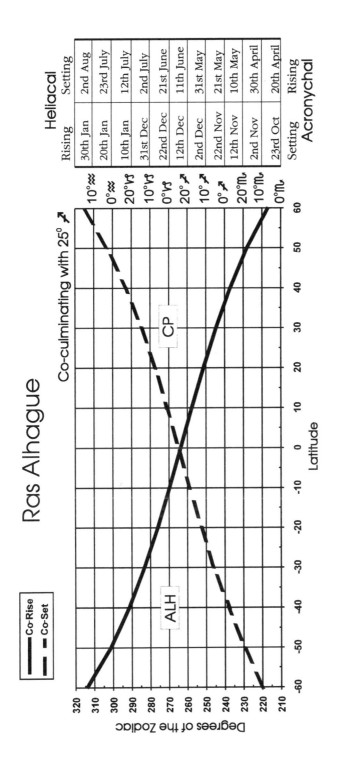

Ras Alhague

Heliacal

	Rising	Setting
10°≈≈	30th Jan	2nd Aug
0°≈≈	20th Jan	23rd July
20°♑	10th Jan	12th July
10°♑	31st Dec	2nd July
0°♑	22nd Dec	21st June
20°♐	12th Dec	11th June
10°♐	2nd Dec	31st May
0°♐	22nd Nov	21st May
20°♏	12th Nov	10th May
10°♏	2nd Nov	30th April
0°♏	23rd Oct	20th April
	Setting	Rising

Acronychal

Co-culminating with 25° ♐

Latitude

Degrees of the Zodiac

CP

ALH

Co-Rise
Co-Set

Paran Map 24. Ras Alhague.

Ras Alhague can be used on all four points for charts between latitudes of 77° South and 77° North. South of that the star never rises and north of that the star never sets and therefore has permanent curtailed passage.

EARLIER OPINIONS

Ptolemy states that the stars in this constellation are like Saturn, with some resemblances to Venus. Robson associates them with misfortune through women, and perverted tastes; Ebertin with drug addicts or overindulgence in druglike substances; also the danger of bites and rabies. Rigor disagrees, talking instead of broad-mindedness, humanitarianism, and "tremendous visualization."

RAS ALHAGUE: THE CONCEPT

John Lennon had his Venus culminating as this star rose, and became known as one trying to heal the world through song, while popularizing the drug culture. Abraham Lincoln had this star rising when his Mercury was at the Nadir, and much of his life was spent trying to heal his country from civil war and slavery. In a similar way, Madam Blavatsky, the 19th-century Russian spiritualist, author, and cofounder of the Theosophical Society, also had Ras Alhague connected to her Mercury, but in her case it was culminating as her Mercury set. She was renowned for her spiritual writings and, although considered by the science of the day to be a fraud, her name lives on as a spiritual teacher. Vincent van Gogh had Ras Alhague setting as his Sun culminated, and he was a great artist, wounded and in need of healing. Healing, teaching, or wounding: these seem to be the themes of this constellation.

RAS ALHAGUE IN THE NATAL CHART

When it appears in your chart, this star suggests you are drawn to the healing profession or have a natural gift in that area. What you choose to heal may not be only living things, but also living ideals. This could lead you into politics or other related activities. The driving force, in any case, will be to repair that which is damaged, to heal.

RAS ALHAGUE AS THE HELIACAL RISING STAR AT BIRTH

Ras Alhague is not on Ptolemy's list, so it cannot be used as the apparent rising star, but if you had it as the cosmic rising star on the day you were born, then the myths and meanings of the great healer and his serpent, and thus his wisdom, will be a part of your life. You may use this gift to become a healer or you may be the one who needs the wisdom of others to be healed.

ORION, GOD ON THE EQUATOR

I fly from you, oh men,
I am not for the earth.
I am for the sky.
I have soared to the sky as a heaven.
I have kissed the sky as a falcon.
I am the essence of a god,
the son of a god.
Behold the faithful and loving Osiris
has come as the stars of Orion, the Beautiful One.
I have come that I may glorify Orion.
My soul is a star of gold
and with him
I will traverse the sky forever.

—*Pyramid text*[161]

AROUND 6000 B.C.E., WHEN THE STARS OF Gemini rose at the spring equinox, the Egyptians, like most other cultures, measured their year by the rising and setting of the brightest stars, notating their calendars with their heliacal risings.

The importance of a heliacal rising star, one that rises just before the Sun, is that the star acts as a herald for the sunrise. The rising Sun was considered by the Egyptians to be the infant Horus in the arms of Isis. As the Sun rose, signifying the return of the god,[162] it appeared to sweep up the star in its light and carry it across the sky. Thus the god mixed his energy with that of the star, and the star was illuminated by the god. By noon the Sun was no longer seen as the infant Horus; rather, it was the adult Horus, or Ra; and at sunset it became Osiris, the god of the underworld.[163]

Lockyer implies that between 6,000–4,000 B.C.E. the importance of the solstice and spring equinox had been established[164] as the beginning of the agricultural cycle, and that the Egyptians would have noted that Orion rose on the important morning of the spring equinox, which was linked to the annual flooding of the Nile.[165] Indeed this connecting of the rising of Orion and the equinox

---

[161] Quoted in Christopher Mann, prod., "The Great Pyramid" (documentary), BBC, 1994.

[162] Lockyer, *Dawn of Astronomy*, p. 36.

[163] Lockyer, p. 25. It is interesting to note that this is the same theme written about by Anonymous of 379 when he says that a star rising will affect the early life, a star culminating will affect the middle years of life, and a star setting will affect the end of life.

[164] Lockyer, *Dawn of Astronomy*, p. 78.

[165] Lockyer, *Dawn of Astronomy*, p. 85.

has been placed at a far earlier time by Sellers, who points out that the last time a star in Orion rose at the equinox would have been about 6,700 B.C.E.[166] Then, as now, the brightest and most spectacular constellation of the night sky was Orion, and the image of this huge humanlike constellation, rising in the predawn light and being scooped up into the fiery boat of the Sun, would have been quite impressive, to say the least.

Orion/Osiris was god.[167] The constellation was not a symbol of god, it *was* god; god's physical place or appearance, in the same way that Sirius in Canis Major was the dwelling place of Isis[168] (see Star Map 14, below). Orion rose with the spring equinox Sun and claimed rulership of the world age. The Egyptians knew him as Osiris and the Pharoahs came from him; they were his physical flesh, and were returned to him. However, as hundreds of years went by, they noted that less and less of the constellation Orion rose before the dawn on the equinox morning. The effects of precession caused the god to slip lower and lower in the sky. So, whereas at one time he was fully risen before sunrise, there came a time when only a part of the constellation was above the eastern horizon before the equinoctial sunrise. The constellation Orion managed to rise for roughly two thousand years

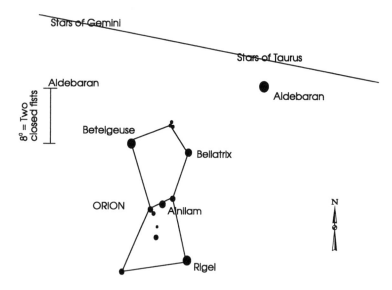

Star Map 14. Orion, god on the equator.

[166] Sellers, *The Death of the Gods in Ancient Egypt* (London: Penguin, 1992), p. 43.
[167] Wallis E. A. Budge, *The Gods of the Egyptians*, vol. 1 (New York: Dover Books, 1969), p. 41.
[168] Budge, *The Gods of the Egyptians*, vol. 2, p. 215.

but the Egyptians knew that their immortal god was moving into the whirlpool, taking the journey across the water as he slipped into the underworld.

Mary Settegast, in her book *Plato Prehistorian*, talks of the death of Osiris occurring in the sixth millennium (the period when the constellation Orion was slipping from the equinox position) as it seemed to influence the spread and design of the pottery of pre-dynastic Upper Egypt.[169] At this time there was a sudden spreading of pottery into other areas, which Settegast suggests is reflected in the myth of the journeys of Isis in seeking her dead husband.

To account for these observations, the Egyptians developed the concept of an immortal god dying and passing on his throne to his son. Now, one of the features of the constellation Orion is that it contains a bright red star called Betelgeuse, found in Orion's right shoulder. By coincidence, the constellation Taurus, the next constellation to herald the dawn of the equinox, also contains a bright red star, by the name of Aldebaran. So, as Osiris died and was replaced by the stars of Taurus, the natural "heir" to the solar throne appeared.[170] This constellation was therefore considered to be the son of Osiris, Horus. Osiris became the god of the underworld or afterlife, and Horus, his son, ruled the new world order. With a religious philosophy that ran for over six thousand years, the Egyptians had to create a religion that would allow for three generations of gods, as three constellations slipped over the equinox.

Many modern theologians/mythologists agree that this precessional movement of Orion is the source of the religious concept of an afterlife given to us by a god who dies. Osiris/Orion is a "prefiguring of Christ."[171] God is immortal. The god also dies, however, in some manner. The dead god then promises us an afterlife in his presence.[172] The following pyramid text captures this Egyptian concept.

> You sleep that you may wake
> You die that you may live.[173]

The constellation Orion is, therefore, an archetype of god. We humans have modeled our male gods on this constellation for probably well over eight thousand years. This is in contrast to the never-setting circumpolar Ursa Major and Minor, the goddess, for goddesses do not die in our philosophy. Goddesses may

---

[169] Mary Settegast, *Plato Prehistory* (New York: Lindisfarne, 1990), p. 156.
[170] Sellers, *The Death of the Gods in Ancient Egypt*, p. 33.
[171] Sellers, *The Death of the Gods in Ancient Egypt*, p. 47.
[172] Sellers, *The Death of the Gods in Ancient Egypt*, p. 122–123.
[173] Pyramid Text, 1,975 B.C.E., quoted in Sellers, p. 127.

fade, but they are immortal. The She-Bear never sets as she circles the pole. However, the male god on the equator and the gods of the ecliptic are subject to the hero's journey of the whirlpool. This one constellation, more than any other group of stars, has affected the human race in a most profound way.

Four thousand years or so later the Greeks modified Orion into a giant, an unwelcome admirer of Artemis. Artemis in turn created a giant Scorpion who stung him on the foot, causing him to go blind.[174] But he regained his sight by watching the sunrise. This myth probably grew from the fact that in the north, as the Scorpion rises, Orion appears to flee by setting. Another version of the story was that Artemis appreciated his advances but was tricked into accidentally killing him. He swam out to sea (a metaphor for the constellation slipping into the sea) where she, mistaking him for driftwood, used him as target practice.[175] He was lost to the sea. Greek stories echo Egyptian mythology, for their Orion stories have the common flavor of Orion dying or going blind and then being reborn through some involvement with the Sun.

STARS OF ORION

The brightest star, though not labeled as alpha, is Rigel; the other stars, in descending order of magnitude are: Betelgeuse, the armpit; Bellatrix, the left shoulder; Mintaka, the belt; Alnilam, middle star in belt; Alnitak, last star in belt; Saiph, in the right thigh; and Thabit, in the sword.

BETELGEUSE

(Alpha Orion. Magnitude variable. RA 06:23:49". Declination 07N24'22". PED = 28° Gemini 03'.) See Paran Map 25, page 167. *An example of how to read the map:* If you were born in Alexandria, Egypt, at a latitude of 31° North then the star rose at about 8° Cancer. If you have a planet at either 8° Cancer or Capricorn, then that planet rose or set with the star. The star also set at 20° Gemini. Therefore, if you have a planet at 20° Gemini or Sagittarius, it would have set or risen as the star set. The star culminates at 28° Gemini so if you have a planet at either 28° Gemini or Sagittarius, then it culminated or was on the Nadir as the star culminated.

At this latitude of 31° North the star has a phase of arising and lying hidden. This period will be from about June 11 (reading the date from the left-hand column of the date box next to 20° Gemini) to June 30 every year (reading the left-hand column of the date box next to 8° Cancer), and is the true or cosmic

---

[174] Grimal, *The Dictionary of Classical Mythology,* p. 330.
[175] Bulfinch, *Myths of Greece and Rome,* p. 238.

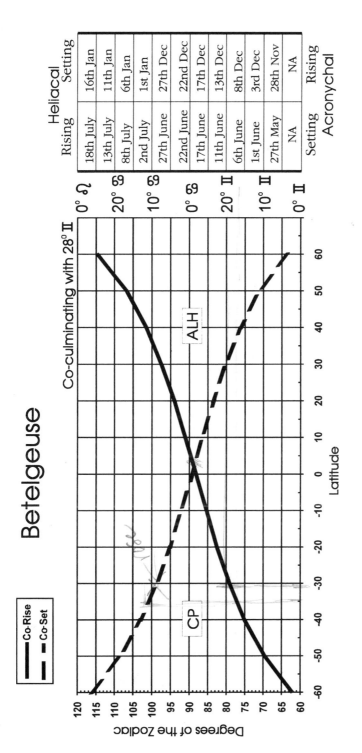

	Heliacal				Heliacal	
	Rising	Setting				
0° ♌	18th July	16th Jan				
20°	13th July	11th Jan				
10°	8th July	6th Jan				
0° ♋	2nd July	1st Jan				
	27th June	27th Dec				
	22nd June	22nd Dec				
	17th June	17th Dec				
20° ♊	11th June	13th Dec				
10° ♊	6th June	8th Dec				
	1st June	3rd Dec				
0° ♊	27th May	28th Nov				
	NA	NA				
	Setting	Rising				
	Acronychal					

Paran Map 25. Betelgeuse.

heliacal rising star about June 30 (reading the date for the rising line at 31° North in the "heliacal rising" column).

Betelgeuse can be used on all four points for charts for all latitudes except for the extremes of the poles.

EARLIER OPINIONS

Ptolemy states that the stars of and near Orion's shoulders are like Mars and Mercury. Robson relates them to martial honor. Ebertin talks of luck, success and everlasting fame. Rigor agrees, and adds rashness and changeability.

BETELGEUSE: THE CONCEPT

Betelgeuse is one of the great stars of the sky and its influence can bring unbridled success without complications. It is in the right hand, armpit, or shoulder of the god, thereby representing that which is clear and strong. Betelgeuse and its companion stars of this constellation are one of the indicators in a chart of fame or success, be it in the local or global community: the person influenced by it is effective, brilliant, and successful.

Because Betelgeuse is such a strong star, it is one of the few stars where one can clearly see its expression change as it affects different angles of the chart.

BETELGEUSE ON THE NADIR

Any star at the Nadir will imply that its effect will not be obvious, as its influence will become apparent in old age or even after death. Both Abraham Lincoln and Martin Luther King have Betelgeuse in this position. Lincoln had his Jupiter rising as Betelgeuse was at the Nadir and, although he had success in his lifetime (for he has many good stars in his chart), Betelgeuse in this position suggests fame that grows after his death. Martin Luther King similarly had Betelgeuse at the Nadir as his Moon rose. He achieved success in his lifetime but it was only in his death that he became immortal.

BETELGEUSE RISING

A star rising gives its energy early in life. The energy may then continue if there are other stars to support it. With Betelgeuse in this position success comes early and may even produce a child prodigy. James Dean is a good example, for he had Betelgeuse rising with his Jupiter and rocketed to fame as an actor before he killed himself in a motor accident.

Marilyn Monroe had Betelgeuse rising as her Mars culminated. Linked with Mars on the MC (that for which one is remembered), she achieved rapid and huge success, not so much for her acting, which would be Venus, but as a sex symbol, which is a Mars expression. She did not have to wait till after her death or when she was middle-aged.

BETELGEUSE CULMINATING

In this position success comes in the middle of life and defines how a person is remembered. Charles Dickens, the Victorian novelist, had Betelgeuse culminating with his Jupiter. This was not the only fixed-star combination in his chart but it showed that he would achieve great success during his lifetime and that his work would live on.

BETELGEUSE SETTING

In this position the energy of the star is expressed later in life. William Blake had his Sun setting with Betelgeuse. He was a great artist and poet who, during his lifetime, had to scratch out a living doing engravings. His name was held in high esteem only in his later life and then after death.

Thus, this star relates to the ability to be successful and to one's work living on. In a sense this star gives a person the opportunity for immortality. Not every person whose chart contains Betelgeuse will rise to great fame but it is an important ingredient to the potential of such fame. A person influenced by it can experience success without having to go through a dark journey of the soul.

BETELGEUSE IN THE NATAL CHART

You will find the planet in contact with Betelgeuse will represent talents or abilities you possess which can be used for joy, success, or even fame. It may be as simple as a Moon or Venus relationship, where a Betelgeuse connection will imply lifelong emotional happiness. Whatever this star touches, it will produce positive results.

BETELGEUSE AS THE HELIACAL RISING STAR AT BIRTH

Potentially both the apparent and the cosmic rising star, Betelgeuse will mark the person with whose Sun it rises with the ability for success. Linked with this personal ambition will be a natural charisma generated through self-confidence. This natural charisma could lead you into a very successful positive life or, depending on the rest of the chart, could suggest a "con man".

RIGEL

(Beta Orion. Magnitude 0.3. RA 05:14:17.6". Declination 08S12'21". PED = 16° Gemini 08'.) See Paran Map 26, page 170. *An example of how to read the map:* If you were born in Wellington, New Zealand, at a latitude of 41° South, then the star rose at about 25° Taurus. If you have a planet at either 25° Taurus or Scorpio, then that planet rose or set with the star. The star also set at 15° Cancer. Therefore, if you have a planet at 15° Cancer or Capricorn, it would have set or risen as the star set. The star culminates at 18° Gemini, so if you have a planet at

Rigel

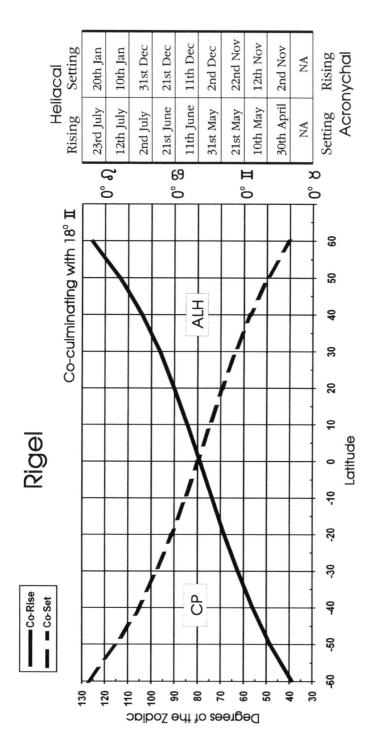

Heliacal		
Rising	Setting	
23rd July	20th Jan	𝟎° ♌
12th July	10th Jan	
2nd July	31st Dec	
21st June	21st Dec	𝟎° ♋
11th June	11th Dec	
31st May	2nd Dec	
21st May	22nd Nov	𝟎° ♊
10th May	12th Nov	
30th April	2nd Nov	
NA	NA	𝟎° ♉
Setting	Rising	
	Acronychal	

Paran Map 26. Rigel.

either 18° Gemini or Sagittarius, then it culminated or was on the Nadir as the star culminated.

At this latitude of 41° South the star has a phase of curtailed passage. This period will be from about November 17 (reading the date from the right-hand column of the date box next to 25° Gemini) to January 5 every year (reading the right-hand column of the date box next to 15° Cancer), and is the true or cosmic heliacal rising star about May 15 (reading the date for the rising line at 41° South in the "heliacal rising" column).

Rigel can be used on all four points for charts for all latitudes except for the extremes of the poles.

EARLIER OPINIONS

Ptolemy says that the stars in Orion that are not in the shoulders are like Jupiter and Saturn. Robson states that they bring riches and glory, along with mechanical ability. Ebertin talks of quick success but the need to wage a continual battle to hold one's position. Rigor agrees with the statements of Robson and adds that Rigel gives ambition.

RIGEL: THE CONCEPT

The brightest star in the constellation is Orion's left toe, touching Eridanus, the River. In ancient Egypt, to be under a pharaoh's foot symbolized being under Osiris's protection. Osiris was gentle, bringing education and civilization to all lands that he conquered. Statues of Osiris show him standing with one foot in front of the other (it varies from left to right), and under his feet are pinioned birds representing his subjects. The pinioned birds were not considered a negative image but rather one of people receiving the wisdom and protection of the civilization that Osiris represented.[176]

Rigel can therefore be thought of as the active, educating side of Orion. Rather than seeing this star only in relation to ambition, as Robson seems to, it is perhaps easier to see the whole picture: the concept of forward development not just for personal gain but, more importantly, for the gain of many. Rigel represents the educator, be it in the local school, in the public sector, or in any field of knowledge. Johannes Kepler had Rigel culminating as Jupiter set and we remember him for his laws of planetary motion. Immanuel Kant, the great eighteenth-century philosopher, was born at the moment that Rigel was on the Nadir, and he also is remembered for his thoughts and ideas. Leonardo da Vinci, another individual that we remember for ideas and inventions, had Rigel setting as his Moon was on the Nadir. Once again, the setting position of the star indicates that this acknowledgment comes late in life or at the end of life.

---

[176] Richard H. Wilkinson, *Reading Egyptian Art* (London: Thames and Hudson, 1992), p. 87.

Bellatrix

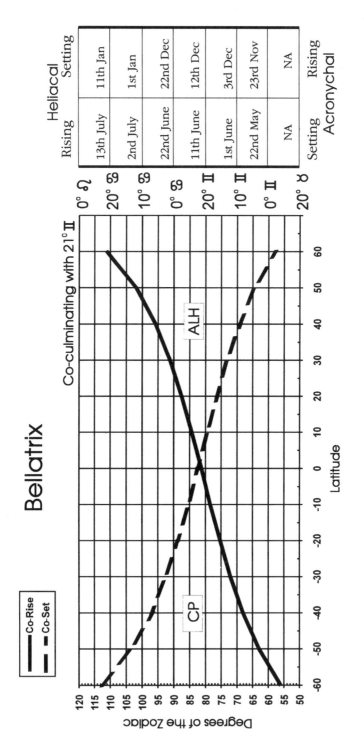

	Heliacal	
	Rising	Setting
0° ♌	13th July	11th Jan
20° ♋	2nd July	1st Jan
10° ♋	22nd June	22nd Dec
0° ♋	11th June	12th Dec
20° ♊	1st June	3rd Dec
10° ♊	22nd May	23rd Nov
0° ♊	NA	NA
20° ♉	Setting	Rising
	Acronychal	

Co-culminating with 21° ♊

ALH

CP

Co-Rise
Co-Set

Degrees of the Zodiac

Latitude

Paran Map 27. Bellatrix.

RIGEL IN THE NATAL CHART

If Rigel effects your chart it poses no problems for you, but it does indicate the desire to learn or to teach, to bring knowledge to others. It could be expressed in your life through a range of meanings, depending on the planet it touches.

RIGEL AS THE HELIACAL RISING STAR AT BIRTH

If you are born with this star as either the apparent or cosmic rising star, you will have a strong connection to the mechanism of civilization and the establishment. There will be a need to teach or expand the worldviews of others, or the need to protect the established worldview, believing that this represents the preferred and better way of life. This perspective will be strong in you, and could at times cause you to clash with unconventional groups of people.

BELLATRIX

(Gamma Orion. Magnitude 1.7. RA 05:24:51.6". Declination 06 S20'44". PED = 20° Gemini 15'.) See Paran Map 27, page 172. *An example of how to read the map:* If you were born in Blackpool, England, at a latitude of 54° North, then the star rose at about 15° Cancer. If you have a planet at either 15° Cancer or Capricorn, then that planet rose or set with the star. The star also set at 3° Gemini. Therefore, if you have a planet at 3° Gemini or Sagittarius, it would have set or risen as the star set. The star culminates at 21° Gemini so if you have a planet at either 21° Gemini or Sagittarius, then it culminated or was on the Nadir as the star culminated.

At this latitude of 54° North the star has a phase of arising and lying hidden. This period will be from about May 24 (reading the date from the left-hand column of the date box next to 3° Gemini) to July 7 every year (reading the left-hand column of the date box next to 15° Cancer), and is the true or cosmic heliacal rising star about July 7 (reading the date for the rising line at 54° North in the "heliacal rising" column).

Bellatrix can be used on all four points for charts for all latitudes except for the extremes of the poles.

EARLIER OPINIONS

Ptolemy states that the stars of the shoulders are like Mars and Mercury. Robson talks of "Quickly Coming or Swiftly Destroying" (his capitals). Ebertin lists qualities such as fighting spirit, courage, ability to organize, but often recklessly. Rigor, however, emphasizes great civil honors for men but, for women, loquaciousness and forcefulness.

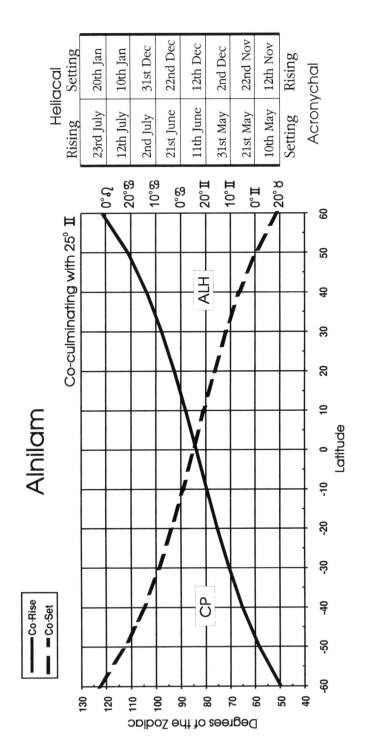

Paran Map 28. Alnilam.

BELLATRIX: THE CONCEPT

Bellatrix is the left shoulder of the god and is known as the Amazon Star or the Female Warrior and at other times, the Conqueror or the Roaring Conqueror.[177] Bellatrix gives the success of its right-sided companion, Betelgeuse, but with a shadow, for the achievement that Bellatrix can promise has a price: that of dealing with some difficult aspects of the psyche. Its pathway to success is not as smooth as with Betelgeuse. Here, personal weaknesses will be exposed, for this is the left, or more shadowy side, of the great god. People with this star will have to experience far more personal growth as the price for their success. If this growth and these insights are ignored, then Bellatrix can imply a downfall.

Marilyn Monroe was born on the day that Bellatrix set with the Sun, so we remember her as a hugely successful but tragic figure. Vincent van Gogh was a Bellatrix person, with Bellatrix setting as his Mars was on the Nadir. Constantly fighting the demons within himself, this great artist suicided. Sir Alexander Fleming, the Scottish bacteriologist who discovered penicillin in 1928, was born at the moment of the rising of Bellatrix. Fleming served as a medical officer during World War I and one wonders if it was his war experience which fueled his desire to find antibacterial substances that were nontoxic to human tissue—again, the potential success indicated by Bellatrix comes only after a journey through darkness.

BELLATRIX IN THE NATAL CHART

An interesting star in a chart, this indicates that you will need to look very seriously at personal weakness and that success, true success, be it spiritually or materially, will only come through personal growth. The angle in the natal chart that the star is occupying will indicate the period of life where this self-awareness and personal growth will be required.

BELLATRIX AS THE HELIACAL RISING STAR AT BIRTH

If you were born on the apparent or cosmic rising of this star, then success is indicated but you will always have to be facing your own demons. This could become a lifestyle, leading you to practice as a therapist or counselor, helping others to face their own personal issues. For you karma is instant; any belief you may have that you can act in a negative fashion for quick results will very soon be dispelled by reality.

ALNILAM

(Epsilon Orion. Magnitude 1.8. RA 05:33:39". Declination 1° S14'. PED = 22° Gemini 46'.) See Paran Map 28, page 174. *An example of how to read the map:* If

---

[177] Allen, *Star Names*, p. 313.

you were born in Minneapolis, USA, at a latitude of 45° North, then the star rose at about 17° Cancer. If you have a planet at either 17° Cancer or Capricorn, then that planet rose or set with the star. The star also set at 5° Gemini. Therefore, if you have a planet at 5° Gemini or Sagittarius, it would have set or risen as the star set. The star culminates at 25° Gemini so if you have a planet at either 25° Gemini or Sagittarius, then it culminated or was on the Nadir as the star culminated.

At this latitude of 45° North the star has a phase of arising and lying hidden. This period will be from about May 24 (reading the date from the left-hand column of the date box next to 5° Gemini) to July 8 every year (reading the left-hand column of the date box next to 17° Cancer), and is the true or cosmic heliacal rising star about July 8 (reading the date for the rising line at 45° North in the "heliacal rising" column).

Alnilam can be used on all four points for charts for all latitudes except for the extremes of the poles.

EARLIER OPINIONS

Ptolemy says that the stars in Orion which are not in the shoulders are like Jupiter and Saturn. Robson talks of Alnilam giving fleeting public honors. Ebertin does not list this star. Rigor agrees with Robson.

ALNILAM: THE CONCEPT

Not very much work has been done on this star astrologically, even though it is one of the twenty-nine stars mentioned by Ptolemy: hence its inclusion. It is the bright buckle of the belt of the god, and any meaning would need to take this symbolism into account. Carl Jung was born on the apparent heliacal rising of Alnilam but, in contrast, so was Benito Mussolini. In working with this star I have not yet found a satisfactory meaning.

PEGASUS, THE WINGED HORSE

HORSES WERE A PART OF THE TRANSITION
that led from the hunter-gatherer (Paleolithic) to the cultivating Neolithic village. They earned their place in the sky because they were the central theme of many cultures, from as early as 12,000 B.C.E.[178] to only a hundred years ago. It is only in recent times that the human race has started to let go of its obsession with the horse.

Little is known of the origin of the horse symbolism in the sky but in Celtic mythology the horse was a most sacred animal and entrusted only to the goddesses. The Celts developed a form of bridle and chariot, and the speed of one's chariot was the measure of one's worth. Men warred with horses and chariots, but the goddess protected and ruled over them. The Morris dancers' traditional horse-head stick or hobbyhorse, symbolizing the ride of the goddess on the white horse—also known as the ride of Lady Godiva[179]—is a simple example of the vestiges of horse-and-goddess mythology still visible in twentieth-century Celtic and English society.

The story of Rhiannon,[180] a Celtic horse-goddess, is a grim reminder of the living presence of Celtic mythology in the collective. Rhiannon was accused of killing her newborn child and the blood of a dog was used as evidence against her. She proclaimed her innocence but was not believed. She was thus punished by having to stay at the gates of the castle and offer any passerby a ride on her back. For twenty years she stayed at the gate and always protested her innocence. Eventually she was proven innocent. This story was played out in modern times in the Australian desert when the story of the horse-goddess Rhiannon was reenacted in the life of Lindy Chamberlain, who was accused of killing her newborn child, after which she protested that a dingo (wild dog) had taken it. After conviction and imprisonment, new evidence found her not guilty. The case caused a global sensation, as if the scattered ancestors of the ancient Celts were instinctually responding to this ancient myth.

Pegasus emerges from the neck of Andromeda (see Star Map 15, p. 178). Only half of him is in the sky: his front legs, wings (to symbolize speed), back, and chest. Four stars make the great square which forms the body and head of the winged horse. The Greeks pictured him as being born from Medusa's neck at the time she was slain by Perseus.[181] Aratus called this constellation divine, for

---

[178] Recent archaeological discoveries indicate that the horse was first harnessed in southwest Europe as early as 12,000 B.C.E.

[179] Walker, *The Woman's Encyclopedia of Myths and Secrets*, p. 411.

[180] Caldecott, *Women in Celtic Myth*, p. 21.

[181] Grimal, *The Dictionary of Classical Mythology*, p. 349.

indeed to the prehistoric world the domestication of the horse must have seemed like a gift from the gods. Pegasus is not the only horse in the sky; next to him is the constellation Equuleus, the Little Horse.

But one senses that Pegasus could have meanings in addition to the domestication of the horse, for Pegasus forms a great square in the sky—the world also being divided into four via the movement of the Sun on its journey (the two equinoxes and the two solstices). This number four was reflected in the view of the Earth as a table floating on a great sea with the North Pole star above it and the South Pole below. This is the table that Zeus in rage slammed with his fist and tilted.[182] Emerging from these four natural points in the solar year were the four compass points and the division of the world into four sections. Squareness was probably one of the earliest religious and philosophical concepts our ancestors developed as they emerged from the circumpolar goddess religions.[183] And

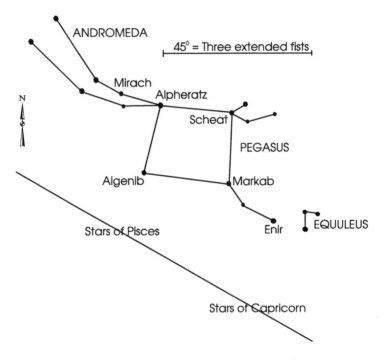

Star Map 15. Pegasus, Andromeda, Equuleus.

---

[182] De Santillana and von Dechend, *Hamlet's Mill,* p. 278.
[183] The Golden Mean, a rectangle formed from the geometry of the arc traveled by the Sun on the day of the summer solstice, has been found in cave drawings in France dating from about 15,000 B.C.E.

with the fading of the goddess and the emerging of the god, the square, or rather a four-sided figure, became increasingly important. A square/golden Mean was used by the Celts who built Newgrange[184] to signify a year. The actual symbol of a square or rectangle signified that the group had knowledge of the year and was proudly chiseled in stone over the lightbox at Newgrange. By the time of the ingress of the equinox into Aries, the developing monotheistic religions built their theology around this number. The Hebrew god of the Old Testament and the god of the Magi and the Cabala, the all-manifesting, full-of-action-and-wrath god is known by this number. In astrology the fourth harmonic, the square aspect, derives its expression of action and speed from this Old Testament god.

Pegasus is also known as "I-iku" or "I-iku Star" which was the measure used in building the perfect, cubed ark of Babylon mythology.[185]

Thus Pegasus can be linked to the Great Magical Square and the mythological and theological concepts of four. At the very least, it is associated with focused action and ability, while also indicating knowledge and learning: the emerging worldview of science.

STARS OF PEGASUS

The brightest star of Pegasus is Markab,[186] with the other main stars being: Scheat, the shoulder; Algenib, in the wings; and Enir, on the nose.

MARKAB

(Alpha Pegasus. Magnitude 2.6. RA 23:04:31.8". Declination 15N10'46". PED = 22° Pisces 47'.) See Paran Map 29, page 180. *An example of how to read the map:* If you were born in Adelaide, South Australia, at a latitude of 35° South, then the star rose at about 27° Pisces. If you have a planet at either 27° Pisces or Virgo, then that planet rose or set with the star. The star also set at 25° Aquarius. Therefore, if you have a planet at 25° Aquarius or Leo, it would have set or risen as the star set. The star culminates at 25° Aquarius, so if you have a planet at

---

[184] Newgrange is in the Boyne Valley, Ireland, and dating from about 3,000 B.C.E. it is considered to be the oldest existing structure in the world. Covering over an acre, it is a large mound considered to be a tomb, but more recently its remarkable sunbeaming construction and stone engravings have given rise to the possibility of it also being a form of calendar and astronomical observatory.

[185] De Santillana and von Dechend, *Hamlet's Mill,* p. 297.

[186] Alpheratz is brighter with a magnitude of 2.2 but in modern times this star is placed in the constellation Andromeda, although astrological indications are that it should still be considered as part of Pegasus.

Markab

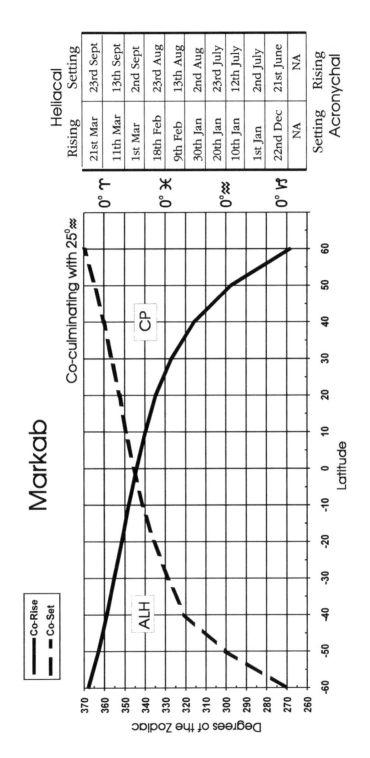

Heliacal	
Rising	Setting
21st Mar	23rd Sept
11th Mar	13th Sept
1st Mar	2nd Sept
18th Feb	23rd Aug
9th Feb	13th Aug
30th Jan	2nd Aug
20th Jan	23rd July
10th Jan	12th July
1st Jan	2nd July
22nd Dec	21st June
NA	NA
Setting	Rising
Acronychal	

0° ♈

0° ♓

0° ♒

0° ♑

Co-culminating with 25° ♒

CP

ALH

— Co-Rise
-- Co-Set

Degrees of the Zodiac

Latitude

Paran Map 29. Markab.

either 25° Aquarius or Leo, then it culminated or was on the Nadir as the star culminated.

At this latitude of 35° South the star has a phase of arising and lying hidden. This period will be from about February 13 (reading the date from the left-hand column of the date box next to 25° Aquarius) to March 17 every year (reading the left-hand column of the date box next to 27° Pisces), and is the true or cosmic heliacal rising star about March 17 (reading the date for the rising line at 35° South in the "heliacal rising" column).

Markab can be used on all four points for charts between latitudes of 74° South and 74° North. South of that the star never rises and north of that the star never sets and therefore has permanent curtailed passage.

EARLIER OPINIONS

Ptolemy says that this star has the nature of Mars and Mercury. Robson talks of it giving honors, but also danger from cuts, blows, fevers, stabs, and violent death. Ebertin links this star to intellectual alertness, mental powers, and a good head for figures; Rigor to good fortune that is subject to disgrace.

It's clear that both Robson and Rigor are drawing on the Greco-Roman myth of Bellerophon, the warrior, that most fortunate and successful young man who was destroyed by his own arrogance. He tried to ride Pegasus to the heavens so he could become a god, but Zeus struck him off the back of Pegasus and he fell to his death.[187]

MARKAB: THE CONCEPT

Markab was seen as the Saddle, that which can be ridden, the anchor point from which one can move. The point of steadiness on a moving object. This star may therefore relate to such steadiness in a person. This seems to be the case with the chart of astronaut Neil Armstrong. On the day that he was born, Markab culminated as his Saturn set. Neil Armstrong was chosen for his historic mission to the Moon because of his steady, stalwart character. He was, so to speak, the saddle upon which the world sat as humankind traveled to, and walked upon, the Moon. The Saturnian involvement indicates that this is his life's work and is how he will be remembered by history. Isaac Newton, the seventeenth-century English mathematician whose work moved the field of mathematics beyond Greek thought and is considered to have laid the foundation for modern physics and mathematics, was born with Markab culminating as his Sun set. Linking this with his connection to the star Thuban discussed under the constellation Draco, we can start to understand that the great treasures that he guards (Thuban) can in some way build a foundation for larger things (Markab).

---

[187] Grimal, *The Dictionary of Classical Mythology*, p. 75.

MARKAB IN THE NATAL CHART

When Markab is placed in your chart you have as a resource the ability to maintain stability under pressure, to be solid and tangible. This may act as a restricting force on you or be a great asset.

MARKAB AS THE HELIACAL RISING STAR AT BIRTH

Markab is not included on Ptolemy's list. However, if it was the cosmic rising star on the day you were born, then it would give your chart great solidness and reliability. This could be a beneficial contact, giving you leadership skills and the ability to handle crises; or it could twist the other way and manifest as a certain stubbornness and a refusal to move or consider other options. Markab was one of Abraham Lincoln's natal heliacal rising stars,[188] and certainly his steadiness steered the American people into a solid union.

SCHEAT

(Beta Pegasus. Magnitude 2.6. RA 23:03:33.2". Declination 28N03'22". PED = 28° Pisces 41'.) See Paran Map 30, page 183. *An example of how to read the map:* If you were born in New York, at a latitude of 41° North, then the star rose at about 29° Capricorn. If you have a planet at either 29° Capricorn or Cancer, that planet rose or set with the star. The star also set at 13° Aries. Therefore, if you have a planet at 13° Aries or Libra, then it would have set or risen as the star set. The star culminates at 15° Pisces, so if you have a planet at either 15° Pisces or Virgo, then it culminated or was on the Nadir as the star culminated.

At this latitude of 41° North the star has a phase of curtailed passage. This period will be from about July 21 (reading the date from the right-hand column of the date box next to 29° Capricorn) to October 6 every year (reading the right-hand column of the date box next to 13° Aries), and is the true or cosmic heliacal rising star about January 18 (reading the date for the rising line at 41° North in the "heliacal rising" column).

Scheat can be used on all four points for charts between latitudes of 61° South and 61° North. South of that the star never rises and north of that the star never sets and therefore has permanent curtailed passage.

EARLIER OPINIONS

Ptolemy links this star to Mars and Mercury. Robson relates it to extreme misfortune, murder, suicide, and drowning. Ebertin implies that if you can get past the mortal accident that awaits you, then Scheat offers a great flow of mental creativity. Rigor alters these meanings by emphasizing turbulence, an

---

[188] Alpheratz was also involved so both stars would have claim to that title.

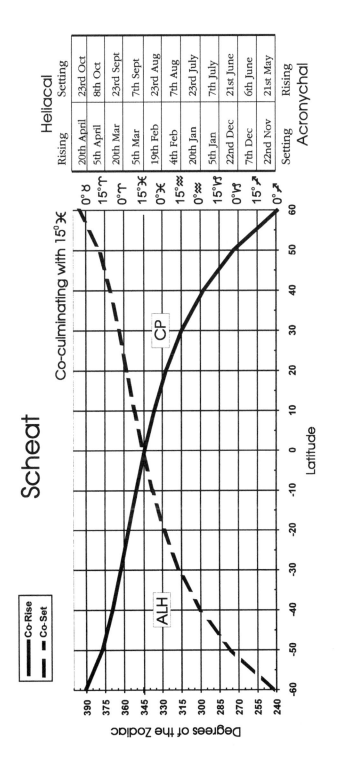

Scheat

Co-culminating with 15° ♓

	Heliacal	
	Rising	Setting
0° ♉	20th April	23rd Oct
15° ♈	5th April	8th Oct
0° ♈	20th Mar	23rd Sept
15° ♓	5th Mar	7th Sept
0° ♓	19th Feb	23rd Aug
15° ♒	4th Feb	7th Aug
0° ♒	20th Jan	23rd July
15° ♑	5th Jan	7th July
0° ♑	22nd Dec	21st June
15° ♐	7th Dec	6th June
0° ♐	22nd Nov	21st May
	Setting	Rising
	Acronychal	

Paran Map 30. Scheat.

unpredictable nature, losing and gaining friends rapidly, and the subject being inclined to fantasize.

SCHEAT: THE CONCEPT

Rigor seems to be giving a description of the character of Bellerophon. Ebertin appears to be closer to the mark with his suggestion of great mental creativity when one realizes that Albert Einstein, Isaac Newton, and Johannes Kepler all had this star in paran with their natal charts. Einstein was born with this star culminating, a very powerful position for a star, and given his chart's involvement with Algol in the constellation Perseus, one can start to understand Einstein's ingenious discoveries about the primal power of the atom (the passion of Algol). In contrast, Newton's Sun set as this star culminated, and linked also to Markab in this same constellation, and Thuban in Draco, one can start to hypothesize that his genius was concerned with the foundation stones of science, the concept of numbers. On the day that Kepler was born, Scheat rose with Mercury. The star also touched Carl Jung, setting as his Venus culminated, showing the mental creativity he channeled into human relationships and how we relate to the world.

Thus we see in Scheat the square of Pegasus, rather than the horse. The square symbolizes the intellect, logic, and thinking, whereas intuition is circular. Scheat appears to represent the very essence of intellect.

SCHEAT IN THE NATAL CHART

Depending on the planet it touches, Scheat implies a love of intellect and the challenge of logic. You will want to think independently and may well have issues about needing to break with conventional thought or philosophy.

SCHEAT AS THE HELIACAL RISING STAR AT BIRTH

Scheat should only be used as the cosmic rising star, as it is too faint to herald the dawn. If it is in this position, it can indicate the gift or the curse of genius. Your education, knowledge, and your use of these skills will be an important part of your identity.

PERSEUS, THE PRINCE

PERSEUS HAS ALREADY BEEN DISCUSSED IN connection with the constellation Andromeda, and also as a member of the royal family which orbits around the North Pole. He was also known as Parash, a horseman, by the Hebrews, or sometimes as Ham, son of Noah[189] (see Star Map 1, p. 48). In the Egyptian cosmology he is Khem, the young black son of Cepheus the king.

STARS OF PERSEUS

The brightest star of Perseus is Mirfak, sometimes called Algenib. Other named stars, in descending order of magnitude, are: Algol, the severed head; and Capulus, a nebula in the sword. All three stars are used in astrology, each symbolizing different facets of a suitor showing off his masculinity via his sword and his trophy.

MIRFAK

(Alpha Perseus. Magnitude 1.9. RA 03:23:58.7". Declination 49N50'25". PED = 1° Gemini 23'.) See Paran Map 31, page 186. *An example of how to read the map:* If you were born in Cairo, Egypt, at a latitude of 30° North then the star rose at about 10° Aries. If you have a planet at either 10° Aries or Libra, then that planet rose or set with the star. The star also set at 20° Gemini. Therefore, if you have a planet at 20° Gemini or Sagittarius, it would have set or risen as the star set. The star culminates at 24° Taurus, so if you have a planet at either 24° Taurus or Scorpio, then it culminated or was on the Nadir as the star culminated.

At this latitude of 30° North the star has a phase of curtailed passage. This period will be from about October 1 (reading the date from the right-hand column of the date box next to 10° Aries) to December 12 every year (reading the right-hand column of the date box next to 20° Gemini), and is the true or cosmic heliacal rising star about April 1 (reading the date for the rising line at 30° North in the "heliacal rising" column).

Mirfak can be used on all four points for charts between latitudes of 40° South and 40° North. South of that the star never rises and north of that the star never sets and therefore has permanent curtailed passage.

---

[189] Jobes, *Outer Space,* p. 227.

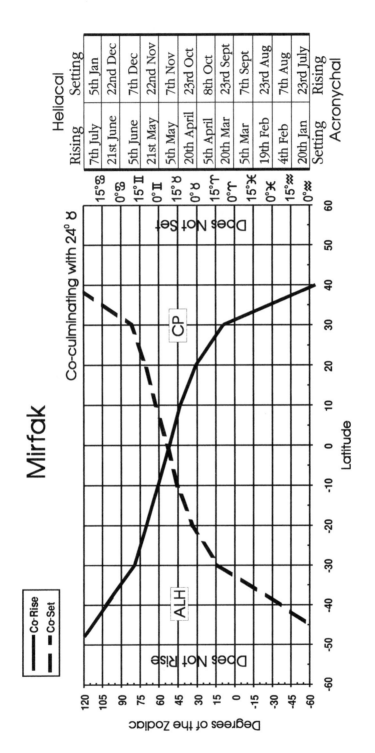

Mirfak

Co-culminating with 24° ♉

	Heliacal	
	Rising	Setting
15°♋	7th July	5th Jan
0°♋	21st June	22nd Dec
15°♊	5th June	7th Dec
0°♊	21st May	22nd Nov
15°♉	5th May	7th Nov
0°♉	20th April	23rd Oct
15°♈	5th April	8th Oct
0°♈	20th Mar	23rd Sept
15°♓	5th Mar	7th Sept
0°♓	19th Feb	23rd Aug
15°♒	4th Feb	7th Aug
0°♒	20th Jan	23rd July
	Setting	Rising
	Acronychal	

Legend:
— Co-Rise
- - - Co-Set

Does Not Set
Does Not Rise

CP
ALH

Degrees of the Zodiac
Latitude

Paran Map 31. Mirfak.

EARLIER OPINIONS

Ptolemy compares the stars in Pegasus to Jupiter and Saturn. Robson, Ebertin, and Rigor do not refer to the star.

MIRFAK: THE CONCEPT

If meaning is going to be placed on this alpha star of Perseus, it needs to be connected to the concept of the young warrior proud of his strength, his hunting and fighting abilities—proud of his trophy.

Muhammad Ali, ex-heavyweight boxing champion, has Mirfak culminating with his Saturn and is seen in society as a fighter, one of the greatest fighters in the history of the sport. Mirfak also culminated as Henry Ford's Mars rose on the day of his birth. Here we see the influence of an enthused, energized Mars, willing to take on all comers, wanting to be active. Martin Luther King had his Moon rising with Mirfak, so he was emotionally charged to fight or to challenge, to push for ideas in which he believed. Linked with another star also active in his chart, Ras algethi,[190] which is an indication of a desire to seek the natural order, to seek correctness, one can see the drive and motivation of this man's life. On another note, Margaret Thatcher, former British prime minister, has Jupiter rising as Mirfak is on the Nadir. Thus she is remembered as a very headstrong, aggressive politician. With this star forming in her chart a powerful combination with Schedar,[191] the star of female sovereignty, it's fitting that her fighting energy was focused toward personal power and reputation.

MIRFAK IN THE NATAL CHART

Mirfak represents young, male energy. It will vary in expression like any star, depending on how it is affecting your chart. However, it is not an area where you will listen to wisdom or take caution. This may well be a strength for you or could lead you to overestimate your physical or mental abilities.

MIRFAK AS THE HELIACAL RISING STAR AT BIRTH

Although Mirfak has a magnitude of 1.9, it was not previously recorded in this position. However, if you were born with Mirfak rising with the Sun, then you will identify yourself with this young, strong, physical energy. You may use this in many ways: it could be a blessing in terms of your physical vitality; or it could be a hindrance by inducing potential recklessness or rashness of action.

---

[190] In the constellation Hercules.
[191] In the constellation Cassiopeia.

ALGOL

(Beta Perseus. Magnitude variable. RA 03:07:51.4". Declination 40N56'02". PED = 25° Taurus 28'.) See Paran Map 32, page 189. *An example of how to read the map:* If you were born in Durban, South Africa, at a latitude of 30° South, then the star rose at about 5° Gemini. If you have a planet at either 5° Gemini or Sagittarius, then that planet rose or set with the star. The star also set at 25° Aries. Therefore, if you have a planet at 25° Aries or Libra, then it would have set or risen as the star set. The star culminates at 18° Taurus, so if you have a planet at either 18° Taurus or Scorpio, then it culminated or was on the Nadir as the star culminated.

At this latitude of 30° South the star has a phase of arising and lying hidden. This period will be from about April 15 (reading the date from the left-hand column of the date box next to 25° Aries) to May 26 every year (reading the left-hand column of the date box next to 5° Gemini), and is the true or cosmic heliacal rising star about May 26 (reading the date for the rising line at 30° South in the "heliacal rising" column).

Algol can be used on all four points for charts between latitudes of 49° South and 49° North. South of that the star never rises and north of that the star never sets and therefore has permanent curtailed passage.

This is a binary star system where a smaller star orbits a larger star, eclipsing that star every 2.86 days. The length of the eclipse is about ten hours, and during that time Algol's magnitude changes from 2.3 to 3.5. Algol appears to blink. Historically, when Algol was dark she was at her worst.

EARLIER OPINIONS

All writers agree that this is the most malific star in the heavens and causes hangings, death by the loss of one's head, and any other foul, demonic deed that could befall the human race.

ALGOL: THE CONCEPT

Algol was called Ras al-Ghul by the Arabs, which means the Head of the Demon, and they considered this female demon to be the wife of the devil.[192] Ptolemy labeled the star as "the brightest one of those in the Gorgon's head."[193] The Chinese called the star Tseih She, meaning Piled Up Corpses.[194] In Talmudic Law she is the first wife of Adam, Lilith, who left him because she refused to be submissive to his needs.[195] Lilith then fled to paradise and became a demof of the wind.

---

[192] Jobes, *Outer Space*, p. 297.
[193] Ptolemy, *The Almagest*, Book 7, p. 239.
[194] Allen, *Star Names*, p. 332.
[195] Barbara Black Koltuv, *The Book of Lilith* (York Beach, ME: Nicolas-Hays, 1986), p. 19.

Algol

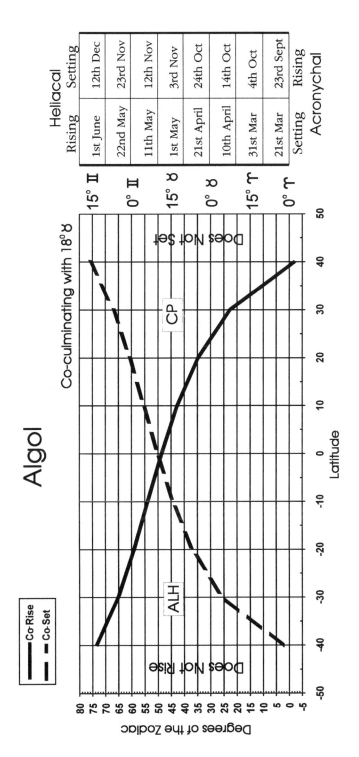

Heliacal		
Rising	Setting	
1st June	12th Dec	15° ♊
22nd May	23rd Nov	0° ♊
11th May	12th Nov	15° ♉
1st May	3rd Nov	0° ♉
21st April	24th Oct	15° ♈
10th April	14th Oct	15° ♈
31st Mar	4th Oct	15° ♈
21st Mar	23rd Sept	0° ♈
Setting	Rising	
	Acronychal	

Co-culminating with 18° ♉

CP

ALH

Does Not Set

Does Not Rise

— Co-Rise
- - Co-Set

Degrees of the Zodiac

Latitude

Paran Map 32. Algol.

She was considered a curse since she gave sexual pleasure and was the cause of all male wet dreams. This eventually led, in the Jewish, Moslem, and Christian cultures, to the suppression in the male of all sexual pleasure, which then led to the suppression of the sexual woman. Algol thus embodied everything that men feared in the feminine. She is not the mother-face of the goddess but rather the passionate lover or the whore. She is female kundalini energy. In the words of Barbara Black Koltuv,

> Eve, destined to be the mother of all those who live and made from Adam's own rib, was not as powerful or primordial as Lilith, whom Adam now meets only at night with nocturnal erections as he lies dreaming. And there is the snare of Lilith's vengeful murderous rage of which man must ever more be wary.[196]

Algol, in other words, is the wild, raw, frightening face of the outraged feminine which has been labeled as demonic or simply evil.

This star seems to contain immense female passion and power. It is the power of the feminine or the potential power of Mother Nature, not to be called evil for being strong. It is a companion star to the nebula Capulus, also in Perseus, which is the male version of this outrage.

Albert Einstein had Algol culminating with his Jupiter on the day he was born, and is remembered for his great work in unleashing the power of the atom. That power itself is not evil, but when it expressed itself in the bombings of Japan, then we saw the destructive power of Algol. John F. Kennedy had Mars culminating with Algol in his chart, and was killed by an assassin's bullet in the head, showing us the more literal side of Agol. O. J. Simpson, United States athlete and actor, born at the moment this star was culminating, also shows the heavy side of this star. He was accused of the brutal murder of his wife and, though he was acquitted, will be remembered as having been connected to this crime. Adolf Hitler had the star setting as his Sun was on the Nadir, so the force of Algol expressed itself in the latter phase of his life and influenced his very identity as it contacted his Sun. In contrast, Wolfgang Amadeus Mozart had his Mercury rising with Algol, so from an early age his expression, thinking, and therefore his music was filled with the passion and intensity of Algol.

ALGOL IN THE NATAL CHART

Algol represents a strong consuming passion that may devour you with anger and rage. If one can contain an unconscious compulsion to take revenge, and focus that passion into a more productive outcome, Algol is one of the most powerful

---

[196] Koltuv, *The Book of Lilith*, p. 16.

stars in the sky. Whatever planet it affects in your chart will be charged with strong, intense, sexual energy that has the potential to be wonderful or, if repressed, to lead to rage or violence.

ALGOL AS THE HELIACAL RISING STAR AT BIRTH

Algol is one of Ptolemy's recorded stars, so it can be either the cosmic or the apparent heliacal rising star. If you are born on the day that Algol rises with the Sun, then your very being is inflamed with passion and intensity. At the very least this will imply that you are a person who will not tolerate injustice. In addition, because you can handle intensity, you will encounter these sorts of situations throughout your life. In a worst case scenario Algol in this position could express itself as the female demon: destroying in a bloody, ruthless manner.

CAPULUS

(A cluster in Perseus with a magnitude of 4.4. RA 02:18:42.4". Declination 57N07'14". PED = 23° Taurus 30'.) See Paran Map 33, page 192. *An example of how to read the map:* If you were born in Bombay, India, at a latitude of 19° North, then the star rose at about 0° Aries. If you have a planet at either 0° Aries or Libra, then that planet rose or set with the star. The star also set at 3° Gemini. Therefore, if you have a planet at 3° Gemini or Sagittarius it would have set or risen as the star set. The star culminates at 7° Taurus, so if you have a planet at either 7° Taurus or Scorpio, then it culminated or was on the Nadir as the star culminated.

At this latitude of 19° North the star has a phase of curtailed passage. This period will be from about September 23 (reading the date from the right-hand column of the date box next next to 0° Aries) to November 22 every year (reading the right-hand column of the date box next to 3° Gemini), and is the true or cosmic heliacal rising star about March 20 (reading the date for the rising line at 19° North in the "heliacal rising" column).

Capulus can be used on all four points for charts between latitudes of 32° South and 32° North. South of that the star never rises and north of that the star never sets and therefore has permanent curtailed passage.

EARLIER OPINIONS

Ptolemy does not mention the star apart from his general statement about Jupiter and Saturn. Robson links it with blindness. Ebertin does not refer to it. Rigor agrees with the statement of blindness and adds turbulence and strong feelings. The association with blindness could come from the fact that Capulus is a nebula and nebulae were used by the Roman army as eyesight tests.[197] If a recruit could see the

---

[197] I have no reference to this except the knowledge passed on to me by tutors in my days of being involved in archery.

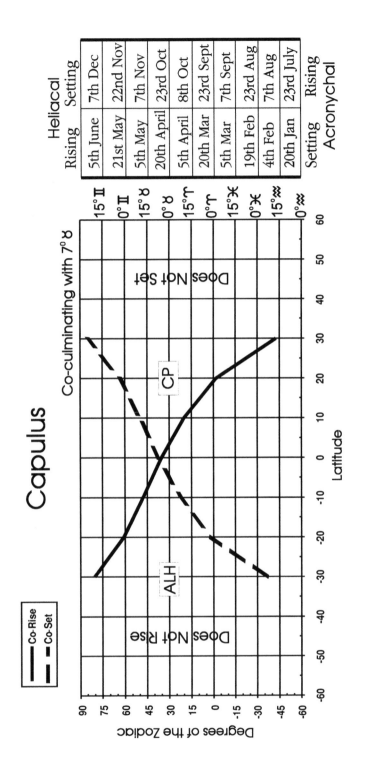

Capulus

Co-culminating with 7° ♉

Heliacal	
Rising	Setting
5th June	7th Dec
21st May	22nd Nov
5th May	7th Nov
20th April	23rd Oct
5th April	8th Oct
20th Mar	23rd Sept
5th Mar	7th Sept
19th Feb	23rd Aug
4th Feb	7th Aug
20th Jan	23rd July
Setting	Rising
Acronychal	

Co-Rise
Co-Set

Does Not Set

Does Not Rise

CP

ALH

Degrees of the Zodiac

Latitude

Paran Map 33. Capulus.

separate stars in the nebula, then he had good sight and could therefore be made an archer or given some position less arduous and expendable than a foot soldier.

CAPULUS: THE CONCEPT

A meaning for this star which may be more accurate than the above could be male sexual energy: focused, direct, penetrating action—a male to complement Algol: focused and passionate, and therefore at times brutal and violent. Jim Jones, the cult leader who instigated the mass suicide of the members of his cult, had Capulus culminating when his Mars rose. His was a ruthless expression of the sword of Perseus. Edward Gein, the mass murderer and cannibal whose crimes and character were used as the bases for the films *Psycho, Chainsaw Massacre*, and *Silence of the Lambs*,[198] had Capulus culminating as his Mercury rose. The nature of the expression of Mercury during Gein's lifetime is not clear, but the fact that his hideous crimes eventually became a model for future literary characters is interesting to note. In contrast to this dark nature of Capulus is the great English poet and painter William Blake. Blake had his Mars rising as Capulus was culminating and he believed that true innocence could not be gained without the bite of experience. It is Capulus in his chart that adds the bite and passion to his work, in a way similar to how Algol was expressed in Mozart's music.

In summary, Capulus energy is clear, decisive, focused, and possibly even ruthless: an "If it can be touched, weighed, or seen, then it has existence" mentality. Perseus's sword is the male kundalini energy, the partner to Algol.

CAPULUS IN THE NATAL CHART

At times Capulus can manifest in ruthlessness and savagery but at other times it can indicate focused, clear action. If you have a strong Capulus, you will need to guard against rash anger and hasty action, for such actions would have far-reaching, negative effects. Maturity hopefully teaches that, by focusing yourself on the desired outcomes, you can obtain the best results. However, you could well struggle with the strength of this male sexual energy.

CAPULUS AS THE HELIACAL RISING STAR AT BIRTH

Capulus is too faint to be used as an apparent rising star. However, if present in your chart as the cosmic rising star, it could indicate that this powerful, action-oriented energy is linked to your personal identity and journey toward personal fulfillment. This could have a very positive expression, by adding vitality to your life, making you a strong, clear person; or it could bring into your personality tendencies to be ruthless or destructive.

---

[198] Lois M. Rodden, *Profiles of Crime* (Yucaipa, CA: Data News Press, 1992), p. 63.

PISCIS AUSTRALIS, THE SOUTHERN FISH

LYING CLOSE TO AQUARIUS IN THE PART of the sky which Aratus named the Water, there is a Fish who drinks the flow from the urn of Aquarius[199] (see Star Map 16, p. 195). This stream-drinking fish is an earlier symbol of life and fertility, for it was the one who carried the egg, drinking the sperm or river of life. This is also the fish in Celtic mythology that holds great wisdom, and has gone through many incarnations as the fish that swallows the ring and the fish which is encountered on the journey the hero takes through the whirlpool.[200] The alpha star, Formalhaut, is a lone, bright star in its part of the starry sky. The Greeks developed, or inherited, rituals around the heliacal rising of this star about 500 B.C.E. when they aligned temples to Demeter with its rising.[201]

The Persians in about 3,000 B.C.E., however, did not see this constellation as a fish but rather considered its alpha star[202] as one of the Royal Stars and called it the Watcher in the South,[203] as it marked their winter solstice. In Persian mythology there is a royal family or pantheon that stems from the time of Zoroaster or Zarathustra, the legendary Iranian prophet whose followers established agricultural practice as a religious doctrine. His name translated into Greek means *Astrothutes*, a "star-worshipper"[204] and his stories, pantheon, and gods seem to capture the meanings of all four Royal Stars of Persia. There is one such character in these stories who was called Zal, who as a baby was sent away by his father, Sam, because of his strange physical appearance: "[his] visage was fair as the sun but [his] hair was white like an old man."[205] The white hair was quite possibly a reference to the winter solstice. Eventually Zal grew into manhood and "his breast was like a hill of silver."[206] Sam was told in a dream to find his forgotten son, which he duly did and welcomed him with open arms. Zal eventually fell in love with the beautiful and highly prized Rudabeh, and the myths tells us of how she loosened her long locks so that Zal could climb to her lofty place of gentle imprisonment. The myth goes on to talk of the lovers being intoxicated with each other, the resulting disapproval by the parents, the couple's dismay but eventual happiness. They married on the

---

[199] Allen, *Star Names*, p. 344.

[200] Miranda J. Green, *Dictionary of Celtic Myth and Legend* (London: Thames and Hudson, 1992), 184.

[201] Jobes, *Outer Space*, p. 320.

[202] It is not certain that Formalhaut is one of the Royal Stars of Persia; however, it is the only bright star in the south that could fit the required position and magnitude.

[203] Allen, *Star Names*, p. 346.

[204] Mary Settegast, *Plato Prehistorian* (New York: Lindisfarne, 1986), p. 211.

[205] *New Larousse Encyclopedia of Mythology* (London: Hamlyn, 1968), p. 322.

[206] *New Larousse Encyclopedia of Mythology*, p. 322.

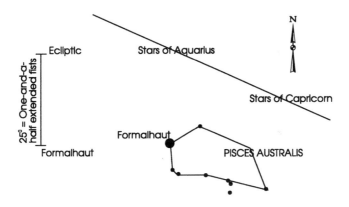

Star Map 16. The Southern Fish.

advice of the astrologers of the court, who warned that Zal was a noble and great person who would give birth to new life, new sons that would rule Persia.

Winter solstice figures generally have personal stories which are based on bringing forth new children or new life, the best example being Christ, who is connected to Christmas, our winter solstice.

STARS OF PISCIS AUSTRALIS

The brightest star in Piscis Australis is Formalhaut. The only other named star also carries the same name, Fum al Hut, which led to confusion among early astronomers.

FORMALHAUT

(Alpha Piscis Australis. Magnitude 1.3. RA 22:57:23.5". Declination 29S38'49". PED = 3° Pisces 09'.) See Paran Map 34, page 196. *An example of how to read the map:* If you were born in Dallas, at a latitude of 33° North, then the star rose at about 8° Aries. If you have a planet at either 8° Aries or Libra, then that planet rose or set with the star. The star also set at 28° Aquarius. Therefore, if you have a planet at 28° Aquarius or Leo, it would have set or risen as the star set. The star culminates at 13° Pisces, so if you have a planet at either 13° Pisces or Virgo, then it culminated or was on the Nadir as the star culminated.

At this latitude of 33° North the star has a phase of arising and lying hidden. This period will be from about February 17 (reading the date from the left-hand column of the date box next to 28° Aquarius) to March 28 every year (reading the left-hand column of the date box next to 8° Aries), and is the true

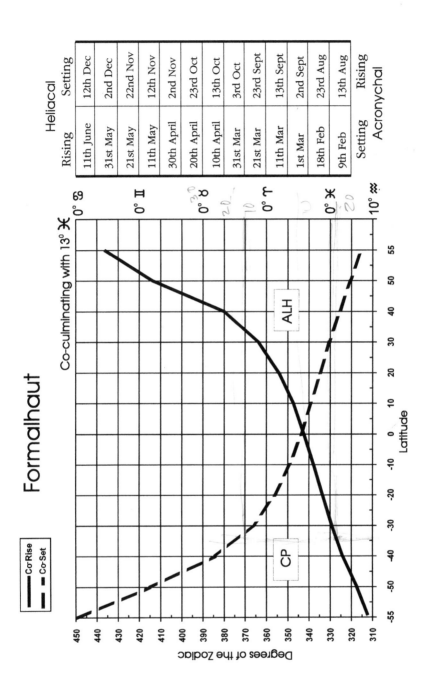

Formalhaut

Co-culminating with 13° ♓

Legend: Co Rise (solid line), Co Set (dashed line)

Labels on graph: ALH, CP

Y-axis (left): Degrees of the Zodiac — 450, 440, 430, 420, 410, 400, 390, 380, 370, 360, 350, 340, 330, 320, 310

X-axis (bottom): Latitude — 55, 50, 40, 30, 20, 10, 0, -10, -20, -30, -40, -50, -55

Right-side zodiac scale: 0° ♋, 0° ♊, 0° ♉, 0° ♈, 0° ♓, 10° ♒

Heliacal		Acronychal	
Rising	**Setting**		
11th June	12th Dec		
31st May	2nd Dec		
21st May	22nd Nov		
11th May	12th Nov		
30th April	2nd Nov		
20th April	23rd Oct		
10th April	13th Oct		
31st Mar	3rd Oct		
21st Mar	23rd Sept		
11th Mar	13th Sept		
1st Mar	2nd Sept		
18th Feb	23rd Aug		
9th Feb	13th Aug		
Setting	**Rising**		

Paran Map 34. Formalhaut.

or cosmic heliacal rising star about March 28 (reading the date for the rising line at 33° North in the "heliacal rising" column).

Formalhaut can be used on all four points for charts between latitudes of 60° South and 60° North. North of that the star never rises and south of that the star never sets and therefore has permanent curtailed passage.

EARLIER OPINIONS

Ptolemy states that Formalhaut is of the same nature as Venus and Mercury. Robson relates it to immortal fame and great success, and to spirituality. Ebertin says that it is either very bad or very good, depending on the natal chart; so he considers it a type of amplifier. Rigor talks of the star being undermining in its influence, and of its manifesting in idealism and spirituality.

FORMALHAUT AS ONE OF THE ROYAL STARS OF PERSIA

I consider the Royal Stars of Persia[207] to be quite unique, for each one seems to represent a trial or a temptation through which the individual must work before true success can be achieved. They form a rocky road with many potential pitfalls or areas where the individual can fall from grace. They are represented in Christian mythology by the scene in the Bible where Christ is tempted by Satan. They are the nemesis the individual must conquer.

Formalhaut is like the Persian character Zal. Out of step with society, he strives to gain the greatest prize in the kingdom, the beautiful Rudabeh and, though there are numerous odds against the couple, their intoxicating, unworldly love for each other wins through. Formalhaut contains a touch of the mystic, a sense of magic, and inspires high ideals or lofty visions. As one of the Royal Stars, it bestows charisma—in particular, in Formalhaut's case, beauty or perfect harmony. An individual with Formalhaut strong in their natal chart will have to clash with mainstream thought in order to achieve these ideals. If the ideal is a noble cause, the person will find personal happiness or success for the benefit of the collective. However, if the ideals or dreams are corrupt in any way, then the downfall is total. The challenge of people strongly influenced by Formalhaut is to maintain the purity of their ideals or dreams.

Abraham Lincoln had Formalhaut culminating with his Mercury; his ideal was to abolish slavery. He had to clash with mainstream thinking and, although he lost his life in the cause, he was successful. Galileo Galilei had Formalhaut culminating with his Sun. His ideals had to do with the laws of physics. He clashed with the Catholic Church, and indeed was made a prisoner in his own house, but he was successful. Adolf Hitler had Formalhaut rising with his Mars. His ideals

---

[207] The others being Regulus, Watcher of the North; Aldebaran, Watcher of the East; and Antares, Watcher of the West.

were for the supremacy of the Aryan race. He gained great power and then lost everything, including the fame and glory he sought for himself as the "führer." Lincoln became the father of his country, Galileo became a father of modern physics, Hitler wanted to be known as a father-figure but ended up in history as The Great Dictator. Formalhaut gives a desire to pursue ideals, and even promises success with those ideals, but only if they are pursued for the collective good. In a totally different example, Formalhaut was active in the chart of John Lennon, for it rose as his Moon culminated. His idealism is expressed in his song "Imagine," and in his intoxication with his second wife, Yoko Ono. In his own way Lennon was a very Zal-like character.

FORMALHAUT IN THE NATAL CHART

If this great star is touching your chart by paran, then you need to be very clear and honest with yourself about your motives in the pursuit of some goal and, as you start to achieve your outcome, it is imperative that personal glory does not become the main driving force. If recognition is forthcoming, it is also important that it is not manipulated for personal glorification. Another side to this star is the bittersweet madness of the poetic mind challenged to remain in the physical world, the child stolen by the fairies who must reject the sweet escape from life and fight to return to the mortal world of life, death, and pain. Formalhaut is one of the great stars in the sky; if affecting your chart, it will have a huge impact on your life.

FORMALHAUT AS THE HELIACAL RISING STAR AT BIRTH

Capable of being either the apparent or cosmic rising, this great star will imbue your life with ideals or mysticism if it touches your chart in this way. Full of goals and dreams, it will add charisma to your life force and promise you much, as long as personal glory is not consciously sought or planned. Laurence Olivier, the great Shakespearean actor, was born on the apparent heliacal rising of this star, and it poured forth from him as he became identified as the greatest Shakespearean actor of his time.

SAGITTA, THE ARROW

ONCE CLUTCHED IN THE CLAWS OF THE
Eagle but now classed as a separate constellation, Sagitta lies as a lone arrow (see
Star Map 2, p. 56). The Greeks claimed it as the arrow shot at the dreaded Stymphalian birds, lying between them still, two of the Stymphalian birds being the
Eagle and the Swan.[208] Other myths link it to the arrow that Hercules used to
killed Zeus' eagle eating the liver of Prometheus.[209] On a calmer note it is also believed to be one of Cupid's arrows.[210] Christian mythology claimed it as one of
the nails of the crucifixion.[211]

STARS OF SAGITTA

None of the stars of Sagitta are named. However, Ptolemy links the constellation
to the energy of Saturn, with a touch of Venus. Robson adds that it gives a keen
mind with an ability for abstract thinking but adds that there is danger of bodily
harm.

---

[208] Allen, *Star Names*, p. 350.
[209] Jobes, *Outer Space*, p. 235.
[210] Jobes, *Outer Space*, p. 234.
[211] Jobes, *Outer Space*, p. 235.

TRIANGULUM, THE TRIANGLE

THERE ARE MANY IMAGES OF INANIMATE instruments in the sky, most of them belonging to the new constellations. However, two ancient triangles are the oldest known nonliving heavenly objects, although the southern one, Triangulum Australe, was only officially named in the sixteenth century.

Triangulum is a small, faint constellation just south of Andromeda that was held in great esteem by the ancients. Aratus called it Deltoton[212] and states how it should be drawn and seen as a right-angle triangle. There are no notable stars, the brightest being only magnitude 3.6 and called Caput Trianguli. The importance of this constellation to the Egyptians, as well as to other cultures who were working with buildings and constructions, was that it symbolized mathematics and geometry. It would be interesting to collect the charts of designers, draftpersons, architects, and mathematicians to see if this star played any role in them.

---

[212] Mair, *Callimachus, Lycophron, Aratus*, p. 225.

TRIANGULUM AUSTRALE, SOUTHERN TRIANGLE

A CONSTELLATION OFFICIALLY NAMED BY Pieter Theodor in the 16th century,[213] it is thought to have been an older constellation acknowledged by the Arabs. It lies south of Ara the Altar and there are no astrologically significant stars in the constellation.

---

[213] Allen, *Star Names*, p. 417.

URSA MAJOR, THE GREAT SHE-BEAR

THE CONSTELLATION URSA MAJOR IS PART of the group of three constellations—the other two being Ursa Minor and Draco— that make up the image of the Goddess and the Dragon (see Star Map 9, p. 134).

Situated around the North Pole, these stars have been held sacred since we first noticed that the whole starry sky moved around one central point. Here, as discussed earlier, is the omphalos used as the original model for the human psyche. This is the unmoving point or the pivot point of the world, thought by most cultures to be a place of the divine, a place which was a gateway to the world of the immortals, from which all life sprang. It was considered the source of the Ganges in Hindu mythology[214] and the place of the Heavenly Mother for the Babylonians. The mythology that pours from this part of the sky for all cultures is almost overwhelming.

Appearing in every star catalog since ancient times, this constellation is probably one of the oldest in human history. Aratus talks of an ancient tale about a bear set in the heavens because it had nurtured the infant Zeus.[215] However, this constellation has featured in many myths over aeons of human existence. Always feminine, this great Bear circles the North Pole, the pivot point of the world, the point of stillness. Here was the source of life itself, and next to this sacred point was placed the great She-Bear goddess. Her first appearance in written history is in the Babylonian creation myth but by that stage she was already ancient.[216] In India the seven stars of Ursa Major were called the Seven Bears and in North America, long before the arrival of the white race, the constellation was known as Paukuuawa or Okuari, both words meaning "bear" in the languages of tribes of the Blackfeet and the Iroquois.[217]

Here was the mother of all life and the protector of all animals, the goddess in one of her original forms.[218] However, by the time of the Greeks she had been reduced in importance and by the days of Homer she had become nothing more than the wood nymph, Callista, raped by Zeus and turned into a bear to protect her from the wrath of Artemis. Trying to reconcile the fact that one of Zeus's conquests was so honored as to be placed in this sacred place in the sky, the Greeks suggested this constellation was Artemis, the She-Bear, who was said to have ruled

---

[214] De Santillana and von Dechend, *Hamlet's Mill*, p. 260.

[215] Mair, *Callimachus, Lycophron, Aratus*, p. 209.

[216] Jobes, *Outer Space*, p. 262.

[217] Jobes, *Outer Space*, p. 264.

[218] She was also known as the Mistress of Animals. Her earliest known representation is a clay figurine of a large naked bearlike woman seated with animals draped over her shoulders and around her throne. The figurine was found at Level II, Catal Huyuk (in central Anatolia) and, dated about 6,000 B.C.E., was thus created at the dawn of pottery in that area.

over all the stars until overthrown by Zeus.[219] This, of course, seems to echo the change from the matrilineal to the patriarchal society. It is interesting to note that she is also most'likely related to She-Bear who rears the hero Paris of Troy.

By Christian times she had become Saint Ursula, a Christian form of a Saxon She-Bear goddess.[220] The mythical Saint Ursula was said to have been accompanied by eleven thousand virgins, a moon goddess surrounded by her stars. It was believed she led these eleven thousand virgins against the Romans, protesting the ways of men, and achieved martyrdom by being slaughtered by the Roman troops. In Britain this constellation was associated with Arthur and his chariot. In the Welsh language *Arth* means "bear" and *Uthyrs* mean "wonderful." This constellation was thought to be the final home and resting place of King Arthur and was connected to the origin of the Round Table, its symbolism being the revolution of the Great Bear (Arthur) around the source of all life (the Holy Grail), the Pole Star.[221].

Still within the Christian tradition, the order of nuns called the Ursulines, formed in 1506, were a group of women dedicated to the education of other women. The size of the original group was the lunar number twenty-eight, and the women were described by Pope Calixtus as "a hotbed of witches."[222] The founder, Angela, received her vision to educate women under the moonlight in an open field and her order persisted in carrying out their duties without the rituals and habits of the Christian church. They seemed to act more as Artemis followers, under the guise of adoring a Christian female saint, than as Christians.

With this constellation, therefore, we are looking at a great-goddess figure whose stories are dimmed through history. Whether the constellation is the great goddess herself, or the mother goddess who nurtures the male god, makes little difference to the concepts for which she stands. She still travels around the North Pole and still represents the protector of all life. The Great She-Bear still moves around the point of stillness.

STARS OF URSA MAJOR

There are seven main stars in the constellation, the brightest being Dubhe, set on the back of the Bear. The others, in descending order or magnitude, are: Merak, Phachd, Megrez, Alioth, Mizar, and Benetnasch. Merak is known as the "Loin"

---

[219] Jobes, *Outer Space*, p. 259.
[220] Walker, *The Woman's Encyclopedia of Myths and Secrets*, p. 1031.
[221] Jobes, *Outer Space*, p. 260.
[222] Walker, *The Woman's Encyclopedia of Myths and Secrets*, p. 1031.

ₛ mentioned by Aratus in his *Phaenomena.* Dubhe and Merak are also
wn as the Pointers, since they point to the North Pole.

DUBHE

(Alpha Ursa Major. Magnitude 2.0. RA 11:03:21. Declination 61N46 44'. PED
= 14° Leo 30'.) No paran map is required for this star. Dubhe culminates at 24°
Virgo.

Dubhe is visible from latitudes north of 28° South and never sets north of
latitude 28° North. *Dubhe* is an abbreviation of the Arabic *Thahr al Dubb al
Akbar,* the Back of the Great Bear.

Dubhe can only be used on all four points for charts between latitudes 28°
South and 28° North. South of that the star never rises and North of that the star
never sets and therefore has permanent curtailed passage.

EARLIER OPINIONS

Ptolemy states that Dubhe is martial in nature. Robson does not mention it.
Ebertin refers to this star as "nasty" and very much like a destructive Mars. Rigor
is a little more positive, indicating that it gives a certain psychic ability or at least
the power to overcome one's enemies.

DUBHE: THE CONCEPT

Could this great and ancient goddess be so destructive? Or can we strengthen
Rigor's comments and look at the concept of strong feminine powers, traditionally those of intuition rather than physical strength. The Great Bear certainly can
overcome all takers, so maybe we are dealing with a star of insight, persistence,
endurance, and passive strength.

For the majority of births, Dubhe can only be used in its culminating position, but if it is influencing your chart it will suggest your strength lies in the
feminine rather than in any action you may take. The best example I have ever
seen of this star is in the chart of Princess Diana. Her Venus was setting as Dubhe
moved into its culminating position. Her strength and social status lay in the fact
that she was the mother of the future heir to the throne. Through all the turbulence of the British royals, she emerged as a sort of virgin mother, a sacred figure.
Here is the expression of the passive, female, nurturing energy of the goddess. If
her position was ever challenged, however, one would then have seen the power
of the angry mother.

DUBHE IN THE NATAL CHART

In a natal chart Dubhe indicates that your greatest strength lies in the position you hold, rather than the actions you take. Quiet strength.

DUBHE AS THE HELIACAL RISING STAR AT BIRTH

Because of its high declination, this star was not used in this manner. However, for births in the equatorial regions, Dubhe may claim this title and would then indicate that your sense of identity is married to this concept of quiet strength.

URSA MINOR, THE LITTLE BEAR

MENTIONED BY ARATUS AS ONE OF THE Bears, it was thought of as the Lesser Bear because, although it is made up of seven main stars, it is considerably dimmer in appearance and also occupies a smaller place in the heavens (see Star Map 9, p. 134). The constellation has also been known as a dog, with the Egyptians calling it the Jackal of Set.[223] In this sense it has been called the Dog's Tail. The Little Bear draws on the same symbolism as the Great Bear, for they both share the sacred pole. The Little Bear was also important as a navigational aid to sixth-century B.C.E. sailors because, along with the stars of Draco, it occupied the important pole position at different times in history. The Greeks incorporated the Little Bear into their mythology as either another wood nymph, apart from Callista or her child, or as Callista herself.

In ancient times the Little Bear was surrounded on three sides by the constellation Draco, the Dragon, and when the brightest star of the Dragon, Thuban, was the pole star in 3,000 B.C.E., the Little Bear was considered to be the wings of the Dragon. The current pole star is Polaris.

STARS OF URSA MINOR

There are seven main stars of Ursa Minor, the brightest being Polaris, called by medieval Arabs, Alracubba. Some of the others that are named, in descending order or magnitude, are: Kochab, Pherkad Major, Pherkad Minor, Yidun, and Farkadain.

POLARIS

(Alpha Ursa Minor. Magnitude 2.1. RA 5:39:27.7". Declination 89N14'14". PED = 27° Gemini 52'.) No paran map is required for this star. Polaris is always at culmination as it is the point of stillness, the celestial pole.

Polaris is named for its current position as the star closest to the North Pole. The pole will move to within a diameter of the Moon from Polaris in about 2,102 C.E. It is visible from the equator upward to the North Pole. For northern hemisphere births this star never sets and therefore has permanent curtailed passage. But for southern hemisphere births it is never visible, and therefore cannot truly be taken into account for any charts.

---

[223] Allen, *Star Names*, p. 450.

EARLIER OPINIONS

Ptolemy declared that the bright stars of Ursa Minor were like Saturn with a dash of Venus. Robson associates Polaris with sickness and disgrace and saw it as an evil star. Ebertin links this star to a sense of guidance, knowing where one wants to be. Rigor connects the star with pioneering, and being a pathfinder.

POLARIS: THE CONCEPT

If meaning is going to be attributed to this star, it must be linked to its long history as a pole star, where it has been used as a guide for centuries by journeyers of both sea and desert. In addition, we have many layers of goddess mythology apply to this area of the sky, and when we combine this with the focus and pathfinding potential of Polaris, we encounter the idea of an emotional or nurturing mission. However, there is no real practical method by which we can use this star when working with visual parans.

THE NEW CONSTELLATIONS

THE SOUTHERN SKIES WERE MAPPED BY Nicholas La Caille from Cape Town, South Africa, in the 18th century. However, the major stars of the southern skies had already been named since antiquity, and placed into constellations, for these stars were visible from the north, as far south as the Southern Cross, at about 60° of declination. This meant that any new constellations could be formed either from the South Pole stars, if there were any, or from the unnamed parts of the sky that were filled with very dim stars.

Aratus 315–245 B.C.E., says of the southern sky:

Other stars, mean in size and feeble in splendour, wheel between the Rudder of Argo and Cetus, and beneath the grey Hare's sides they are set without a name. For they are not set like the limbs of a fashioned figure.[224]

And then later he adds:

Now the other stars are grouped in clear figures and brightly shine, but those beneath the hunted Hare are all clad in mist and nameless in their course.[225]

Aratus explains that it is not necessary to know the name of every star or for every piece of the sky to be filled with a constellation. For both northern and southern hemispheres he sights empty places in the sky where figures are not formed. It should be remembered that in his day the use of the stars for astrological and meteorological purposes was a major function of society, so his reluctance to add other constellations is a reflection of his belief in the importance of these sky figures.

Aratus lists forty-four constellations that, by the time of Ptolemy, had increased to forty-eight. However, in modern times we have eighty-eight constellations, exactly double the number listed by Aratus. Some of these are new and consist of dim stars, or are in areas that Aratus says are best left unnamed. Others have been formed by breaking up old constellations. There were also many more constellations formed by would-be namers. However, the International Astronomical Union settled on eighty-eight, and by 1930 had clearly defined the boundaries of all modern constellations.

---

[224] Mair, *Callimachus, Lycophron, Aratus*, p. 237.
[225] Mair, *Callimachus, Lycophron, Aratus*, p. 237.

It should be remembered that modern astronomers like La Caille, and eventually the International Astronomical Union, were naming and shaping figures in the sky with no concern for the astrological implications. The IAU was fueled by the need for easy definition of a star's location, and La Caille was, most likely, driven by the need to name a new world. So although some authors offer astrological interpretations of all of these modern constellations, based largely on the nature of the animal or object figured, these interpretations should be taken with a very large grain of salt.

For the sake of completeness, I have included all the new constellations, who named them, and any history attached to them. Occasionally a bright star was moved from an ancient constellation into a new grouping. I have kept that star in the new grouping and delineated it by its more ancient roots. Unless otherwise noted, Allen and Jobes are the sources of the formalizing of these constellations.

ANTILIA, THE AIR PUMP

This constellation lies between Vela, the sails of the Argo, and Hydra. It was formed by La Caille in 1763. Its brightest star has a magnitude of 6.7.

APUS, THE BIRD OF PARADISE

Formally introduced by Bayer in the seventeenth century, although he did not create it. The Chinese called it the Little Wonder Bird. It lies just 13° from the South Pole and does not contain any significant stars. Its brightest star has a magnitude of 3.9.

CAELUM, THE CHISEL

Lying between Columba the Dove, and Eridanus the River, it was formed by La Caille in 1763. Its brightest star has a magnitude of 4.0.

CAMELOPARDALIS, THE GIRAFFE

First mapped by Bartschius in 1614 and named The Camel, which he saw as the beast that had brought Rebecca to Isaac, it later became latinized to *Camelopardalis* which means Giraffe. It stretches from Polaris, the pole star, to Perseus. Its brightest star has a magnitude of 4.0.

CHAMAELEON, THE CHAMELEON

Formed by Bayer and sitting south of Carina, the Keel of the Argo, its brightest star has a magnitude of 4.2.

CIRCINUS, THE COMPASSES

Formed by La Caille, it is close to the feet of the Centaur. It is meant to be associated with the constellation Norma, the Square and the Level, as this is a drafting compass. Its brightest star has a magnitude of 3.5.

COLUMBA NOAE, THE DOVE OF NOAH'S ARK

Formally published by Royer in 1679. Early works place the stars of this constellation among the stars of Canis Major, but Royer cut the constellation in two, taking two stars from Canis Major and renaming them Alpha and Beta Columba Noae to avoid confusion with stars in the Argo. The two stars are Phact and Wezn.

PHACT

(Alpha Columba Noae. Magnitude 2.5. RA 05:39:27.7". Declination 34S04'25". PED = 21° Gemini 28'.) See Paran Map 35, page 211. *An example of how to read the map:* If you were born in Boston, USA, at a latitude of 42° North, then the star rose at about 12° Leo. If you have a planet at either 12° Leo or Aquarius, then that planet rose or set with the star. The star also set at 10° Taurus. Therefore, if you have a planet at 10° Taurus or Scorpio, it would have set or risen as the star set. The star culminates at 25° Gemini so if you have a planet at either 25° Gemini or Sagittarius, then it culminated or was on the Nadir as the star culminated.

At this latitude of 42° North the star has a phase of arising and lying hidden. This period will be from about April 27 (reading the date from the left-hand column of the date box next to 10° Taurus) to August 3 every year (reading the left-hand column of the date box next to 12° Leo), and is the true or cosmic heliacal rising star about August 3 (reading the date for the rising line at 42° North in the "heliacal rising" column).

Phact can be used on all four points for charts between latitudes of 55° South and 55° North. North of that the star never rises and south of that the star never sets and therefore has permanent curtailed passage.

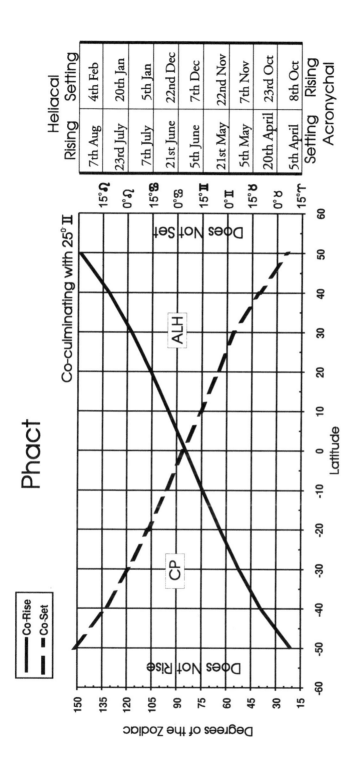

Paran Map 35. Phact.

EARLIER OPINIONS

Ptolemy does not mention the star, although he talks of the bright stars in the Argo, the constellation which contained Phact in Ptolemy's day, as being like the stars of Jupiter and Saturn. Robson, Ebertin, and Rigor all indicate that the person influenced by this star has artistic talents and is very harmonious, with Ebertin talking of a touch of genius and mediumship.

PHACT: THE CONCEPT

It is obvious that Robson, Ebertin, and Rigor are drawing on the symbolism of the dove to derive their meanings of artistic talents and harmony. But this star used to be part of the Argo on the top of the bow, crashing through the waves in waters uncharted. The symbolism here should not be the seventeenth century peaceful dove but rather the ancient quest for adventure. Carl Jung had Phact rising as his Moon culminated. He spent his life trying to chart the unknown waters of the human psyche. Leonardo da Vinci had Phact rising as his Sun culminated. This was not related so much to Leonardo's art, but rather his plans for flying machines, submarines, and bicycles.

Phact is one of many examples where modern alterations to a constellation have become incorporated into the delineation of the star with no thought to the thousands of years that humans have projected other symbolism onto that part of the sky.

PHACT IN THE NATAL CHART

When Phact is connected to your chart it adds the element of exploration, of seeking the unknown and of being prepared to move into uncharted waters. It can be a bold risk-taking statement if, for example, it is connected to Mars; on the other hand it could be the exploration of intellectual pursuits if connected with Mercury.

PHACT AS THE HELIACAL RISING STAR AT BIRTH

Phact was not traditionally used in this way but if it is the Cosmic rising star in your chart, then recognise that the desire to seek and explore will become a lifestyle and a major component of your personal identity.

DORADO, THE GOLDFISH

Formed by Johann Bayer in 1624, Dorado is close to the South Pole and its brightest star has a magnitude of 3.1.

FORNAX, THE FURNACE

Another constellation formed by La Caille, made from stars in the southern bend of the River, Eridanus. The Chinese had also noted this group of stars and had called it Heaven's Temporary Granary, Tien Yu. Its brightest star has a magnitude of 3.6.

GRUS, THE CRANE

Originally belonging to Piscis Australis, this constellation was formed by Bayer in 1603. The brightest star Al nair, the Bright One in the Fishes Tail, has a magnitude of 2. Ptolemy talks of the bright stars of Piscis Australis as being of the nature of Venus and Mercury. Robson says it gives a love of astronomy as well as the tendency of being kind, watchful, and idealistic. If Al nair was going to be used astrologically, it would probably be wise to stay within its more ancient symbolism of the Southern Fish, whose alpha star is Formalhaut, one of the Royal Stars of Persia.

HOROLOGIUM, THE PENDULUM CLOCK

Lying between the River Eridanus and the Keel of the Argo, Carina, this was also called the Horoscope. Its brightest star has a magnitude of 3.8.

HYDRUS, THE MALE SERPENT

This was the last snake to be added to the heavens and should not be confused with its ancient counterpart, Hydra. This constellation was invented by Bayer in 1603[226] and lies between Horologium, the clock, and the Tucana. Its head points to the South Pole. Its brightest star has a magnitude of 2.7. It was considered to be the mate of Hydra. It does not contain any named stars.

INDUS, THE INDIAN

Another of Bayer's constellations, it lies south of the Microscope and its brightest star has a magnitude of 3.1.

---

[226] Jobes, *Outer Space*, p. 192.

LACERTA, THE LIZARD

Formed by Hevelius (1611–1687) from the stars between Cygnus and Andromeda, Lacerta was formerly known as the Scepter and Hand of Justice, meant to
relate to the French king Louis XIV. Its brightest star has a magnitude of 3.9.

LEO MINOR, THE LITTLE LION

Formed by Hevelius from stars between Leo and Ursa Major, the Lion and the
Bear. There is one star in it that is named and that is Praecipua, with a magnitude of 4.0.

LYNX, THE LYNX

Created by Hevelius at the feet of Ursa Major, its brightest star has a magnitude
of 4.4., and Hevelius himself said that one needed to be Lynx-eyed to see the
constellation.

MENSA, THE TABLE MOUNTAIN

One of La Caille's constellations formed between the South Pole and the southern pole of the ecliptic. La Caille saw this as symbolic of the Table Mountain in
Cape Town where he had performed all of his observations. Its brightest star has
a magnitude of 5.3.

MICROSCOPIUM, THE MICROSCOPE

Another of La Caille's constellations formed in 1752, it is south of Capricornus
and west of Piscis Australis, the Southern Fish. Its brightest star has a magnitude
of 4.8.

MONOCEROS, THE UNICORN

Resting between the two Dogs in a largely vacant area of the sky, it is believed to
have been mapped first by Bartschius who named the area Unicornu. However, it

was first sighted as a horselike creature in the seventeenth century. Its brightest star has a magnitude of 3.6.

MUSCA, THE FLY

Another of La Caille's constellations, although it seems to have a blurred background. Known also as The Bee, it lies south of the Southern Cross. Its brightest star has a magnitude of 2.9.

NORMA, THE LEVEL AND THE SQUARE

Lying close to the sting of the Scorpion between Ara the Altar, and Lupus the Wolf, it was originally part of those three constellations. However, La Caille altered it to its present grouping. Its brightest star has a magnitude of 4.6.

OCTANS, THE OCTANT

Published by La Caille in 1752, this constellation actually marks the South Pole with one of its stars which has a magnitude of 5.8 and so is almost invisible to the naked eye. It is currently only 45' away from the Pole. Its brightest star has a magnitude of 3.8.

The ancients believed that the South Pole was more thickly populated with stars than the North Pole and wrote with authority about the Bears that supposedly orbited the South Pole. The Arabs gave it the same healing powers as the North Pole, saying that if you looked at the North or South Pole for a period of time, it would heal you.

PAVO, THE PEACOCK

Formed by Bayer, this lies between 60 and 70 degrees of southern declination. The stars were unnamed. However, in recent times the alpha star has been given the name Peacock and has a magnitude of 1.9. One would like to link this with the ancient tradition of the peacock, the sacred bird of Juno, but this is a modern addition. The constellation is only four hundred years old and the naming of the alpha star has only occurred this century. Robson, however, still gives meaning to the constellation Pavo, saying that it gives a love of display and vanity, clearly drawing on the symbolism of the physical bird itself.

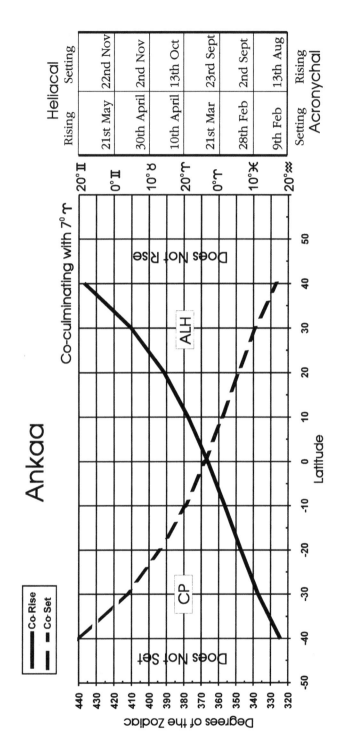

Heliacal			
Rising	Setting		
21st May	22nd Nov		
30th April	2nd Nov		
10th April	13th Oct		
21st Mar	23rd Sept		
28th Feb	2nd Sept		
9th Feb	13th Aug		
Setting	Rising		
Acronychal			

Ankaa

Co-Rise
Co-Set

Paran Map 36. Ankaa.

If the alpha star Peacock is going to be used astrologically, then it is important to try and find the early history, if any, of this part of the sky.

PHOENIX, THE PHOENIX

Another modern addition by Bayer which lies between the Southern Fish and the River, Eridanus. The naming of this constellation fits in with much older traditions—the Chinese, Egyptians, Indians, and Persians all having myths linking the stars in this group with a bird that symbolized some form of cyclic regeneration.[227]

Ankaa, also known as Nair al Zaural, the Bright One in the Boat,[228] is the only named star in the constellation and, although the constellation is new, it appears to be the formalization of a much older tradition.

ANKAA

(Alpha Phoenix. Magnitude 2.4. RA 00: 27'. Declination 42S18'. PED = 14° Pisces 47'.) See Paran Map 36, page 216. *An example of how to read the map:* If you were born in Cairns, Australia, at a latitude of 17° South then the star rose at about 20° Pisces. If you have a planet at either 20° Pisces or Virgo, then that planet rose or set with the star. The star also set at 2° Taurus. Therefore, if you have a planet at 2° Taurus or Scorpio, it would have set or risen as the star set. The star culminates at 7° Aries so if you have a planet at either 7° Aries or Libra, then it culminated or was on the Nadir as the star culminated.

At this latitude of 17° South the star has a phase of curtailed passage. This period will be from about September 12 (reading the date from the right-hand column of the date box next to 20° Pisces) to October 24 every year (reading the right-hand column of the date box next to 2° Taurus), and is the true or cosmic heliacal rising star about March 10 (reading the date for the rising line at 17° South in the "heliacal rising" column).

Ankaa can be used on all four points for charts between latitudes of 47° South and 47° North. North of that the star never rises, south of that the star never sets and therefore has permanent curtailed passage.

EARLIER OPINIONS

Robson is the only author to cite the constellation and he states that it gives ambition and possibly lasting fame.

---

[227] Allen, *Star Names*, p. 336.
[228] Allen, *Star Names*, p. 336.

ANKAA: THE CONCEPT

Not a great deal of work has been done with this star but it does seem to carry a sense of transformation or transcending. Joseph Campbell, the famous mythologist and author, had Ankaa culminating with his Sun, indicating that the star was connected to his life work, his career, his mark in the world. Joseph Campbell raised our collective consciousness to a higher level with his understanding, teachings, and writings about the importance of myths. It is connected to his Sun, so it is a part of his identity, how he defines himself, and because it is culminating it is how we define him. In stark contrast, it is also connected to the chart of Patty Hearst, the daughter of a wealthy American industrialist who disappeared only to reappear as a SLA[229] terrorist. She had Ankaa culminating when her Moon was on the Nadir. Her contact is all lunar, emotional, and feeling, and she was radically transformed by these feelings.

ANKAA AS THE HELIACAL RISING STAR AT BIRTH

Ankaa was not used as the heliacal rising star. However, if it is the cosmic rising star at birth, then Ankaa's influence would be connected to your Sun, the center of your being. You may well seek to change things, to alter the way things are. The ability to do this would be part of your definition of self.

PICTOR, THE PAINTER

Formed by La Caille and meant to be a painter's palette, Pictor lies just south of Columba the Dove. Its brightest star has a magnitude of 3.5.

RETICULUM, THE RETICLE

Reticulum is a very small constellation lying between Horologium and the keel of the Argo. It was added by La Caille but thought to have been formed by Isaak Habrecht of Strassburg. Its brightest star has a magnitude of 3.3.

SCULPTOR, THE SCULPTOR

Formed by La Caille, it lies between Cetus the Whale, and the Phoenix. Its brightest star has a magnitude of 4.2.

---

[229] Symbionese Liberation Army.

SCUTUM, THE SHIELD

Lying between the end of the Hydra and the head of Sagittarius, the Shield was formed to commemorate the victory of John Sobieski, king of Poland, against the Turks in 1683. Its brightest star has a magnitude of 4.0.

SEXTANS, THE SEXTANT

Sextans was placed in the sky by Hevelius to honor the sextant he had used in making stellar measurements from 1658 to 1679. It lies on the back of Hydra between it and the constellation Leo. Its brightest star has a magnitude of 4.1.

TELESCOPIUM, THE TELESCOPE

Formed by La Caille in 1752, it sits just south of Corona Australis. Its brightest star has a magnitude of 3.5.

TUCANA, THE TOUCAN

Another of Bayer's constellations, known originally under its English name, but later latinized. It lies close to the South Pole with its tail near Achernar, alpha Eridanus. It has no named stars. Its brightest star has a magnitude of 2.8.

VOLANS, THE FLYING FISH

Volans was named by Johann Bayer in 1624. It is close to the South Pole and its brightest star has a magnitude of 3.9.

VULPECULA, THE FOX

This was once called the Fox and the Goose, placed in the sky by Hevelius between Sagitta the Arrow and Cygnus the Swan. There seems to be only one named star, Anser, with a magnitude of 4.4.

Part 3

THE ZODIAC, THE RING OF LIFE

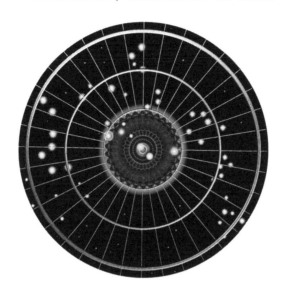

THE ZODIAC CONSTELLATIONS

THE ZODIAC IS THE GREAT RING OF LIFE.
It is composed of the constellations through which the Sun moves, showing the world the twelve faces of the god, or the twelve primary ingredients or archetypes of life. These can be read on the material plane as a commentary on the lives of humankind, or on the spiritual plane, showing modern astrologers the mixture and blending of the human psyche. But the constellations of the zodiac, the actual star groupings, are different from the 30° sections of the sky which make up the tropical zodiac and the two should never be confused; the latter measure the position of the Sun in relationship to the seasons and the former refer to the actual fixed stars themselves.

Around two thousand years ago these two zodiacs were aligned, but the tropical zodiac was measured from the point of the northern hemisphere spring equinox. By the time of Ptolemy and Vettius Valens, the tropical zodiac took its meanings from the seasons of the year, the "seasons" of our own individual lives, and later—as the concept of the human collective evolved in the 20th century—from the "seasons" of the development of human culture. From these "seasons," which were locked into the tropical zodiac by tying the point 0° Aries to the spring equinox, we have evolved the meanings of the twelve tropical zodiac signs. As astrologers, we seek to reveal or explore these meanings in the examination of an individual's birth chart.

Thus the astrological meanings of the tropical zodiac signs can probably be traced to the seasons, the unfolding rhythm of life. Any influence that the fixed stars in the constellations on the ecliptic had on the "sun signs" was probably minimal. So the stories and history contained in the constellations on the ecliptic were cut adrift from Western astrology about the time of Ptolemy, and have remained in stasis since that time, giving us the physical pathway of the sun's yearly movement, even though they no longer contribute to "sun sign" meanings.

ARIES, THE RAM

AS THE STARS OF ARIES THE RAM BECAME the heliacal rising constellation for the spring equinox, thus placing it in the lead position of the zodiac, the concept of the tropical zodiac was also taking shape. Therefore Aries became the leading sign of the tropical zodiac, a designation that has never been altered even though the stars of Aries have long since lost this lead role, now belonging to the stars of Pisces.[1]

History shows us that when the spring equinox moves into a new constellation, a new age and a new god emerge. This god is either the son of the older god, or a new concept represented by a new god, which springs forth from the collective unconscious. With the movement of the equinox from the stars of Taurus into the stars of Aries, which occurred in about 2,000 B.C.E., the movement was away from the sacred bull of the Egyptians and the god Horus (who had many forms—one of which was the bull)[2] toward gods of a more Arian nature. To the people of the Euphrates this new god was known as Tammuz Daum-uzei, the Only Son of Life, with the emphasis on the word *only*. The Israelites, thought to have emerged from Canaan, came forth with their god El, whose name was changed to YHWH (I am that I am)[3] at the time when Moses led the Israelites out of Egypt. These gods were One-God monotheistic concepts with YHWH

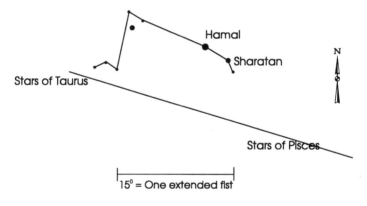

Star Map 17. Aries, the Ram.

---

[1] Through precession the Sun's position at the equinox appears to shift backward through the zodiac. Once, around the time of Christ, the Sun rose with the stars of Aries. Now, the stars with which it rises are those of early Pisces. Later, when the Sun rises among the stars of Aquarius, anywhere from twenty to five hundred years from now, depending on your point of view, it will be known as the age of Aquarius.

[2] Wallis E. A. Budge, *The Gods of the Egyptians*, vol. 1 (New York: Dover Books, 1969), p. 493.

[3] Magnus Magnusson, *BC—The Archaeology of the Bible Lands* (London: British Broadcasting Corporation, 1977).

(Yahweh) using the blood of a lamb to mark and save his people from his wrath. The new Arian gods were solo creatures who shared their glory with no other.

The Egyptians by now were moving into their third god as they moved into what is called the period of the New Empire,[4] which culminated with the position of the "king of the gods and lord of the thrones of the two lands",[5] the god Amen-Ra. He was a new type of god for the Egyptians, for he also shared his glory with no other god. He was supreme.[6] Amen-Ra was a god with many forms, one of which was ram's horns, and he was called "Lord of the Head," and the Egyptians linked him to the stars of Aries[7] since now those stars rode the Chariot of the Sun.[8] He was the virile male and the holy phallus; stories or images of a ram in the thicket are considered by some to be sexual metaphors.[9] Ram imagery in the Old Testament is also linked to Yahweh. Indeed it is this image of a ram in a thicket which saves Abraham from sacrificing his son Isaac on the command of Yahweh. This was an important story for the new monotheistic religion as it showed that the male god of the ram desired animal sacrifices rather than the more ancient practice of human sacrifices.[10] The ram was sacred to the Israelites, who sacrificed the paschal lamb each year at Passover as a substitute for the primitive sacrifices of firstborn sons which Yahweh originally demanded in Exodus 13:2.[11]

The Greeks, who were growing in power in this period, adopted Amen-Ra as their Zeus[12] and developed the story of Jason and the Golden Fleece. The ram became the magical animal that transported Phrixus and Helle, the children of Athamas, to the safety of Colchis to escape the wrath of their stepmother, Ino. Helle, the daughter, fell from the beast's back and died, but the male child, Phrixus, survived. The ram was sacrificed in thanksgiving, his image placed in the heavens and his golden fleece hung in the grove of Ares.[13]

---

[4] About 2,000 B.C.E.

[5] Wallis E. A. Budge, *The Gods of the Egyptians*, vol. 1 (New York: Dover Books, 1969), p. 174.

[6] Budge, *The Gods of the Egyptians*, vol. 2, p. 5.

[7] Jobes, *Outer Space*, p. 124.

[8] The stars of Aries rising with the spring equinox.

[9] Barbara Walker, *The Woman's Encyclopedia of Myths and Secrets* (San Francisco: HarperSanFrancisco, 1983), p. 841.

[10] Walker, *The Woman's Encyclopedia of Myths and Secrets*, p. 841.

[11] Walker, *The Woman's Encyclopedia of Myths and Secrets*, p. 526.

[12] The cult of Zeus is believed by archaeologists to be the final dying phase of the cult of Zagreus, possibly first originating in the seventh millennium B.C.E.

[13] Grimal, *The Dictionary of Classical Mythology* (Cambridge: Blackwell Reference, 1986), p. 371.

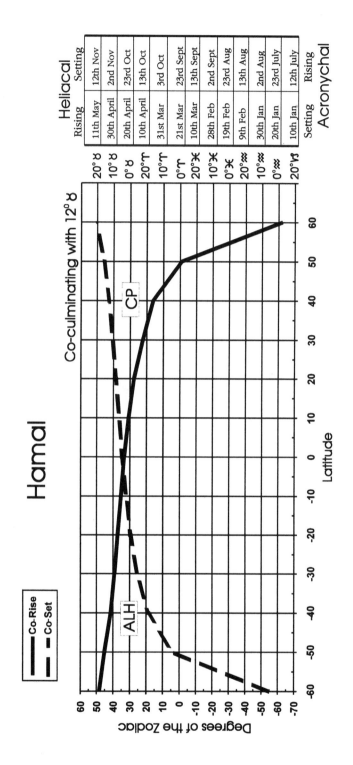

Paran Map 37. Hamal.

STARS OF ARIES

The brightest star of Aries is Hamal, the base of the eastern horn of the Ram. Other named stars, in descending order of magnitude, are: Sharatan and Mesarthim, both on the west horn.

HAMAL

(Alpha Aries. Magnitude 2.2. RA 02:06:54.3". Declination 23N26'18". PED = 6° Taurus 58'.) See Paran Map 37, page 226. *An example of how to read the map:* If you were born in Cape Town, South Africa, at a latitude of 34° South, then the star rose at about 10° Taurus. If you have a planet at either 10° Taurus or Scorpio, then that planet rose or set with the star. The star also set at 22° Aries. Therefore, if you have a planet at 22° Aries or Libra it would have set or risen as the star set. The star culminates at 12° Taurus, so if you have a planet at either 12° Taurus or Scorpio, then it culminated or was on the Nadir as the star culminated.

At this latitude of 34° South the star has a phase of arising and lying hidden. This period will be from about April 12 (reading the date from the left-hand column of the date box next to 22° Aries) to April 30 every year (reading the left-hand column of the date box next to 10° Taurus), and is the true or cosmic heliacal rising star on April 30 (reading the date for the rising line at 34° South in the "heliacal rising" column).

Hamal can be used on all four points for charts between latitudes of 66° South and 66° North. South of that the star never rises. North of that the star never sets and therefore has permanent curtailed passage.

EARLIER OPINIONS

Ptolemy states that the stars of the head of Aries are of the nature of Mars and Saturn. Robson associates them with brutishness and premeditated crime. Ebertin lists Hamal as *El Naith* and refers to it as a difficult star causing danger. Rigor takes it one step further and relates it to "perverted" tastes.

HAMAL: THE CONCEPT

As a new religion arrives, its followers will try to cast grave aspersions on the outgoing or older religion. Aries and the Ram were a religious concept; indeed, in the Jewish religion they still are. When the age of Pisces was born and the god of Fishes, son of the Ram, was enthroned, the old horned god of the Ram was labeled as Satan, the most evil.[14] The astrological meaning of Hamal may have suffered the same censorship and so the star became associated with evil.

---

[14] Walker, *The Woman's Encyclopedia of Myths and Secrets*, p. 841.

By peeling off the discrimination of Christianity, Hamal can be seen as a forceful star of action and independence, a little like the meaning of the tropical zodiac sign, Aries. Instead of being evil and perverted, it seems to enhance any planet it contacts with the strength of independence. This may have negative or positive consequences.

Joan of Arc was born with her Mercury culminating as Hamal rose. Thus the independent and forceful influence of Hamal affected her Mercury at an early age (rising). As a young peasant girl she insisted she be taken to the French heir to the throne and that he listen to what she believed were her "messages from God."

Madam Blavatsky, the nineteenth-century Russian spiritualist and author who was a cofounder of the Theosophical Society, had Hamal culminating as her Jupiter set. Jupiter tends to magnify a star and a culminating star expresses itself in the middle, or active, adult part of one's life. In Blavatsky's case, Hamal expresses itself in her life through her highly critical attitude to the mainstream thinking of the day, as well as through her vigorous and very active promotion of different ideas and philosophies. Indeed she is remembered today primarily for establishing the Theosophical Society.

HAMAL IN THE NATAL CHART

When Hamal is in your chart it indicates a certain independence and strength of will. This could manifest as the simple but useful ability to be focused and direct, or it could be expressed as temper or frustration and the inability to deal with authority figures within the family or in the career.

HAMAL AS THE HELIACAL RISING STAR AT BIRTH

Hamal is not of sufficient magnitude to herald the dawn. However, it can be used as the cosmic rising star. Here Hamal will be at its strongest, linked to the Sun, your very identity. You will be very focused, very motivated, and will prefer to act or think in a way which separates you from others. Lacking diplomacy, you may be a forceful leader or a tyrant. A lovely example of this is in the chart of William Shatner, the actor who played Captain James T. Kirk of the starship *Enterprise* in "Star Trek." He was born at the time when Hamal was the cosmic rising star for Montreal, Canada, his place of birth, and his role as the mythical starship captain captured the minds of millions as he became a symbol of the human urge to explore.

TAURUS, THE BULL

THE BULL IS THE SECOND SYMBOL OF A god in the heavens, the first symbol being Orion. As the spring equinox slipped into the stars of Taurus around 4,500 B.C.E., The Bull with its red eye became Horus,[15] the son of Osiris to the ancient Egyptians.[16] During this equinox shift from the stars of Orion to Taurus, many gods of the ancient world appeared that were connected with or incarnated as bulls. The Phoenician bull-god, called father of men was given the title of *El*, meaning "bull," but which translates into English as the word "god."[17]

El was worshipped throughout Syria where the Persians labeled the great red star in the eye of the Bull as their watcher of the east.[18] For them a great ancient cult surfaced, involving a figure called Mithras[19] who was a god of the first order, one of military valor without rival, said to ride the solar chariot across the sky.[20] He was also known as or linked with Ahura Mazda,[21] a Persian savior figure known as the bull slayer, a humanized version of the Bull who seized a great wild bull by the horns and rode him to exhaustion, after which he slayed the bull whose wounds and spilled blood produced life for the earth.[22] His worship involved a baptism of bull's blood where the initiate stood in a pit underneath a slotted platform and was showered with the blood of a sacrificial bull slaughtered on top of the platform. The initiate would bathe in this blood, making sure that it touched eyes, ears, mouth, and body, and drink it as a sacramental act. Thus the initiate emerged from this pit cleansed of sin, washed clean by the blood of the bull.[23]

The Egyptians also annually slew a sacred bull in atonement for the sins of the realm.[24] The concept was that the blood of one god, or the symbol of that god, could cleanse the sins of many. From this ritual arose the belief that blood had to be spilled if sins were to be forgiven, thus probably dictating that thousands of years later Christ was to die a bloody death. However, after two thousand or so years the spring equinox slipped from Taurus the Bull into Aries the Ram, heralding the birth of yet another new god, this time emerging from the

---

[15] Horus was seen as the divine falcon but is linked to stars of Taurus.

[16] Jane B. Sellers, *The Death of the Gods in Ancient Egypt* (London: Penguin, 1992), p. 112.

[17] Walker, *The Woman's Encyclopedia of Myths and Secrets*, p. 125.

[18] Richard Hinckley Allen, *Star Names; Their Lore and Meaning* (New York: Dover, 1963), p. 385.

[19] The earliest cave paintings of this figure are thought to date from 23,000 B.C.E.

[20] *New Larousse Encyclopedia of Mythology* (London: Hamlyn, 1968), p. 311.

[21] *New Larousse Encyclopedia of Mythology*, p. 314.

[22] Settegast, *Plato Prehistorian* (New York: Lindisfarne, 1986), p. 112.

[23] Walker, *Encyclopedia*, p. 126.

[24] Walker, *Encyclopedia*, p. 126.

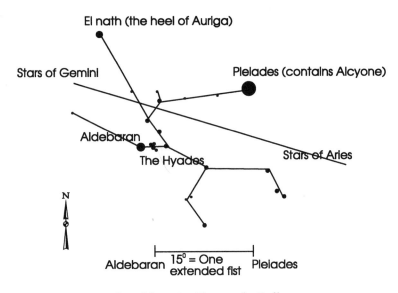

Star Map 18. Taurus, the Bull.

Israelites. They distinguished themselves from the bull-worshippers by using the blood of the lamb as a sacred fluid and symbol. For Moses was leading his people, chosen with lamb's blood, to a new religion. This was the new world age marked by Aries and thus a new god was required. Returning from Mount Sinai with the new laws of the new world order, Moses was angered that his chosen people were looking backwards to the bull (Golden Calf) instead of forward to the lamb.[25]

In other mythology, too, as the Bull began to slip from the equinox to make way for Aries, the bull took on a more negative sense: in the Greek myth of Jason, for example, who had to tame a fiery bull in order to pass one of the tests toward claiming the Golden Fleece of Aries[26] (the incoming god). Another example is the Minotaur, placed in a labyrinth by King Minos. Part bull, part man, the Minotaur fed on sacrifices of human flesh until conquered by Theseus, who came out of the labyrinth and into the light.[27] The bull in these myths is seen as darkness or antilife, as it becomes the symbol of old religion making way for the god of Aries.

---

[25] G. de Santillana and Hertha von Dechend, *Hamlet's Mill* (Boston: Nonpareil Books, 1977), p. 60.

[26] Bulfinch, *Myths of Greece and Rome* (New York: Penguin, 1979), p. 153.

[27] Bulfinch, *Myths of Greece and Rome*, p. 181.

The bull has also charged through Irish culture and produced the great epic and heart of their mythology, *The Tain,* which is the story of The Donn or Brown Bull in mortal conflict with the White Bull[28]—darkness against light.

The Bull as a god has long since lost his power, having slipped from the equinox position around 2,000 B.C.E., but it is from this period that the mythological symbolism was firmly stamped upon his celestial image.

STARS OF TAURUS

The brightest star of Taurus is Aldebaran but the constellation also contains two asterisms: the Pleiades, a cluster of seven stars in the shoulder of the Bull; and the Hyades, a cluster of five to seven visible stars on the forehead of the Bull.

ALDEBARAN

(Alpha Taurus. Magnitude 1.1. RA 04:35:37.4". Declination 16N29'53". PED = 9° Gemini 05'.) See Paran Map 38, page 232. *An example of how to read the map:* If you were born in Toronto, Canada, at a latitude of 44° North, then the star rose at about 17° Gemini. If you have a planet at either 17° Gemini or Sagittarius, then that planet rose or set with the star. The star also set at 6° Gemini. Therefore, if you have a planet at 6° Gemini or Sagittarius it would have set or risen as the star set. The star culminates at 10° Gemini so if you have a planet at either 10° Gemini or Sagittarius, then it culminated or was on the Nadir as the star culminated.

At this latitude of 44° North the star has a phase of arising and lying hidden. This period will be from about May 27 (reading the date from the left-hand column of the date box next to 6° Gemini) to June 8 every year (reading the left-hand column of the date box next to 17° Gemini), and is the true or cosmic heliacal rising star about April 8 (reading the date for the rising line at 44° North in the "heliacal rising" column).

Aldebaran can be used on all four points for charts between latitudes of 74° South and 74° North. South of that the star never rises, north of that the star never sets and therefore has permanent curtailed passage.

EARLIER OPINIONS
Ptolemy states that Aldebaran has the nature of Mars. Robson indicates that the star can give great honor but says that this honor will not last. Ebertin claims it gives great energy and that the person influenced by it can achieve many things

---

[28] Thomas Kinsella, trans., *The Tain* (Oxford: Oxford University Press, 1989).

Aldebaran

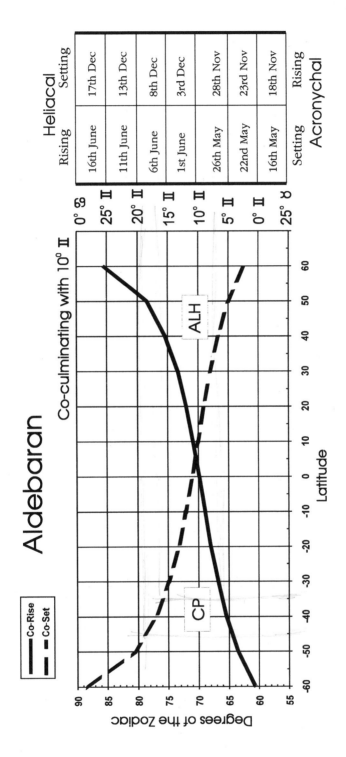

Heliacal	
Rising	Setting
16th June	17th Dec
11th June	13th Dec
6th June	8th Dec
1st June	3rd Dec
26th May	28th Nov
22nd May	23rd Nov
16th May	18th Nov
Setting	Rising
Acronychal	

Paran Map 38. Aldebaran.

but will make enemies. Rigor agrees with Robson and then adds that the person will tend toward turbulence and lack of stability. ← non taurean

ALDEBARAN: THE CONCEPT

Aldebaran is one of the great stars in the sky, one of the Royal Stars of Persia, the Watcher in the East, the great cornerstone marking the spring equinox. In this capacity Aldebaran was the god Mithras, or Ahura Mazda, the slayer of the cosmic bull. Mithras was a great military god who gave victories to his followers but only if they followed the strictest procedure in his worship.

This procedure is also reflected in the writings and worship of the god-prophet Zarathustra, of Persian (Iranian) origin, who was said to have learned wisdom from Ahura Mazda. His name means "star worshipper" and his teachings were meant "to restore the belief in the sanctity of the material world, and ultimately, it is said, to restore the earth to its original state of perfection."[29] Whether Aldebaran is connected to Mithras or Zarathustra, or possibly even both, we are able to derive a more three-dimensional meaning for Aldebaran from these ancient beliefs and customs, which emphasize success linked to integrity of morals and objectives. Mithras was a warrior king who also bore the title "lord of contracts."[30] He considered all exchanges as sacred and therefore oversaw the business of his followers, insisting on their honesty and purity, failing which the follower was condemned to an ordeal of fire. This was usually expressed by having the suspected person run through a tunnel of fire, where their survival meant their innocence.

The four Royal Stars of Persia are all very powerful stars and each one offers the possibility of glory, success, or happiness, but only if a particular nemesis can be overcome. In the case of Aldebaran, this challenge is one of integrity and honor. Greatness can be achieved but the individual will be challenged on issues of integrity and purity of their thoughts and dealings. If they fail this test they lose everything.

The English king Edward VIII had Aldebaran rising with his Jupiter on the day he was born. Heir to the English throne, he fell in love with a divorcee. By British law he could not retain the monarchy if he married her. His most logical option would have been to follow in the footsteps of other kings and have her as his mistress. However, he refused to take this option and abdicated so that he could marry the woman he loved. Faced with an issue of integrity, he rose to the occasion.

Galileo Galilei also had contact with Aldebaran. His Mars set with Aldebaran on the day he was born. Late in his life he rebelled against the Church and

---

[29] Settegast, *Plato Prehistorian*, p. 219.

[30] Jason Cooper, *Mithras* (York Beach, ME: Samuel Weiser, 1996), p. 3.

announced that the Earth orbited around the Sun. He did this with the knowledge that he would be arrested and imprisoned. Fortunately for him, he was imprisoned in his own house due to his old age rather then being put through the ordeal of fire to test his theories. This is a nice example of the energy of the (setting) star, expressing itself in the later part of life.

George Bernard Shaw, the great Irish playwright and author, had Aldebaran exactly rising in his chart at the moment of his birth, and lived according to principles in which he believed. A small example of this was the vegetarianism for which he was famous.[31] He was also a teetotaler and was meticulous in not allowing any alcohol to be used in the preparation of any food. He lived by his morals and beliefs and would not allow his integrity to be challenged, almost embodying this side of Aldebaran.

A military example of Aldebaran is Niccolo Machiavelli, the fifteenth-century statesman, writer, political theorist and, at times, military general. He was born with two contacts to Aldebaran: his Moon culminated with the star and his Mercury rose with it. In a sense, he represents the fall of Aldebaran. He rose in status within the diplomatic, military, and administrative power base of fifteenth-century Italy. When his allies lost power to the Medici, he was accused of conspiracy against the new government and tortured to admit guilt. However, being innocent, Machiavelli refused to confess, and was eventually released but lived the rest of his life in poverty. Although labeled a traitor, spy, and immoral person, history tells us that he was an upright honest citizen with very high integrity and beliefs.[32] Here is the honor and glory of Aldebaran, but also the fall, which implies that somewhere in Machiavelli's life he succumbed to temptation.

ALDEBARAN IN THE NATAL CHART

The presence of Aldebaran in a chart indicates that you will have to face moral dilemmas which challenge your integrity. Success will be presented to you. However, along the journey you will be tempted to compromise your position, to go against your own integrity. Be aware that when this star is involved, any compromising of your integrity will have negative results and all that is gained could be lost very rapidly.

ALDEBARAN AS THE HELIACAL RISING STAR AT BIRTH

Aldebaran can be both the apparent and the cosmic rising star, and will be at its strongest in this position. You will be characterized by strong principles, ethics, things about which you feel strongly. These principles are a vital part of your suc-

---

[31] Followers of Ahura Mazda were also very strict vegetarians.

[32] *The New Encyclopedia Britannica*, vol. 7 (Chicago, 1986), p. 629.

cess but you will be challenged on them. You will have to fight to maintain the purity of what you believe, and any wavering of your integrity could cause you to lose ground rapidly.

EL NATH

(Beta Taurus. Magnitude 2.1. RA 05:22:56". Declination 28°N 34'. PED = 21° Gemini 53'.) See Paran Map 39, page 236. *An example of how to read the map:* If you were born in Dallas, USA, at a latitude of 33° North, then the star rose at about 18° Gemini. If you have a planet at either 18° Gemini or Sagittarius, then that planet rose or set with the star. The star also set at 27° Gemini. Therefore, if you have a planet at 27° Gemini or Sagittarius it would have set or risen as the star set. The star culminates at 22° Gemini so if you have a planet at either 22° Gemini or Sagittarius then it culminated or was on the Nadir as the star culminated.

At this latitude of 33° North the star has a phase of curtailed passage. This period will be from about December 7 (reading the date from the right-hand column of the date box next to 18° Gemini) to December 17 every year (reading the right-hand column of the date box next to 27° Gemini), and is the true or cosmic heliacal rising star about June 5 (reading the date for the rising line at 33° North in the "heliacal rising" column).

El Nath can be used on all four points for charts between latitudes of 61° South and 61° North. South of that the star never rises, north of that the star never sets and therefore has permanent curtailed passage.

EARLIER OPINIONS

Ptolemy talks of this star having the nature of Saturn and partly Mercury. Robson says that it gives good fortune. Ebertin does not list the star but uses the name El Nath for the alpha star of Aries. Rigor does not list the star.

EL NATH: THE CONCEPT

El Nath is the tip of the horn, the point of attack. It was viewed as the force of the Bull, thereby having power over the waters, or blood of life, and thus it can symbolize a great and terrible weapon, a potentially destructive skill that can be used to destroy or to give life. Henry Kissinger, the United States statesman who won the Nobel Peace Prize for his work in averting wars, has El Nath rising with his Mercury. Here the star is concerned with the weapons of war but in striving for peace rather than for aggression. In stark contrast to this, in mundane astrology, El Nath rose with the planet Uranus in 1945 over the latitudes of Japan, that country experiencing the deadliest weaponry of the modern age, the atom bomb.

El nath

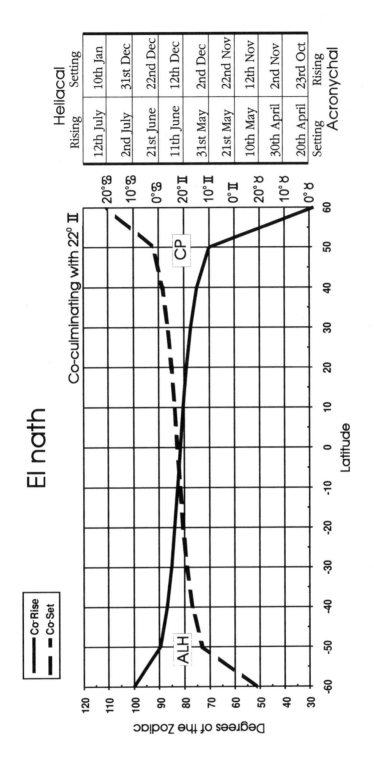

Heliacal			
Rising	Setting		
12th July	10th Jan		
2nd July	31st Dec		
21st June	22nd Dec		
11th June	12th Dec		
31st May	2nd Dec		
21st May	22nd Nov		
10th May	12th Nov		
30th April	2nd Nov		
20th April	23rd Oct		
Setting	Rising		
Acronychal			

Co-culminating with 22° ♊

CP

ALH

Co-Rise
Co-Set

Latitude

Degrees of the Zodiac

Paran Map 39. El Nath.

EL NATH IN THE NATAL CHART

If El Nath is making a contact in your chart, then at some level of your life there will be issues of the use, or non-use, of weapons. These "weapons" may manifest in a love of martial arts or, more simply, a sharp-edged tongue that you learn to use or curb.

EL NATH AS THE HELIACAL RISING STAR AT BIRTH

Ptolemy believed El Nath cannot herald the dawn, so it should only be used as the cosmic rising star. In this position, like any star, it is at its strongest, so the whole issue of weapons, war, and peace becomes linked to your very sense of personal identity. This does not necessarily have to have a negative expression, since you also may work vigorously for peace.

THE PLEIADES

The Pleiades is a small cluster of stars, which takes up less than one degree in the sky, about the width of one finger. Nevertheless, without a doubt it has claimed more poetry, scientific writings, recordings, and myths than any other constellation. The themes expressed for the Pleiades vary from "a Narrow Cloudy Train of Female Stars," as described by Manilius,[33] to the Chinese "Seven Sisters of Industry,"[34] to the children of Atlas, or seven doves who take ambrosia to the infant Zeus,[35] the seven daughters of Pleione,[36] and even a Hen with her Chickens.[37] The Pleiades were also a major calendar pivot point, their heliacal rising and setting being the official beginning, and later the ending, of a season. In Babylon the heliacal rising heralded the beginning of the new year.[38] This grouping of stars seems also to be linked by the Celts to the Fates, as an old oral custom forbade women to sew on the days when the Pleiades were either the heliacal or acronychal (first star to rise in the east after sunset) rising—just in case they broke their thread and accidentally snapped the thread of life for the human race.

The Celts also used the acronychal rising of the Pleiades to mark their month of mourning for dead friends. Prayers for the dead were said on the first day of what we now know as November. This custom is still echoed today with All Hallows Eve (October 31), All Saints Day (November 1), and All Souls Day

---

[33] Allen, *Star Names*, p. 391.

[34] Allen, *Star Names*, p. 393.

[35] Gertrude and James Jobes, *Outer Space: Myths, Name Meanings, Calendars* (New York: Scarecrow Press, 1964), p. 337.

[36] Jobes, *Outer Space*, p. 338.

[37] Allen, *Star Names*, p. 399.

[38] Walker, *The Woman's Encyclopedia of Myths and Secrets*, p. 803.

(November 2),[39] still celebrated as the feast days of the dead, and reflected also in Remembrance Day (Veterans Day in the U.S.), November 11, the day given to the mourning of the dead of World War I.

To pre-Vedic India they were the seven mothers who judged men and sometimes wounded them with moon-shaped razors. To the Egyptians they were seven goddesses whom the dead had to encounter and by whom they had to be judged.[40] Under the Greeks, the Pleiades were part of an early cult of Aphrodite, who gave birth to seven daughters and turned them into a flock of doves that became the seven stars of the Pleiades. The leader of these doves was a dove-goddess, Alcyone, who was said to bring good weather for the planting season.[41] The seven visible stars of the Pleiades were also seen as a smaller version of the great She-Bear goddess, Ursa Major, with her seven stars.[42]

STARS OF THE PLEIADES

The main star of the Pleiades is Alcyone, the other named stars being Maia, Electra, Merope, Taygete, Celaeno and Sterope.

ALCYONE

(Eta Taurus. Magnitude 3.0. RA 03:37:10.9". Declination 24N05'17". PED = 29° Taurus 18'.) See Paran Map 40, page 239. *An example of how to read the map:* If you were born in Brest, France, at a latitude of 48° North, then the star rose at about 18° Taurus. If you have a planet at either 18° Taurus or Scorpio, then that planet rose or set with the star. The star also set at 4° Gemini. Therefore, if you have a planet at 4° Gemini or Sagittarius it would have set or risen as the star set. The star culminates at 3° Gemini so if you have a planet at either 3° Gemini or Sagittarius, then it culminated or was on the Nadir as the star culminated.

At this latitude of 48° North the star has a phase of curtailed passage. This period will be from about November 9 (reading the date from the right-hand column of the date box next to 18° Taurus) to November 26 every year (reading the right-hand column of the date box next to 4° Gemini), and is the true or cosmic heliacal rising star about May 5 (reading the date for the rising line at 48° North in the "heliacal rising" column).

Alcyone can be used on all four points for charts between latitudes of 66° South and 66° North. South of that the star never rises, north of that the star never sets and therefore has permanent curtailed passage.

---

[39] Jobes, *Outer Space*, p. 338.
[40] Walker, *The Woman's Encyclopedia of Myths and Secrets*, p. 803.
[41] Walker, *The Woman's Encyclopedia of Myths and Secrets*, p. 804.
[42] Jobes, *Outer Space*, p. 337.

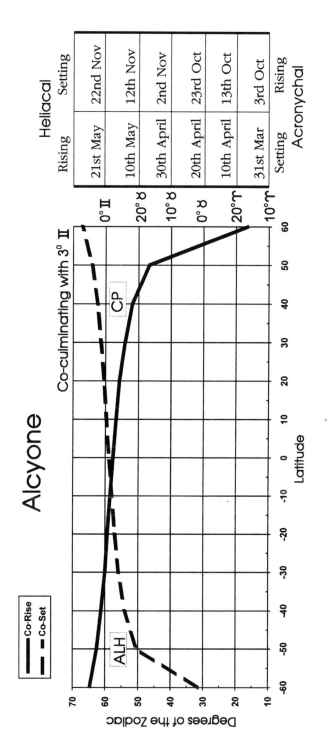

Paran Map 40. Alcyone.

EARLIER OPINIONS

Ptolemy states that the nature of the stars in the Pleiades is similar to that of the Moon and Mars. Robson does not view them favorably, seeing the stars as wanton, ambitious, and causing turbulence, and suggests they are linked to blindness. Ebertin talks of honor and glory but also warns quite strongly of eyesight problems, possibly even blindness. Rigor basically agrees with Robson and Ebertin.

ALCYONE: THE CONCEPT

All clusters in astrology traditionally cause eye problems or blindness. Lilly, in *Christian Astrology*, states that the eyes will be affected if certain parts of a chart are connected to different nebulae, and lists the Pleiades and Facies in Sagittarius as some of the culprits.[43] Yet historically they can well mean the exact opposite. Facies was named the face of the Archer or the Archer's eye,[44] and these types of star clusters were often used as eyesight tests for archers, since someone with bad eyesight would only have been able to see the nebula as a blurry fuzz. It is possible that nebulae could also relate to the seeking of inner vision, or third eye, rather than literal blindness. In my practice I have never felt on safe ground predicting eyesight problems with the placement of a nebula in the chart. However, I have found that the client will have a very strong desire to seek inner knowledge, and in a few cases the client has actually discussed the concept of a third eye.

In addition to Alcyone's links to vision, physical or mystical, there is also a strong connection to the Fates and the judgment of the dead, bringing in a ruthlessness when dealing with those who have not fulfilled necessary requirements, a potential for ruthlessness or judgmental anger. In working with this star, then, look past the doves of the Greeks.

Sigmund Freud was born on the day that Alcyone culminated with Mercury. The insightful but at times judgmental energy of Alcyone was linked to Freud's ideas and writings, indicating that he had great insights into his chosen subject. The star culminating means this inner vision and insight was expressed in his adulthood, the prime of his life.

ALCYONE IN THE NATAL CHART

If you have Alcyone contacts in your natal chart, there will be a sense of vision or insight via the planet with which it is involved, with a caution against making rash judgements or being narrow-minded to the point of becoming blind to the obvious. You have the potential for real insight and understanding, so it is important that you do not use this to make harsh judgments.

---

[43] William Lilly, *Christian Astrology* (London: Regulus Publishing, 1985), p. 581.
[44] Allen, *Star Names*, p. 359.

ALCYONE AS THE HELIACAL RISING STAR AT BIRTH

Alcyone is at its most powerful expression in this position and indicates that strong spiritual and visionary skills are connected to the chart. If this is part of your chart, it will imply that your very sense of personal identity is intertwined with these artistic, visionary, but judgmental characteristics. Alcyone is not cited by Ptolemy as the apparent rising star but history tells us that it did fulfil this role.

There are two contrasting examples of Alcyone in this position. The first is Jim Jones, the spiritual leader who led his flock of over five hundred followers to mass suicide in Guyana. He was born on the day of the cosmic rising of Alcyone. Here is an example of spiritual vision turned judgmental and ruthless. The second example is Leonardo da Vinci, born on the apparent heliacal rising, and in his inventions and art we experience the visionary nature of the star.

THE HYADES

The Hyades are a small group of six to seven visible stars which seem to cloud the forehead of Taurus. They are located so close to Aldebaran that they will generally be rising and setting in the same degrees as that royal star. For this reason there is no separate paran map for the Hyades. Of the stars themselves there seems to be no astrological significance. However, the nebula as a whole holds a considerable amount of mythology.

The main star is named El Nath, the Butting One,[45] located at the base of the north horn and a different star from the El Nath situated at the tip of the horn, referred to earlier. Heavily represented in ancient literature, this cluster is one of the few stellar objects mentioned by Homer. The Hyades seems to be linked with rain, water, and storms, most likely because, in classical times, their heliacal rising occurred in late November or early December, the beginning of winter.[46] The word *hyades* is a form of the Greek (hydor) for rain or water. The Greeks also saw them as daughters of Atlas and teachers of the infant Dionysus, the heir to Zeus' throne, raised into the heavens in appreciation.[47] In China they were worshipped as Yu Shi, the ruler of rain,[48] even though their wet season did not correspond to their rising. The Hyades embodies the concept of all things related to water, as this is its constant symbolism throughout the ancient world.

However, the Babylonians called this cluster the Jaws of the Bull, because in their creation epic it represented the jawbone used like a boomerang by Marduk

---

[45] Allen, *Star Names*, p. 390.
[46] Allen, *Star Names*, p. 387.
[47] Jobes, *Outer Space*, p. 323.
[48] Jobes, *Outer Space*, p. 325.

to destroy heavenly monsters.[49] The Pleiades were thought of as a net[50] that could catch monsters or enemies, and the Hyades were the great weapon of the gods used to kill monsters. In a remake of the story of the Babylonian Marduk, the biblical figure Samson used the weapon of the Hyades to kill the Philistines.[51]

Aldebaran is considered to be the *lucida*, or bright star, of The Hyades.[52] Lilly's claim that the Hyades rising or culminating in a chart implies military honor[53] is more than likely a confusion by that author, or earlier authors who were Lilly's sources, between the royal star Aldebaran, which has strong connections to military figures, and the actual nebula itself.

---

[49] De Santillana and von Dechend, *Hamlet's Mill*, p. 166.

[50] The story of Hephaestus catching Venus and Mars in a net so he could mockingly display them to the other gods is more than likely a myth-history of a Venus-Mars conjunction in the Pleiades.

[51] De Santillana and von Dechend, *Hamlet's Mill*, p. 166.

[52] Jobes, *Outer Space*, p. 323.

[53] Lilly, *Christian Astrology*, p. 620.

GEMINI, THE TWINS

KNOWN AS THE TWINS IN MOST ANCIENT writings, these two companion stars and their resulting constellation embody for the human psyche the wonder of twins.

Dylan and Lleu, twin powers of dark and light, were born from Arianhrod, the Celtic goddess of the Star Wheel.[54] Ahura Mazda[55] and Ahriman were god and devil, born simultaneously from Zurvan's womb.[56] In the Bible the twins are Cain and Abel. For the Egyptians, the god of the morning star and light was Horus, and the god of the evening star was his evil brother, Set,[57] who represented darkness. Set was also connected to the never-setting circumpolar stars that the Egyptians considered to be the realm of the female Hippopotamus, wife of Set, constellations we now know as Ursa Major, Minor and Draco.[58] Thus the ancient Egyptian conflict of Horus/Osiris and Set can be seen as the struggle of the god to overcome the goddess, or the light to overcome the dark, which is the dawn extinguishing the light of the circumpolar stars.[59]

The Greeks also applied the concepts of the morning and evening with their twins, Castor and Pollux. Castor was connected to the morning star and was the horseman; Pollux, the boxer, was connected to the evening star and was associated with thieves and darkness.[60] Thus Castor was of the light and Pollux was of the dark.

Twins represent the concept of polarity: where there is light there is dark; for every push forward there is a step that also has to be taken backward. The larger the positive effect, the greater the shadow with which one has to deal. As Jungian analyst Robert Johnson says,

> We all are born whole and, let us hope, will die whole. But somewhere early on our way, we eat one of the wonderful fruits of the tree of knowledge, and things separate into good and evil."[61]

---

[54] Green, *Dictionary of Celtic Myth and Legend* (London: Thames and Hudson, 1992), p. 34.

[55] Ahura Mazda is discussed in the section on the constellation Taurus. This god was also known as Ormazd.

[56] *New Larousse Encyclopedia of Mythology*, p. 315.

[57] Budge, *The Gods of the Egyptians*, vol. 2, p. 243.

[58] Lockyer, *The Dawn of Astronomy* (Kila, MT: Kessinger, 1992), p. 146.

[59] Lockyer, p. 151.

[60] Jobes, *Outer Space*, p. 179.

[61] Robert A. Johnson, *Owning Your Own Shadow* (San Francisco: HarperSanFrancisco, 1993), p. 4.

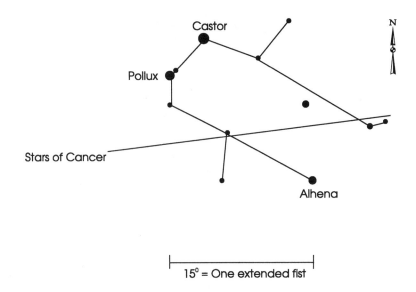

Star Map 19. Gemini, the Twins.

The human is a balance of behavior patterns, some placed on the side of what Johnson calls "civilization," and the others placed on the darker side of ourselves, the Shadow. No traits can be discarded and Johnson points out that if there is an indulgence of the civilized side, then the left, or shadow, will need expression also. This implies that if you have a success or a movement forward in your life, you will need to balance that with an adjustment to your shadow. You may project this onto another and see that person as evil or hateful, or you may recognize that you are dealing with your personal Set or Cain or Pollux. Your ability to understand your own shadowy twin is directly connected with your ability to become whole or holy.

The morning star was also known as Lucifer (light-bearer) and the evening star, Vespers (evening).[62] Lucifer's expulsion from heaven and into the whirlpool is possibly the mythological retelling of the slipping of Castor into southern declinations.

There are many paired stars in the heavens, each set implying a wholeness divided into two, the civilized and the shadow. Gemini, however, is the most well known heavenly pair.

---

[62] *The New Encyclopedia Britannica*, vol. 7, p. 542.

STARS OF GEMINI

Castor and Pollux are the two brightest stars, the twin of the light, Castor, being the alpha star. See Star Map 19, page 244. The other named stars, in descending order of magnitude, are: Alhena, in Pollux's heel; Wasat, in the middle of the constellation very close to the ecliptic; Mebsuta, Castor's knee; and Tejat, also known as Propus, the toe or front of Castor's left foot.

CASTOR

(Alpha Gemini. Magnitude 1.6. RA 07:34:15.8". Declination 31N53'52". PED = 19° Cancer 33'). See Paran Map 41, page 246. *An example of how to read the map:* If you were born in London, at a latitude of 51° North, then the star would never set. It would culminate at 21° Cancer, so if you have a planet at either 21° Cancer or Capricorn, then it culminated or was on the Nadir as the star culminated, but this would be the only way you could work with Castor at that latitude.

Castor can be used on all four points for charts between latitudes of 58° South and 58° North. South of that the star never rises, north of that the star never sets and therefore has permanent curtailed passage.

POLLUX

(Beta Gemini. Magnitude 1.2. RA 07:44:59.6". Declination 28N02'14". PED = 19° Cancer 33'.) See Paran Map 42, page 247. *An example of how to read the map:* If you were born in London, at a latitude of 51° North, then the star rose at about 12° Cancer. If you have a planet at either 12° Cancer or Capricorn, then that planet rose or set with the star. The star also set at 9° Leo. Therefore if you have a planet at 9° Leo or Aquarius, it would have set or risen as the star set. The star culminates at 23° Cancer so if you have a planet at either 23° Cancer or Capricorn, then it culminated or was on the Nadir as the star culminated.

At this latitude of 51° North the star has a phase of curtailed passage. This period will be from about January 2 (reading the date from the right-hand column of the date box next to 12° Cancer) to February 8 every year (reading the right-hand column of the date box next to 9° Leo), and is the true or cosmic heliacal rising star about July 4 (reading the date for the rising line at 51° North in the "heliacal rising" column).

Pollux can be used on all four points for charts between latitudes of 72° South and 72° North. South of that the star never rises, north of that the star never sets and therefore has permanent curtailed passage.

Castor

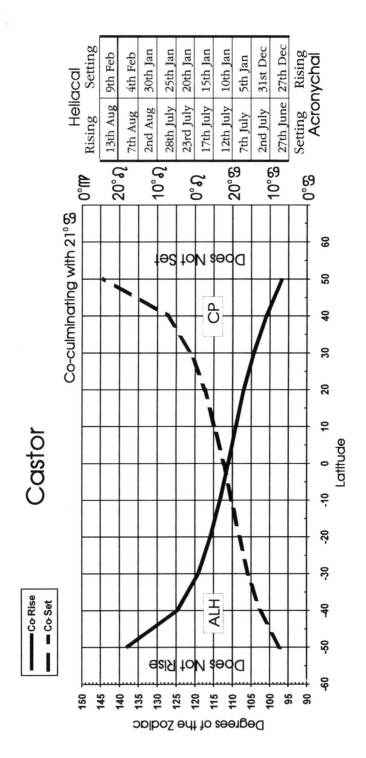

Heliacal		Co-culminating with 21° ♋
Rising	**Setting**	
13th Aug	9th Feb	0° ♍
7th Aug	4th Feb	20° ♌
2nd Aug	30th Jan	10° ♌
28th July	25th Jan	0° ♌
23rd July	20th Jan	20° ♋
17th July	15th Jan	
12th July	10th Jan	
7th July	5th Jan	10° ♋
2nd July	31st Dec	
27th June	27th Dec	0° ♋
Setting	**Rising**	
	Acronychal	

Co-Rise
Co-Set

Does Not Set

CP

ALH

Does Not Rise

Latitude

Degrees of the Zodiac

Paran Map 41. Castor.

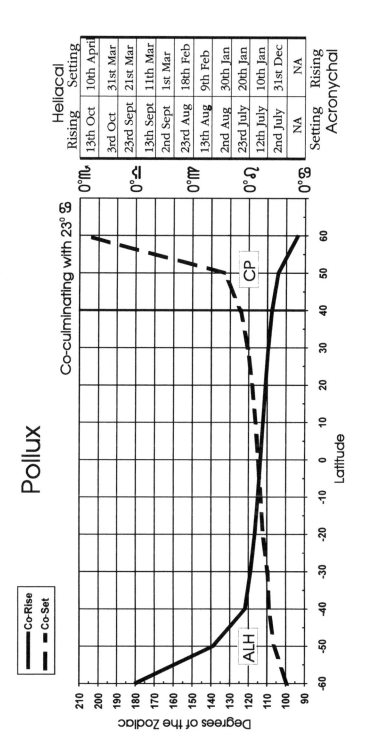

Paran Map 42. Pollux.

EARLIER OPINIONS

Ptolemy states that the star called Apollo (Castor) is like Mercury, with the star called Hercules (Pollux) of a nature similar to Mars. Robson says that Castor is linked to keen intellect and success in law and publishing, but warns that it is prone to violence, while Pollux is crafty, spirited, rash, and connected to poisons. Ebertin says that Castor is blessed with good manners, refinement, and excellent morals, while Pollux is the "wicked brother," brutish, violent, and cruel. Rigor states that Castor is violent and mischievous, while Pollux gives a love of sport, brave but possibly rash and cruel.

CASTOR AND POLLUX: THE CONCEPT

These two stars are twins and although it might be nice to split them into the good guy, Castor, and bad guy, Pollux, a more useful view is that their influence involves working with polarity. William Blake had Castor setting as his Saturn rose and he spoke about reconciling the two sides of himself, expressing this in his work. Robert Johnson quotes him as saying "that we should go to heaven for form and to hell for energy—and marry the two."[63]

In addition, it would seem that Castor and Pollux, while struggling with their polarities, produce writers. Apart from the poet and artist William Blake, a great many writers have either Castor or Pollux active in their charts: the novelist James Joyce, songwriter John Lennon, poet William Wordsworth, novelist Lewis Carroll, novelist George Eliot, poet Alfred, Lord Tennyson, and novelist Charles Dickens, to name but a few.

Castor and Pollux are probably not about writing itself, or the urge to write, but, rather, successful storytelling by one who has a knowledge of mixing good and evil, overlapping them until both are changed and whole. Writers who can do this will be successful. Again, Castor and Pollux are about the blending of opposites, the recognition of opposites, and the building of bridges between them.

Castor and Pollux, in true Gemini tradition, also provide us with a handy ruler in the sky. Because the two stars are exactly 4.5 degrees apart, they are used by seafarers as a guide for measuring angles and can be used by stargazers for calibrating hand and finger width, as described in Appendix A.

CASTOR AND POLLUX IN THE NATAL CHART

If only one of the pair are present in your chart, it will imply all of the above concepts but with a leaning toward that particular polarity. If Castor is the active star,

---

[63] Johnson, *Owning Your Own Shadow*, p. 38.

then you will seek the bright side of the story or situation. You are aware of the polarity but from the bright side of the subject. However, if Pollux is present, then there is the same awareness of opposites or polarity but now you will find yourself embroiled in the more shadowy side of the issues, with the pain or angst of the situation always seeming to be present. You seem to come at the issue from its problematic side.

CASTOR AND POLLUX AS THE HELIACAL RISING STAR AT BIRTH

Both stars can be used as the apparent, as well as the cosmic, rising star and if linked with the Sun in this manner, they will shape your identity so that your lifestyle, or the meaning of your life, will be a journey through a valley of polarities. There will be a driving need to seek out information or events and blend them into the pattern of your beliefs. You will be driven to explore polarities.

ALHENA

(Gamma Gemini. Magnitude 1.9. RA 06:34:48". Declination 16N27. PED = 8° Cancer 24'.). See Paran Map 43, page 250. *An example of how to read the map:* If you were born in Niagara Falls, Canada, at a latitude of 43° North, then the star rose at about 14° Cancer. If you have a planet at either 14° Cancer or Capricorn, then that planet rose or set with the star. The star also set at 2° Cancer. Therefore, if you have a planet at 2° Cancer or Capricorn, it would have set or risen as the star set. The star culminates at 13° Cancer so if you have a planet at either 13° Cancer or Capricorn, then it culminated or was on the Nadir as the star culminated.

At this latitude of 43° North the star has a phase of arising and lying hidden. This period will be from about June 23 (reading the date from the left-hand column of the date box next to 2° Cancer) to July 6 every year (reading the left-hand column of the date box next to 14° Cancer), and is the true or cosmic heliacal rising star about July 6 (reading the date for the rising line at 43° North in the "heliacal rising" column).

Alhena can be used on all four points for charts for all latitudes except for the polar regions.

EARLIER OPINIONS

Ptolemy states that the stars in the feet of Gemini have the nature of Mercury and some of Venus. Robson states that they are artistically inclined, but there is

Alhena

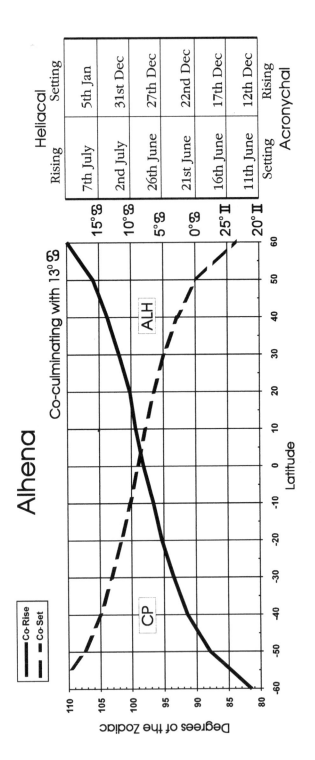

Heliacal	
Rising	Setting
7th July	5th Jan
2nd July	31st Dec
26th June	27th Dec
21st June	22nd Dec
16th June	17th Dec
11th June	12th Dec
Setting	Rising
Acronychal	

15° ♋
10° ♋
5° ♋
0° ♋
25° ♊
20° ♊

Co-culminating with 13° ♋

ALH

CP

Co-Rise
Co-Set

Degrees of the Zodiac

Latitude

Paran Map 43. Alhena.

danger of injuries to the feet. Ebertin sees this star as having a spiritual, along with artistic or scientific, influence. Rigor does not mention the star.

ALHENA: THE CONCEPT

The original or earliest name recorded for this star is Arabian,[64] the Proudly Marching One. They also called it The Mark, or Brand, referring to the brand on the side or neck of the camel.[65]

The tradition of the god with the wounded heel seems to come from the Egyptian belief that at the solstice and equinox, the Sun god touched and rested on the Earth, thus connecting himself to the physical world. But, as the physical world was considered to be impure,[66] he wounded his heel in the process. So Alhena represents the heel of an immortal or sacred one who touches the Earth. The name of Proudly Marching One sits well with Alhena, as the star of movement and determination. In another way it can also be linked with the Mark of Cain. Cain is the one who defied the system and was thus allowed to live. Cain defied god and murdered his perfect, obedient brother, yet the Lord's punishment was to send Cain out into the world to breed. He was marked so that no one would hurt him. Cain became a very important piece of "livestock," from whom, the Old Testament says, we are all descended.[67]

Alhena was culminating as Mars rose on the day and in the place that Nelson Mandela was born. Born into an apartheid South Africa, he fought for years for the rights of black South Africans, and although he spent many years in prison, he never lost sight of his mission. Eventually, in 1995 he was appointed the first South African president under their new anti-apartheid constitution. Alhena is not the only star active in his chart but what Alhena gives to his Mars is unshakeable determination and pride, the sort of pride that can eventually win through great adversity.

James Cook, the famous British naval captain, navigator, and explorer, was born with Alhena setting as his Mars rose. With the star setting its expression should be seen in the latter part of his life or seen as his life's work. Cook was renowned for opening up the New World, as well as charting unknown areas from the shores of Canada to the ice fields of the Antarctic. Cook was killed on a Hawaiian island while trying to find the elusive northeast passage between the Pacific and the Atlantic. He was the never-satisfied explorer who had very strong ideas of how seamen should be treated, and his paper on the prevention of scurvy was awarded high honors from the Royal Society in England. He also laid down

---

[64] Allen, *Star Names*, p. 234.
[65] Jobes, *Outer Space*, p. 297.
[66] Jobes, *Outer Space*, p. 239.
[67] Genesis 4: 17–26.

new standards on seamanship, cartography, and how to deal with native populations. It is said of him that "he had peacefully changed the map of the world more than any other single man in history."[68]

ALHENA IN THE NATAL CHART

To have Alhena in your chart it to have a cause to follow, a belief for which you will march. This marching may hurt you at times, but the difficulties that it causes you will be considered small in return for the goals you are trying to achieve. These goals may have physical expression or they may be linked to intellectual ideals, depending on the way Alhena connects with your chart.

ALHENA AS THE HELIACAL RISING STAR AT BIRTH

This is not one of the stars cited by Ptolemy as potentially heralding the dawn. However, it can still be used as the cosmic rising star. In this position in your chart, your personal identity is tied to the energy of pride and determination. This indicates that you are very focused, very driven, and should be able to achieve. Arrogance may shadow these abilities, however, as you may feel that you have a divine right to reform or correct situations.

---

[68] *The New Encyclopedia Britannica*, vol. 3, p. 597.

CANCER, THE CRAB

AROUND THE TIME 4000 B.C.E., THE HELIACAL rising stars for the solstice were still the stars of Leo, giving the Sun rulership of this summer sign. However, by about 2000 B.C.E. the stars of Cancer had assumed this role, and although they were faint and dim, they were an important grouping that had to be acknowledged. It was here that the Sun, having reached its southernmost point of rising on the horizon, would turn on its path and begin its journey northward. It was the Chaldeans who officially linked this constellation to the Crab, apparently because of this sideways movement of the Sun as it entered this constellation.[69] See Star Map 20, below.

The Egyptians, however, linked the constellation to the Scarab Beetle (see figure 21, p. 254), a symbol of immortality, rising from the dead and settling "upon the empty throne in the boat of Ra,"[70] a place where the Sun god was born again. This may well be the source for the later belief that this group of stars was the source of all life and a portal, the place where human souls entered into the Earth's material realms. In contrast, the stars of Capricorn, the winter solstice, were seen as the place of departure or death.[71]

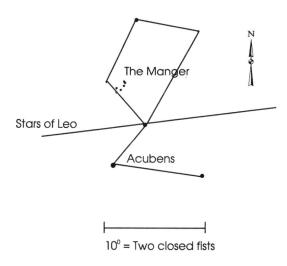

Star Map 20. Cancer, the Crab.

[69] Jobes, *Outer Space*, p. 131.

[70] Budge, *The Gods of the Egyptians*, vol. 1, p. 356. To the Egyptian mind, when the Sun rose with a certain constellation at the equinox it was described as being in the Boat of Ra. Any reference to an empty throne indicates that an age has changed and a new god or energy will come and rule the heavens.

[71] De Santillana and von Dechend, *Hamlet's Mill*, p. 242.

Figure 21. The scarab beetle, the Egyptian hieroglyph for resurrection and life.

Later Greek mythology had Dionysus, driven mad by the heat of the Sun, taken across a marsh by two asses whom he rewarded by placing them as an asterism in this constellation. Many years later this same theme was repeated by the Christians, who called this constellation the Manger and the Two Asses, symbolizing the nativity scene of Christian mythology.[72]

As time passed, and this faint constellation no longer heralded the summer solstice, the importance of the Crab and its mythology faded. From its role as the important Gateway of Souls, giver of all life, it became a crab the Greeks said was sent by Hera to help the Hydra who was in mortal combat with Hercules.[73] Hercules crushed the crab and Hera, in thanks for the crab's obedience, placed it in the heavens. The allocation of the crab to such a sacred place implies that the Greek myth was a vestige of a story about a crab or scarab beetle of far greater stature. If we remove the Greek myth, and the Christian overlay about the holy manger, we return to the concept of the scarab beetle, the symbol of life and resurrection. To the Egyptians this was the third form of the Sun god Ra, known as Khepera, who in their creation myths was the force rising from the primeval water, Nu, and the source of all life.[74] The stars of Cancer, therefore, are linked to the concept of life. One may travel through death but one is born again via these faint but important stars. Truly, in this sense, the stars of Cancer are the cradle of life.

Stars of Cancer

The brightest star of Cancer is Acubens, on the claws, the other named stars being: Asellus Borealis and Asellus Australis, the northern and southern donkeys; The Manger, sometimes called the Beehive or Praesepe, a nebula on the head of the crab; and Tegmine, at the base of the shell.

---

[72] Allen, *Star Names*, p. 109.
[73] Grimal, *Classical Mythology*, p. 197.
[74] Budge, *The Gods of the Egyptians*, vol. 1, p. 355.

ACUBENS

(Alpha Cancer. Magnitude 4.4. RA 08:59'. Declination 11N51'. PED = 12° Leo 57'.). See Paran Map 44, page 256. *An example of how to read the map:* If you were born in Budapest, Hungary, at a latitude of 47° North, then the star rose at about 17° Leo. If you have a planet at either 17° Leo or Aquarius, then that planet rose or set with the star. The star also set at 4° Leo. Therefore, if you have a planet at 4° Leo or Aquarius, it would have set or risen as the star set. The star culminates at 12° Leo so if you have a planet at either 12° Leo or Aquarius, then it culminated or was on the Nadir as the star culminated.

At this latitude of 47° North the star has a phase of arising and lying hidden. This period will be from about July 26 (reading the date from the left-hand column of the date box next to 4° Leo) to August 9 every year (reading the left-hand column of the date box next to 17° Leo), and is the true or cosmic heliacal rising star about August 9 (reading the date for the rising line at 47° North in the "heliacal rising" column).

Acubens can be used on all four points for charts for all latitudes except for the extremities of the poles.

EARLIER OPINIONS

Ptolemy states that the stars of the claws of Cancer are of the nature of Saturn and Mercury. Robson indicates that the star is connected to liars and criminals. Ebertin does not list the star. Rigor reads Saturn-Mercury in a more positive light and associates Acubens with a logical mind, strength, perseverance and good organization.

ACUBENS: THE CONCEPT

Acubens is the alpha star of Cancer and therefore it might well carry the symbolism of the scarab beetle of Egypt, linking the star to the ability to come through difficult circumstances. Resurrection is the key concept and it may translate to a certain perseverance which does not clash with Ptolemy's Saturn-Mercury combination. However, the star is far more than just perseverance. This star is linked with the energy of giving life, the gateway of life.

Pope John Paul II has Acubens culminating with his Jupiter, indicating that his lifework has to do with the laws of life, the laws of the teaching of resurrection. He is not the only pope who has been involved with this star. However, another face to this concept of resurrection is present in the chart of Michelangelo. He had Acubens and Pollux (the beta star of Gemini, which indicates creativity but via the shadowy or more painful path) both setting as his Neptune culmi-

Acubens

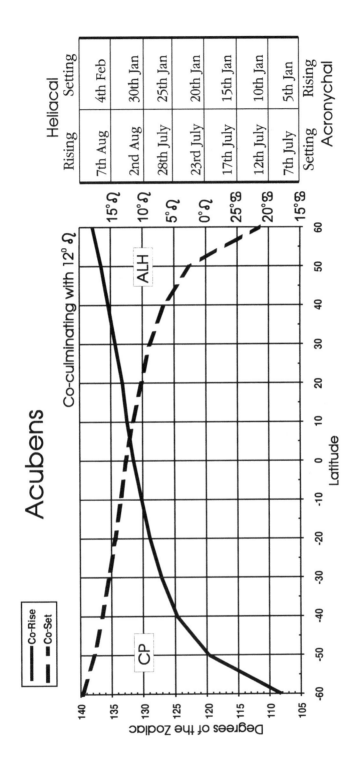

Heliacal	
Rising	Setting
7th Aug	4th Feb
2nd Aug	30th Jan
28th July	25th Jan
23rd July	20th Jan
17th July	15th Jan
12th July	10th Jan
7th July	5th Jan
Setting	Rising
Acronychal	

Co-culminating with 12° ♌

ALH

CP

Co-Rise
Co-Set

Degrees of the Zodiac

Latitude

15° ♌
10° ♌
5° ♌
0° ♌
25° ♋
20° ♋
15° ♋

Paran Map 44. Acubens.

nated. Generally such statements are generational and belong to the collective rather than being personal, but the Sistine Chapel and its representation of the Last Judgment and thus the resurrection of all souls was a major artistic statement made by Michelangelo on behalf of the collective. Here is the combined energy of both Acubens and Pollux, the sense or knowledge of resurrection linked with a creative drive. A marked contrast to this is the cult leader, Jim Jones, who convinced all his followers to commit suicide in the hope of a better life. He had Acubens rising with his Mars, while at the same time Capulus (the nebula in the sword of Perseus, male aggression and violence) was culminating. It is Capulus and Mars that indicate the violent nature of his actions. However, it is the presence of Acubens which gives this violence its resurrectional, religious twist of leading people to their deaths in hope for a better life in "Heaven."

ACUBENS IN THE NATAL CHART

By itself Acubens is not a star with a strong presence. It may well sit quietly in your chart, shaping some of your spiritual attitudes and giving you a sense or belief in the concepts of resurrection, either religiously or in the form of an optimistic outlook on life; to survive at all cost. You may be involved with the bringing in of new life, or with helping in the process of death. The expression will depend greatly on how the star is present in your chart.

ACUBENS AS THE HELIACAL RISING STAR AT BIRTH

Acubens is far too faint to herald the dawn, although it could be used as the cosmic rising star. If it is in this position, the star will be linked to your very sense of self, how you see yourself, how you define yourself. So a love of life and a respect for life on a spiritual or biological level will hold a strong position in your beliefs and may well be the major driving force in your life.

THE MANGER

(RA 08:41'. Declination 19N39'.) This is a faint nebula which was seen in ancient times as the cradle of life, the point where life emerged. It was also called the Crib.[75] Aratus, however, links it to predictions of rain saying that, when dim in the sky, it is an indication of a storm approaching.[76] Most fixed stars have some form of weather prediction linked to them for the obvious reason that at any given location their positions in the sky are fixed in relationship to the seasons. On February 1, 1953, the Netherlands experienced their worst storms and

---

[75] Allen, *Star Names*, p. 113.
[76] A. W. and G. R. Mair, *Callimachus, Lycophron, Aratus* (Cambridge: Harvard University Press, 1989), p. 277.

flooding since 1421. During that period, at that latitude, Pluto was rising with Acubens (and therefore with the Manger), as Achernar (the major star of Eridanus the River) was culminating. Achernar relates to fire and flood; its link, via Pluto's rising, with Acubens and the Manger gave the Netherlands their worst floods in over five hundred years.

LEO, THE LION

AROUND 6,000 TO 3,000 B.C.E., THE STARS of Leo were the heliacal rising stars of the summer solstice, linking this constellation with hot summers and the longest days. This connection, occurring during the dawn of writing, permanently linked Leo with the Sun. Recognized as a lion by the Persians, Syrians, Babylonians, and Egyptians, and then later by the Turks and the Jews,[77] this constellation seems to have been seen as a lion from the beginning of cultivation and civilization. See Star Map 21, page 260.

The earliest known use of the lion as a symbol appears to be Sekhmet, the sister form to Bast-Hathor of Egyptian mythology. She was a sphinx-lioness symbolizing wrathful destruction and an active aggressor against her father's enemies. She sat beside Ra and poured forth blazing fire that scorched and consumed his enemies, or else used fiery darts to strike them from afar.[78] At all times in Egyptian mythology the lion is linked to a goddess, aggressive, assertive, known by many titles and names, the "Lady of Flame" or "great lady, holy one, powerful one," for example.[79] The rank and status of this lion goddess is expressed in a vignette from the Egyptian *Book of the Dead*, chapter 164:

> . . . thou lady of red apparel, queen of the crowns of the South and North, only One, sovereign of her father, superior to whom the gods cannot be, thy mighty one of enchantment (words of power) in the Boat of Millions of Years . . .[80]

The Nile flooded in the period of Leo's heliacal rising, and so the life-giving waters of the Nile were also connected with the great fiery goddess. Thus she was called upon to protect the precious water in the same way that she would fight for her father. The goddess lion's head would often be sculpted on the irrigation gates that opened to allow the Nile into the fields.[81] In this manner the Egyptians saw the Lion as a guardian of water, a belief still echoed in fountains which use a lion's head as a font.

However, as Leo moved from its summer solstice position, and Egyptian culture declined, it started to lose its importance in the same manner as Cancer when it slipped from prominence. By 243 B.C.E. the lion had lost the tuft of its

---

[77] Allen, *Star Names*, p. 253.
[78] Budge, *The Gods of the Egyptians*, vol. 1, p. 515.
[79] Budge, *The Gods of the Egyptians*, vol. 1, p. 517.
[80] Budge, *The Gods of the Egyptians*, vol. 1, p. 518.
[81] Jobes, *Outer Space*, p. 194.

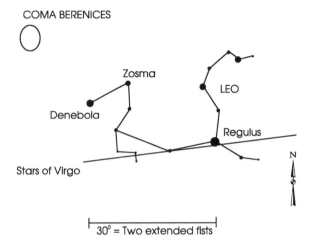

COMA BERENICES

Zosma

LEO

Denebola

Regulus

N

Stars of Virgo

30° = Two extended fists

Star Map 21. Leo, the Lion.

tail and this group of stars was redefined as Coma Berenices, with both the Egyptian and Greek cultures claiming creation of the event.[82]

The stars of the lion no longer claiming the important solstice position, the Greeks and Romans associated the constellation with the Nemean Lion that Hercules killed. The Nemean Lion was no ordinary beast but a grandchild of Gaia, Mother Earth, and the child of a destroying Moon goddess[83] (remnants of the destroying Sun goddess of the Egyptians, but by this period the Moon, not the Sun, was associated with the goddess). He was a giant, magical lion whose coat was impenetrable to the masculine weapons of sword or spear. In Greek mythology this lion had laid waste to the countryside around the town of Nemea. One of Hercules' labors was to kill this lion. After his weapons proved ineffective, he cornered the beast, wrapped his arms around its back and squeezed the lion to death.[84]

It is possible to think of the Nemean Lion (grandchild of Gaia) as a representative of the matrilineal culture, and its activities around the town of Nemea imply that the worship of the goddess, or practice of a non-Zeus-centered religion, was still active in that area. Hercules, whose main duty seemed to be to destroy all the symbols of older religions, was sent to rout these "pagans," in the same manner that the Christian Church in the Middle Ages killed nine million men and women, mostly in the countryside, because these people were supposed to believe in an older religion.

---

[82] Jobes, *Outer Space*, p. 195.
[83] Walker, *The Woman's Encyclopedia of Myths and Secrets*, p. 721.
[84] Grimal, *The Dictionary of Classical Mythology*, p. 197.

Later, the Romans imported the symbol of the lion into Britain, where it was portrayed on their coins as a lion led by a woman, once again an echo of the older Egyptian symbol of the lioness-goddess. They saw the Virgin and the Lion as two constellations, not only physically wed together but also mythologically. She was known in Britain as the "Lady who Ruled Lions," and became a symbol of the early divinity. By the end of the Dark Ages the lion was being used as a symbol of sovereignty in Britain, and by the twelfth century was the only animal shown on Anglo-Norman shields.[85] To the Christians this constellation was the lion who Daniel faced in his den.

STARS OF LEO

Regulus, the heart of the lion, is the brightest star, with other named stars, in descending order of magnitude: Denebola, in the tail; Algeiba, in the mane; and Zosma, on the back of the lion.

REGULUS

(Alpha Leo. Magnitude 1.3. RA 10:08:05". Declination 11N59'35". PED = 29° Leo 08'.) See Paran Map 45, page 262. *An example of how to read the map:* If you were born in Colombo, Brazil, at a latitude of 25° South, then the star rose at about 29° Leo. If you have a planet at either 29° Leo or Aquarius, then that planet rose or set with the star. The star also set at 0° Virgo. Therefore, if you have a planet at 0° Virgo or Pisces, it would have set or risen as the star set. The star culminates at 28° Leo so if you have a planet at either 28° Leo or Aquarius, then it culminated or was on the Nadir as the star culminated.

Because Regulus is located on the ecliptic, and rises and sets with approximately the same degree of the zodiac, it has no phases. In other words, for all but polar latitudes it will rise and set every day, never appearing not to rise or set. Its true heliacal rising will be around August 22 and its acronychal rising, rising as the Sun sets, well be six months later, about February 18.

Regulus can be used on all four points for charts of all latitudes except for the extremities of the poles.

EARLIER OPINIONS
Ptolemy states that the star in the heart of the Lion is like Mars and Jupiter. Robson links the star to violence and destructiveness, saying that the star may give honor

---

[85] Allen, *Star Names*, p. 254.

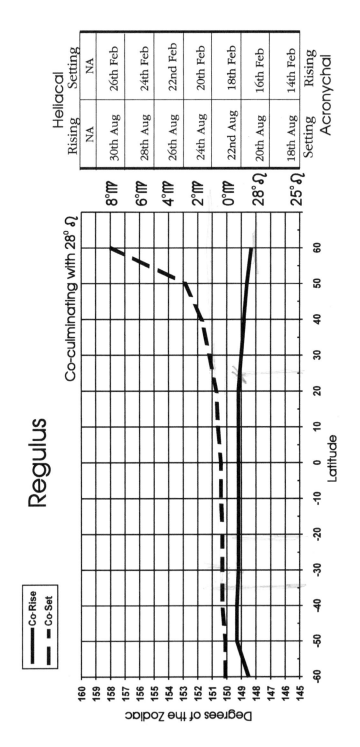

Regulus

	Heliacal	
	Rising	Setting
	NA	NA
8° ♍	30th Aug	26th Feb
6° ♍	28th Aug	24th Feb
4° ♍	26th Aug	22nd Feb
2° ♍	24th Aug	20th Feb
0° ♍	22nd Aug	18th Feb
28° ♌	20th Aug	16th Feb
25° ♌	18th Aug	14th Feb
	Setting	Rising
	Acronychal	

Co-culminating with 28° ♌

— Co-Rise
– – Co-Set

Latitude

Degrees of the Zodiac

Paran Map 45. Regulus.

but that it is short lived. Ebertin links the star to royal properties and a noble mind, frankness and courage. Rigor agrees with Robson, saying that the star gives the ability to command and to be successful but that any greatness suffers an "eclipse."

REGULUS: THE CONCEPT

As one of the Royal Stars of Perisa, this is one of the great historical stars of the sky. The Persians saw it as the Watcher in the North which was linked to their mythical king Feridun, who once, in their mythology, ruled the entire known world. He was a good and great king whose origins were similar to Zeus. Like Zeus he was raised apart from his family, suckled on a sacred cow, and in adulthood claimed the throne via a great battle. He is an image also very much like Osiris in Egyptian mythology: teaching; bringing peace and civilization; and giving laws to his people. In his old age he decided to divide his great kingdom among his three sons. The two oldest fell upon and murdered their younger brother in order to take his lands, and this act so grieved Feridun that he took revenge upon his two elder sons. The resulting battle was the end of his kingdom and the end of the golden days of Feridun.[86]

The importance of this story is that it shows us the myth behind the military honors and successes of Regulus. Like the other three Royal Stars, a person whose chart it affects can gain great success but only by facing a particular nemesis. For Regulus, this nemesis is revenge. You may gain a great deal of success in your chosen field but if you ever stoop to take revenge, then you lose power, position, and standing in the community.

Regulus indicates power and success and so is active in the charts of successful people. But the higher this star takes a person, the more they must guard against revenge. A modern leader who mirrored the story of Feridun was the long-running Labor Party prime minister of Australia, Bob Hawke. He has Regulus setting with his Mercury. After many years in office he was forced to retire because he had promised to "divide up his kingdom" with a younger man, his treasurer, Paul Keating. In his forced retirement he wrote his memoirs in which he took revenge on members of his own party. This revenge caused him to fall from grace, so where once he had a right to be seen as one of the great men of his party, he is now considered a weakened figure. Regulus's connection with his natal Mercury, and in the setting position, states that he will feel the desire to seek revenge in his old age via the spoken or written word, but it is also a warning that he will lose all power if he succumbs to this desire.

REGULUS IN THE NATAL CHART

Always strong and hot in nature, this star will make its presence felt in a chart. Much depends on how it connects to the chart, but its meaning will have to do

---

[86] *The New Larousse Encyclopedia of Mythology,* p. 323.

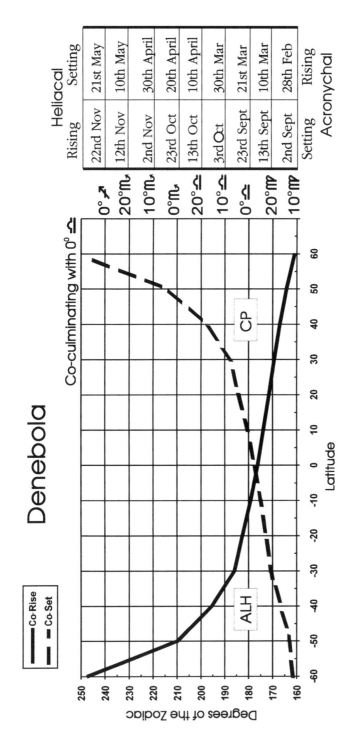

Paran Map 46. Denebola.

with the striking for success and the potential for ambitions to be fulfilled. However, at the same time it will suggest issues of revenge, always tempting and testing a person. If, out of anger or hurt, the person takes revenge, then as promised with all Royal Stars, there is a falling from grace. This temptation will occur at the time of life indicated by the angle[87] in the chart that Regulus has activated. If revenge is taken then there is a loss of what has been gained. This loss may be public or private.

REGULUS AS THE HELIACAL RISING STAR AT BIRTH

To be born with one of the Royal Stars in this position will put great strain on the rest of the chart, for you will be pushed to succeed, to shine, or to move forward in your life. This may fit well with the rest of your chart, in which case, you should step out, as success is yours. However, it may contradict other needs, in which case, by taking pride in small things, the deep pressure to shine that Regulus will apply to you can be eased. With Regulus in this position in your chart you should aim high but with the awareness of the danger of revenge. Regulus can be used as both the apparent and the cosmic rising star.

DENEBOLA

(Beta Leo. Magnitude 2.2. RA 11:48:46.8. Declination 14N36'10". PED = 20° Virgo 55'.) See Paran Map 46, page 264. *An example of how to read the map:* If you were born in Venice, Italy, at a latitude of 46° North, then the star rose at about 15° Virgo. If you have a planet at either 15° Virgo or Pisces, then that planet rose or set with the star. The star also set at 28° Libra. Therefore if you have a planet at 28° Libra or Aries, it would have set or risen as the star set. The star culminates at 0° Libra so if you have a planet at either 0° Libra or Aries, then it culminated or was on the Nadir as the star culminated.

At this latitude of 46° North the star has a phase of curtailed passage. This period will be from about March 5 (reading the date from the right-hand column of the date box next to 15° Virgo) to April 15 every year (reading the right-hand column of the date box next to 28° Libra), and is the true or cosmic heliacal rising star about September 7 (reading the date for the rising line at 46° North in the "heliacal rising" column).

Denebola can be used on all four points for charts between latitudes of 75° South and 75° North. South of that the star never rises, north of that the star never sets and therefore has permanent curtailed passage.

---

[87] The Ascendant signifying early life; the MC, the middle of life; and the Descendant, old age.

EARLIER OPINIONS

Ptolemy states that the stars in the tail of Leo are like Saturn and Venus. Robson links Denebola with swift judgment leading to despair and regrets, but also to nobility, daring, and self-control. Ebertin talks of this star indicating major catastrophes in mundane charts, and in a natal chart indicating exciting events which can be negative or positive. Rigor agrees with Robson almost word for word.

DENEBOLA: THE CONCEPT

Denebola seems to take on the symbolism of the Nemean Lion, for just as the Nemean Lion was possibly symbolic of the goddess worship still practiced in rural areas, this star indicates in some degree "being out of step" or being out of the mainstream of thought, not conforming, by living on the fringe.

Denebola was culminating as the Sun was rising on the day that George Eliot was born. She was a British novelist of the nineteenth-century who used a male pseudonym in her writing and went against all convention by living with a married man for many years. Leonardo da Vinci had Mercury rising as Denebola was setting. Leonardo invented flying machines four hundred years before the Wright brothers and is known in history (Denebola setting in his chart) as a man whose ideas (Mercury) were well ahead of his time. Another example is that of Henri de Toulouse-Lautrec, a famous nineteenth-century French artist who had Mars culminating as Denebola rose. In this case the star's energy was expressed in Lautrec's earlier life through the vehicle of Mars. In his childhood he had two separate accidents that broke both his left and right thighbones, respectively. These accidents left him a cripple, so he devoted his life to his art and became famous for his observations of Parisian society. Because of his childhood injuries, he played the role of the outsider looking in at the rich and flamboyant people of his day.

DENEBOLA IN THE NATAL CHART

Denebola adds an element of nonconformity, seeing the world differently in some way. This may have very good results leading to a great deal of success, but generally this success will be on the edge of the establishment, out of step with the main point of view. Or, it could be very negative, implying that you are not open to the views of the collective and tend toward dictatorial attitudes. More simply, you could find that you hold opinions different from others, which causes frustration. Awareness of this, and listening to other opinions, will be of benefit, not necessarily to change your mind but merely to enable you to understand other points of view.

DENEBOLA AS THE HELIACAL RISING STAR AT BIRTH

As one of the stars on Ptolemy's list Denebola can be used both as the apparent as well as the cosmic rising star. In either position, it will emphasize that you see the world differently from others and would be well advised to listen to them, particularly if your ideas might disturb other people. However, Denebola can also suggest an ability to discover or invent because you see the world through a different lens.

ZOSMA

(Delta Leo. Magnitude 2.6 RA 11:13:48.9". Declination 20N33'10". PED = 10° Virgo 37'.) See Paran Map 47, page 268. *An example of how to read the map:* If you were born in Saint George, Bermuda, at a latitude of 32° North, then the star rose at about 9° Virgo. If you have a planet at either 9° Virgo or Pisces, then that planet rose or set with the star. The star also set at 5° Libra. Therefore, if you have a planet at 5° Libra or Aries, it would have set or risen as the star set. The star culminates at 20° Virgo so if you have a planet at either 20° Virgo or Pisces, then it culminated or was on the Nadir as the star culminated.

At this latitude of 32° North the star has a phase of curtailed passage. This period will be from about February 26 (reading the date from the right-hand column of the date box next to 9° Virgo) to March 25 every year (reading the right-hand column of the date box next to 5° Libra), and is the true or cosmic heliacal rising star about September 1 (reading the date for the rising line at 32° North in the "heliacal rising" column).

Zosma can be used on all four points for charts between latitudes of 69° South and 69° North. South of that the star never rises, north of that the star never sets and therefore has permanent curtailed passage.

EARLIER OPINIONS

Ptolemy states that the stars in the Lion are of the nature of Saturn and Venus. Robson says Zosma's influence brings an alert mind but also unhappiness and fear of poison. Ebertin agrees with Robson and adds melancholy and illness. Rigor agrees with the above but also adds a love of life.

ZOSMA: THE CONCEPT

Zosma is the place on the back of the Nemean Lion where the latter was crushed by Hercules. This myth is a symbol of the point in Greek and Roman mythology where nonestablishment concepts or beliefs were extinguished. Its meaning is similar to the great Celtic myth of Macha (referred to in connection with Auriga the Charioteer), the Celtic marker in history of this transition of power from the feminine to the masculine, from one way of life to another. Zosma itself is not feminine but rather it belongs to those whom the establishment, either directly or indirectly, makes powerless. Generally it does not belong in the charts of the rich and famous, unless they become so victimized. It is present in the charts of

Zosma

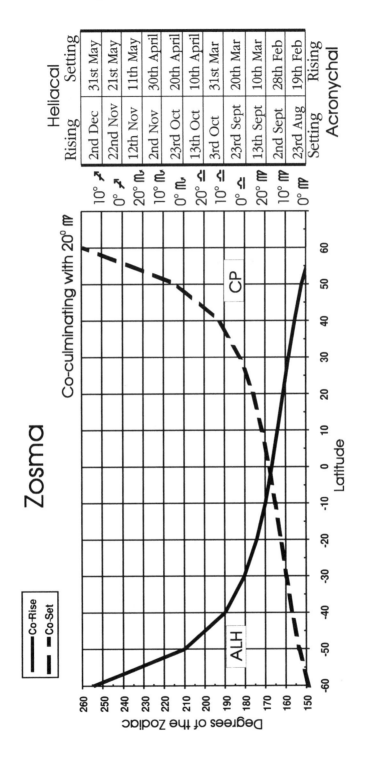

Co-culminating with 20° ♍

	Heliacal	
	Rising	Setting
10° ♐	2nd Dec	31st May
0° ♐	22nd Nov	21st May
20° ♏	12th Nov	11th May
10° ♏	2nd Nov	30th April
0° ♏	23rd Oct	20th April
20° ♎	13th Oct	10th April
10° ♎	3rd Oct	31st Mar
0° ♎	23rd Sept	20th Mar
20° ♍	13th Sept	10th Mar
10° ♍	2nd Sept	28th Feb
0° ♍	23rd Aug	19th Feb
	Setting	Rising
	Acronychal	

Legend: — Co-Rise - - Co-Set

Paran Map 47. Zosma.

victims, of people who are abused by the system. It is not an "evil" star, but its presence means that the particular planet with which it is connected will potentially be abused in some way.

John F. Kennedy had Zosma culminating with his Moon. The culmination implies that the star's energy will be expressed in the middle years of life, in Kennedy's prime. Its connection to his Moon, which is considered to be one of the most sensitive points for a fixed star,[88] links it to his emotional life; firstly, in his private life, and secondly, because he was the president of the United States, to his people. This star might have resulted in Kennedy putting effort into helping the victims of society, but his assassination shows he himself became the victim.

The fateful TWA flight of July 17, 1996, which exploded shortly after take-off from New York, occurred on the day, for that latitude, that Saturn rose as Zosma set and Facies (the nebula in the face of Sagittarius and one of the most violence-inducing stars in the sky) culminated. The combination of Zosma, Facies, and Saturn suggests lasting consequences (Saturn) of a violent act (Facies) against innocent people (Zosma), accidental or intentional.

Anastasia of Russia was also connected to Zosma; her Mars and Zosma culminated together. Whether she was murdered as a member of the czar's family during the Russian revolution, or whether she survived and lived to fight on for recognition, her life as a victim of society was totally dictated by Zosma.

ZOSMA IN THE NATAL CHART

The planet that is involved with Zosma will potentially involve suffering, perhaps through the person's naivete allowing them to be led into a victimizing situation, or perhaps by their working as a social worker or caregiver. This is not a star of glory and fame but rather of the invisible work of dealing with the victim in oneself or in others. Azaria Chamberlain, the infant who was taken by a dingo in the Australian desert and whose mother, Lindy Chamberlain, was accused of killing her, was born at the moment Zosma rose. Azaria's whole short life, and the events after her death, was dominated by this star.

ZOSMA AS THE HELIACAL RISING STAR AT BIRTH

Zosma can only be used as the cosmic rising star. It is a difficult placement, as your life will be intertwined with issues of minority group needs or victims of society. You, personally, may have to guard against being abused by the system. Or your beliefs or lifestyle may put you at a disadvantage and will become one of your life lessons. Mother Teresa was born on the cosmic rising of Zosma and indeed she devoted her life to helping the victims of society.

---

[88] Anonymous of 379, *The Treatise on the Bright Fixed Stars*, trans. Robert Schmidt (Berkeley Springs, WV: Golden Hind Press, 1994), p. 1.

VIRGO, THE VIRGIN

LOST IN ANTIQUITY AND MYTHOLOGICALLY
connected to Leo, the ancient goddess in the sky was probably part of the original six zodiac constellations[89] and is considered by some astronomers to be over 15,000 years old in human awareness[90] (which was about the time the spring equinox occurred in this constellation). See Star Map 22, page 271. The earliest expression of Virgo was about 2,900 B.C.E. with the construction of the Egyptian sphinx, believed to be a celebration and adoration of the two zodiac signs through which the sun traveled at the time of summer and the harvest. The sphinx had the head of the great harvest goddess and the body of a lion.[91] However, Lockyer, in the late 19th century, implied that the sphinx may be far older than this date.[92]

The Egyptians drew her on their Denderah zodiac, larger than she is now and with no wings but clearly a goddess. They saw her as the thousand-named goddess Isis, wife of the dead Osiris and mother of the god Horus.[93] She was seen as holding a wheat sheaf in her hand, which she dropped to form the Milky Way. She ruled the summer solstice about 5,000 B.C.E., when time began for the human race.[94] The Golden Age was said to have ended when this goddess no longer governed the solstices, for the Egyptians saw this shift in the constellation of the summer solstices as a crisis: they believed the goddess had left the earth to return to heaven in distress at the behavior of the humans of the Silver Age. The Milky Way, which was formed by the wheat dropping from the sheaf in her hand, is a piece of mythology reflecting the early belief that the Milky Way was the burned out passage of the Sun, before humans discovered precession.[95] For at that stage there was no reason to assume that the path of the precession of the equinox was defined by the ecliptic.

The early Arabs called her Al Adhra al Nathifah, the Innocent Maiden. She was also known as the Pure Virgin and the Chinese knew her as the Frigid Maiden, which seems to be an unkind literal translation from the Chinese. To the Greeks she was Demeter, goddess of the harvest, who withdrew herself and her seasons from the Earth when Pluto abducted her daughter. They also saw her as Erigone, a maiden who became so distressed at the ways of the human race that she hanged herself. By the time of Christianity she had become Mary holding the Child.[96]

---

[89] Norman J. Lockyer, *The Dawn of Astronomy* (Kila, MT: Kessinger, 1992), p. 404.
[90] Jobes, *Outer Space*, p. 272.
[91] Jobes, *Outer Space*, p. 274.
[92] Lockyer, *Dawn of Astronomy*, p. 83.
[93] Allen, *Star Names*, p. 462.
[94] De Santillana and von Dechend, *Hamlet's Mill*, p. 59.
[95] De Santillana and von Dechend, *Hamlet's Mill*, p. 245.
[96] Allen, *Star Names*, p. 464.

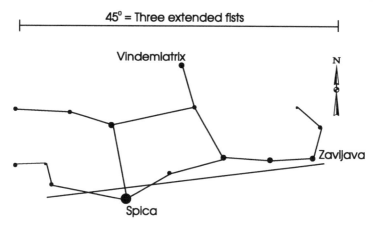

Star Map 22. Virgo, the Virgin.

Whatever image is chosen from across time and cultures, what is contained in Virgo is the archetype of the harvest-bringing goddess, pure and good, independent of the masculine. She gives the four seasons and is the source of the fertile Earth. Her emphasis at the time of harvest linked her to the gifts of the harvest and the cycles of the Earth, rather than the more worldly pursuits of commerce and trade. Her purity was reflected in the concept of virginity. However, the earliest forms of this goddess are not "virginal" in the modern sense of the word. The older meaning of virgin was a woman who owned her own body and was therefore free to love whomever she desired. Virgo is a fruitful, fertile goddess, not a virginal, innocent adolescent.[97]

STARS OF VIRGO

The brightest star of Virgo is Spica, with some other named stars, in descending order of magnitude: Zavijava, marking the top of the wing; and Vindemiatrix, in the arm.

SPICA

(Alpha Virgo. Magnitude 1.2. RA 20:39:25". Declination 11S08'. PED = 23° Libra 09'.) See Paran Map 48, page 272. *An example of how to read the map:* If

---

[97] Virgo also contains the 12th lunar mansion, known as Al-Simak, that originally contained the star Spica (see Allen, p. 467). Because of this bright star, this mansion was considered barren and later in astrology this concept was reflected over the whole tropical zodiac sign. However, the constellation of Virgo has always been linked with fertility.

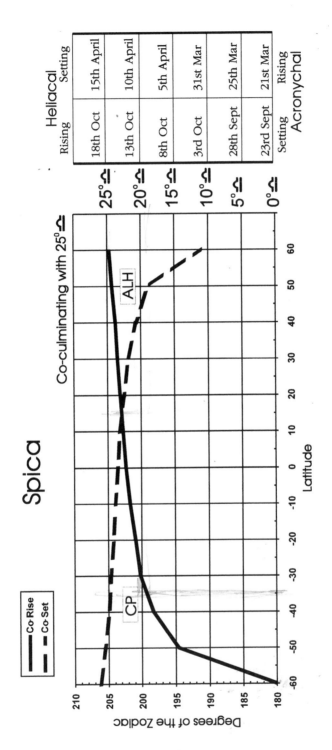

Paran Map 48. Spica.

you were born in Fuji, Japan, at a latitude of 35° North, then the star rose at about 24° Libra. If you have a planet at either 24° Libra or Aries, then that planet rose or set with the star. The star also set at 22° Libra. Therefore, if you have a planet at 22° Libra or Aries, it would have set or risen as the star set. The star culminates at 25° Libra so if you have a planet at either 25° Libra or Aries, then it culminated or was on the Nadir as the star culminated.

At this latitude of 35° North the star has a phase of arising and lying hidden. This period will be from about October 14 (reading the date from the left-hand column of the date box next to 22° Libra) to October 17 every year (reading the left-hand column of the date box next to 24° Libra), and is the true or cosmic heliacal rising star about October 17 (reading the date for the rising line at 35° North in the "heliacal rising" column).

Spica can be used on all four points for charts for all latitudes except for the extremities of the poles.

EARLIER OPINIONS

Ptolemy states that Spica resembles Venus, and Mars somewhat as well. Robson talks of the star giving honor and fame and links it to scientists, writers, painters, and musicians. Ebertin agrees with Robson, but also adds that the star can result in unfruitfulness and injustice for the innocent. Rigor, however, sees it as all positive.

SPICA: THE CONCEPT *Spica, the professional*

Seen as the wheat sheaf in the hand of the goddess, Spica was considered a symbol of her gifts to humankind. These gifts were originally harvest and bounty. The wheat sheaf, therefore, symbolized human knowledge of cultivation, a gift from the goddess. In present times this type of knowledge is not venerated, so if Virgo was created in the twentieth century, she might well be holding a silicon chip. Spica, the wheat sheaf, is the symbol of knowledge and insights which are respected. Spica is, therefore, not connected with any particular field or profession, but rather shows the potential for brilliance in whatever it touches in a chart.

Sir Isaac Newton, the great physicist and creator of calculus, was born at the moment that Spica was rising. In this position the brilliance of Spica affects his whole chart and his whole life. It represents how he is seen; it is part of his definition of himself. The Egyptians would say that he belonged to Spica, he was an embodiment of Spica. Many people are born with this star in that position and obviously they do not all have the scientific mind of Isaac Newton. Having a star in such a position does not guarantee success but it does indicate the possibility.

Wolfgang Amadeus Mozart had Spica culminating with his Jupiter, and his Sun set as Spica was on the Nadir. In this example, the culmination with Jupiter suggests a magnification of Spica, brilliance in the prime of life. Mozart is not just considered another composer, he is considered to be one of the greatest musical geniuses ever to have existed. The combination of Spica on the Nadir with his Sun insured that after his death his work would live on, for a star on the Nadir represents how a person is remembered after their death, and Spica on the Sun indicates that he will be seen as a brilliant composer.

SPICA IN THE NATAL CHART

Spica represents a gift of brilliance, a hidden or obvious talent, skill, or ability that is out of the ordinary. The word "gifted" applies to strong Spica people, and whatever this star touches, it will illuminate in some way. If you have Spica in your chart, consider the angle it is touching as well as the planet with which it is involved. The angle will give you the timing and the planet will indicate the style of the brilliance or gift that Spica holds in your chart.

SPICA AS THE HELIACAL RISING STAR AT BIRTH

Spica can be used as both the apparent and the cosmic rising star, and in this position can be the mark of a gifted person who truly does have something to contribute to the world. If Spica is supported by other strong, successful, fixed stars, then one is looking at fame and possibly even glory. If your Sun rose with Spica, then you can and should try to stretch yourself, as Spica is indicating that you have a talent or an insight that may be quite special.

VINDEMIATRIX

(Epsilon Virgo. Magnitude 3.3. RA 12 59'40". Declination 11N14'. PED = 9° Libra 15'.) See Paran Map 49, page 275. *An example of how to read the map:* If you were born in Durban, South Africa, at a latitude of 30° South, then the star rose at about 0° Scorpio. If you have a planet at either 0° Scorpio or Taurus, then that planet rose or set with the star. The star also set at 8° Libra. Therefore, if you have a planet at 8° Libra or Aries, it would have set or risen as the star set. The star culminates at 17° Libra so if you have a planet at either 17° Libra or Aries, then it culminated or was on the Nadir as the star culminated.

At this latitude of 30° South the star has a phase of arising and lying hidden. This period will be from about September 30 (reading the date from the left-hand column of the date box next to 8° Libra) to October 23 every year (reading the left-hand column of the date box next to 0° Scorpio), and is the true or cosmic heliacal rising star about October 23 (reading the date for the rising line at 30° South in the "heliacal rising" column).

Vindemiatrix can be used on all four points for charts for all latitudes except for the extremities of the poles.

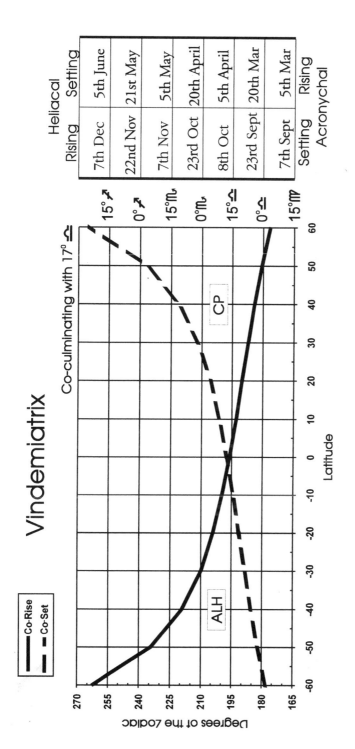

Vindemiatrix

Heliacal		
Rising	Setting	
7th Dec	5th June	
22nd Nov	21st May	
7th Nov	5th May	
23rd Oct	20th April	
8th Oct	5th April	
23rd Sept	20th Mar	
7th Sept	5th Mar	
Setting	Rising	
Acronychal		

Co-culminating with 17° ♎

CP

ALH

— Co-Rise
-- Co-Set

Degrees of the Zodiac

Latitude

15° ♐
0° ♐
15° ♏
0° ♏
15° ♎
0° ♎
15° ♍

Paran Map 49. Vindemiatrix.

EARLIER OPINIONS

Ptolemy states that this star is like Saturn and Mercury. Robson states that this star belongs to Libra, not Virgo, and that it is a most "evil" star, causing disgrace, stealing, wanton folly, and often causing natives to become widowers. Ebertin links it to mental concentration and says that it is good for architects and businessmen. Rigor agrees with Robson.

VINDEMIATRIX: THE CONCEPT

The name Vindemiatrix means Grape Gatherer, for it was said to be the heliacal rising signal to harvest the grapes. And even as precession removed Vindemiatrix from this important calendar date, the Greeks and Romans maintained her identity as the Grape Picker. The star, although dim in our time, was considered a major star by ancient writers and seems to have been recognized and named, possibly even before the formation of the zodiac.[98] Aratus refers to Vindemiatrix:

> Above both her shoulders at her right wing wheels a star, whereof the name is the Vintager—of such size and with such brightness set, as the star that shines beneath the tail of the Great Bear.[99]

It would seem that statements made by Robson and Rigor concerning the evil nature of the star are not supported in its history. Vindemiatrix no longer seems to hold its strength or power in our times, for not only has it dimmed in magnitude but also in effect. Vindemiatrix was connected with the time of harvest and therefore implies a time of action, a time to pick what one has sown. Marie Curie, the Polish-born French physicist who, along with her husband Pierre, discovered the new element radium and then managed to extract a small sample of it from hundreds of tons of pitchblende, was born with Mars, Saturn, and Mercury conjunct and setting with Vindemiatrix. She is generally remembered for her remarkable "harvest" of the new element.

VINDEMIATRIX IN THE NATAL CHART

This star will not force its mark onto your life, like the great Spica or one of the Royal Stars. However, it will show that you are a collector or gatherer. You will be action oriented, not in an Aries-Mars manner but in a gentler way, focused on taking the time to harvest what you have planted, to patiently collect the things that you like or need. Art collectors, stamp collectors, people who gather facts or things are expressions of this star.

---

[98] Allen, *Star Names*, p. 471.
[99] Mair, *Callimachus, Lycophron, Aratus*, p. 217.

VINDEMIATRIX AS THE HELIACAL RISING STAR AT BIRTH

Although not cited by Ptolemy as a herald of the dawn, historically this s
be used as both the apparent and the cosmic rising star. In this position in y
chart you will be able to make the most of your resources, as you will instinc-
tively gather and collect the things, facts, or people that you need to achieve your
goals. Gathering will be a major theme in your life.

IBRA, THE SCALES

THE CLAWS OF THE SCORPION BECAME
nd the time of the Greek and early Roman empires. Ara-
llation as the Claws of the Scorpion and called them "the
of light."[100] However, well before Aratus this part of the sky
t or lamp representing the Assyrian god Bir. Bir was known
as 1 a... d of fire or great light who was believed to be found among
these stars.[101] Other images picture the stars as a lamp held by the scorpion, a type
of light-and-dark symbol similar to the yin/yang symbol of the *I Ching*.

The Romans claimed they added this sign, bringing the number of the zodiac signs to twelve.[102] But it should be remembered that, from at least 2,000
B.C.E., there were twelve signs with one, Scorpio, broken into two parts: the Scorpion and the Claws of the Scorpion. The Romans saw Libra as a symbol of justice ruled by their goddess, Astraea (Virgo), who held the Scales in her hands.[103]
She is still used today to represent the law and courts. See Star Map 23, below.

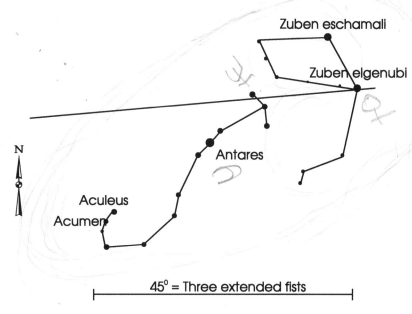

Star Map 23. The giant Scorpion, Libra and Scorpio.

[100] Mair, *Callimachus, Lycophron, Aratus*, p. 215.
[101] Jobes, *Outer Space*, p. 200.
[102] Allen, *Star Names*, p. 270.
[103] Allen, *Star Names*, p. 270.

A possible origin of the association of the scales of Libra with justice could be Babylonian and Egyptian theology, where the souls of the dead are weighed in a great scale. The Scorpion was seen as the gateway to the afterlife, which was then followed by the scales of judgment. Justice, death, final judgment: this is the essence of this part of the sky.

STARS OF LIBRA

Libra's brightest star is Zuben Elgenubi, the southern scale, with the other named stars, in descending order of magnitude: Zuben Eschamali, the northern scale; and Zuben Hakrabi, sometimes called Graffias, which lies on the tip of the northern scale.

ZUBEN ELGENUBI

(Alpha Libra. Magnitude 2.9. RA 14:50:35.3". Declination 16S01'09". PED = 14° Scorpio 23'.) See Paran Map 50, page 280. *An example of how to read the map:* If you were born in Antipolo, Philippines, at a latitude of 15° North, then the star rose at about 14° Scorpio. If you have a planet at either 14° Scorpio or Taurus, then that planet rose or set with the star. The star also set at 16° Scorpio. Therefore, if you have a planet at 16° Scorpio or Taurus, it would have set or risen as the star set. The star culminates at 15° Scorpio so if you have a planet at either 15° Scorpio or Taurus, then it culminated or was on the Nadir as the star culminated.

Because Zuben Elgenubi is located on the ecliptic and rises and sets with approximately the same degree of the zodiac, it has no phases. In other words, for all but polar latitudes, it will rise and set every day, never totally disappearing from the night sky. Its true heliacal rising will be around November 6 and its acronychal rising, rising as the Sun sets, well be six months later, about May 4.

Zuben Elgenubi can be used on all four points for charts between latitudes of 74° South and 74° North. South of that the star never rises, north of that the star never sets and therefore has permanent curtailed passage.

EARLIER OPINIONS
Ptolemy states that the stars "in the middle of the claws" are like Saturn and to a certain degree like Mars. Robson defines Zuben Elgenubi as causing malevolence, violence, disease, lying, and (among other things) danger from poison. Ebertin sees this as a negative star, particularly if one is born at night, and says it causes bad health but, along with its northern partner, gives immortality to one's name. Rigor agrees word for word with Robson.

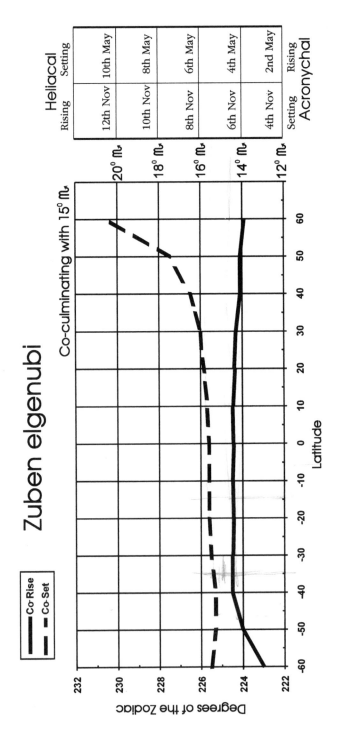

Zuben elgenubi

Co-Rise
Co-Set

Co-culminating with 15° ♏

	Heliacal	
	Rising	Setting
20° ♏	12th Nov	10th May
18° ♏	10th Nov	8th May
16° ♏	8th Nov	6th May
14° ♏	6th Nov	4th May
12° ♏	4th Nov	2nd May
	Setting	Rising
		Acronychal

Paran Map 50. Zuben elgenubi.

ZUBEN ESCHAMALI

(Beta Libra. Magnitude 2.7. RA 15:16:43.4. Declination 09S21'44". PED = 18° Scorpio 40'.) See Paran Map 51, page 282. *An example of how to read the map:* If you were born in Marseilles, France, at a latitude of 43° North, then the star rose at about 14° Scorpio. If you have a planet at either 14° Scorpio or Taurus, then that planet rose or set with the star. The star also set at 5° Sagittarius. Therefore, if you have a planet at 5° Sagittarius or Gemini, it would have set or risen as the star set. The star culminates at 21° Scorpio so if you have a planet at either 21° Scorpio or Taurus, then it culminated or was on the Nadir as the star culminated.

At this latitude of 43° North the star has a phase of curtailed passage. This period will be from about May 3 (reading the date from the right-hand column of the date box next to 14° Scorpio) to May 26 every year (reading the right-hand column of the date box next to 5° Sagittarius), and is the true or cosmic heliacal rising star about November 5 (reading the date for the rising line at 43° North in the "heliacal rising" column).

Zuben Eschamali can be used on all four points for charts for all latitudes except for the extremities of the poles.

EARLIER OPINIONS

Ptolemy states that the stars in the "the points of the claws" are like Jupiter and Mercury. Robson associates them with honor, distinction, and ambition, Ebertin agrees with Robson and sees the northern scale in a more positive light, regarding the whole constellation as a form of Gemini—a type of study in polarities—saying that Zuben Eschamali gives honor and distinction. Rigor adds to the list "psychic preferment."

ZUBEN ELGENUBI AND ZUBEN ESCHAMALI: THE CONCEPT

These stars are a pair and therefore have a common theme, with one star showing us the light, brighter side and the other showing the more shadowy side. These stars are strongly involved in social reform or social justice. The southern scale, Zuben Elgenubi, which is labeled as the negative star, seems, from my own research work, to bestow higher ideals than its northern partner. Zuben Elgenubi was active in the chart of Martin Luther King, culminating as his Sun rose. John Lennon had the star on his Nadir as his Saturn and Jupiter culminated. Abraham Lincoln had the star setting as his Moon culminated, and Karl Marx had the star setting as his Sun rose.

The supposedly blessed northern scale, on the other hand, although expressing itself as interest in social reform, seems to have a more direct and sometimes negative manifestation. Mao Tse-Tung had it setting with his Mars and Benito Mussolini had it setting when his Sun was at his nadir. Zuben Eschamali is

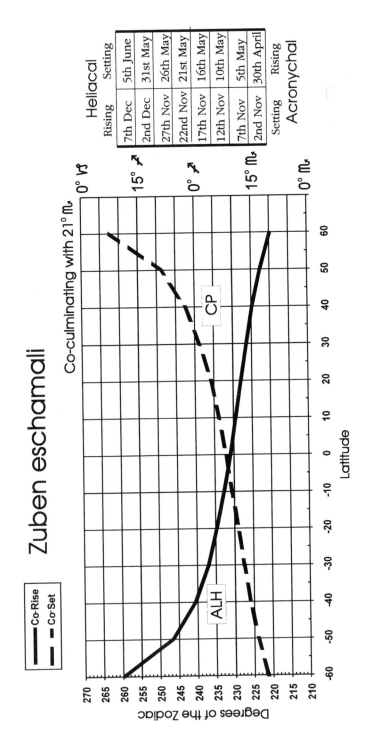

Paran Map 51. Zuben Eschamali.

not a negative star but it will show the more shadowy or material side of social reform or justice.

Zuben Elgenubi seems to differ from its partner in that its prime motive is not personal gain. This is the lighter side of the issue, the person who can be involved with reform and resist the temptation for personal gain or power. Zuben Eschamali can be just as effective in the community but will be connected to a strong personal gain or power motive. The local councillor who seeks to help his or her community, but also wants the status of being on the council, is a positive example of Zuben Eschamali. However, the councillor wanting the position in order to act in a corrupt way is a negative expression of the star.

ZUBEN ELGENUBI OR ZUBEN ESCHAMALI IN THE NATAL CHART

Either star will give a social orientation to the chart, indicating that you will want to be involved in groups, be they those of national reform, politics and the law, or simply a hobby or social group. The angle the star is on will indicate the time in your life when you will become so involved, and the natal planet will show you the style or nature of this involvement. Robert Graves, the author and mythologist, had Zuben Elgenubi culminating as his Mercury set, thus indicating that in the prime of his life he would use his Mercury in some way to aid society in an exploration of the mythology of many cultures.

ZUBEN ELGENUBI OR ZUBEN ESCHAMALI AS THE HELIACAL RISING STAR AT BIRTH

Both stars can be used as the apparent as well as the cosmic rising stars. Here, the need to be involved as a reformer with a project or a group will be very strong. If the star is Zuben Elgenubi, then these actions will involve sacrifice in some way, acts done for the joy of giving, whereas in the case of Zuben Eschamali you will have a more mercenary relationship to the project—you help it and it helps you.

SCORPIUS, THE SCORPION

SCORPIUS, KNOWN TO ASTROLOGERS AS the most southern constellation of the zodiac. It once contained the stars of ʟ.ora, known as the Claws of the Scorpion, and once the Scorpion lost its claws its contact with the ecliptic became minimal. See Star Map 23, p. 278. The Sun only spends nine days among the stars of Scorpius, the other twenty-one days among the stars of the constellation Ophiuchus, the Serpent Holder. Because of Scorpio's ancient claim to the Ring of Life, however, it may have lost its physical place on the ecliptic, but not its hold on the human imagination.

From 5,000 B.C.E. to approximately 1,000 B.C.E. in the northern hemisphere, the Sun was among the stars of the Great Scorpion, Scorpio, and Libra during the autumn equinox. As one of the signs of an equinox, it was considered one of the four gateways to the otherworld, a bringer of darkness, for as the Sun entered this constellation, it moved into the southern hemisphere and the dark part of the year began. Lockyer[104] links the constellation to the Babylonian myth of Marduk, the god of light, struggling to overcome Tiamat, a watery monster of darkness, and suggests that this myth shows the great antiquity of the sign. In Egyptian mythology the Sun was Horus/Osiris; the myth of the Scorpion killing Osiris and sending him to his midwinter death only to be reborn again in the form of Horus, is a myth describing the annual journey of the Sun through this constellation. Thus the Scorpion, well established in the zodiac by 4,000 B.C.E. if not even earlier,[105] became linked to darkness and death. From these sources the Greeks developed the myth that the Scorpion killed a great giant called Orion[106] (in Egypt, Osiris and/or his son Horus), which was also supported by the visual evidence in northern hemisphere autumn skies where the Scorpion rose while Orion set.[107] Orion, therefore, was seen as fleeing the Scorpion.

To the Egyptians, the Scorpion with its red flashing heart was one of the great symbols of life and death and, as there can be no life without death, it was the Scorpion who showed the way down into the underworld. The Scorpion was one of the four main points of the calendar: Aquarius, the winter solstice; Taurus, the spring equinox; Leo, the summer solstice; and Scorpio, the autumn equinox. These were the four cardinal[108] points and the symbols for them were

---

[104] Lockyer, *Dawn of Astronomy*, p. 397.

[105] Lockyer, *Dawn of Astronomy*, p. 407.

[106] Grimal, *The Dictionary of Classical Mythology*, p. 330.

[107] The situation in the southern hemisphere is the opposite. In the spring months, as Orion rises the Scorpion sets.

[108] The modern "cardinal" signs of Aries, Cancer, Libra, and Capricorn, of the tropical zodiac, are so considered because they are defined by the Sun's movement on the ecliptic as it crosses the equator or reaches its greatest northern or southern declination.

often placed on the four cardinal points of a tomb, that is north, south, east and west. Christians later adopted these four points as the four angels of the Apocalypse, and the Magi thought of them as the four archangels. Scorpio, guarding the west, eventually became the archangel Gabriel, whose element is water.[109]

The Celts celebrated the Sun's entry into these stars with their feast of Samhain,[110] a great gathering at Tara to celebrate the end of summer. But the eve of Samhain was considered a night of darkness in which the souls of the dead would roam the earth, for it was on that night that the Celts believed the gateway between the otherworld and the world of the living was open.

There is an old Celtic parable about a scorpion and a frog. The scorpion asked the frog if he would carry him across the river on his back. The frog was alarmed and said that he feared the scorpion would sting him. The scorpion assured the frog that that would be foolish, for if he stung him as they crossed the river, they would both die. The frog could see the logic of this and so agreed to carry the scorpion. Halfway across the river the frog felt the scorpion sting him and as the frog started to sink, he called out in his death throes: "Why have you done this? Now we will both die." The scorpion's reply was simple: "I could not help myself, it is in my nature."

The Persians, Syrians, and Greeks all view it as a dark and fearful sign. Scorpio lost its claws to Libra around the time of Ptolemy, although Ptolemy still used the name "The Claws of the Scorpion" in his *Tetrabiblos*.

STARS OF SCORPIO

The brightest star of Scorpio is Antares, with other named stars in descending order of magnitude: Graffias, on the head; Dschubba, also on the head; and a nebula with two visible stars, Shuala and Lesath, also known as Acumen and Aculeus respectively, in the sting.

ANTARES

(Alpha Scorpius. Magnitude 1.2 RA. 16:29:5". Declination 26S25'12". PED = 9° Sagittarius 04'.) See Paran Map 52, page 286. *An example of how to read the map:* If you were born in Faisalabad, Pakistan, at a latitude of 31° North, then the star rose at about 11° Sagittarius . If you have a planet at 11° Sagittarius or

---

[109] Aleister Crowley, *777 and Other Qabalistic Writings of Aleister Crowley* (York Beach, ME: Samuel Weiser, 1977), p. 16.

[110] Green, *Dictionary of Celtic Myth and Legend*, p. 187.

Antares

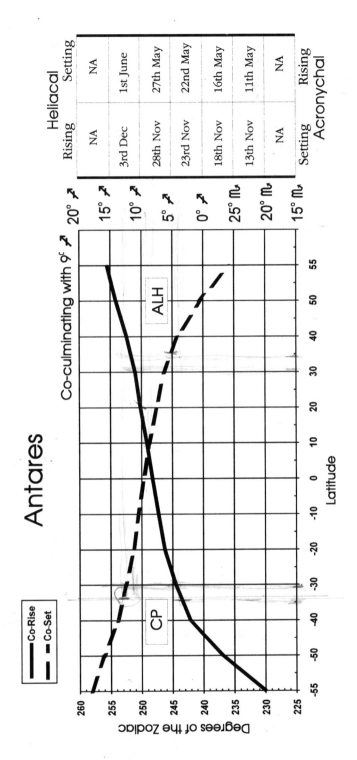

Heliacal		
Rising		Setting
NA		NA
3rd Dec		1st June
28th Nov		27th May
23rd Nov		22nd May
18th Nov		16th May
13th Nov		11th May
NA		NA
Setting	Acronychal	Rising

Paran Map 52. Antares.

Gemini, then that planet rose or set with the star. The star also set at 6° Sagittarius. Therefore, if you have a planet at 6° Sagittarius or Gemini it would have set or risen as the star set. The star culminates at 9° Sagittarius so if you have a planet at either 9° Sagittarius or Gemini, then it culminated or was on the Nadir as the star culminated.

At this latitude of 31° North the star has a phase of arising and lying hidden. This period will be from about November 29 (reading the date from the left-hand column of the date box next to 6° Sagittarius) to December 2 every year (reading the left-hand column of the date box next to 11° Sagittarius), and is the true or cosmic heliacal rising star about December 2 (reading the date for the rising line at 31° North in the "heliacal rising" column).

Antares can be used on all four points for charts between latitudes of 73° South and 73° North. North of that the star never rises, south of that the star never sets and therefore has permanent curtailed passage.

EARLIER OPINIONS

Ptolemy states that Antares is similar to Mars and Jupiter. Robson sees it as a most negative star, talking of destructiveness, evil, and "danger of fatality." Ebertin says that it makes people tough and pugnacious, as well as good for military careers. Rigor adds keen mentality and courage but also warns of self-destruction.

ANTARES: THE CONCEPT

This star is the Heart of the Scorpion[111] and is one of the great stars of the sky. It is a Royal Star of Persia and was known as the Watcher of the West. To the Persians this star was the god of the dead, Yima. For the Egyptians, the west was also the land of the dead, for the Sun sets in the west, the light dies there. In the Egyptian *Book of the Dead* the souls start their journey to the afterlife by traveling westward.

As a Royal Star, Antares offers great success, worldly or otherwise. However, it also indicates that the person may well cause their own undoing, like the scorpion on the frog's back in the Celtic parable. The natural desire of this star to generate success by going through a cleansing life-and-death experience can cause a person to seek this intensity even when it is not required.

Joan of Arc is a good example of the expression of Antares. When she was born, Mars rose as Antares was on the Nadir. Antares' link to her Mars led her to great success at the tender age of 19 years old. But her Mars was also her undoing. She refused to let go of the military and the conquest of France after the dauphin was crowned, even though the crowning of the dauphin was her holy

---

[111] Jobes, *Outer Space*, p. 304.

mission, divinely given to her when she was only 14. The results of her continuing activity eventually led to her capture by the English, and execution. With Antares linked to her Mars via the Nadir, we remember her as a sacred or holy warrior.

Two examples of Antares connected to Mercury are the murder mystery writer, Agatha Christie, and the prime minster of South Africa, Nelson Mandela. In both their charts Mercury was culminating as Antares rose. The former expressed the energy of Antares by writing about the world of murder and obsessive investigation, while the latter used this energy to hold a vision of freedom for all of South Africa, in the face of huge adversity.

ANTARES IN THE NATAL CHART

A powerful star, its presence in your chart will imply that you will go to extremes, intentionally or unintentionally. Success will come, as this is one of the Royal Stars, but only through continually putting your efforts to the test and honing them through the fires of experience. The planet in contact with Antares will indicate how this energy will be expressed in your life. The danger is that you will seek drama simply for the thrill, and if this happens, it can lead to the loss of all that has been gained.

ANTARES AS THE HELIACAL RISING STAR AT BIRTH

Antares is potentially abrasive or ruthless in this position, and you will need to allow yourself to be obsessive while recognizing that others may not be as driven as yourself. The essence of Antares firstly to create, and then to use human drama as a whetstone can be a problem, for if you become distracted by the whetstone, then what has been created will be destroyed. Antares can be used as both the apparent as well as the cosmic rising star.

ACULEUS

(M6 Scorpius. Magnitude 5.3. RA 17:36:48". Declination 32S11'. PED = 25° Sagittarius 02'.) See Paran Map 53, page 289.

ACUMEN

(M7 Scorpius. Magnitude 3.2. RA 17:50:44". Declination 34S48'. PED = 28° Sagittarius 03'.) See Paran Map 54, page 290. *An example of how to read the map:* If you were born in Athens, Greece, at a latitude of 38° North, then the star rose at about 5° Capricorn . If you have a planet at 5° Capricorn or Cancer, then that planet rose or set with the star. The star also set at 21° Sagittarius. Therefore, if you have a planet at 21° Sagittarius or Gemini, it would have set or risen as the

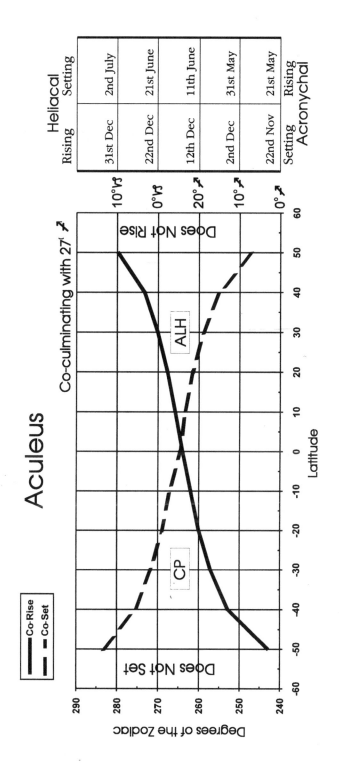

Heliacal		Acronychal	
Rising	Setting	Rising	Setting
31st Dec	2nd July	21st May	22nd Nov
22nd Dec	21st June	31st May	2nd Dec
12th Dec	11th June	11th June	12th Dec
2nd Dec	31st May	21st June	22nd Dec
22nd Nov	21st May	2nd July	31st Dec

Paran Map 53. Aculeus.

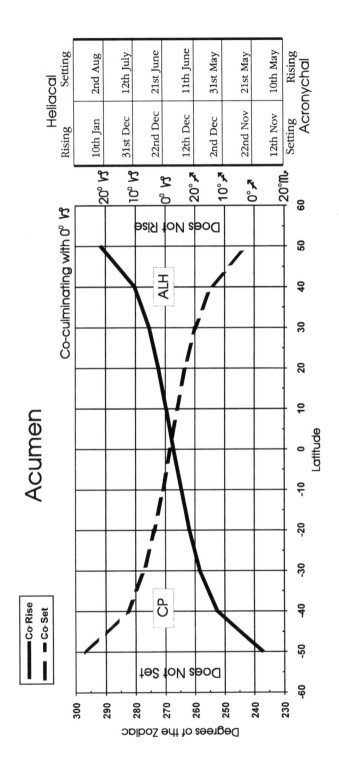

Paran Map 54. Acumen.

star set. The star culminates at 0° Capricorn so if you have a planet at either 0°Capricorn or Cancer, then it culminated or was on the Nadir as the star culminated.

At this latitude of 38° North the star has a phase of arising and lying hidden. This period will be from about December 12 (reading the date from the left-hand column of the date box next to 21° Sagittarius) to December 27 every year (reading the left-hand column of the date box next to 5° Capricorn), and is the true or cosmic heliacal rising star about December 27 (reading the date for the rising line at 38° North in the "heliacal rising" column).

Aculeus can be used on all four points for charts between latitudes of 58° South and 58° North. North of that the star never rises, south of that the star never sets and therefore has permanent curtailed passage.

Acumen can be used on all four points for charts between latitudes of 55° South and 55° North. North of that the star never rises, south of that the star never sets and therefore can only be used as it culminates.

EARLIER OPINIONS

Ptolemy states that the stars in the nebula in the sting of the Scorpion are like Mars and the Moon. Robson talks of blindness when they're in contact with a luminary. Ebertin does not list them. Rigor splits the two stars and says that Aculeus gives eyesight problems but also leadership ability, while Acumen gives eyesight problems, illness, and extreme disfavor.

ACULEUS AND ACUMEN: THE CONCEPT

Once again this is a nebula and therefore traditionally linked to blindness. However, as previously stated, the references to eyesight can be read metaphorically as comments on insight or inner vision. These stars as a pair have also been known as the Fish Hook[112] and, like other pairs of stars, they represent a single concept expressed in shades of light and dark. In the work that I have done with these two stars, and in keeping with the nature of the constellation, Aculeus and Acumen tend to be linked to attacks, not necessarily physical, but mental, verbal, or spiritual.

Acumen carries the negative or shadowy side, so it has to do with attacks that weaken, that can eventually damage the person: Vincent van Gogh, Marilyn Monroe, Mozart, to name just a few. Aculeus leans toward the less destructive style of attack, the sort the individual can endure and use to harden or strengthen themselves. Margaret Thatcher and Edward VIII of England have Aculeus in their charts.

---

[112] Allen, *Star Names*, p. 370.

ACULEUS OR ACUMEN IN THE NATAL CHART

If either of these stars is present in your chart, you will find yourself being either challenged, or subject to eroding or destructive gossip. This could even manifest as threats to your health. This influence represents the sting of the scorpion, and if you lash out or get angry, then potentially you can damage yourself. To ignore gossip and always deal with problems up front in the clear light of day is the pathway you should tread.

ACULEUS OR ACUMEN AS THE HELIACAL RISING STAR AT BIRTH

These two stars were not used in this position as they were too faint to act as heralds of the dawn. However, they can be used as the cosmic rising stars and, so placed in your chart, will have an impact on your sense of being. Your life path will be strewn with enduring attacks and, more importantly, you will need to learn to overcome obstacles placed there either by yourself or by others.

SAGITTARIUS, THE ARCHER

SAGITTARIUS IS KNOWN AS THE ARCHER and indeed that is the major emphasis in this constellation. See Star Map 24, below. Cuneiform tablets from the Euphrates call it the Strong One or the Giant King of War—the archer god of war.[113] To the Persians it was Kaman, to the Turks it was Yai, and in Syria it was Kertko, all names signifying a bow or bow and arrow. The Egyptians saw it as a hand holding an arrow[114] and Aratus called it the Wielder of the Bow.[115]

The animal part of the constellation was added in the classical period, when it was called a satyr (a wild beast, part man, part animal) and was always displayed as a very threatening figure. This was also the satyr sent to destroy Gilgamesh in his great mythical epic.[116] Over time, as the bow was no longer considered the feared weapon that it once was, the Archer became more friendly and the beast turned into a centaur which became the focus instead of the weapon. By modern times it seems to have been forgotten that, when Zeus, of

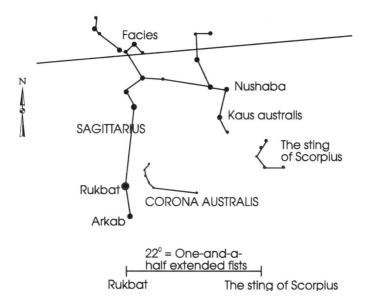

Star Map 24. Sagittarius, the Archer.

[113] Jobes, *Outer Space*, p. 235.
[114] Allen, *Star Names*, p. 352.
[115] Mair, *Callimachus, Lycophron, Aratus*, p. 231.
[116] Jobes, *Outer Space*, p. 236.

Greek mythology, wanted to place Chiron in the heavens, he could not displace Crotus, the cruel, wild beast of Sagittarius, and so was forced to place Chiron far to the south in the constellation Centaurus.[117] Sagittarius is therefore the equivalent of a modern combat soldier carrying the latest in attack weaponry, with the gentle, teaching, healing Chiron belonging to the constellation Centaurus.

The archer in ancient times was a feared and powerful warrior, able to fight from afar rather than face-to-face with a sword. Picked for his sharp eyesight and steadiness of stance and strength, he was the "green beret" of the squad, a most important and powerful piece in the game of war. In the Middle Ages the losing army's archers were often put to the sword on the pretext that they were cowards, not facing the men they killed. The reality, however, was that the enemy wished to destroy such a powerful weapon.[118] Thus, the soldier of Sagittarius was cruel, stormy, wild, and feared, and this is reflected in some of his stars.

STARS OF SAGITTARIUS

The brightest star of Sagittarius is Rukbat; the other named stars, in descending order of magnitude, are: Arkab, uniting the leg to the heel; Al Nasl, also called Nushaba, the point of the arrow; Kaus Meridionalis, the middle of the bow; Kaus Australis, the southern part of the bow; Ascella, the armpit; Kaus Borealis, the northern part of the bow; and a nebula called Facies, in the face of the Archer.

Of all these named stars, only two seem to be used in astrology: the alpha star Rukbat; and the very dim, almost invisible nebula, Facies.

RUKBAT

(Alpha Sagittarius. Magnitude 4.1. RA 19:23:33". Declination 40S37'32". PED = 15° Capricorn 56'.) See Paran Map 55, page 295. *An example of how to read the map:* If you were born in Pica, Chile, at a latitude of 20° South, then the star rose at about 10°Capricorn. If you have a planet at either 10° Capricorn or Cancer, then that planet rose or set with the star. The star also set at 0° Aquarius. Therefore, if you have a planet at 0° Aquarius or Leo, it would have set or risen as the star set. The star culminates at 24° Capricorn so if you have a planet at either 24° Capricorn or Cancer, then it culminated or was on the Nadir as the star culminated.

At this latitude of 20° South the star has a phase of curtailed passage. This period will be from about July 2 (reading the date from the right-hand column

---

[117] Jobes, *Outer Space*, p. 146.

[118] Medieval Archery Research Project, University of Arkansas Web site http://comp.uark. edu.

Rukbat

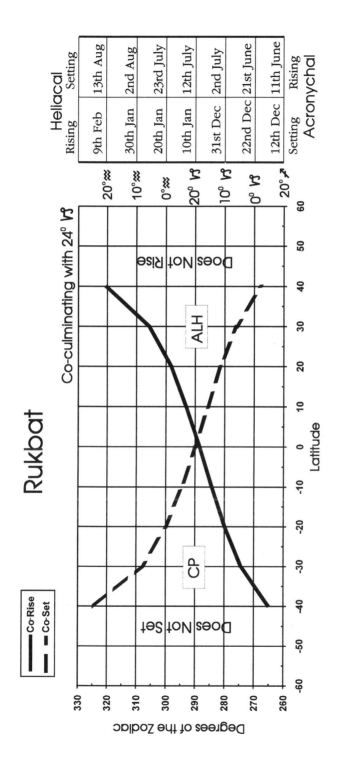

Heliacal		Acronychal
Rising	Setting	
9th Feb	13th Aug	
30th Jan	2nd Aug	
20th Jan	23rd July	
10th Jan	12th July	
31st Dec	2nd July	
22nd Dec	21st June	
12th Dec	11th June	
Setting	Rising	

Paran Map 55. Rukbat.

of the date box next to 10° Capricorn) to July 23 every year (reading the right-hand column of the date box next to 0° Aquarius), and is the true or cosmic heli-acal rising star about December 31 (reading the date for the rising line at 20° South in the "heliacal rising" column).

Rukbat can be used on all four points for charts between latitudes of 49° South and 49° North. North of that the star never rises, south of that the star never sets and therefore has permanent curtailed passage.

EARLIER OPINIONS

Ptolemy states that the stars of the feet have the nature of Jupiter and Saturn. Robson, Ebertin, and Rigor do not list the star. However, Robson works with Pelagus, a small star in the shaft of the arrow, which he says gives truthfulness; Ascella, which brings good fortune and happiness; and Manubrium, which is a part of the nebula Facies. Ebertin does work with "The Bow of the Archer," say-ing that it gives a sense of justice, and mental stimulation. Rigor works with Kaus Borealis, saying almost the exact same words as Ebertin.

RUKBAT: THE CONCEPT

If any of these stars are going to be used, it may be relevant to link them with their original symbolism: Rukbat, possibly, a symbol of steadiness—the archer's stance; and Ascella, the armpit, possibly a symbol of strength; with the stars of the bow linked to intervention and force. Rukbat is the only one of these with which I have worked and it does seem to imply steadiness or solidness.

An interesting example is Muhammad Ali who has Rukbat rising as his Mars culminates. The Mars and the culminating position show that this is how we see him, a fighter, a boxer, indeed one of the greatest boxers in the history of the sport. Rukbat shows that he was steady and stable, from a young age, both mentally and (most importantly) physically, a necessary requirement for such an occupation. In contrast to Muhammad Ali is the figure of Laurence Olivier, who had a very similar combination. He was born on the day that Mars culminated with Rukbat. Laurence Olivier is not a boxer, but consistency and solidness in his acting was one of his points of greatness; and we might postulate that the Mars influence was behind his being a Shakespearian specialist, playing the kings and warriors involved in the tragedy of life.

The examples Muhammad Ali and Laurence Olivier are fine illustrations of how one should not take stars simply as keywords but rather look more deeply at their concepts to see how the person is using that energy.

RUKBAT IN THE NATAL CHART

If Rukbat is in your chart it will add steadiness and consistency. This could turn to stubbornness, but generally it means you can use the energy to give yourself strength. Be prepared to work toward long-term goals rather than looking for the shortcut. This represents skill in your chart, not a hindrance.

RUKBAT AS THE HELIACAL RISING STAR AT BIRTH

Rukbat can be used as both the apparent as well as cosmic rising star and in either position it is a "Rock of Gibraltar" statement, representing qualities of consistency and steadiness: the ability to maintain your stance, be it physically or philosophically.

FACIES

(M22 Sagittarius. Magnitude 5.9. RA 18:36:03". Declination 23S55'38". PED = 7° Capricorn 36'.) See Paran Map 56, page 298. *An example of how to read the map:* If you were born in Arnhem, The Netherlands, at a latitude of 52° North, then the star rose at about 6° 30' Capricorn. If you have a planet at either 6° 30' Capricorn or Cancer, then that planet rose or set with the star. The star also set at 8° Capricorn. Therefore, if you have a planet at 8° Capricorn or Cancer, it would have set or risen as the star set. The star culminates at 15°Capricorn so if you have a planet at either 15° Capricorn or Cancer, then it culminated or was on the Nadir as the star culminated.

Because Facies is located on the ecliptic and rises and sets with approximately the same degree of the zodiac, it has no phases. In other words, for all but polar latitudes it will rise and set every day, never going through a period where it will appear not to rise or set. Its true heliacal rising will be around December 28 and its acronychal rising (rising as the Sun sets) will be six months later, about June 27.

Facies can be used on all four points for charts between latitudes of 66° South and 66° North. North of that the star never rises, south of that the star never sets and therefore has permanent curtailed passage.

EARLIER OPINIONS

Ptolemy states that the stars of the face of the Archer have the nature of the Sun and Mars. Robson talks of blindness and sudden death. Ebertin sees Facies as a very spiritual star but also links it to weak eyesight. Rigor links the star to violence, eyesight problems, and leadership skills.

FACIES: THE CONCEPT

All nebulae in astrology indicate blindness, as has already been discussed under the Pleiades in Taurus. However, this blanket statement is not that applicable in the modern astrologer's consulting room. In addition, keenness of eyesight is a physical feature of the archer, and thus it is logical that this nebula in the face of the Archer should related to good eyesight or sharpness of eyesight.

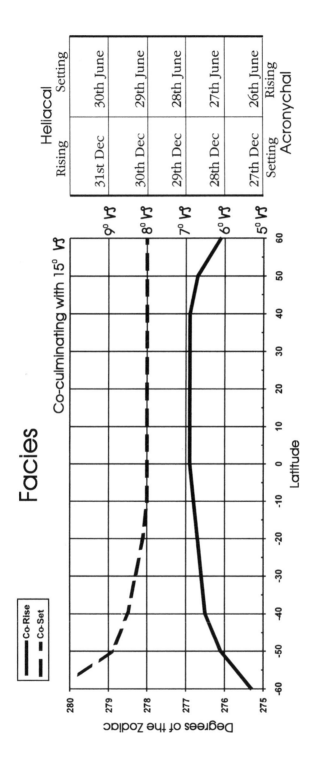

Paran Map 56. Facies.

The eyesight of the ancient archer was an expression of the quality of the weapon. One could never have nearsighted archers. Facies represents the penetrating stare of a lethal weapon. It is one of the most difficult, and possibly the most violent, objects in the heavens. It gives a penetration of action that has no regard for others, and can therefore make a great leader or a dictator. The other side of Facies is the individual who may be the victim of the archer's stare.

John Lennon was born at the moment Facies was culminating. He was cut down by the archer's stare. In this case all the archaic warnings of a violent death were fulfilled. Margaret Thatcher, former British prime minister, is a Facies person. She had Facies culminating as her Sun set. The Falklands War showed her Facies traits, as her first and only reaction was to attack. Adolf Hitler had Facies in combination with his Moon and Jupiter, and he manifested the total cruelty of the war machine on full display. Facies can be cruel and ruthless, and its darkest shadow is the evil of war. But it can also be very strongly focused and, if balanced, can imply a nondiplomatic but achieving person.

FACIES IN THE NATAL CHART

Facies in a chart will indicate that the planet it touches will be very focused and driven, and that you will need to be aware that the push to achieve goals and aims may well become ruthless. If Facies is the only difficult star in a chart, then it will suggest being focused. However, if other difficult stars are also present, then issues of ruthlessness and even cruelty could be a problem.

FACIES AS THE HELIACAL RISING STAR AT BIRTH

Having a magnitude of 5.9 means that Facies is barely visible to the naked eye, so traditionally would not be used as the apparent rising star. It could, however, still be used as the cosmic rising star. In this position it will give great focus and even forcefulness to the sense of identity.

CAPRICORN, THE GOAT

ARATUS CALLED THIS CONSTELLATION THE Horned Goat to distinguish it from the Auriga, the charioteer who carried a nursing goat. In Persia, Arabia, and Syria it was also known as the Goat and sometimes as the goat-footed Pan. At the time when the winter solstice occurred among its stars, around 3,000 to 2,000 B.C.E., it was known as the southern gate of the Sun. See Star Map 25, page 301.

It appears that as early as 1,000 B.C.E. the goat had taken on its fish tail. A Babylonian planisphere shows it in this fashion. The sea-goat or goat-fish was known in early Babylonian times as the god Ea, He of Vast Intellect and Lord of the Sacred Eye.[119] Ea was the protector of his people, and from his place in the sky the great rivers flowed, giving life. Periodically he would rise from these waters, take on human form, and teach the people the knowledge they needed for civilization. He was another Osiris-like god: caring, educating, and civilizing. He was charged with this mission by his brothers who, along with him, had suffered at the hands of their ruthless, oppressive parents, who wanted to destroy the human race their children had created. Ea castrated his father, Apsu, and severed his sinews, imprisoning the pieces of flesh in an earthen prison. Ea then became the ruler of Earth, which he managed from his watery realm. The myth goes on to talk of how humans started to fail Ea, and how he was eventually overthrown by his brother Bel . Unhappy with humans, Bel sent a great deluge—the precession of a sign through the equinox—to wipe out the population and start a new world order. Ea, however, once again saved the human race by urging them to construct an ark.[120] Ea was therefore the preserver of the human race and was given the title Kerubu, which later became Cherub. Being of the water he was often represented as a fish, and sometimes as a snake, and may eventually have ended up in the Garden of Eden as the snake in the Tree of Life, encouraging learning and knowledge rather than blissful ignorance.[121]

Whenever Ea roamed the earth he took the form of a goat, until he eventually won the right to govern that part of the heavens he now holds. Ea was considered the Father of Light[122] and his celebrations, dating back to 15,000 B.C.E., were carried out wearing goat skins.[123]

---

[119] *New Larousse Encyclopedia of Mythology*, p. 51.
[120] Jobes, *Outer Space*, p. 138.
[121] Jobes, *Outer Space*, p. 138.
[122] Bel, his brother, was also known to carry this title.
[123] Jobes, *Outer Space*, p. 139.

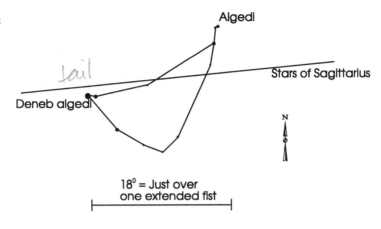

Star Map 25. Capricorn, the Goat.

The Greeks saw Capricorn as the sea-goat that nurtured and fed the infant Zeus but they failed to resolve the problem of the goat that nursed Zeus in the constellation of Auriga. They linked the stars of Capricorn with cold and storms because of their connection with winter in the northern hemisphere. They also took this ancient god and created Pan, telling legends of how the great Pan dove into the water and developed a fish tail.[124]

Clearly this constellation involves an ancient and powerful god whose myths of castrations and ark-building are reflected in the mythology of later cultures. He seems to hold center stage as the original savior of the human race, and still carried out this role in the time of the Jews, or rather the beginning of monotheism when the equinox had precessed into Aries. The early Jews considered the goat sacred and a savior. Every year the sins of the people would be placed on the head of a goat that would then be killed or hunted. The sacrifice of the goat was seen as a way of being absolved from sin and from this practice comes the concept of the scapegoat.[125] However, the scapegoat is Ea, the ancient Father of Light, who saves us from floods and is devoted to protecting the human race by suffering for us in order for our sins to be absolved.

By Christian times, the snake and the Horned One were considered the very essence of evil because they represented a previous religion, even though the new god of Pisces behaved like Ea or the scapegoat by carrying the sins of the human race.

---

[124] Allen, *Star Names*, p. 136.
[125] Jobes, *Outer Space*, p. 139.

STARS OF CAPRICORN

The alpha star of Capricorn is Giedi, also called Algedi, in the horn of the goat. Other named stars, in descending order of magnitude, are: Dabih, which is actually two stars marking the base of the horn; Nashira, which means in Arabic the Bringer of Good Tidings, in the tail; and Deneb Algedi, also in the tail.

The stars of Capricorn are quite dim, the Alpha star, Giedi, having a magnitude of only 3.2. It seems that the only star in astrological use is Deneb Algedi.

DENEB ALGEDI

(Delta Capricornus. Magnitude 3.1. RA 21:44:16". Declination 16°S21'. PED = 22° Aquarius 50'.) See Paran Map 57, page 303. *An example of how to read the map:* If you were born in Good Hope, South Africa, at a latitude of 32° South, then the star rose at about 22° Aquarius. If you have a planet at either 22° Aquarius or Leo, then that planet rose or set with the star. The star also set at 27° Aquarius. Therefore, if you have a planet at 27° Aquarius or Leo, it would have set or risen as the star set. The star culminates at 25° Aquarius so if you have a planet at either 25° Aquarius or Leo, then it culminated or was on the Nadir as the star culminated.

At this latitude of 32° South the star has a phase of curtailed passage. This period will be from about August 15 (reading the date from the right-hand column of the date box next to 22° Aquarius) to August 21every year (reading the right-hand column of the date box next to 27° Aquarius), and is the true or cosmic heliacal rising star about February 11 (reading the date for the rising line at 32° South in the "heliacal rising" column).

Deneb Algedi can be used on all four points for charts between latitudes of 73° South and 73° North. North of that the star never rises, south of that the star never sets and therefore has permanent curtailed passage.

EARLIER OPINIONS

Ptolemy states that the stars of the tail of Capricorn are like Saturn and Jupiter. Robson says that Deneb Algedi causes sorrow and happiness, life and death, and beneficence and destructiveness. Ebertin states that Deneb Algedi was formerly called Nashira, yet these are two different stars in the goat's tail, so it is not clear which star he is referring to. However, he goes on to link the star with wisdom and integrity, and adds that the person influenced by it will be a legal adviser or counselor. Rigor agrees with Robson.

DENEB ALGEDI: THE CONCEPT

If this star is going to be used in astrology, then the symbol of the law giving, justice-oriented god trying to civilize his people is probably the best tool for

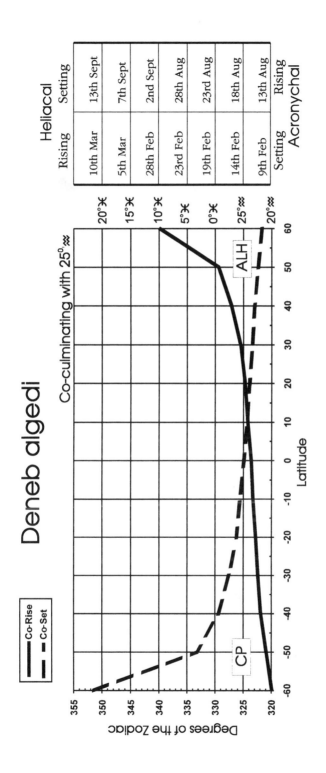

Paran Map 57. Deneb algedi.

approaching it, since this would reflect its long history. This is the star of a person who is a benefic ruler, one who is trying to use wisdom and knowledge to protect and help the people around them. Mother Teresa of India had two contacts with Deneb Algedi: when her Moon rose the star was culminating, and when her Sun culminated the star was rising. So this concept of the ancient, protecting god is connected to both her luminaries.

DENEB ALGEDI IN THE NATAL CHART

Deneb Algedi bestows a sense of justice, of wanting to be a "savior." By itself this is not a strong star and it needs to be linked to the stars of either Libra—for social reform—or one of the Royal Stars—for power—before you put too much emphasis on it. However, it does suggest the desire to help, not by serving but by leading.

DENEB ALGEDI AS THE HELIACAL RISING STAR AT BIRTH

With a magnitude of only 3.1, this star is really too dim to be a herald of the dawn. But if it is the cosmic rising star, then its natural sense of justice, and desire to help will become a part of your identity.

AQUARIUS, THE WATER CARRIER

AROUND 4,000 B.C.E. AQUARIUS WAS ONE of the four major points of the zodiac, holding the position of the winter solstice. See Star Map 26, page 306. Since that time, if not earlier, this sign has been identified as a giant urn pouring water into the sky. Thousands of years later Aratus called this part of the sky The Water.[126] Aquarius was seen to govern the huge cosmic sea that now contains the constellations of Pisces the Fishes, Cetus the Whale, Capricornus the Sea-Goat, Delphinus the Dolphin, Eridanus the River, Piscis Australis the Southern Fish, and Hydra the Water Serpent.

The Babylonians called the stars of Aquarius the Seat of the Flowing Water[127] and saw it as the source of the rain that caused the great deluge of their creation myth. Following this theme, and linked with the fact that it was the winter solstice constellation, they also called it the God of Storms.

In Egypt, where rainfall was negligible, the Nile was the source of all water and therefore all life. The Nile is the most predictable and reliable river in the world, flooding annually every July through to October, pouring life-giving water and silt over the Nile Valley floor. Thus the river was seen as a god or goddess and a most sacred life-giving entity. At the time of the flooding, Aquarius was the heliacal setting constellation, meaning that as the Sun rose, Aquarius set on the western horizon. From this visual fact the Egyptians saw the Water Carrier as dipping his urn into the Nile, his pot displacing the water that caused the flooding; or, more simply that he leaned down and poured his water into the Nile.

The usual image of Aquarius comes from this Egyptian concept of the river god pouring the contents of his urn into the Nile while holding a norma nilotica, a rod for measuring the rising waters of the Nile.[128] By the Middle Ages he was thought of as John the Baptist,[129] matching an ancient Babylonian image of a man pouring water and holding a towel.[130] This simple change from a river-measuring rod to a towel degrades Aquarius from a river god to an attendant in a bathhouse. The Greeks did not place any of their mythology onto this great and ancient constellation, except to link him to Ganymede, Zeus's cupbearer.[131]

Whatever his name, he has been associated with water, be it life-giving floods and rain or life-taking storms and deluge. The Greek astrologer Valens (second century C.E.) listed Eridanus the River as part of Aquarius, seeing the

---

[126] Mair, *Callimachus, Lycophron, Aratus*, p. 239.

[127] Allen, *Star Names*, p. 47.

[128] Allen, *Star Names*, p. 49.

[129] Jobes, *Outer Space*, p. 115.

[130] Allen, *Star Names*, p. 45.

[131] Jobes, *Outer Space*, p. 114.

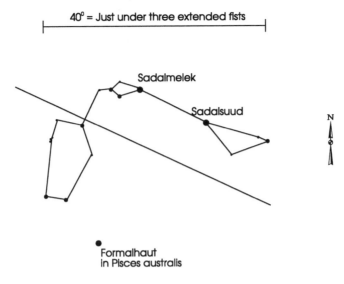

Star Map 26. Aquarius, the Water Carrier.

mighty Water Carrier emptying his urn to create the river. Now we see Eridanus as coming from the feet of Cetus, the Whale, while Aquarius pours his water into the mouth of the Southern Fish, Piscis Australis.

STARS OF AQUARIUS

The brightest star is Sadalmelek, on the right shoulder. Some other named stars, in descending order of magnitude, are: Sadalsuud, on the left shoulder; Sadachbia, on the inner edge of the urn; Skat, in the leg; and Ancha, the hip.

SADALMELEK

(Alpha Aquarius. Magnitude 3.2. RA 22:03:12". Declination 0N34'. PED = 3° Pisces 04'.) See Paran Map 58, page 307.

Sadalmelek can be used on all four points for charts for all latitudes.

EARLIER OPINIONS

Ptolemy states that the stars in the shoulders of Aquarius are like Saturn and Mercury. Robson talks of persecution, lawsuits, sudden destruction, and the death penalty. Ebertin does not list any stars from Aquarius. Rigor agrees with Robson.

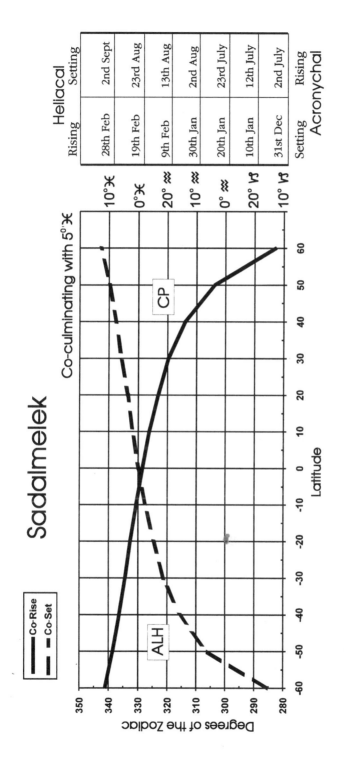

Sadalmelek

Co-culminating with 5° ♓

Legend:
— Co-Rise
- - Co-Set

Degrees of the Zodiac (vertical axis): 350, 340, 330, 320, 310, 300, 290, 280

Latitude (horizontal axis): -60, -50, -40, -30, -20, -10, 0, 10, 20, 30, 40, 50, 60

CP

ALH

Heliacal		
Rising	Setting	
28th Feb	2nd Sept	10° ♓
19th Feb	23rd Aug	0° ♓
9th Feb	13th Aug	20° ♒
30th Jan	2nd Aug	10° ♒
20th Jan	23rd July	0° ♒
10th Jan	12th July	20° ♑
31st Dec	2nd July	10° ♑
Setting	Rising	
Acronychal		

Paran Map 58. Sadalmelek.

SADALSUUD

(Beta Aquarius. Magnitude 3.1. RA 21:28:56". Declination 5S48'. PED = 22° Aquarius 42'.) See Paran Map 59, page 309. *An example of how to read the map:* If you were born in Calcutta, India, at a latitude of 23° North, then the star rose at about 16° Aquarius. If you have a planet at either 16° Aquarius or Leo, then that planet rose or set with the star. The star also set at 25° Aquarius. Therefore, if you have a planet at 25° Aquarius or Leo, it would have set or risen as the star set. The star culminates at 26° Aquarius so if you have a planet at either 26° Aquarius or Leo, then it culminated or was on the Nadir as the star culminated.

At this latitude of 23° North the star has a phase of curtailed passage. This period will be from about August 6 (reading the date from the right-hand column of the date box next to 16° Aquarius) to August 18 every year (reading the right-hand column of the date box next to 25° Aquarius), and is the true or cosmic heliacal rising star about February 5 (reading the date for the rising line at 23° North in the "heliacal rising" column).

Sadalsuud can be used on all four points for charts for all latitudes except for the extremities of the poles.

EARLIER OPINIONS

Ptolemy states that, as with Sadalmelek, Sadalsuud is like Saturn and Mercury. Robson simply says that it causes trouble and disgrace. Ebertin does not list the star. Rigor talks of strange events which are probably scandalous but also visionary and original.

SADALMELEK AND SADALSUUD: THE CONCEPT

Both Sadalmelek and Sadalsuud are considered lucky by their Arabian namers. Indeed their names refer to forms of luck, *Sadalmelek* meaning "Lucky One of the King" and *Saladsuud* meaning "Luckiest of the Lucky."[132] Linking these meanings with the symbolism of the Water Carrier as bringer of life-giving water and/or rain, it is probably wiser to see these two stars as indicating a bringer of good events or news, rather than the death and destruction indicated in the literature. These are a pair of stars, so once again their meaning is expressed in polarity.

SADALMELEK OR SADALSUUD IN THE NATAL CHART

Not an overly strong influence but, depending on the planet and angle involved, these two stars should make things flow in the area indicated. Life-giving water will be poured onto a thirsty situation. Some may call such an ability luck, but

---

[132] Allen, *Star Names*, p. 51.

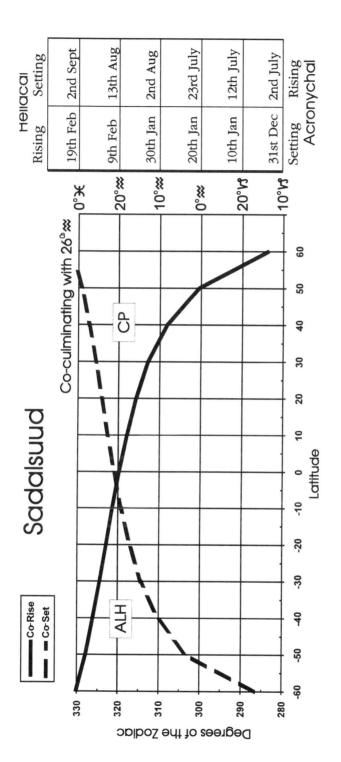

Sadalsuud

Co-culminating with 26°♒

	Heliacal	
Rising		Setting
19th Feb		2nd Sept
9th Feb		13th Aug
30th Jan		2nd Aug
20th Jan		23rd July
10th Jan		12th July
31st Dec		2nd July
Setting		Rising
	Acronychal	

0°♓
20°♒
10°♒
0°♒
20°♑
10°♑

CP

ALH

Co-Rise
Co-Set

Degrees of the Zodiac

330
320
310
300
290
280

Latitude

-60 -50 -40 -30 -20 -10 0 10 20 30 40 50 60

Paran Map 59. Sadalsuud.

really it's knowing how to win through, to find happiness. This is not a pair of stars to indicate a brilliant or tragic career but rather, when present in charts, particularly connected with the luminaries or Jupiter, the person will be fortunate or lucky at times in their life. And although one may see it in the charts of lottery winners, the stars do not seem to be connected with the luck of winning money but, rather, the luck of finding happiness in one's life.

SADALMELEK OR SADALSUUD AS THE HELIACAL RISING STAR AT BIRTH

With their magnitudes around 3.2 and 3.1, respectively, these two stars were never used as morning heralds. However, as cosmic rising stars their presence could imply a strong life force, as the great water giver mixes his energy with the vitality of the Sun. The Arabs would simply define the person as lucky.

PISCES, THE FISHES

PISCES MOVED INTO THE LEAD POSITION
in the Ring of Life around two thousand years ago, when the spring equinox heliacal rising slipped from Aries the Ram to Pisces the Fishes. There was never a clear distinction between these two constellations, as Pisces is so large, its two Fish reaching through the sky actually encompass the stars of Aries. See Star Map 27, page 312.

The coming of the age of Pisces, the new world order, was eagerly awaited, heralded in 6 B.C.E. by a triple conjunction of Saturn and Jupiter in Pisces. In his fourth *Eclogue*, Virgil announced it would be the return of the golden age.[133] This conjunction was the astronomical highlight of the time, eagerly awaited and watched, and was later named, in Christian mythology, the Star of Bethlehem.[134]

But the fish was an ancient symbol long before it was adopted by the new god. It represented wisdom and was recognized as a female sign. The symbol for the fish was derived from the yoni. The Chinese Great Mother, called Kwan-yin, Yoni of Yonis, often appeared as a fish goddess.[135] The Celts considered that eating fish would put new life in a womb.[136] Their hero, Tuan, was eaten by a fish and the fish in turn was eaten by the queen of Ireland who, in the fullness of time, gave birth to him. Thus to eat of the salmon was also to grow in wisdom.

The Greeks incorporated the fish as a sacred symbol through Aphrodite, in her form as a fish goddess called Aphrodite Salacia.[137] She was depicted as a fertile mother nursing a child, and her temples always contained ponds of fish. Her followers would eat fish on her holy day, which was Friday. They were known as the fish eaters, and this custom was adopted by the Catholic Church who decreed that the eating of fish on a Friday, considered abstinence from meat, was a holy act required of its followers.

As the spring equinox moved into Pisces, the ram god sent his son, Christ, to save the world, and he became the god of fishes. He was a fisherman fishing for men's souls. His disciples were fishermen and one of his miracles, which proved him god, was the miracle of the loaves and fishes, where he was said to have fed five thousand on just a few fish and some bread. The new

---

[133] De Santillana and von Dechend, *Hamlet's Mill*, p. 244.
[134] This association is more of an attempt by Christianity to claim Christ as the herald of the new age, rather than having any real basis in historical facts.
[135] Walker, *The Woman's Encyclopedia of Myths and Secrets*, p. 313.
[136] Green, *Dictionary of Celtic Myth and Legend*, p. 184.
[137] Walker, *The Woman's Encyclopedia of Myths and Secrets*, p. 314.

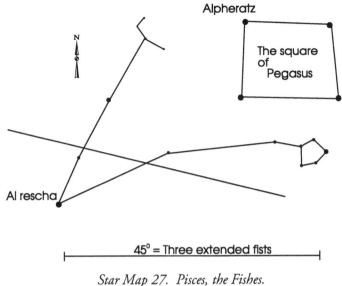

Star Map 27. Pisces, the Fishes.

religion adopted the sign of the Fish as their symbol. The cross belonged to the pagans and was not incorporated into Christian symbolism until after the sixth century C.E.[138]

The arrival of any new age heralds more than just a change of gods, for it represents a change in the way humans see the world. One of the features of the Piscean new world order was that our concept of time and its cyclic nature became altered in our collective mind. The new god now ruled forever, and thus everything was measured before or after his incarnation. However, the concept of cycles, of there being an heir to every throne, that had been part of the myths of the Bull (Taurus) and the Ram (Aries), ended with Pisces. For Christ had no children and the only way to acknowledge the whirlpool created by precession was to talk about a second coming—who would ostensibly be the new god of Aquarius. For several centuries after Christ, Christians believed the second coming was immanent, forgetting that the cycle was several thousand years long. The cyclic order was crumbling, for the new god ruled forever. As previously mentioned, it was announced that the great Pan was dead, and Plutarch mused, in about 60 C.E., that oracles had ceased to give answers.[139] For our logic, under the new god, was no longer cyclic; therefore oracles could no longer predict. Euclidean geometry, logic, linear time, and the separatism of science had begun.

---

[138] Walker, *The Woman's Encyclopedia of Myths and Secrets*, p. 188.
[139] De Santillana and von Dechend, *Hamlet's Mill*, p. 341.

STARS OF PISCES

There are no bright stars in the constellation Pisces. The alpha star, Al Rescha, seems to be the only named star, and marks the knot in the united cords of the Fishes.

AL RESCHA

(Alpha Pisces. Magnitude 4.0. RA 01:59:28". Declination 2N31'. PED = 28° Aries 41'.) Sec Paran Map 60, page 314. *An example of how to read the map:* If you were born in Meda, Portugal, at a latitude of 41° North, then the star rose at about 14° Taurus . If you have a planet at 14° Taurus or Scorpio, then that planet rose or set with the star. The star also set at 27° Aries. Therefore, if you have a planet at 27° Aries or Libra, it would have set or risen as the star set. The star culminates at 3° Taurus so if you have a planet at either 3° Taurus or Scorpio, then it culminated or was on the Nadir as the star culminated.

At this latitude of 41° North the star has a phase of arising and lying hidden. This period will be from about April 18 (reading the date from the left-hand column of the date box next to 27° Aries) to May 5 every year (reading the left-hand column of the date box next to 14° Taurus), and is the true or cosmic heliacal rising star about May 5 (reading the date for the rising line at 41° North in the "heliacal rising" column).

Al Rescha can be used on all four points for charts for all latitudes.

EARLIER OPINIONS

Ptolemy called Al Rescha the "bright star in the knot," so it seems as if Al Rescha has dimmed since his day. He said that it has the nature of Mars and is moderately like Mercury. Robson, Ebertin, and Rigor do not list this star.

AL RESCHA: THE CONCEPT

Al Rescha seems to take its major symbolism from the concept of the knot, the point of contact between the two ancient fish. Therefore, it signifies the point of contact between two points of knowledge, the joining of different concepts to create wisdom and understanding. John Addey, the English astrologer who linked harmonics with Western astrology, had Al Rescha connected to his Sun. His Sun set as Al Rescha was on the Nadir, indicating that his work will live on. Carl Jung also had Al Rescha active in his chart. As his Jupiter rose, Al Rescha set. Jung linked mythology, ritual, and symbols to the makeup of the human mind. Al Rescha has to do, then, with bringing two things together, marrying two concepts to create great understanding.

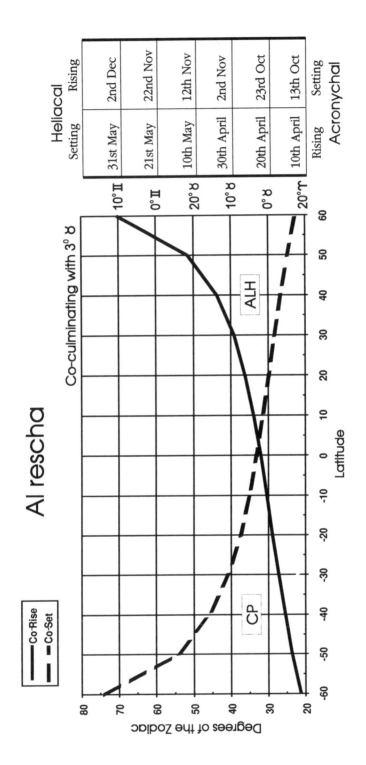

Paran Map 60. Al rescha.

AL RESCHA IN THE NATAL CHART

Al Rescha is a gentle star indicating that you will be seeking different connections, looking at things in a different light, joining separate concepts together to gain a greater understanding. The planet being affected will indicate the area of your life where you will seek these unions, and the angle that the star touches will indicate the timing of these unions in your life.

AL RESCHA AS THE HELIACAL RISING STAR AT BIRTH

Since Al Rescha only has a magnitude of 4, it is far too dim to use as a visual herald to the dawn. However, if it is the cosmic rising star, then the need to find unusual connections in the search for how the world, mind, and soul work will be a major theme in your life.

Part 4

STAR PHASES

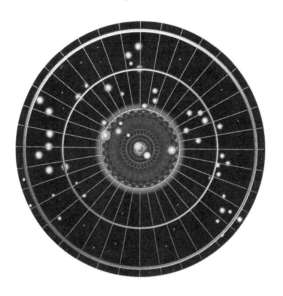

THE SUN AND THE STARS

STAR PHASES HAVE NOT BEEN USED IN astrology for nearly two thousand years. Yet this technique was the predominant method used when fixed stars held the center stage of an astrologer's life.[1] As we became disconnected from the sky, the importance of star phases faded, not because of faulty technique but because it was a visually based system. The "phasing" of a star—that is to say its rising with the Sun on a particular calendar date, its period of visibility in the night sky and its period of invisibility when it was not present in the night sky—was one of the major tools for defining the calendar, the seasons, and the weather.[2] In addition, the periods when a star was missing from the night sky, and its subsequent return, provided foundations for both myths and religious practices that the Egyptians raised to their highest form of expression.[3]

The phases of the stars are the result of the combination of three factors: The first is that the stars do not reside on the ecliptic and will therefore co-rise and co-set for a given latitude on different degrees of the ecliptic. The second is that the Sun, which defines the ecliptic, will rise and set with the same degree of the ecliptic for a particular day. And the third and most obvious factor, is that stars are only visible when the Sun is below the horizon.

DETERMINING THE PHASE OF A STAR

The phases of a star describe that star's current status with regard to its visibility for a particular location. There are two types of phase cycles through which a star can move: one contains the period which is called curtailed passage; and the other contains the period called arising and lying hidden. The phase a star will go through depends on two points: whether a star has either northern or southern declination; and whether the observer is in the northern or southern hemisphere. Southern declination stars observed in the southern hemisphere will travel through the phase which contains curtailed passage. Northern declination stars observed in the northern hemisphere will also travel through the phase which contains curtailed passage.

---

[1] Robert Hand, introduction to Ptolemy's *The Phases of the Fixed Stars*, vol. 3, trans. Robert Schmidt (Berkeley Springs, WV: Golden Hind Press, 1994), p. iii.

[2] Ptolemy, *The Phases of the Fixed Stars*, p. 10.

[3] See Norman J. Lockyer, *The Dawn of Astronomy* (Kila, MT: Kessinger, 1992).

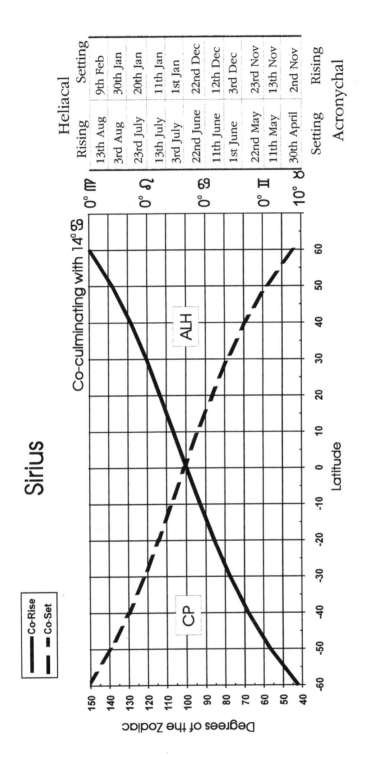

Figure 22. *Paran map for Sirius.*

THE RULE FOR DETERMINING CURTAILED PASSAGE

If a star is observed from the same hemisphere (northern or southern latitude) as its declination (north or south), it will appear to travel through a period of curtailed passage.

This is when a star appears in the night sky at sunset and will not set during the course of the night. Thus it appears not to touch the earth and it is said to be in a phase of curtailed passage. Circumpolar stars therefore, are stars in a permanent state of curtailed passage. If, on the other hand, a star with southern declination is observed at northern latitudes, then it will have a phase of arising and lying hidden, as will a star with a northern declination observed from the southern hemisphere.

THE RULE FOR DETERMINING A PHASE OF ARISING AND LYING HIDDEN

If a star is observed from the hemisphere opposite (northern or southern latitude) from its declination (north or south), it will appear to travel through a period of arising and lying hidden.

This is when a star will rise and set while the Sun is still above the horizon. Thus at night the star will not appear to be in the sky. Hence it is said to be arising and lying hidden, rising, but hidden by the daylight.

THE STAR PHASE THAT CONTAINS THE PERIOD OF ARISING AND LYING HIDDEN

Consider that Sirius, with a declination 16° 42'25" South, is being observed from a latitude 40° North and will therefore go through a phase of arising and lying Hidden.

Looking at the paran map for Sirius (figure 22, p. 320) for a latitude 40° North the map indicates that Sirius will co-rise with about 9° Leo. However, it will co-set with 10° of Gemini. Similarly, at 20° North Sirius will co-rise with 23° Cancer and co-set 27° Gemini. Depending on the latitude, Sirius, like any other star, will co-rise with a different zodiacal degree to that with which it co-sets. This is because the star is transcribing across the sky a different arc from the Sun.

ACRONYCHAL SETTING—THE BEGINNING OF INVISIBILITY

At a latitude of 40° north, when the transiting Sun is at 0° Gemini, the Sun will rise before Sirius, which co-rises with 9° Leo. However, as the Sun sets at about 0° Gemini on that day, Sirius, which co-sets with 10° Gemini, would become visible in the early evening light, low in the west, just about to set. This period is called acronychal setting, setting when the Sun sets, and marks the beginning of the phase of arising and lying hidden. See figure 23, p. 322.

TRUE ACRONYCHAL SETTING

Ten days later, when the transiting Sun is at 10° Gemini, the Sun will rise before Sirius, which co-rises with 9° Leo. However, the Sun will set at 10° Gemini, which is the setting degree for Sirius (see figure 24, p. 322). Thus Sirius will be

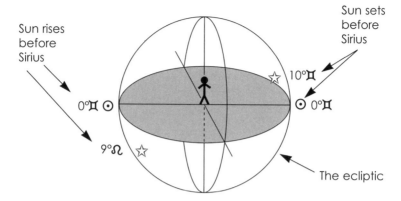

Figure 23. The acronychal setting of Sirius. Latitude 40° North.

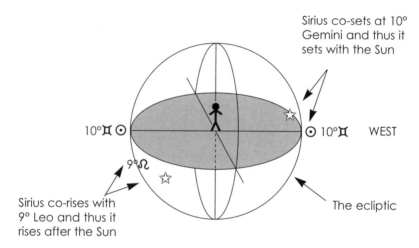

Figure 24. The true acronychal setting of Sirius. Latitude 40° North with the Sun at 10° Gemini.

setting with the Sun and consequently will not be visible. This is called the true acronychal setting and is the mathematical beginning of the period of arising and lying hidden. The Sun rises before Sirius and sets with Sirius. Thus, for the entire time that Sirius is above the horizon it is daylight and the star cannot be seen.

About thirty-five days later the Sun will be at 15° Cancer. Once again the Sun will rise before Sirius because Sirius does not rise until 9° Leo is on the Ascendant. The Sun will also set at 15° Cancer *after* Sirius has set at 10° Gemini. Sirius, therefore, has both risen and set while the Sun is above the horizon (see figure 25, p. 323). It is not visible and is considered to be arising and lying hidden. Indeed

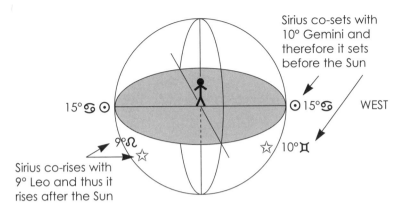

Figure 25. Sirius in a phase of arising and lying hidden. Latitude 40° North with the Sun at 15° Cancer.

any position for the Sun between 10° Gemini and 9° Leo would give the same results.

TRUE HELIACAL RISING—THE END OF INVISIBILITY

Another twenty-five days pass and now the Sun is at 9° Leo, now rising with Sirius. This is called true heliacal rising, rising with the sun, and marks the mathematical end to the period of arising and lying hidden.

The Egyptians also called this the cosmic rising, for the star was seen to blend its light with the Sun. The Sun will set at 9° Leo after Sirius which had set with 10° Gemini (see figure 26, p. 324).

VISIBLE HELIACAL RISING

Another 10 days or so, and the Sun will be at 20° Leo. Sirius will rise before the Sun, co-rising with 9° Leo, and set before the Sun sets. However, Sirius will be visible in the early morning sky for a short period before sunrise. This is known as the visible heliacal rising phase, also called the apparent heliacal rising phase for Sirius, which marks the visible end to the period of arising and lying hidden (see figure 27, p. 324).

It was a period of great celebration when a major star like Sirius reappeared as the heliacal rising star, for this marked its return to the world of the living, the end of its period of darkness or invisibility. The star was thought to go into the underworld and its heliacal rising was a rebirth, a return of its energy to the planet. The heliacal rising dates for important stars were well recorded and if on the day of the heliacal rising the star rose with a wandering star, a planet, that would be a sign or an omen. This is an important point to remember when applying the modern uses of fixed stars and will be discussed later.

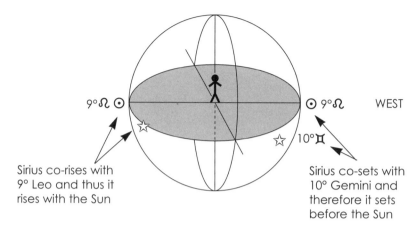

Figure 26. The true heliacal rising of Sirius. Latitude 40° North with the Sun at 9° Leo.

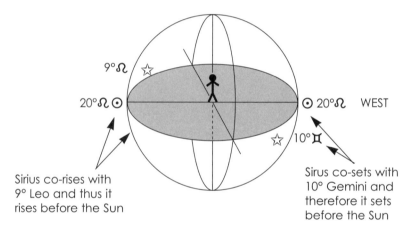

Figure 27. The visible heliacal rising of Sirius. Latitude 40° North with the Sun at 20° Leo.

THE TIME OF PASSAGE

This is the period of time when Sirius is visible in the night sky and, at some time during the night, will rise or set. The star is seen to have passage, that is to say, contact, with the horizon line. This period will last from the heliacal rising through to the acronychal setting.

In summary: At a latitude of 40° North, Sirius will be invisible, not appearing in the night sky, for the period of time that it takes the Sun to travel from 10° Gemini to 9° Leo—or, for a latitude of 20° North, the time it takes the Sun to travel from 27° Gemini to 23° Cancer. This period of time of invisibility is marked on the appropriate side of the paran map as "ALH" (see figure 22, p. 320).

FINDING THE LENGTH OF THE PERIOD OF ARISING AND LYING HIDDEN

Refer again to the map for Sirius (figure 22, p. 320) at a latitude of 40° North: The area contained in the map between the setting line and the rising line is representative of the length of time that Sirius is not visible. Marked by the letters ALH, it can be seen that the closer an observer is to the equator (0° latitude), the smaller this area is and thereby the shorter the period of time when the star is not visible.

By reading first the date in the heliacal rising column for the setting of Sirius, and the date from the same column for the rising of Sirius, the following is obtained: 40° North: Sirius setting line corresponds to June 1 (the date in the heliacal rising column), while the rising line corresponds to about August 1. Thus, Sirius for a latitude of 40° North will have a period of arising and lying hidden from June 1 to August 1. For a latitude of 20° North, the setting line corresponds to about June 20 and the rising line corresponds to about July 15. So for a latitude of 20° North, Sirius will not be visible in the night sky from June 20 to July 15.

But what if we looked at a latitude of 40° South? Now we would be looking at a southern declination star in the southern hemisphere, so there is no period of arising and lying hidden. Sirius will be seen every night of the year but there will be a period where it will appear not to rise or set during the night. Instead it will be in the night sky at sunset and still be visible in the night sky at dawn. This period is called curtailed passage.

THE STAR PHASE THAT CONTAINS THE PERIOD OF CURTAILED PASSAGE

Using Sirius again: According to the paran map for a latitude of 40° South, Sirius will co-rise with 9° Gemini and co-set with 10° Leo. This is the reverse, or rather mirror image, of the northern hemisphere example. See figure 22, p. 320.

ACRONYCHAL RISING—THE BEGINNING OF CURTAILED PASSAGE

The acronychal rising is when a star rises as the sun sets and marks the beginning of the period of curtailed passage. In the case of Sirius at 40° South, this will be when the sun sets as 9° Gemini rises. In other words, when the Sun sets at 9° Sagittarius, Sirius will appear to rise. See figure 28, p. 326.

CURTAILED PASSAGE

Moving forward through the calendar, if the Sun is at 15° Sagittarius as it sets 15° Gemini will be rising and Sirius, co-rising with 9° Gemini, would have already risen. So as the sky darkens and the stars appear, Sirius will already be visible. See figure 29, p. 326.

At sunrise the next morning the Sun will rise at about 16° Sagittarius, which means that 16° Gemini will be setting (see figure 30, p, 327). Sirius, however, which co-sets with 10° Leo, would still be visible in the sky. So the Sun will set with Sirius already risen and visible in the early night sky and the Sun will rise

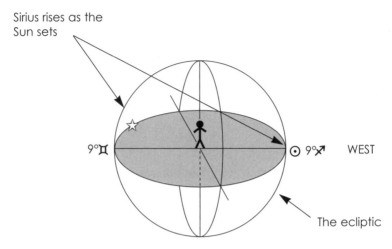

Sirius rises as the
Sun sets

9°♊

☉ 9°♐   WEST

The ecliptic

Figure 28. The acronychal rising of Sirius. Latidue 40° South.

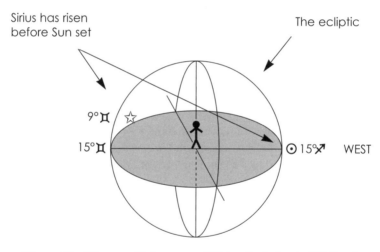

Sirius has risen
before Sun set

The ecliptic

9°♊

15°♊

☉ 15°♐   WEST

Figure 29. The curtailed passage of Sirius for latitude 40° South.

before Sirius sets. Thus for the whole night Sirius will neither rise nor set, but will be visible all through the night. This is called curtailed passage and is marked on the paran maps as "CP."

HELIACAL SETTING—THE END OF THE PERIOD OF CURTAILED PASSAGE

Moving forward through the calendar until the Sun is at 10° Aquarius, as the Sun sets at 10° Aquarius, 10° Leo will be rising and Sirius will be in the night sky, having risen at 9° Gemini. As the Sun rises on the following day, at about 10° Aquar-

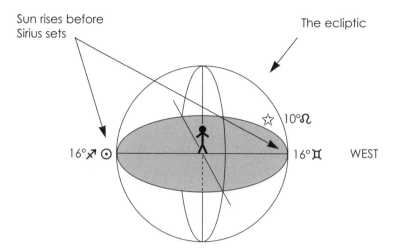

Figure 30. The curtailed passage of Sirius for latitude 40° South.

ius, 10° Leo will be setting. Thus Sirius will be setting (heliacal setting), and this is the end of the period of curtailed passage (see figure 31, p. 328). Sirius will be starting to set as the Sun rises, thus the star will just start to touch the horizon.

THE TIME OF PASSAGE

The *time of passage* is the period of time when Sirius is visible in the night sky, and some time during the night rises or sets. The star appears to "have passage," that is to say, contact, with the horizon line. This period will last from the heliacal setting to the acronychal rising of the star. In the above example, for Sirius observed at 40° South, its time of passage will be from the Sun at 10° Aquarius until the Sun reaches 9° Sagittarius. So the period of curtailed passage will last while the Sun travels from 9° Sagittarius to 10° Aquarius.

DETERMINING THE LENGTH OF TIME A STAR IS IN ITS PERIOD OF CURTAILED PASSAGE

The period of curtailed passage for any star can be determined by reading the heliacal setting column on the paran maps (see figure 22, p. 320). Starting with the rising line for 40° South, the corresponding date is about December 1. Then, using the setting line at 40° South, the corresponding date is January 30. So at latitude 40° South, Sirius has a period of curtailed passage from December 1 to January 30, whereas for a latitude of 20° South the period of curtailed passage for Sirius is from about December 15 to about January 15.

When a star is in its phase of curtailed passage, it does not visibly touch the earth; that is, it does not appear to touch the horizon line. And although there is very little written concerning the meaning of this phase, it can be hypothesized that the star's influence is less concerned with the affairs of the earth, for the star

Sirius appears to
set as the Sun rises

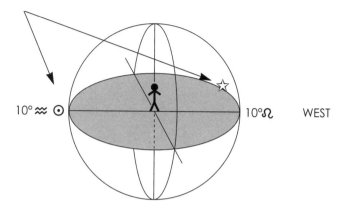

$10° \approx \odot$ $10° \Omega$ WEST

Figure 31. Heliacal setting of Sirius for latitude 40° South.

has moved temporarily into the realm of the immortal circumpolar stars, appearing never to set and thus beyond the affairs of humans.

TRUE OR APPARENT PHASES

With star phases, one can work with visual or apparent phases, or true phases, or that which the Egyptians called cosmic risings. For example, the apparent heliacal rising of a star is its *visual* rising just before the sun. The star itself could be anything from 8° to 11° in front of the rising Sun. Similarly, for the apparent heliacal setting, which is the star that sets just before the dawn light spreads across the sky, the star will be 7° to 10° before the opposition to the Sun. Apparent phases are based on visual facts.

True phases, on the other hand, are not based on the visual concept but rather on a *mathematical* one. The true or cosmic rising of a star is the day that it rises exactly when the Sun is on the horizon.[4] The Egyptians used the term "heliacal" only for visual risings and settings, whereas the term "cosmic" was used for the true risings.[5] However, by Ptolemy's time, both risings with the Sun were defined as heliacal, one true, the other apparent.[6] Both types of rising were used from the earliest of times.

All the maps in this book are for the true phases, and the apparent phases can be calculated by adjusting the dates accordingly. In Ptolemy's time this adjustment was the following: In the case of stars of the first magnitude, for heliacal

---

[4] It would seem that no allowances were made for the size of the sphere of the Sun.
[5] Lockyer, *The Dawn of Astronomy*, pp. 121, 160.
[6] Ptolemy, *The Phases of the Fixed Stars*, p. 4.

risings and settings, a difference of 11° was commonly used if the star and the Sun were on the same horizon. If they were on opposite horizons, then a depression of 7° was used.[7] For stars of the second magnitude, the values were 14° and 8.5°, respectively.[8] Thus for a first magnitude star:

- The apparent heliacal rising would be when the star rose about 11° before the Sun. Sun and star both on the eastern (rising) side of the horizon.
- The apparent acronychal setting would be when the star sets about 11° after the Sun. Sun and star both on the western (setting) horizon.
- The apparent heliacal setting would be when the star was about 7° from setting as the Sun rose. The Sun (east) and the star (west) on opposite horizons.
- The apparent acronychal rising would be when the star had risen about 7° as the Sun was setting. The Sun (west) and the star (east) on opposite horizons.

The dilemma of which phase to use was an unanswered question. Ptolemy states:

> For appearing is the manifestation of a figuration at once definite (on the horizon) and apparent, and of the figurations set out, the true ones make the times themselves unclear, while the apparent ones make the places of the Sun unclear.[9]

In other words, for true phases, one is not precisely certain when the star is on the horizon, since it is lost in the Sun's light, and with apparent phases, one is equally uncertain of the exact position of the Sun because it has not risen.

DETERMINING THE TRUE HELIACAL RISING OR SETTING FOR A STAR

Each paran map can be used to find the true phases of the star for any given latitude. Figure 22 (p. 320) is the map for Sirius. At a latitude of 40° North, the rising line indicates Sirius will rise at that latitude at about 9° Leo. Moving across the row to the heliacal rising column, the date given is August 3. However, the point being shown by the map is a little before the line for August 3, so a more accurate reading would be August 1. Therefore, Sirius's true heliacal rising at a latitude of 40° North occurs on August 1.

Look at the setting line and travel across to the heliacal setting column. The date there is December 3. Therefore, Sirius's true heliacal setting at a latitude of 40° North occurs on December 3.

---

[7] The number of degrees before or after the exact opposition.
[8] Lockyer, *The Dawn of Astronomy*, p. 121.
[9] Ptolemy, *The Phases of the Fixed Stars*, p. 4.

DETERMINING THE TRUE ACRONYCHAL RISING OR SETTING FOR A STAR

Using the acronychal headings to the columns, Sirius at 40° North sets at 10° Gemini, and in the acronychal setting column, the date is June 1. Therefore: Sirius's true acronychal setting at a latitude 40° North occurs on June 1.

Now look at the Sirius rising line and cross to the row for acronychal rising. The date given is January 30. Once again the intersection point on the map is a little before this, so call the date January 28. Therefore, Sirius's true acronychal rising at a latitude 40° North occurs on January 28.

THE STARS TO USE TO DETERMINE THE HELIACAL RISING STAR OF THE DAY

In determining the nature of a particular day by establishing what stars were the heliacal rising or setting, a natural question arises: which stars to use? There are eight thousand visible stars, so this question is best answered by Ptolemy, who says:

> As for our not inserting some of the fainter of the stars named by the ancients . . . one must concede, if the question is not weighty, that especially the last and first phases of such small stars are altogether phantasms because they are hard to distinguish and hard to consider anyway. . . . Then, it is quite clear that, since this first publication is submitted by us only as far as fixed stars of the first and second magnitude for the reasons set out . . .[10]

Ptolemy goes on to explain that other, fainter stars would only be in conflict with the brighter stars and points out that it would be incorrect to have the heliacal rising attributed to a faint star when it is also the heliacal rising of a bright star.

Table 1 (page 331) lists Ptolemy's stars of the first and second magnitude and should be used as a guide for determining which stars can be the heliacal rising star for the day of birth. Appendixes C and D also contain paran maps of the heliacal rising and acronychal setting of all major stars to aid the astrologer in finding this information for any date and location.

Further support of the use of just a limited number of fixed stars is given in the list of key stars for the Babylonians, twenty-eight in all,[11] a number important also in the Egyptian calendar of star risings and in the number of lunar mansions.

---

[10]Ptolemy, *The Phases of the Fixed Stars*, p. 9.
[11] Lockyer, *The Dawn of Astronomy*, p. 408.

Table 1. Ptolemy's Stars.

1st Magnitude Stars	2nd Magnitude Stars
Capella (Auriga)	Algol* (Perseus)
Wega (Lyra)	Menkalinan† (Auriga)
Arcturus (Bootes)	Deneb (Cygnus)
Regulus (Leo)	Alphecca (Corona Borealis)
Denebola (Leo)	Castor (Gemini)
Aldebaran (Taurus)	Pollux (Gemini)
Procyon (Canis Minor)	Alpheratz (Andromeda)
Beletguese (Orion)	Altair (Aquila)
Spica (Virgo)	Bellatrix (Orion)
Rigel (Orion)	Alphard (Hydra)
Sirius (Canis Major)	Zuben eschamali (Libra)
Formalhaut (Piscis Australis)	Zuben elgenubi (Libra)
Achernar** (Eridanus)	Alnilam (Orion)
Canopus (Carina)	Antares (Scorpius)
Rigel Kentaurus (Centaurus)††	Rukbat (Sagittarius)

* Ptolemy just says "the bright star in Perseus." The brightest star is Marfak, but common opinion is that Ptolemy was referring to Algol.

† The star is not included in this text as Capella and El Nath, which are included, are also from Auriga.

** Ptolemy says here "the last star in Eridanus." In his day this was the star Acamar. However, this star only has a magnitude of 3 and therefore it is strange that he would include it on his list of first magnitude stars. In modern times the constellation was extended to end with Achernar, a star with a magnitude of 0.4. Since this is such a bright star, it can be concluded that this is the star to which Ptolemy was referring.

†† Also called Toliman.

SUMMARY OF DEFINITIONS

There are two types of star phases:

- *arising and lying hidden.* Occurs when a star is observed from a latitude that is in the hemisphere opposite from its declination.
- *curtailed passage.* Occurs when a star is observed from a latitude that is in the same hemisphere as its declination.

THE PERIODS OF STAR PHASES

Heliacal rising: The rising of a star with the Sun. This marks the end of the period of arising and lying hidden. This is a most important period of the cycle and marks the reappearance of a star after a period of absence from the night sky.

Heliacal setting: The star setting as the Sun rises. This marks the end of the period of curtailed passage and therefore the beginning of the period where a star can touch the earth.

The period of passage: The time of the calendar when a star rises or sets during the night. It will therefore seem to touch the earth and be involved with mortals.

Acronychal setting: The star is setting with the Sun. This marks the beginning of the period of arising and lying hidden.

Acronychal rising: The star is rising as the Sun sets. This marks the beginning of the period of curtailed passage.

Arising and lying hidden: The period when the star is missing from the night sky. It rises after sunrise and sets before sunset.

Curtailed passage: The period when the star is permanently in the night sky, having risen before the Sun sets and not setting until after dawn.

The two types of phases can be represented as follows:

Arising and lying hidden phase: For stars which are observed from the hemisphere opposite from their declination. See figure 32, below.

Curtailed passage phase: For stars that are observed from the same hemisphere as their declination. See figure 33, p. 333.

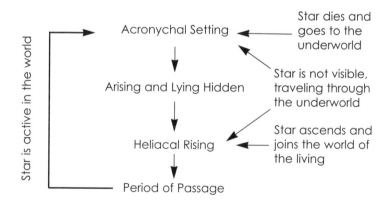

Figure 32. The stages in the phase of arising and lying hidden.

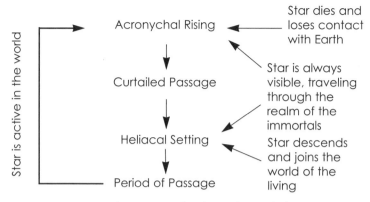

Figure 33. The stages in the phase of curtailed passage.

STAR PHASES IN NATAL AND MUNDANE ASTROLOGY

Due to the phenomena of star phases some stars disappear for a time from the night sky and the first sign of their reappearance, if they have been arising and lying hidden, will be their rising just before the dawn. To the Egyptians, any rising celestial object belonged to Horus and was an expression of Horus.[12] Thus the heliacal rising star was the return of that version of the god and therefore such a return needed to be watched for and celebrated. Obviously any particular star would, apart from the effects of precession, always rise before the dawn for the same period in the calendar from one year to the next, and indeed the Egyptian calendar was based on these risings.[13] But because these risings were also linked to Horus, the calendar was interwoven into the fabric of religious practice. Great temples were built to be aligned with the heliacal risings of certain stars: Annu, aligned to Capella around 5,000 B.C.E.; Tyre, aligned to Wega around 3,000 B.C.E.;[14] and the temple known as Seti II, built at Karnak,[15] was aligned to the rising of Canopus for the period around 1,300 B.C.E.—to name a few. The starlight would, with the aid of polished stones and gold, shine on the darkened statue of the god or goddess,[16]

---

[12] Lockyer, *The Dawn of Astronomy*, p. 149.

[13] The Egyptian calendar is confusing as it contained three types of years: The Vague, 365 days; the Sacred, based on the rising of Sirius; as well as the True year, based on the rising of the Nile. The Sacred year, by coincidence, was the exact same length as the Julian year.

[14] Lockyer, *The Dawn of Astronomy*, p. 161.

[15] Lockyer, *The Dawn of Astronomy*, p. 184.

[16] Temples aligned to the rising light were dedicated to the goddess, while the western, or dying light was the domain of the gods.

indicating the beginning of the period when the immortal had returned to the world and could be touched by mere mortals. However, the azimuth[17] of a star rising is very sensitive to precession, and a temple would only fulfil this function for a few hundred years. To cater to this, the Egyptians would either build a new temple next to the old one but with an alignment changed by just a few degrees, or shift the old temple to the new alignment. It was because of this that early archaeologists considered the Egyptians to be symmetrophobic, that is, to hate symmetry, since their temples would stand next to each other but at slightly different angles, a detail which seemed offensive to the French and English eye. However, the alignment to the heliacal risings of stars was considered by the Egyptians to be of far greater importance than humankind's natural desire for symmetry.

This practice of temple alignment to stars was also carried into the Greek culture. Many of their temples have been found to align to an important star. For example, the rising of Spica was acknowledged by the alignment of the temple of Diana at Ephesus around 715 B.C.E. and two of the temples on the Acropolis were aligned to the rising of the Pleiades, one showing a later alignment time than the other.[18]

It is difficult to find any astrological writings giving meanings to the phases but it is clear from Egyptian theology as well the architecture that the times of a star's contact with the world, that is to say, when it has passage, were considered the period where humans could interact with its energy. In addition, the last star that rose before the early morning light filled the sky (the heliacal rising star) was considered the star or god/goddess whose influence was the major one for that period. There are many stars that rise but the number that were said to claim the day or the period of the calendar was reduced to twenty-four stars by the Egyptians, increased to twenty-eight or thirty by the time of Ptolemy. All of these stars are first or second magnitude and therefore have sufficient strength to be seen just before the dawn and, because of their number, were generally considered to rule for about a two week period. A heliacal rising star would govern the period until the next helical rising star came into view.

This information of star phases and particularly of heliacal risings can be re-applied, tentatively, to the use of fixed stars in modern astrology, as long as we are aware that (although this is one of the oldest, if not *the* oldest astrological technique in the history of the subject) it has been neglected for so long that most of its meaning has been forgotten. We are therefore building up techniques based on very old foundations which, although they are historically solid, still have uncertain parameters.

---

[17] A point on the horizon usually expressed as a compass bearing.
[18] Lockyer, *The Dawn of Astronomy*, p. 424.

STAR PHASES IN NATAL ASTROLOGY

Egyptian tradition, as already discussed, implies that the period when a star has passage, that is to say, when it rises or sets visibly in the night sky, is the period of greatest influence of the star on the mortal world. The height of the star's expression during this period will be when the star becomes the apparent heliacal rising star. For mortals like ourselves who live and deal with this world and who are represented by our natal charts, this is the period when we can interact with the star, where the star's energy can be used in a growing, developing, less fatalistic manner. This is the time when you are in closer contact with the star.

What this implies in modern astrology is that one can take a more psychological approach to the delineation of the star when it has passage.

WHEN A STAR IS OF CURTAILED PASSAGE OR ARISING AND LYING HIDDEN

For stars that are in either a period of curtailed passage or arising and lying hidden there is a lack of contact with the Earth, for they do not visually touch the horizon. In this situation the star tends to express itself more fatefully, with the individual concerned being unable to influence the theme of the star. The meaning of such a star is more black and white, very much in the older style of fixed star use. The star may therefore raise you to great heights but also dash you on the rocks of failure. There is less human control over a star that is without passage, whether because of its phases or because it is circumpolar in that latitude. Whichever way, it is more difficult to work with stars that do not touch the horizon.

THE APPARENT HELICAL RISING STAR FOR THE DATE AND PLACE OF BIRTH

In addition to a star's phase ability to adjust the expression of a star, the apparent heliacal rising star for the date and time of birth can also be considered, for everyone is born with a particular star ruling the day, according to its being the apparent or true heliacal rising star. In practice this means that you will be working with a sunrise chart and using orbs of 10° to 14° while looking for the last bright star to rise *before* sunrise. Indeed the orb used is not relevant, as you are looking for a bright star that has just risen (apparent) or is just rising (true). You are looking for the star that "ruled" the period of time in which you were born.

For example, Albert Einstein was born in Ulm, Germany, latitude 48° 30'North and Longitude 10° 00' East, on March 14, 1879.[19] See chart 2, page 336. On the morning of his birth, the true heliacal rising star for the day was Hamal, the alpha star of Aries. Hamal is the true heliacal rising star for 48° 30' North from about March 12 to 17 every year. At the same time as Hamal rises

---

[19] Blackwell's Data Set, Astrolabe.

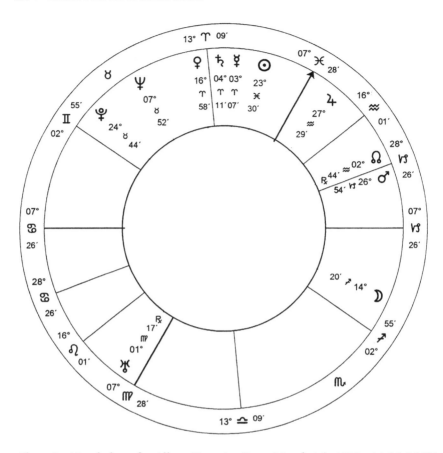

Chart 2. Natal chart for Albert Einstein. Born March 14, 1879; 11:30 LMT (10:50 UT) Ulm, Germany; 48N24 10E00. Geocentric, Tropical, Regiomontanus Houses, True Node. Data from Blackwell. Source: From the civil registry.

with the Sun for that latitude, Betelgeuse culminates while being in a phase of "having passage." Every year in the middle of March, for that latitude, Hamal rises with the Sun as Betelgeuse culminates. So Albert Einstein was a mixture of Hamel and Betelguese, according to the phases of the stars.

Hamal's meaning is to be able to do one's own thinking, to be independent, not one of the group. To dare to be different. Betelgeuse is one of the great stars of the sky and implies great success. It has passage, so this success can be personal and controlled in his life.

Now, the important point to be aware of is that *every* March 14 in the city of Ulm, Germany, for around one hundred years plus or minus from Einstein's birth, this will be the case, and clearly there are no other great geniuses born on that calendar date. What makes it special for Einstein was that this energy of greatness and independence was linked to particularly strong aspects in his chart. One of the interesting features of Einstein's chart is that he has Mercury conjunct Saturn and this conjunction was linked to the heliacal rising star for that period, for the Saturn-Mercury conjunction rose with Hamal (see figure 34, below). So he was touched by both stars. He has a personal contact with the heliacal rising situation on the day of his birth. Both Hamal and Betelgeuse are focused into his chart via his Mercury and Saturn. There were probably other children born on that day at that latitude with Einstein's conjunction. Why he was affected and not the others is one of the great unanswered questions of astrology.

The technique displayed here is very ancient and is fundamentally the acknowledgment of the importance of the heliacal rising star at birth. We can hypothesize that this star has an imprint on the natal chart and magnifies this imprint if, firstly, any other major star is on an angle at sunrise and, secondly and most importantly, we personalize this stellar energy by interpreting the star's contact with transiting and natal planets. Note that in Einstein's chart the Saturn-Mercury conjunction is in his 10th house, yet we are not concerned with this. We are looking at what was on the angles at sunrise.

Another example is the day of birth of Neil Armstrong, born August 5, 1930, at latitude 40° 31' North. At that latitude the heliacal rising of Sirius occurs in late July and early August. During its heliacal rising for this latitude Alpheratz also culminates. Alpheratz at this time is just entering its period of curtailed passage.

Sirius is the brightest star in the sky and is powerful almost to the point of being destructive to the individual. With Sirius, the individual does not count. It

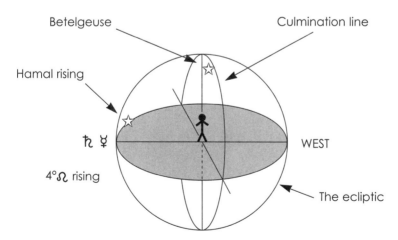

Figure 34. Betelgeuse culminating as Hamal rises. March 14, 1879, Ulm, Germany. Latitude 48° 30' North.

is transforming and makes sacred all that it touches, whether this be to the betterment or detriment of the individual. Alpheratz can be thought of as Pegasus, the flying Horse, its original constellation. It represents speed, movement, going faster, further than anybody else. The fact that Alpheratz was entering a curtailed passage period could emphasize its meaning, making its expression more extreme. These two stars have been coming together at this latitude for at least two hundred years. However, on this particular day of Neil Armstrong's birth, as the Sun rose with Sirius and Alpheratz reached culmination, the transiting true north Node also culminated, thereby linking his chart to the potential defined by these two stars. Once again there would have been other people born with links to this pattern but that does not detract from the fact that the first man to travel further and faster than any other human was born on this heliacal rising combination. The presence of Sirius shows us that, although it was the work of thousands that put Neil Armstrong on the Moon, he was the person chosen to become the symbol of this human achievement. He was the one who physically walked on the Moon. He was the one placed in the saddle of Pegasus.

Margaret Thatcher, the first woman to become a British prime minister and since made a baroness, was born on October 13, 1925, at latitude 52° North 55'. For this date, at that location, the apparent heliacal rising star is Alphecca. The true heliacal rising occurred about ten days earlier but no other bright stars had yet risen with the Sun, so the days were still ruled by Alphecca. The meaning of Alphecca is very simply to be handed a crown. To be given a prize. Margaret Thatcher has many other fixed stars active in her chart that indicate the position that she gained. However, being born with the heliacal rising of Alphecca indicates the seeking of nobility.

In summary, the heliacal rising star under which you are born is a statement about your life. It influences your persona and the outcomes or goals that you seek. If, for a particular location, other bright stars are also on an angle at the time of sunrise, then those stars will blend themselves to the heliacal rising star. In addition, if there are any transiting planets or luminaries also on an angle at the same time, then your fate is tied to these stars.

PHASES IN MUNDANE ASTROLOGY

This was one of the very first practices in astrology. Great importance was placed by the Egyptians on the heliacal rising of a star and particularly if any other stars or planets were involved, as this was an omen of things to come. Stars were seen to rule and affect nations, and although we may like to think that a nation can amend the expression of the fixed stars to which it is connected, these stars are very potent.

WORKING WITH HELIACAL RISINGS IN MUNDANE ASTROLOGY

Ignoring the effects of precession, stars will rise on a given calendar date at a given parallel of latitude, sometimes with other major stars either culminating or setting at the same time. For graphs of the heliacal rising of stars for any latitude or degree of the zodiac see Appendixes C and D. For example, at a latitude of 35° North Sirius rises as Achernar is culminating. Achernar is the star whom the Greeks considered to be the son of Apollo, the son who is cast from the sky to his death because he was setting the Earth and the sky alight. This star is very much about destructive fire and water, literally or metaphorically. Sirius was the most important star in the ancient world, the brightest star in the sky. This star defined the Egyptian year and religious festivals and was called "The Scorcher." It has the ability to transform everything it touches, raising it to brilliance or sacredness.

The true heliacal rising of Sirius for 35° North in this century is July 28. And every year at that latitude on that day, as Sirius rises with the Sun, Achernar will be culminating. This combination of stars is very violent at the best of times, and will occur every year, but it will only erupt when a slow-moving transiting planet becomes involved via paran to the two stars.

Between the years of 1943 and 1947 Pluto was involved in the heliacal rising of Sirius at this latitude. Pluto was at early degrees of Leo, so as the Sun rose in late July and early August the combination of stars and planets was Sirius, Achernar, and Pluto. On August 6, 1945, Hiroshima, a city on that latitude, was destroyed by nuclear attack. Within three days, on August 9, Nagasaki was also destroyed. Although a little lower in latitude, this city was also at that time being affected by the same stars. The astrological reason as to why this happened in 1945 and not one of the other years has to do with the star El Nath, which is associated with weapons. In 1945 Uranus was also rising with El Nath at those latitudes. However, what is not obvious is why Hiroshima and Nagasaki, and not some other location on this latitude, were attacked. This may be answered by geodetic astrology.

As already stated, a star will rise on a particular date for a particular latitude. Thus Sirius will rise in early August *only* for a latitude of about 35° North. However, geodetic methods emphasize longitude. In geodetic astrology a point is taken on the Earth's surface to represent 0° Aries. Once this is established, then the rest of the 360° of the zodiac can be laid out on the equator moving in an easterly direction. Generally the starting point for such an Earth-based zodiac is the prime meridian, the longitude line of 0° passing through Greenwich, England. Thus if a planet was transiting through 10° Aries, placed on a map of the world that planet would be transiting at 10° East in longitude. Thus the marriage of these two fields of astrology, fixed stars with geodetic, may finally give us a system which yields precise locations, as one indicates latitudes and the other longitudes. Indeed in this period, using the prime meridian, Greenwich, as 0°, Aries places transiting Pluto over Japan by geodetic principles. Thus by fixed stars calculation the emphasis is on Pluto, Sirius, and Achernar for August, 1943 to 1947, at a latitude of 35° North; and by geodetic astrology we have an emphasis on Pluto for the dates of early August, 1943 to 1947, at a longitude of about 130° East. Hiroshima's coordinates are 34°30' North 132° 30' East.

This example examines a time when transiting Pluto was involved with those stars, but obviously the parallel of 35° North is very sensitive around early August, particularly if there are slow-moving planets or, indeed, any difficult planetary combination transiting through early degrees of Leo.

Baghdad, capital of Iraq, is at a latitude of 33° 20' North and so is also under the influence of Sirius and Achernar in early August every year. In 1990, while Sirius was the heliacal rising star, there was a Mars-Pluto opposition. This opposition occurred at the degrees of the culmination of Menkar. Menkar represents the collective unconscious and is probably one of the most difficult stars in the heavens. On August 2, 1990, Saddam Hussein began his invasion of Kuwait. He went to war under the heliacal rising of Sirius and the culmination of Achernar, with disastrous consequences for his country.

This latitude is also affected at other times. During mid-April every year at the heliacal rising of Hamal, the alpha star of Aries, a most difficult star named Facies also culminates. Facies is the face of the Archer. It represents a war machine, a combat soldier, ruthless and, at worst, very violent. From about April 9 to 23, Hamal is at first the true heliacal rising star, and later the apparent heliacal rising star, with no other bright star laying claim to the Sun. Around April 17–19 every year Facies culminates with the sunrise which is ruled by Hamal.

So this period of time for this latitude of 35° North is also a sensitive time, being a combination of headstrong energy, Hamal, and the potential ruthlessness of Facies. In 1995 for this latitude, in this sensitive period, transiting Mars, Neptune, and Uranus all moved into a paran relationship with Menkar. Once again Menkar raised its ugly head. On April 19, 1995, the bombing of the governmental office building in Oklahoma City occurred. Okalahoma City is at a latitude of 35° 30' North.

Another example involves the city of San Francisco, at 37° 35' North. This city, although a few degrees higher in latitude, has this same combination of Hamal heliacally rising as Facies culminates. Hamal is the true heliacal rising star on April 9 and (as in Oklahoma City) holds that position for about two weeks. Similar to Oklahoma City, the few days from the 17th to 19th of April are very sensitive, as this is the culmination of Facies. In 1906 there was a transiting Uranus-Neptune opposition which was within one degree of being exact. The zodiacal degrees at which this opposition was occurring were the same degrees of culmination and Nadir for Facies. On April 18, 1906, a great earthquake occurred at the very moment that Facies culminated with this opposition. If ancient astrologers had been living in that city at that time, they would have spotted that potential date years before the earthquake.

In this brief examination of the latitudes from about 33° to 38° North, the dates of early August and mid-April are emphasized by history: Hiroshima, Nagasaki, and the invasion of Kuwait in early August; and the San Francisco earthquake and the Oklahoma bombing in mid-April. These examples are dramatic and violent but not all fixed stars are going to yield these results; it is just that history records wars and disasters, rather than good news. These examples of natal charts and historical events imply that this most ancient method of working with fixed stars may still be very applicable in our modern world.

In Appendices C and D there are graphs and tables to enable you to determine the heliacal rising star for any date in this century.

SUMMARY OF WORKING WITH STAR PHASES

- The heliacal rising star will influence the day and thereby the natal chart.
- Any other star on an angle at that time will blend its energy with the heliacal rising star.
- Any planet or luminary involved with these stars, via paran, will personalize the energy of the stars into the natal or mundane chart.
- Stars linked to any other planet or luminary via visual parans will have their hardest, more fatalistic effect if they are in a phase of curtailed passage or arising and lying hidden.
- Stars linked to any other planet or luminary via paran will have a more psychological than fatalistic effect if they are in a phase of having passage.

Star phases are both the oldest system we have for working with fixed stars, as well as the newest, so the key is experimentation and documentation.

Part 5

FIXED STARS AND THE NATAL CHART

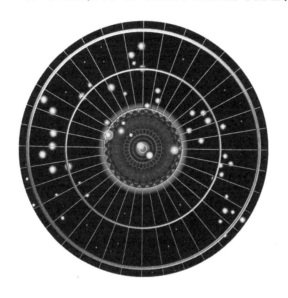

WORKING WITH FIXED STARS

FIXED STARS ADD ANOTHER COMPONENT
to the chart. A natal star list or map for a birth time and place, while very different from a horoscope, will still contain a great deal of information concerning the individual. Also, such a star list will not be entirely dependent upon an accurate time of birth, unless you are only focusing on the stars on the angles at the precise moment of birth.

The first step in working with fixed stars is to determine which ones are forming paran relationships to your chart. You can create this list either by working with the paran maps provided for each star or by using an appropriate software package to generate this list for you. Once you have this list, you need to sort it into rising stars, culminating stars, setting stars, and stars on the Nadir, which divides a life into four periods, the first three being those effective during a person's life and the last being the summation of the life work. Hence one can consider the first twenty-five years of life as the early years (rising), the years from the late twenties till about sixty as the middle years (culminating), and the years after the early sixties as the later years (setting).[1]

Having constructed this list, you will then need to use the graphs in Appendix C to find the heliacal rising star that was active at the time of birth, as well as checking the paran maps for each star on the list to determine if the individual stars have passage or not. Stars that do not have passage, i.e., that are in a phase of arising and lying hidden or curtailed passage, will be much stronger and should be delineated in a more black-and-white fashion. Remember also that if a star never rises for a location, then it cannot be used at all.

The following is a set of examples of natal star lists. The first examples are famous people, to make it easier for you to see the workings of the different stars in particular lives. The later examples are of ordinary people, the sort of people who consult an astrologer and are not necessarily going to rule the world. These later star examples have come from my own client files.

ADOLF HITLER

To modern society Hitler represents the face of evil and fascism and for that reason is a good example with which to begin, since we would expect to see difficult stars in his chart. Hitler was born on April 20, 1889 at 5:37 P.M. GMT in Braunau

---

[1] These periods are just a rule of thumb, but if a person dies early, then his or her short life is not divided into three periods, but is seen as not moving past the rising stars.

am Inn, Austria, 48°N 15' by 13°E 02'.[2] The following are his fixed star parans using an orb of 0° 30' and the list of sixty-four stars delineated in this text. The parans have not been applied to Uranus, Neptune, Pluto, or the Nodes.

HELIACAL RISING STAR

Hamal,[3] in Aries is similar to Albert Einstein's birth. Hamal's meaning in this position is about a person who is very independent, not a group-oriented person. This individual will put a great deal of energy into projects—but not necessarily in a diplomatic way.

Rising (a star rising on the ascendant as a planet is on the same or another angle)
Wega (Lyra) rising as his Mercury set: curtailed passage.
Formalhaut (Piscis australis) rising as his Mars rose: arising and lying hidden.
Arcturus (Bootes) rising as his Jupiter was on the Nadir: curtailed passage.

Culminating (a star culminating as a planet is on the same or another angle)
Facies (Sagittarius) culminating as his Moon culminated: always has passage.
Menkar (Cetus) culminated as his Mars culminated: has passage.

Setting (a star setting as a planet is on the same or another angle)
Algol (Perseus) setting as his Sun was on the Nadir: permanent curtailed passage.
Denebola (Leo) setting as his Mercury was rising: curtailed passage.
Phact (Columba Noae) setting as his Mercury was set: arising and lying hidden.
Denebola (Leo) setting as his Venus rose: curtailed passage.

On the Nadir (a star on the IC as a planet is on the same or another angle)
Aldebaran (Taurus) on the Nadir as Saturn set: has passage.

Looking at this list of stars, the first point to note is the number of powerful stars present: Formalhaut and Aldebaran, two of the Royal Stars of Persia; and Wega the great star of Orpheus' Lyre. And linked to all this power are three of the most difficult stars in the sky: Algol, the head of the gorgon; Facies, the ruthless face of the archer; and Menkar, the terrifying energy of the collective unconscious unleashing its expression into the conscious world. It is not unusual for a chart to pick up a relationship with any one of these stars but these three, combined with the power-giving potential of the Royal Stars, makes for a very unusual and potentially formidable combination.

---

[2] Blackwell's Data Set, Astrolabe.
[3] According to Ptolemy, Hamal is too faint to herald the dawn but it does seem that it is worth noting the presence of the alpha star of Aries.

HITLER'S YOUTH—THE RISING STARS

The symbolism of the rising stars will be expressed in childhood and young adulthood and then will form a part of the very fabric of the person.

Hitler's Mercury set as Wega rose. Wega is the magical, charismatic star and having it linked to Mercury implies either magical ideas or fantasies, as well as the ability to talk, to charm, to have charisma by the spoken or written word. This skill would have been with Hitler from his early childhood. He was therefore a naturally skilled, charismatic orator who had the potential of creating the magic of Orpheus's music with his voice: hypnotic and entrancing. This is further emphasized by the star being in curtailed passage: the star has less contact with the Earth and is therefore more extreme or less easily modified by life's experiences.

To add to this charm, Formalhaut rose with his Mars. Formalhaut is the Royal Star that relates to idealism and noble causes. All Royal Stars relate to action, with the person keen to achieve or to follow a cause. If you have a strong Formalhaut, you will be prepared to go against society in the pursuit of your dreams, lofty ideals, or visions. Being a Royal Star, the pathway will be narrow but potentially very successful. The narrowness of the path or nemesis that must be overcome is the tendency to be corrupted along the path toward these high ideals and plans, allowing the ideals to lose touch with reality. Thus Formalhaut seeks the purity of its ideals but must keep them grounded. However, the star is in a phase of arising and lying hidden, so the potential for these ideals to be disconnected from the reality of human life is greatly increased. In this case the connection to Mars implies that young Hitler was motivated to take action on his political beliefs. The foundation for these beliefs came from his childhood and later these ideals took shape in his adult life. Since the star is a Royal Star, he was not going to be an armchair philosopher, but rather a man who actively sought the expression of his dreams.

The third rising star was Arcturus, which rose as his Jupiter was on the Nadir. Arcturus is the alpha star of Bootes, the hunter-gatherer turned cultivator. It represents a person who is prepared to try something new. A person who is willing to take a risk to create a new way of life. Jupiter simply amplifies any star with which it is involved. This combination talks of a person who will be seeking a new path, a new way of doing things or a new lifestyle. The star is in a period of curtailed passage, so the journey on which he leads his people is not necessarily one based on worldly practicality.

These three stars together describe Hitler's ability to speak and convince others of the greatness or loftiness of his ideals and dreams that he then put into action. He was seen as the leader of a new age, of a new way of being. These were skills and ideals that were there from an early age. The charm and power that is the energy of Alpheratz is the human archetype or driving force to create a better life.

THE PRIME OF HITLER'S LIFE: THE STARS CULMINATING

The symbolism of these stars will be expressed in the prime of his life and represent the cause he lives for, his career.

Facies culminated with the Moon and it always has passage as it is very close to the ecliptic. Facies is a most difficult star and defines either the victim of ruthless violence or the perpetrator. Linked with the Moon, we may simply be looking at a strong emotional loss in the prime of Hitler's life. However, when it is linked with the stars that are rising in this chart, implying a charismatic leader, we may well believe he is going to be assassinated as the victim of the Archer's stare. But history tells us that the ideals and plans that so motivated him had to do with the purity of a race, and so meant pursuing political ideals at the expense of other races and cultures. This was the emotional drive in Hitler, the link to his Moon, showing us that this was what he strongly believed would bring him the greatest happiness.

The culmination of Menkar with Mars is also alarming when viewed in the light of the other stars active in his chart. Menkar has passage but it is grouped with so many other difficult stars that this does not really help. Here is the star that represents the beast from the collective unconscious. Linked with Mars it describes a person who acts as the vehicle for the eruption of the collective emotions into the conscious world, either as the victim or the perpetrator.

These two stars are culminating. So the prime of Hitler's life, what he seeks, the things he wants to achieve, are expressed by these two most violent stars which are linked to the charismatic and idealistic stars of his youth. This gives him power, power to bring his dreams into reality and the ability to succeed. However, these dreams are filled with idealism and as such belong to the artist, not the politician. For the lofty ideals of Formalhaut are not the necessary ingredients for a politician who needs to represent all people, not just his or her personal goals. So the fixed stars indicate that he will seek a violent pathway for the fulfilment of those dreams, either as a victim or as an aggressor. He will become either the noble figure who is cut down in his prime or the noble figure who cuts down others who stand in his way.

THE LATER PART OF HITLER'S LIFE: THE STARS SETTING

The symbolism of these stars will be expressed in the later part of his life, in his old age or at the end of his life. They are the summation or results of his life work. As we know, Hitler did not live past the war, and died in his mid-50s, so he would have been only approaching the expression of his setting stars.

Algol, with Curtailed Passage, set as his Sun was on the Nadir. This is the head of the gorgon, considered by many astrologers to be the most evil star in the sky, and it is linked to his Sun. Hitler is seen as evil, or at one with the gorgon, the beast, the thing to be feared. His Mercury and Venus are linked to Denebola, the star in the tail of Leo. Denebola represents going against society, being out of step, and it is in a phase of curtailed passage: hence its meaning is emphasized. As the war drew to a conclusion Hitler was starting to lose power. His followers were starting to see his ideals and dreams as incorrect or "out of step" and the magic spell of his oratory was breaking down.

HITLER'S LIFEWORK: THE STARS ON THE NADIR

The meaning of stars on the Nadir is very similar to that of the setting stars in that it is expressed in the later part of life or after death. They represent the summation or results of one's life work, how one is remembered.

Generally, any star that is forming a culminating relationship with a planet on the MC or IC will form this same relationship on the Nadir. Hitler had Mars culminating with Menkar. About twelve hours later, when Mars was on the Nadir, Menkar was there also. Thus these paran relationships are going to be duplicated, firstly, with the star culminating and, secondly, with the star on the Nadir. You may read them in both places if you wish or you may choose to read just one position. I tend to read them with the star culminating but feel free to experiment. I only look at stars on the Nadir if they are there at the times when a planet is rising or setting.

Aldebaran, which has passage, was on the Nadir as Hitler's Saturn set. Saturn with any star relates to what you can build with that star, how you are seen to use it. Aldebaran is one of the Royal Stars of Persia and is the eye of the Bull in Taurus. This is a great star, which has its basis in integrity and fairness. With Aldebaran having passage, Hitler would have been given many opportunities throughout his life to act with fairness and consideration, for the star describes the correct way to deal with others, not only in business and politics but in all walks of life. If this is compromised, then the star, like any Royal Star, will suggest a downfall. Hitler's lifework did not come to pass because that lifework, based on his political ideals, was flawed in the eyes of Aldebaran. It is this combination of Aldebaran with Saturn which tells us that this political, charismatic figure must work for the common good of all or suffer the total loss of all that he held precious. For Aldebaran is connected with the god Ahura Mazda and the fate of any person who broke his rules was an ordeal by fire. In a strange twist, Hitler served as a lesson about the dangers of fascist pathways: a lesson from Aldebaran.

In conclusion, if the young Hitler had come to you to have a look at his fixed stars, you would have praised the visions and ideals of his youth but emphasized that his lifework would come to nothing if he did not act with fairness to all. Being aware of the violence of his middle years, you may have tried to steer him away from the public arena, urging him to write or paint and to avoid the political stage. However, being aware that the violence was there, you could have advised him to write about or depict in painting a level of society that was being victimized, in the hope that this would handle the energy of these turbulent stars. It would have been a difficult consultation. In all the years I have been working with fixed stars this way, Hitler's combination of stars is the darkest I have ever seen.

It is important to remember that one difficult fixed star by itself does not cause too many problems but, rather, it is the combination of stars that takes the main focus. If Hitler had not had all the power and charisma of Formalhaut and Wega focused into his Mars and Mercury, respectively, he would not have had the ability to sway others to his way of thinking. Without that, the violent stars of his middle years would have had a very different expression.

PABLO PICASSO

A totally different figure from Hitler, but just as passionate and intense, is Pablo Picasso. Picasso died recognized as one of the world's greatest artists. He died in glory, not in flames. He was born on October 25, 1881, at 11:33 P.M. GMT in Malaga, Spain, 36°N45' 04°W26'.[4] (orb used, 00° 30'). Uranus, Neptune, Pluto, and the Nodes are not used.

HELIACAL RISING STAR: THE STAR OF PICASSO'S LIFE, HIS ESSENCE
Alphecca (Corona Borealis), and in the same period, Spica (Virgo). Since Spica is the brighter star, it would most likely have claimed this period.

Rising (his youth)
Alpheratz (Pegasus) rising as his Moon culminated: has passage.
Regulus (Leo) rising as his Mercury was on the Nadir: always has passage.
Scheat (Pegasus) rising as his Jupiter was on the Nadir: has passage.
Sirius (Canis Major) rising as the Ascendant rose, thus it was rising at the moment of birth: has passage.

Culminating (his prime and middle years)
Thuban (Draco) culminating as his Sun culminated (Thuban is always in a phase of curtailed passage).
Hamal (Aries) culminating as his Sun was on the Nadir: curtailed passage.

---

[4] Lois Rodden, Astro Data II (Tempe, AZ: AFA, 1988). This is dirty data. However, apart from Sirius rising with his Ascendant, any change in birth time will not affect the other fixed stars. Stars via parans are very sensitive to location but not so much to time. We do know Picasso's place of birth is correct.

Canopus (Argo) culminating as Venus rose: has passage.
Arcturus (Bootes) culminating as Mars set: has passage.

Setting (the later part of his life)
Zuben Elgenubi (Libra) setting as Saturn rose: always has passage.
Menkar (Cetus) setting as Saturn set: has passage.

On the Nadir (his life work)
Murzims (Canis Major) was on the Nadir as Venus set: has passage.

Note: Most of Picasso's stars have passage but most of Hitler's did not. Stars that have passage can be worked with and modified, for there is a far greater human element involved with the star's expression.

HELIACAL RISING STAR—THE STAR OF HIS LIFE, HIS ESSENCE
Spica represents a great gift or talent and to be born on its apparent heliacal rising indicates that Picasso was born with this gift. Every year at that latitude, at that time, Spica is the heliacal rising star. Thus by itself it will give a drive or a desire to express this gift, but without the support of other stars it would only struggle, not necessarily manifest. Picasso has other powerful stars to support Spica, so in his life we can see the brilliance of Spica.

PICASSO'S YOUTH—THE RISING STARS
This is a most powerful combination of stars. If he was born when Sirius was rising, then Sirius is one of the major stars in his chart. Sirius is the brightest star in the sky and has passage at the time of his birth. Sirius suggests greatness but only if one totally surrenders to its force. It is the Scorcher that burns off mortal flesh, giving immortality. The burning of the mortal flesh can be a very difficult experience. For Picasso, however, Sirius has passage, which greatly reduces its tendency to "burn." Many people are born with Sirius rising and not all of those undergo its journey. However, if they strive to fulfill a passion and devote their life to their goals, then Sirius gives them success but at the cost of their own private life. This star potentially implies that the young Picasso has a great gift or talent and that if he starts to use it, he will have to sacrifice his life to this skill or talent.

Regulus (which always has passage) rose as his Mercury was on the Nadir. This is one of the Royal Stars and is the Heart of the Lion in Leo. It is powerful, will seek action, and promises success, provided revenge is not taken. Linked with his Mercury, it implies that this success will come via writing or some kind of communication. The presence of a Royal Star always implies action and the potential for greatness or success.

Scheat is the star of intellect and thinking and is in the constellation Pegasus. In combination with his Jupiter, which acts as an amplifier, this implies that the young Picasso will be bright and sharp of intellect. It has passage, so his bright intellect will stay connected to the world. He will watch and learn.

Alpheratz rose with his Moon. Alpheratz is the navel of Pegasus but modern astronomers place it in the constellation Andromeda. This star gives a love of freedom, a love of movement, a love of expression and, linked to his Moon, shows Picasso's emotional need for independence. However, since the star has passage, he will be able to find this love of independence without needing to become a loner.

These four stars together, particularly Sirius, Regulus, and Scheat all rising in his chart, portray a very bright young boy whose gifts and talents would have been present and recognized. Thus, Picasso would have been getting recognition from an early age and the nature of his talent would begin to express itself, not in his middle years, but right from birth. History tells us that by the age of 10 he was creating his first paintings and by the age of 15 he was being hailed as an artistic genius.

THE PRIME OF PICASSO'S LIFE : THE STARS CULMINATING

Thuban (always of curtailed passage), in the constellation Draco, is linked to his Sun, his identity. Culminating is the only connection this star can make with his chart as it is circumpolar. Thuban is the treasure chest, the guardian or creator of a treasure. It represents hoarding, stockpiling, collecting, and so on. This star does not relate to art, or even talent, but given the rising stars already discussed, Picasso's works will either be worth a great deal or he will be prolific. Indeed both of these statements are correct. He created more than twenty thousand pieces of art and each of his creations had great value, even during his own lifetime. He is the only artist to have been hung in the Louvre while still living.

This driving force to create also floods into his Canopus-Venus combination. Canopus is the great bright star in the south, which would only have risen for a short period for Picasso's place of birth, and it had passage. It is the pathfinder, the forger of a new way, the pilot on the Argo. This star is linked to his Venus, so its energy goes into his relationship as well as his art. Once we know he is an artist, we can see that he will create a new style of art. Cubism was one of them but he also forged pathways in sculpture, engraving, and collage. And because Canopus had passage, Picasso created a path that others could follow. The addition of Hamal, which is in a phase of curtailed passage, also linked to his Sun, shows us the freethinking, independent, possibly headstrong person he would have needed to be to create these new styles or themes. Here is the star without passage, here is the ungrounded star in his freethinking spirit but linked to so many other grounded stars that it helps him break free of the established ideas in art, rather than causing any difficulties. Arcturus, which does have passage, complements Hamal, for it relates to the same concepts. It is linked to his Mars, motivating him to press forward into new areas, new ways of doing things.

So his middle years, built on the talent of his youth, are firstly about pushing into new areas and using his talent in ways that it had not been used before (Hamal, Canopus, and Arcturus all indicate this); and secondly, his ability to compile a large body of work or for his work to be of great value (Thuban with his Sun).

Now if Picasso did not have these stars that were rising (his talents) but simply had the stars that were culminating, he would still have been successful but maybe as a collector or curator of precious things. He would still bring to his work original thinking and independent action. However, he would not have been the great artist that we know. These stars of his middle years are not about his art but his motivation.

THE LATER PART OF PICASSO'S LIFE: THE STARS SETTING

Zuben Elgenubi, with passage, describes practical social reform or involvement, working for or on behalf of groups for a positive outcome. By the age of 63 Picasso had joined his first political party, the Communist Party, and his lithograph "The Dove" (1949) was adopted as the symbol of The World Peace Congress. Zuben Elgenubi is linked to his Saturn and his image of the dove for world peace has lived on. Saturn is also connected to Menkar, the star we encountered in Hitler's chart in Cetus the whale, the beast of the unconscious. In this case Menkar is not linked with other violent stars and has passage. Thus Menkar can express itself as the artist who represents the collective. Great artists tap into the collective; otherwise their work is not recognized. It was on Picasso's ninetieth birthday that his work was hung in the Louvre. Society had claimed him as the greatest living artist in the world and the greatest artist of the twentieth century.

The stars in this position imply that he does not create new themes or start new ideas in his later years. This has all been done in his youth and in his prime. Indeed it was in his later years that he focused on painting works based on the great masters, as well as continuing to sculpt and to engrave.

If we changed his chart so that the stars that were rising were setting instead, then his great talent would have come out in his later years. If we moved the stars that were culminating to the setting position, then the great body of his work and his new styles and themes would not have come out until his later years. When you are working with a person's fixed stars, what is important is the period of life when the stars start to express themselves. This is a major part of the delineation.

There is just one lone star in this position. This star is Murzims, which has passage, and it is linked to his Venus. His art is his life. It is a simple statement. Murzims is in Canis Major and is called the Announcer, indicating something to say. This star tells us that Picasso's lifework lives on. He had a statement to make through his art and we continue to hear his message even after his death. If none of the other great stars were present in his chart, this simple statement would have meant very little, but coming at the end of a great life, it implies that he is remembered and that his work lives on.

CHARLIE CHAPLIN

Charlie Chaplin is the great English film director, actor, producer, and composer who was world famous for his most loved character, The Tramp, in silent films. He was born on April 16, 1889 at 8:00 P.M. GMT in London, England, 51°N31' 00°W06'.[5] (orb used, 00° 30'). Uranus, Neptune, Pluto, and the Nodes are not used.

HELIACAL RISING STAR: THE STAR OF HIS LIFE, HIS ESSENCE
No heliacal rising star.

Rising (his youth)
Mirach (Andromeda) rising as Venus was on the Nadir: permanent curtailed passage.
Facies (Sagittarius) rising as Mars was on the Nadir: always has passage.
Facies (Sagittarius) rising as Jupiter rose: always has passage.
Aldebaran (Taurus) rising as Saturn was on the Nadir: has passage.

Culminating (his prime and middle years)
Menkar (Cetus) culminating as Venus culminated: has passage.
Zosma (Leo) culminating as Venus set: curtailed passage.
Zuben Elgenubi (Libra) culminating as Mars was on the Nadir: always has passage.
Zuben Elgenubi (Libra) culminating as Jupiter culminated: always has passage.

Setting (the later part of his life)
Acumen (Scorpio) setting as the Moon set: permanent curtailed passage.
Hamal (Aries) setting as Mars set: has passage.

On the Nadir (his life work)
Sualocin (Delphinus) was on the Nadir as the Sun set: has passage.

---

[5] Lois Rodden, Astro Data II, AFA, 1988.

Sirius (Canis Major) was on the Nadir as Mercury rose: has passage.
Sirius (Canis Major) was on the Nadir as Venus rose: has passage.

CHAPLIN'S YOUTH: THE RISING STARS

Charlie Chaplin's childhood and youth are expressed by the following stars: Facies, the ruthless face of the Archer; Aldebaran, the great Royal Star of Persia, which talks of success but only through honesty and integrity; and Mirach, the beta star of Andromeda, which is connected to harmony and receptivity. When he was 7 years old, in 1896, Charlie's mother was forced into a workhouse and later became insane and was sent to Cane Hill lunatic asylum. Charlie and his elder brother were sent to an orphanage for destitute children. This was not a easy time for Charlie and the presence of Facies, connected to both his Mars and his Jupiter, indicates a violent and difficult childhood. In his autobiography he talks of these as very unhappy years.

Mirach was also involved in his early years. It is in a phase of permanent curtailed passage, so its expression will be stronger, and it was linked to his Venus. Like Venus, it is receptive, seeking harmony, being open to the flow of events and giving rhythm. This seems to be an emphasis or indication of his talents as an actor and his ability to gain rapport with characters or situations. By the age of 15 Charlie had gone on the road with a traveling troupe of actors and was already showing talent in this area.

Aldebaran has passage and its presence with his Saturn makes a strong but simple statement: if he can maintain his honesty and not move into criminal activity, in all likelihood being exposed to it in his childhood, then he can grow from these experiences and gain great success by using his insight or knowledge of that lifestyle. There is a very strong chance that he will be able to do this as the star has passage, which makes working with the star easier. Years later his character portrayal of the poor, homeless, but honorable Tramp captured the heart of the world. Aldebaran's presence in his childhood indicates an opportunity to move beyond his expected fate of a lowerclass, or even criminal-class Londoner.

THE PRIME OF CHAPLIN'S LIFE: THE STARS CULMINATING

Menkar, which has passage, represents the beast of the collective unconscious. This star is combined with Zosma, which is in a phase of curtailed passage and is the star in Leo which represents the point on the back of the Lion which was broken by Hercules. It describes being a victim or being involved with victims in some way, and this star is very strong in Chaplin's chart because it does not touch the horizon. These two stars are both connected to his Venus. His personal life was often stormy. He was married four times and his divorces were sensationalized in the media. However, the symbolism of these two stars also expressed themselves in his acting, for his greatest roles were those where he portrayed the victims of society.

Zuben Elgenubi always has passage and is one of the Scale stars of Libra. It represents an involvement with social issues, in either a noble way or without seeking personal gain. This star is combined with both Chaplin's Mars, his motivation to make political comments through his work, and Jupiter, which amplifies this. Just before the outbreak of World War II he wrote, produced, and directed the film *The Great Dictator*, a ridicule of Hitler and his political views. Later he took this one step further by urging the United States to support the Russians in their fight against Hitler, a view that led him to be accused of crimes against the state, as the U. S. government feared he was a communist. Note also that Menkar and Zosma symbolism were active as he became cast as the traitor by U. S. society.

THE LATER PART OF CHAPLIN'S LIFE: THE STARS SETTING

Charlie Chaplin has only two setting stars involved in his chart: Acumen, one of the stars in the tail of the Scorpion, which is the sting of the Scorpion; and Hamal, the alpha star of Aries. The first point to note is that in Charlie Chaplin's chart, stars rising, culminating, or on the Nadir are far more powerful than those that are setting, indicating that Charlie's early life, his prime, and indeed even how his life is viewed are more successful than the later years of his life. So although this was not a negative period for him, it was not a period where he achieved anything major.

Acumen is the sting of the Scorpion, which slowly weakens, and in Charlie's chart it is of curtailed passage so its sting is quite strong. It is linked to his Moon and implies that the political charges of which he was accused and proven innocent were based on emotions rather than fact. With Acumen of curtailed passage, however, he was forced to leave the U. S. although he was innocent. If Acumen's partner star, Aculeus, had been the influence then the attack would have strengthened Charlie and, after proving his innocence, he might have gone on to make more social comments through films. Hamal linked to his Mars gave him the strength to handle the hurt of these attacks and by this stage, being a very wealthy man, he was able to live his life in the way he chose. However, in his later years, he did very little creative work.

CHAPLIN'S LIFEWORK: THE STARS ON THE NADIR

This period, the end of his life and how he is seen after his death, is symbolized by two stars: Sirius, the brightest star in the sky, the alpha star of Canis Major; and Sualocin, the alpha star of the Dolphin, connected with playfulness or naivete but also with mastery of one's medium. Both stars have passage, so they are gentler in their expression. Charlie Chaplin started to gain awards in the very twilight of his life. In 1971, when he was 82 years old, he was allowed to return to the United States to receive an Academy Award. He was also made a commander of the Legion of Honor at the Cannes Film Festival.

Sirius contacting his Mercury and Venus implies he will be remembered and honored for his acting and writing. Sirius is the Scorcher, and brings immortality, often at the expense of the individual. The addition of Sualocin linked to his Sun shows that he is remembered for his most famous character, The Tramp: innocent, naive, and playful.

Charlie Chaplin's stars indicate a very difficult childhood but one that can be used as a creative source if he can maintain his integrity. They go on to capture the great activity and success of his middle years, as long as he is involved in, or expressing to the rest of the world, the plight of the poorer class of society and his own political opinions. They indicate that the later years of his life are not that successful or productive. However, his life work will be honored and remembered.

EVERYDAY CLIENTS

Generally an astrologer's clients are not the wealthy, rich, and famous, but rather the common people of everyday life, some more successful than others. The following examples are from my own files and serve to give insight into the method of delineating fixed stars in the everyday situation of the consulting room.

CLIENT 1: A MALE AGED IN HIS EARLY 50S

This man worked in manufacturing until he was 35, then decided to use his life to help others. He left his employment and worked with the homeless and poor of society. He has now devoted his life to working for his religion by designing liturgy, organizing conferences, and being an advisor to different parishes.

At the moment of his birth, Altair was on the Nadir. This is the alpha star of Aquila the Eagle and is connected to a certain boldness of action. At the same time, this boldness is linked to human rights or human relationships. This star on the client's Nadir at birth has passage and indicates that the client will be remembered by his family or his community or globally as a person who did things his own way, and in this manner achieved a level of success fueled by a love or caring for humanity.

Heliacal rising star: the star of his life, his essence
No Heliacal Rising Star.

Rising (his youth)
No stars rising with any planets.

Culminating (his prime and middle years)
Diadem (Coma Berenices) culminating as the Mercury rose: has passage.
Rukbat (Sagittarius) culminating as Mars was on the Nadir: curtailed passage.

Setting (the later part of his life)
Alphecca (Corona Borealis) setting as Jupiter set: has passage.

On the Nadir (his life work)
Mirach (Andromeda) was on the Nadir as Mercury rose: has passage.

THE CLIENT'S YOUTH: THE RISING STARS
None to analyze.

THE PRIME OF THE CLIENT'S LIFE: THE STARS CULMINATING
Now in his early 50s, we can still consider that the client is in his middle years but toward the later part of them. Diadem is the alpha star of Coma Berenices and symbolizes quiet sacrifice. It has passage, so this sacrifice will not be severe or painful.

The reason that my client left a well-paid position in manufacturing was to help others, to counsel, to talk, and even to write about them, for he co-authored a number of books on theology using examples from the work he was doing with the people of the streets. The addition of Rukbat, the feet of the Archer, represents steadiness and calmness, and linked to his Mars, adds great solidness. My client is known for his ability to stay calm, to ignore conflicts, and to bring a steadying influence to the people around him. Indeed one of his major jobs is as a troubleshooter and people-organizer. However, the star is in the phase of curtailed passage and his steadiness can at times turn into inaction, refusing to be decisive or get involved, which has caused him problems from time to time.

THE LATER PART OF THE CLIENT'S LIFE: THE STARS SETTING
There was only one star setting with any of his planets on the day of his birth, and this was Alphecca, which set at the same time as his Jupiter and has passage. Alphecca is the major star of Corona Borealis and is the crown of achievements, but in a quiet way. There is advancement and success but based on a love of others. In this case it is connected to Jupiter, which amplifies its symbolism. Given the history of my client, we could predict that in the later part of his life he will achieve some of his dreams of genuinely helping people or of making a difference. He may do this through his writing or through his work. However, this

achievement will be done quietly, without seeking any real public recognition. It is in his later years where he gains the success that he quietly seeks.

THE CLIENT'S LIFEWORK: THE STARS ON THE NADIR
Mirach was the only star on the Nadir when any of the planets were on other angles. It occupied the Nadir as Mercury rose, and has passage. Mirach is the beta star of Andromeda and is a symbol of harmony and receptivity, active in Charlie Chapin's chart. Linked to my client's Mercury it implies that he will be remembered either for an important work that he writes in the later years of his life, or simply remembered by his family as a quiet, caring man who would always listen to the ideas of others and help and counsel wherever he could.

In summary, then, my client's list of fixed stars tells me, the astrologer, that he will lead a normal life, fulfilling his fate or family expectations until the middle years of his life, when the themes of helping, caring, and sacrifice become the major focus. These similar themes are repeated in the later period, as well as in the summary or completion of his life. In addition, the fixed stars indicate that he should continue with his writing and his work, for it would appear that in later years success comes quietly to him.

CLIENT 2: A MALE IN HIS MID-20s

This is a young man in his mid-20s whose ambition is to become a writer. He failed to gain entrance into university, packed his bags, and set off to a new city to start life as a writer. He supported himself through modeling work after being discovered in a coffee shop by a modeling agency who paid him well. After several years of struggling for the big break, he realized he had to find better work but did not want to let go of the writing passion.

HELIACAL RISING STAR: THE STAR OF HIS LIFE, HIS ESSENCE
He was born on the cosmic rising of Regulus (the Sun and Regulus rose together). Castor (Gemini) was also the apparent heliacal rising star. Both stars will be important for his life.

Rising (his youth)
Zuben Elgenubi (Libra) rising as the Moon was on the Nadir: always has passage.
Procyon (Canis Minor) rising as Venus rose: has passage.

Culminating (his prime and middle years)
Regulus (Leo) culminating as the Sun culminates: always has passage.
Alphecca (Corona Borealis) culminating as Sun sets: has passage.
Acumen (Scorpio) culminating as Jupiter culminates: has passage.

Betelgeuse (Orion) culminating as Jupiter is on the Nadir: has passage.
Rigel (Orion) culminating as Saturn culminates: has passage.

Setting (the later part of his life)
Sualocin (Delphinus) setting as Venus rose: has passage.

On the Nadir (his life work)
No stars on the Nadir.

HELIACAL RISING STAR: THE STAR OF THE CLIENT'S LIFE, HIS ESSENCE

This young man was born at a very auspicious time. Regulus gives him the power and the potential to reach far greater heights than the family into which he was born. In addition, Castor makes a claim on him and indicates that he has potential as a writer and/or a communicator. Every child born at his date and place, every year, will have these two stars in their chart. What personalizes this power is how the rest of his planets link with other stars.

All his stars have passage, so all of them should be delineated in a softer, more "user-friendly" fashion.

THE CLIENT'S YOUTH: THE RISING STARS

Zuben Elgenubi is one of the Scales of Libra and is connected with social reform and involvement. Linked to this young man's Moon it seems to imply that, like many young people, he is emotionally driven by his political ideals. Because of the Moon's involvement, this also talks of his mother and what he learns from her in his childhood. His mother is a very active person who freely gives her time to minority groups, believing very strongly in social reform. However, Procyon rising with his Venus is far more interesting. Procyon is the star that rises before the great Sirius, the Dog Star. It symbolizes rapid success but short-lived opportunities, for its bright rising light is quickly outshone by the rising of Sirius. Procyon is connected to his Venus and his discovery in a coffee shop by an international modeling agency because he had the look they were after is an expression of this star. However, these modeling opportunities will not last or lead to a career because they are symbolized by Procyon. If they had been symbolized by Sirius, or one of the Royal Stars of Persia, then this would be an indication of a long-term, successful Venus-type career.

THE PRIME OF THE CLIENT'S LIFE: THE STARS CULMINATING

He has not yet reached this period in his life but it should be by far the most successful and productive of his life. Regulus and Alphecca both linked to the Sun indicate that he will achieve a great deal of success (Regulus), but only if he devotes himself to his work rather than seeking fame and success (Alphecca). Regulus will give him recognition but will also tempt him to take revenge at some stage. Acumen, one of the stars of the sting of Scorpio, is connected to his Jupiter, so with his success will come attack, and this attack will smite him, tempting him to lash back and take revenge (Regulus). However, if he takes this step he will lose all that he has gained.

Betelgeuse is also culminating and connected to his Jupiter and this is an indication that he will be victorious, and can aim his sights on some very large dreams and ambitions. Rigel, the foot of Orion, the educator, the teacher, the one who teaches, is connected to his Saturn, implying that he can use in a very practical way the lessons he has learned in his writing or in his work.

These middle years will be his most successful and he was advised to work very hard in this period, as this would be the period in his life when he could gain the most.

THE LATER PART OF THE CLIENT'S LIFE: THE STARS SETTING

There is only one star setting and this is Sualocin, the alpha star of the Dolphin, discussed in relation to Charlie Chaplin. In this case it is linked to Venus. The lack of great stars in this period of his life implies that the success of his prime is not carried over into his old age. Like Charlie Chaplin, who was made powerless by both the technologies of the talking movies as well as the politics of the time, this client will not produce any great work or achievement in the later years of his life. He will not be unhappy about this, as Sualocin indicates the playfulness of the dolphin and, linked with Venus, it implies that he may explore some new creative medium without the driving force to succeed in it. However, it is important that he make the most of the years from 25 to his early 60s.

THE CLIENT'S LIFEWORK: THE STARS ON THE NADIR

There are no stars on the Nadir. At this stage of my research I would not say that he was not going to be remembered in any way, or that his life work stands for nothing within his family or globally just because there are no stars connected to his Nadir. Indeed I expect this young man may well become noted as a writer. Many of the stars that are culminating in his chart are also on the Nadir with the same planets: the Sun, for example, which culminates with Regulus, is also on the Nadir with Regulus, so this may well relate to his lifework.

• • •

In summary, when looking at a person's list of fixed star parans, the astrologer is not only getting natal information, but timed information, and therefore knowledge of when stars are going to be influential. For example, with this young man we can see that his modeling work is not his correct career and will be short-lived. We can also see the great potential of his middle years, and can therefore encourage him to work hard at his writing or whatever it is that is driving him. We also see that in that period he will be attacked and will be tempted to seek revenge, a response which he must avoid at all cost. In his later years there are no great works or new achievements but a sort of gentle contentment to play with new mediums or ideas.

USING FIXED STARS AS A PREDICTIVE TOOL

BECAUSE OF THE FACT THAT A STAR'S location on a particular angle gives not only the type of energy or symbols with which you are dealing but also, via the angle, the period in your life when the star's influence will be experienced, an astrologer can predict by using stars. The nature of the prediction is in the manner shown for the last example (the young writer). By seeing life in three sections (young years, middle years, and old age) and noting the stars' activity in those periods, a broad overview can be formed. In the last example we do not know if the young, ambitious writer will succeed at his writing, but we do know that he will succeed at something, and furthermore that that success will not follow him into his old age.

This type of predictive work opens up new areas. A solar return is a chart for the moment when the Sun returns to its location in the zodiac at birth. This zodiac may be one based on the stars themselves (sidereal) or based on the position of the Sun in relationship to the equator (tropical). Such a return traditionally gives predictions for the period from one birthday to the next and is therefore valid for only twelve months. Therefore, the angles of the return will refer to the early part of the year (rising), the middle part of the year (culminating), the end of the year (setting), and the year in review (Nadir).

A simple example of this application is to look at the solar return of Jackie Kennedy for the year when John F. Kennedy was assassinated. Jackie Kennedy was born July 28, 1929, 2:30 P.M. EDT, Southhampton, New York, 40N53, 72W23.[6] So any return for her would cover the period from July 28 of one year to the next. In looking at the fixed star parans for her solar return[7] for Washington, which was her home at that time in 1963, we find the following.

HELIACAL RISING STAR

I do not use the concept of a heliacal rising star with solar returns, for unless the person moves around a great deal the same star will be the heliacal rising star from one year to the next.

Rising (the first four months after her birthday, July 28 to the end of November.)
Alphecca (Corona Borealis) rising as Venus culminates: has passage.
Diadem (Coma Berenices) rising with Mars: has passage.

---

[6] Lois Rodden, *Profiles of Women* (Tempe, AZ: AFA, 1979).
[7] This return was done in the tropical zodiac. The only difference between a tropical or sidereal return is the time, thus the angles will vary but the links of stars to planets will not change.

Antares (Scorpio) rising as Mars culminates: has passage.
Pollux (Gemini) rising as Mars is on the Nadir: curtailed passage.

Mars is highlighted by its involvement with the following: Diadem, to make a sacrifice; Antares, one of the Royal Stars of Persia, the Heart of the Scorpion, intensity, drama, rebirth and obsession, whether it has passage or not; and Pollux, which is normally a star of writing or communication but is always linked with a painful journey. The painful journey of Pollux is emphasized for Jackie as the star is at a phase of curtailed passage. At the same time her Venus is connected to Alphecca: fruitfulness or quiet success. At the beginning of this solar return she was pregnant and her husband was in power as president of the United States. By the end of this four-month period, her child had died a few days after birth and her husband had been assassinated.

Culminating (This is the second four-month period, from the end of November, 1963 till the end of March, 1964.)
Antares (Scorpio) culminating as Mercury set: has passage.
Antares (Scorpio) culminating as Saturn rose: has passage.
Schedar (Cassiopeia) culminating as Venus rose: permanent curtailed passage.

These are not the only stars culminating in her solar return but they are the most important, for the great Heart of the Scorpion is culminating, and contacting both Mercury and Saturn. This indicates the obsession of grief, the mind totally occupied with the tragic shock of the previous four months. The star Schedar is curtailed of passage and thus becomes unworldly, growing in the strength of its expression, the queen, and is a star that demands or gains respect through quiet dignity. Here is the American people's love and respect for her as she strove to handle her grief. She was turned into a sacred figure of dignity and respect.

Setting (This is the final four-month period, from the end of March, 1964 to her birthday in July, 1964.)
Menkar (Cetus) setting as the Moon rose: has passage.
Aculeus and *Acumen* (Scorpio) setting as Mercury was on the Nadir: both have passage.
Algol (Perseus) setting as Mars culminated: permanent curtailed passage.

Menkar is the great beast of the unconscious. Jackie was not only the victim of a collective unconscious act but also seen as the public figure of the nation's grief. Aculeus and Acumen are the stings of the Scorpion and, linked to Jackie's Mercury, are symbols of her pain and mental state. The presence of Algol, connected to her Mars and curtailed of passage, adds to the ugliness of this period, showing the anger and rage she must have felt at this time.

Nadir (The summation of this year for her.)
Algol was on the Nadir as Venus set: permanent curtailed passage.

This is the summation of her year, the year in review. Algol represents the dark, painful rage of the feminine and, linked to Jackie's Venus, shows that the year is a year of pain, anger, and loss of relationships. She is also seen by the public as the tragic widow. With the star being of curtailed passage, the human Jackie Kennedy is lost to this larger concept. She became the person grieving for the nation, her own identity lost.

Such a solar return stands out because of the large number of difficult and heavy stars. However, any solar return can be examined in this manner and, remember, one difficult star does not make for a tragedy. As always with fixed star work, it is the combination of stars which must be considered, as well as their individual meanings.

APPENDICES

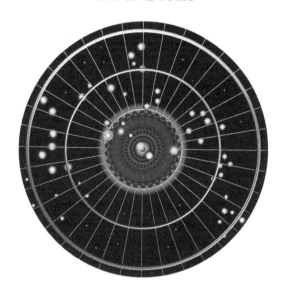

APPENDIX A:
LOCATING, MEASURING,
AND NAMING THE STARS

STARS ARE LOCATED ON THE CELESTIAL sphere (see figure 35, p. 370) in a similar way to how cities or places are located on the terrestrial sphere. As a location on Earth will have a longitude, so the location of a star will have right ascension. Right ascension is measured either in hours or degrees and begins at the intersection of the ecliptic with the equator for the March (vernal) equinox. Each hour of right ascension is equivalent to fifteen degrees and it gains in time or degrees as it moves toward the east. Thus there are up to twenty-four hours or 360° of right ascension. When right ascension is given for the stars in this book it is expressed in hours.

Declination is identical to terrestrial latitude and as such is measured in degrees and minutes north or south of the equator. If a star has a declination that is the same as the latitude of a city, then that star will pass directly over the city in the course of a day. For example, London has a latitude of 51°N31'. Any star with a declination of 51° or 52° North will pass directly over London in the course of twenty-four hours.

KNOWING IF A STAR
WILL RISE AND SET FOR YOUR LOCATION

If you are aware of the latitude of your location, you can ascertain whether a star will rise and set by knowing a star's declination. Subtract the latitude of your location from 90°. If a star's declination is greater than the result, it will either not be visible for that location or it will never set.

For example, the latitude of London is 51°N31'. Call this 52° and subtract it from 90°; the answer is 38°. Any star south of declination 38° South will not be visible for London. In addition, any star which is north of declination 38° North will never set. Thus for London the stars that can rise and set will have declinations between 38° South and 38° North. This is a rule of thumb and there will always be a degree or so of doubt, depending on your altitude above sea level. Also, your local terrain will affect your ability to see stars that only skim the horizon for your location. (See Appendix B for further information.)

MAGNITUDE OF A STAR

Stars vary in their brightness, and in order to describe this, the ancient astronomer Hipparchos two thousand years ago devised a system where the

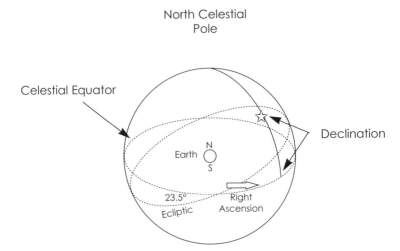

North Celestial
Pole

Figure 35. The celestial sphere.

brightest stars were considered the most important. These brightest stars were labeled magnitude 1. The dimmer stars were then labeled in decreasing importance as magnitude 2, 3, 4, 5, and 6, stars of the sixth magnitude being barely visible to the human eye. This system has been refined in modern times, yet astronomy still uses this basic system. A star of magnitude 1 is still brighter than one of magnitude 2. A star that is magnitude 1 is 2.51 times brighter than a star of magnitude 2. Similarly a star of magnitude 2 is 2.51 times brighter than a star of magnitude 3. To cater for very bright stars or the Sun and the Moon, negative magnitudes have been introduced. Sirius and the Sun are the two brightest stars in the sky and Sirius has a magnitude of –1.46 while the Sun is –26.85.

NAMING OF STARS

Although many stars have proper names, they are also named firstly by the constellation to which they belong and then, secondly, by their relative brightness compared to other stars in the same constellation. The brightest star will be labeled alpha (α) while the second brightest star will be called beta (β), and so on down the Greek alphabet. If there are more stars than letters in the alphabet, then the remaining stars are given a number.

THE STAR INFORMATION
THAT IS LISTED IN THE PARAN MAPS

For each star there is a set of information. For example, if we look at Alpheratz:

Alpheratz. Alpha Andromeda. Magnitude 2.2. RA 00:08:09". Declination 29N03'50" PED= 13° Aries 37'.

- The most commonly accepted proper name is given first, followed by its constellation name: Alpha Andromeda, which means in this case that the star is in the constellation Andromeda and that it is the brightest star in the constellation.
- Magnitude 2.2 is telling you that it is not a very bright star but still easily visible to the human eye.
- The RA 00:08:09" is expressed in hours, minutes and seconds and is telling you that the star is located just a little east of the vernal equinox—the intersection of the ecliptic and the equator.
- Declination 29N03'50" means that the star is 29° north of the equator.
- PED = 13° Aries 37' is saying that, for the year 2000 C.E., when this star is projected via lines of longitude or RA from the poles of the equator,[1] the point where this projection will cut the ecliptic is at 13° Aries 37'.

USING YOUR KNOWLEDGE
AS AN ASTROLOGER TO LOCATE THE STARS

Right ascension and declination will not be of great help to the average person who is standing outside on a starry night trying to identify stars.

The first step when faced with a starry sky is to locate the pole. If you are in the northern hemisphere, this will be the North Pole, and for those in the south, of course, it will be the South Pole. As astrologers you will know the latitude of your current location and this latitude will be the altitude of the pole above the horizon. For example, if you are just outside London at a latitude 51° North, face north and using your hand (a closed fist measuring 4° and an extended fist—a fist with the thumb and little finger extended—measuring 15°), measure 51° up from the horizon. Your hand measurement should finish on the stars of Ursa Minor.

---

[1] For a listing of the projected degrees using the poles of the ecliptic see Appendix E.

If you are in the southern hemisphere, then face south and measure up from the horizon the number of degrees of your latitude. Note that you will be looking at a fairly empty place in the sky. However, scout around and see if you can spot the Southern Cross.

Once you have located the pole, look at the star maps given for each constellation and locate your circumpolar constellations. Take one constellation at a time and become visually familiar with them. Learn to recognise these constellations. Measure them with your hand and by using the maps become familiar with some of the individual names of stars.

Your next step is to locate the points that are east and west of you. If you are facing the South Pole, then the location square of that and to your left will be east, whereas for those in the northern hemisphere, east will be on your right hand side as you face the North Pole. The ecliptic arcs from east to west. However, it will be highly unlikely that it will be pass directly over your head. It is a moving arc but it will always be traveling from approximately east to west.

Use your astrological knowledge to decide what zodiac constellations should be visible. For example, if the Sun is in the sign of Taurus,[2] then the constellations of Scorpio and those either side of it will be above the horizon at night. Look for these constellations on the arc of the ecliptic using the star maps to help you.

KEY POINTERS

Some constellations are very bright and obvious and can help you find fainter constellations. Scorpio is a most brilliant constellation, stretching across the night sky when the Sun is traveling through the signs of Pisces, Aries, Taurus, Gemini, Cancer, and Leo. At its center is the red star Antares, which looks like Mars to the untrained eye. Once you have seen the great Scorpion, you will always be able to locate it.

Opposite Scorpio is the constellation Taurus. This constellation contains the large red star Aldebaran, the eye of the Bull, with the Pleiades on its shoulder. Aldebaran will be rising at sunset (acronychal rising) when the Sun moves though the sign of Sagittarius in December, and then is visible in the night sky roughly from December through to June.

Next to Taurus is Gemini with the bright stars of Castor and Pollux, exactly 4° 30' apart. Use them as a gauge for your hand and fingers. Just south of them will be the very visually obvious constellation Orion containing the red star Betelgeuse.

---

[2] This is the tropical zodiac, which means that the Sun is among the stars of Aries.

By learning how to recognize these few very easily seen constellations you will then be able to use your hand and the star maps provided to explore the rest of the heavens. Finding your way around the night sky will take more than just one night, but if you concentrate on one or two constellations at a time, you will quickly be able to look up at a sky and recognize constellations and individual stars. Once you get started you may want to invest in a few simple tools such as one of the many different planetarium software packages and a compass.

APPENDIX B:
STARS THAT RISE AND
SET FOR ANY GIVEN LATITUDE

FOR ANY GIVEN LATITUDE A NUMBER OF stars will never rise, some will never set, and others will appear to rise and set. When a star is never going to rise for your location, you might want to consider leaving it out of the chart work. In addition, stars that do rise and set for your location will have phases and are considered to be interacting with the Earth. A simple method for deciding if a single star will rise or set is given in Appendix A. However, the following list of the major stars, with the latitudes at which they will either never rise or never set, will enable you to see at a glance all the stars that do not rise or set.

An example of how to use Table 1 (pages 375–376). If you are observing the sky from New York City, at a latitude of 42° North, then using the "Never Sets" column, look down until you find the last latitude less than 42° North. It is Mirfak that never sets for latitudes north of 40°. All the stars from Mirfak to the top of the table to Deneb Adige will never set for this location. Using the "Never Rises" column, look down until you find a star listed for less than 42° North. This star is Canopus. Canopus will not rise for latitude north of 37°so *all* the stars listed from Canopus to Acrux will not rise for the latitude of New York. All the stars between Mirfak and Ankaa will rise and set for New York.

Another example using a location in the southern hemisphere. If you are observing the sky from Adelaide, South Australia, at a latitude of 35° South, using the "Never Sets" column, look down until you find a latitude less than 35° South. It is Achernar that never sets for latitudes south of 32°. All the stars from Achernar to the bottom of the table or Acrux, will never set for this location. Using the "Never Rises " column, look down until you find a star listed for less than 35° South. This star is Schedar. Schedar will not rise for latitudes south of 33°, so *all* the stars listed from Schedar to Deneb Adige will not rise for the latitude of Adelaide. All the stars between Schedar and Achernar will rise and set for Adelaide.

Table 1. Stars that Never Rise or Set.*

North Pole Never Sets	South Pole Never Rises	Star	Constellation
32°N	32°S	Deneb Adige	Cygnus
32°N	32°S	Capulus	Perseus
33°N	33°S	Schedar	Cassiopeia
40°N	40°S	Mirfak	Perseus
43°N	43°S	Capella	Auriga
49°N	49°S	Algol	Perseus
51°N	51°S	Wega	Lyra
54°N	54°S	Mirach	Andromeda
58°N	58°S	Castor	Gemini
60°N	60°S	Alpheratz	Andromeda
61°N	61°S	Scheat	Pegasus
61°N	61°S	El Nath	Taurus
63°N	63°S	Alphecca	Corona Borealis
66°N	66°S	Hamal	Aries
66°N	66°S	Alcyone	Taurus
69°N	69°S	Zosma	Leo
70°N	70°S	Arcturus	Bootes
72°N	72°S	Diadem	Coma Berenices
72°N	72°S	Pollux	Gemini
74°N	74°S	Markab	Pegasus
74°N	74°S	Alhena	Gemini
74°N	74°S	Aldebaran	Taurus
74°N	74°S	Sualocin	Delphinus
75°N	75°S	Ras Algethi	Hercules
75°N	75°S	Denebola	Leo
77°N	77°S	Ras Alhague	Ophiuchus
79°N	79°S	Regulus	Leo
79°N	79°S	Spica	Virgo
79°N	79°S	Vindemiatrix	Virgo

Table 1. Stars that Never Rise or Set (continued)

81°N	81°S	Altair	Aquila
81°N	81°S	Acubens	Cancer
82°N	82°S	Betelgeuse	Orion
86°N	86°S	Menkar	Cetus
87°N	87°S	Al Rescha	Pisces
89°N	89°S	Sadalmelek	Aquarius
88°S	88°N	Alnilam	Orion
85°S	85°N	Procyon	Canis Minor
84°S	84°N	Sadalsuud	Aquarius
83°S	83°N	Bellatrix	Orion
82°S	82°N	Rigel	Orion
81°S	81°N	Alphard	Hydra
81°S	81°N	Zuben Eschamali	Libra
74°S	74°N	Zuben Elgenubi	Libra
73°S	73°N	Sirius	Canis Major
73°S	73°N	Antares	Scorpius
73°S	73°N	Deneb Algedi	Capricornus
72°S	72°N	Murzims	Canis Major
71°S	71°N	Alkes	Crater
66°S	66°N	Facies	Sagittarius
60°S	60°N	Formalhaut	Piscis Australis
58°S	58°N	Aculeus	Scorpius
55°S	55°N	Acumen	Scorpius
55°S	55°N	Phact	Columba Noae
49°S	49°N	Rukbat	Sagittarius
47°S	47°N	Ankaa	Phoenix
37°S	37°N	Canopus	Carina
32°S	32°N	Achernar	Eridanus
29°S	29°N	Toliman	Centaurus
29°S	29°N	Agena	Centaurus
26°S	26°N	Acrux	Crux

*Note: The "Never Sets" column starts at the North Pole and moves to the South Pole, and the "Never Rises" column starts at the South Pole and moves to the North Pole.

APPENDIX C:
HELIACAL AND ACRONYCHAL
ZODIAC MAPS

THE FOLLOWING ARE THE PARAN MAPS
for determining the true or apparent heliacal rising and the acronychal settings
for any solar position of the zodiac. These graphs are for every star discussed in
this text. If you prefer to work with just the first magnitude stars then see Appendix D.

The graphs are based on the natal positions of the Sun which, of course,
can be translated to a calendar date. The graphs are used as in the following
examples.

FINDING THE HELIACAL RISING STAR

EXAMPLE: A PERSON BORN WITH
THE SUN AT 15° ARIES AT A LATITUDE OF 35° NORTH

Using the graph for Aries, look up the natal position of the Sun for the latitude
of birth. This is marked on the graph in figure 36 (p. 378).

The point for 15° Aries at 35° North can be seen to be just above Formalhaut and Algol. To find the heliacal rising star *lower* your gaze towards the latitude line. The first star line you encounter will be the heliacal rising star for that
period in that location. In this example it is two stars, Formalhaut and Algol.
What the graph is telling you is that Formalhaut and Algol co-rose at about 10.5°
of Aries, about 4° in front of the Sun. To find the stars before these two, we
would have to go to the Pisces graph and find out what the first star would be at
this latitude. If you look at that graph you will notice that these are the first two
bright stars to rise for some time.

Now, if the same person were born at a latitude of 35° South rather than
north, the 15° Aries line would still be used, but now under –35 (figure 36).
When you move down the graph the star line you encounter is that of Scheat. So
the heliacal rising star would be Scheat. Scheat co-rose with 7° Aries, therefore
Scheat was 8° in front of the rising Sun and would be a bright star rising just before the dawn light spread through the sky.

For Taurus, Gemini, and Cancer there are two graphs for each sign as there
are so many bright stars that co-rise in these signs. Use both graphs and select the
star that best fits in terms of its degrees in front of the Sun.

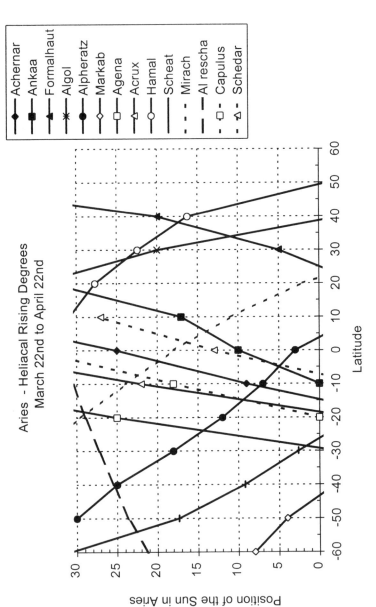

Figure 36. Aries stars rising at dawn.

FINDING THE ACRONYCHAL SETTING STAR

EXAMPLE: A PERSON BORN WITH
THE SUN AT 15° ARIES AT A LATITUDE OF 35° NORTH

Using the same example as before, the acronychal setting star can be determined. This is the star setting just after the Sun sets. Now use the Aries graph for the acronychal setting.

Using the line for 15° Aries, move to the column for 35° North in figure 37 (p. 380) in the same manner as for the heliacal graph. Once you have located this position you will then need to *raise* your gaze or finger up to the top of the graph until you encounter a star. The star found in this example is Alpheratz. The Sun will set at 15° Aries but Alpheratz co-sets at about 22° of Aries and will therefore set just after sunset.

Now looking at 35° South, move to the column for 35° South in figure 37 in the same manner as for the heliacal graph. Once you have located this position you will then need to *raise* your gaze or finger up to the top of the graph until you encounter a star. You will see that the true acronychal setting stars are both Formalhaut and Algol, co-setting with 15° Aries, and the apparent acronychal setting star would be Hamal, co-setting with about 23° Aries and thus setting after the Sun.

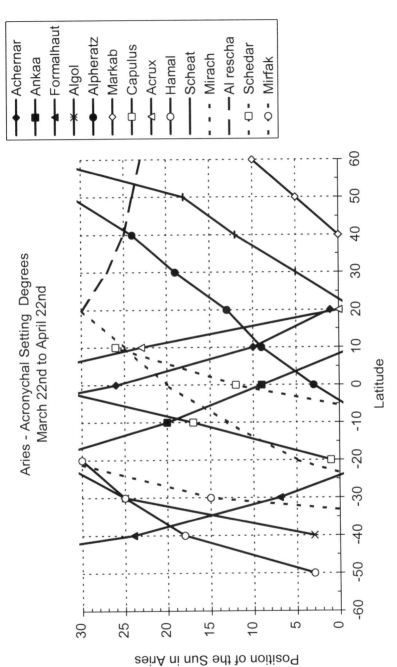

Figure 37. Aries stars setting with the Sun.

FINDING YOUR OWN
HELIACAL RISING OR ACRONYCHAL SETTING STARS

What follow are the heliacal rising and acronychal setting graphs for all the stars discussed in this book (see pages 382–411). By following the method given earlier in this appendix, you will be able to determine the heliacal rising or acronychal setting stars for any given date or place.

These maps have been constructed for the year 2000 C.E., and precession will affect their accuracy but in a way that cannot be easily taken into account. However, the heliacal rising or acronychal setting star will be quite a few degrees in front of or behind the Sun, so one could use these maps for a span of 1500 C.E. to 2500 C.E. with confidence, as long as you realized that for cosmic or true rising then the span will be from 1900 C.E. to 2100 C.E., approximately.

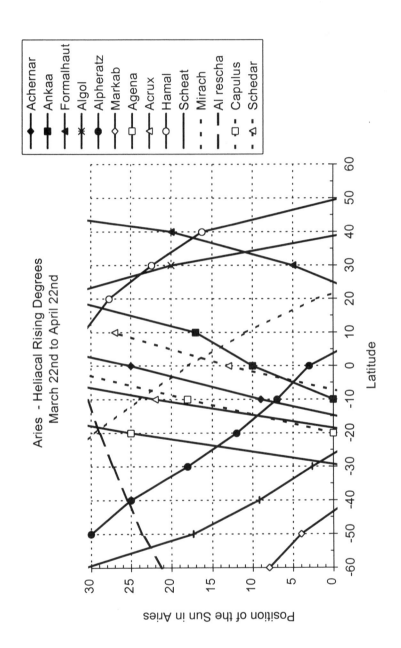

Aries - Heliacal Rising Degrees
March 22nd to April 22nd

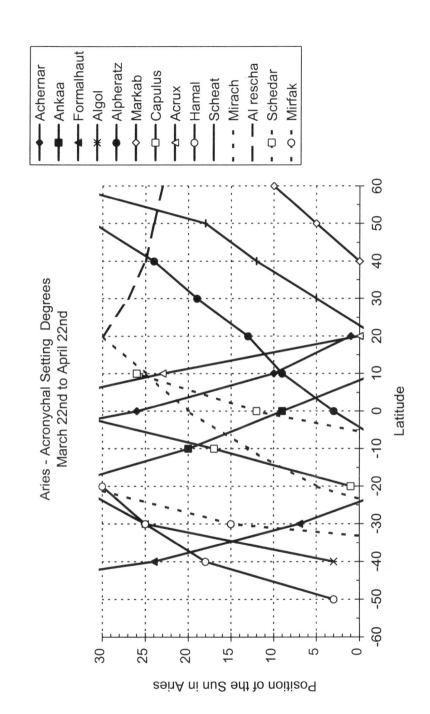

Aries - Acronychal Setting Degrees
March 22nd to April 22nd

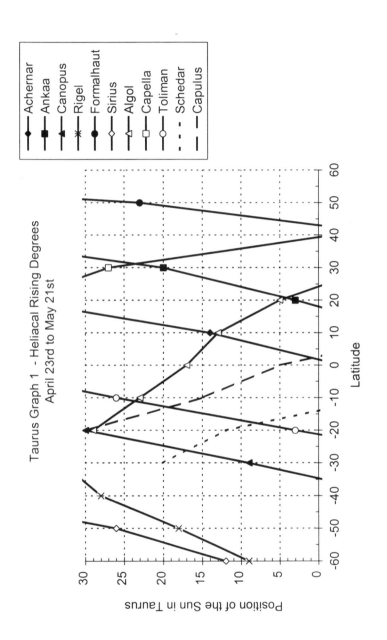

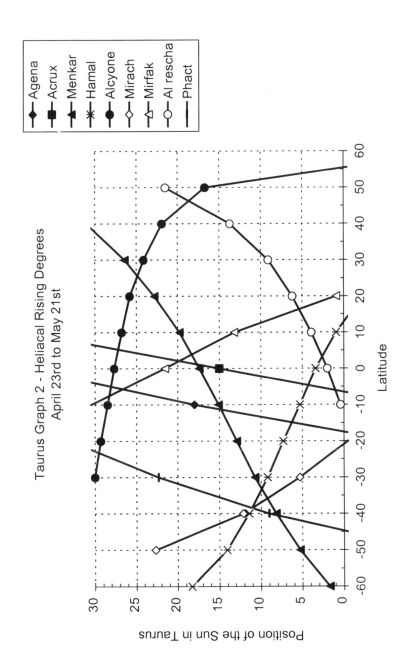

Taurus Graph 2 - Heliacal Rising Degrees
April 23rd to May 21st

Position of the Sun in Taurus

Latitude

Agena
Acrux
Menkar
Hamal
Alcyone
Mirach
Mirfak
Al rescha
Phact

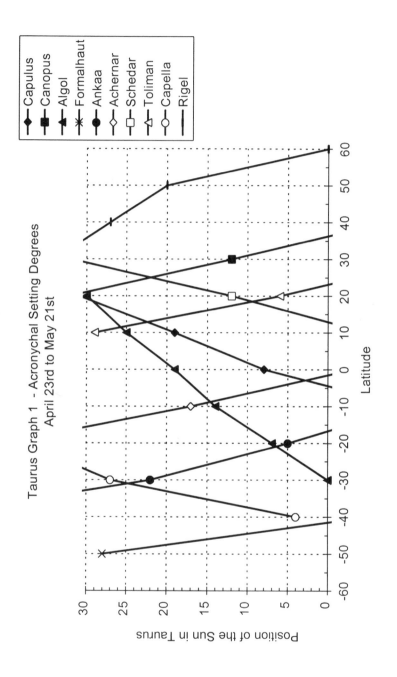

Taurus Graph 1 - Acronychal Setting Degrees
April 23rd to May 21st

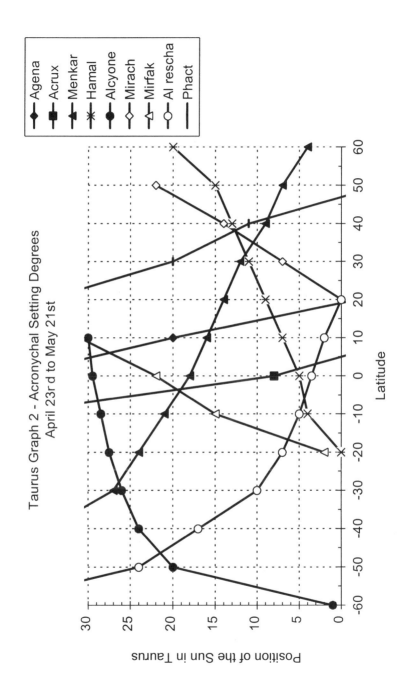

Taurus Graph 2 - Acronychal Setting Degrees
April 23rd to May 21st

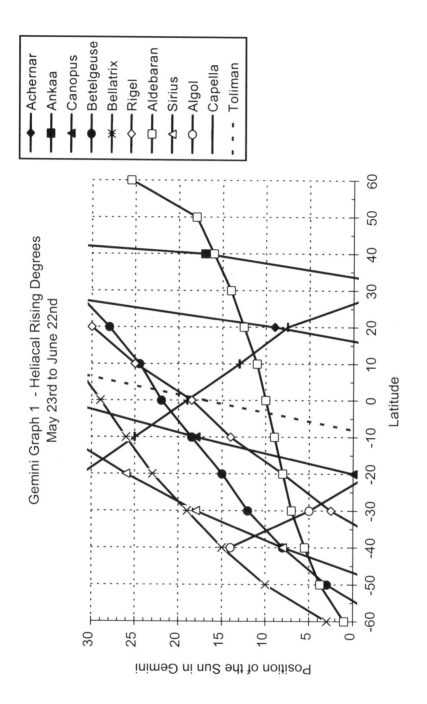

Gemini Graph 1 - Heliacal Rising Degrees
May 23rd to June 22nd

Position of the Sun in Gemini

Latitude

Achernar
Ankaa
Canopus
Betelgeuse
Bellatrix
Rigel
Aldebaran
Sirius
Algol
Capella
Toliman

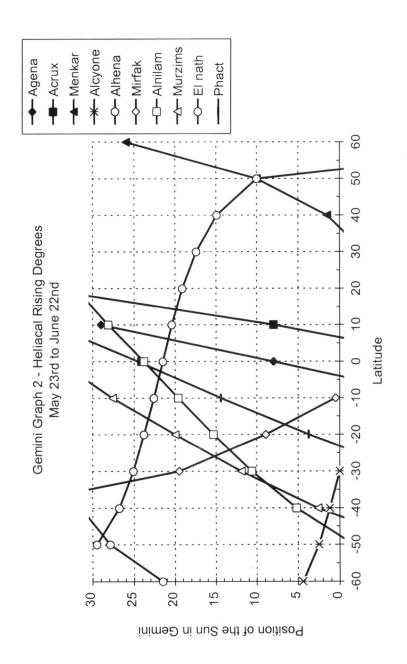

Gemini Graph 2 - Heliacal Rising Degrees
May 23rd to June 22nd

Position of the Sun in Gemini

Latitude

Agena
Acrux
Menkar
Alcyone
Alhena
Mirfak
Alnilam
Murzims
El nath
Phact

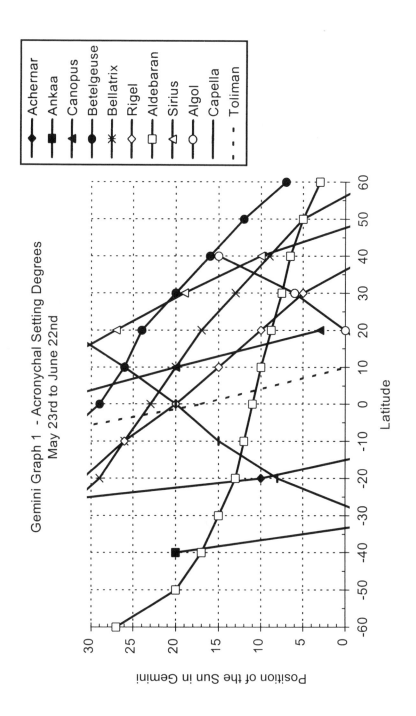

Gemini Graph 1 - Acronychal Setting Degrees
May 23rd to June 22nd

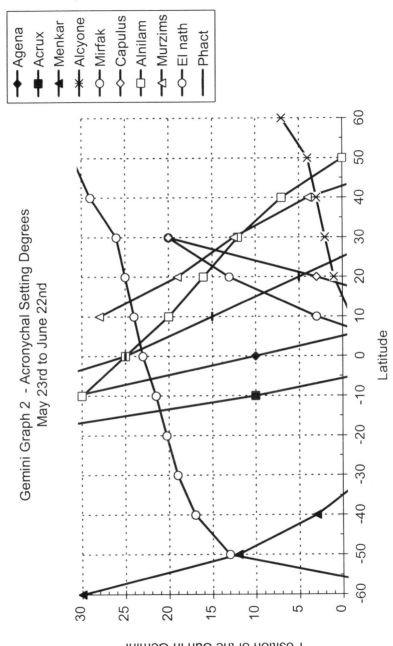

Gemini Graph 2 - Acronychal Setting Degrees
May 23rd to June 22nd

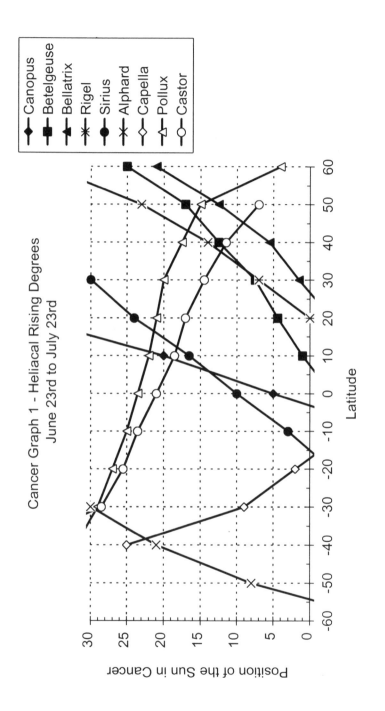

Cancer Graph 1 - Heliacal Rising Degrees
June 23rd to July 23rd

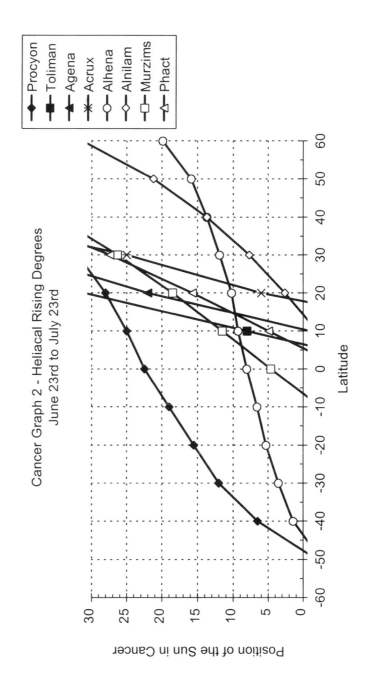

Cancer Graph 2 - Heliacal Rising Degrees
June 23rd to July 23rd

Legend: Procyon, Toliman, Agena, Acrux, Alhena, Alnilam, Murzims, Phact

Position of the Sun in Cancer

Latitude

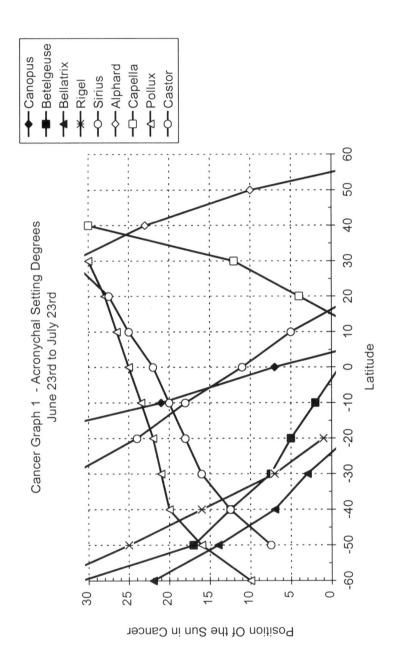

Cancer Graph 1 - Acronychal Setting Degrees
June 23rd to July 23rd

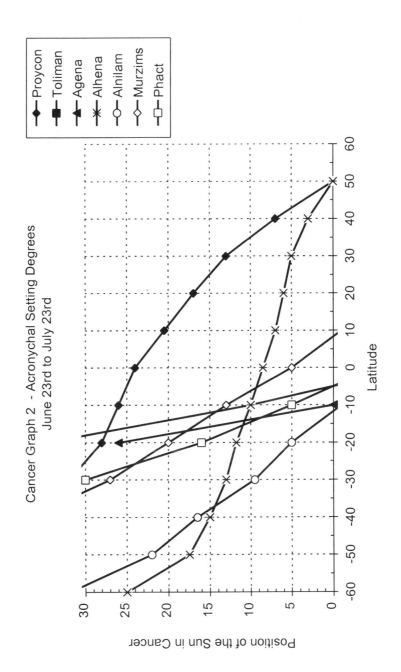

Cancer Graph 2 - Acronychal Setting Degrees
June 23rd to July 23rd

Position of the Sun in Cancer

Latitude

Proycon
Toliman
Agena
Alhena
Alnilam
Murzims
Phact

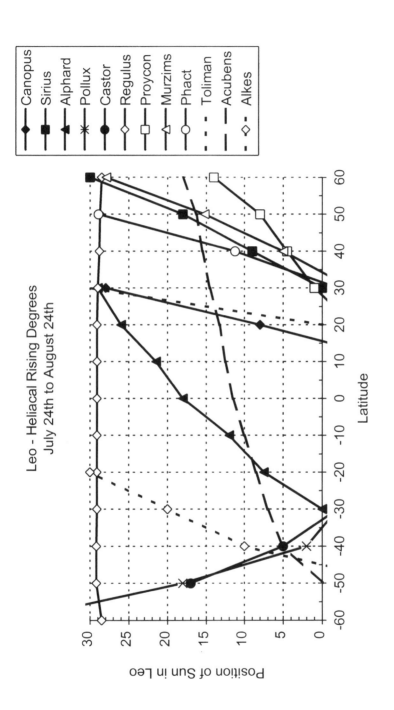

Leo - Heliacal Rising Degrees
July 24th to August 24th

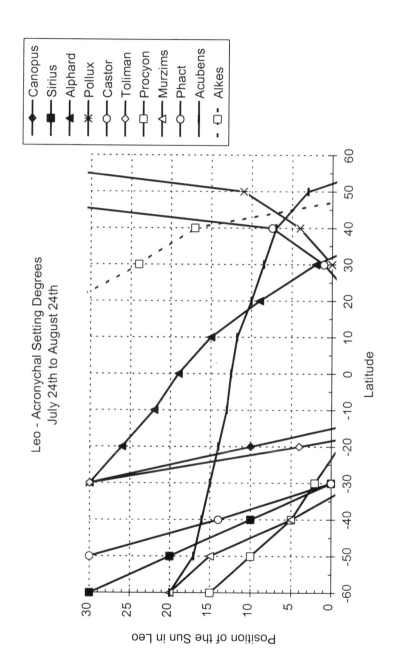

Leo - Acronychal Setting Degrees
July 24th to August 24th

Legend: Canopus, Sirius, Alphard, Pollux, Castor, Toliman, Procyon, Murzims, Phact, Acubens, Alkes

Position of the Sun in Leo

Latitude

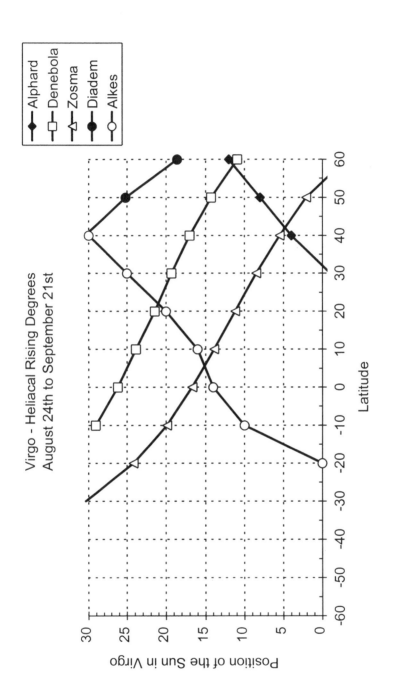

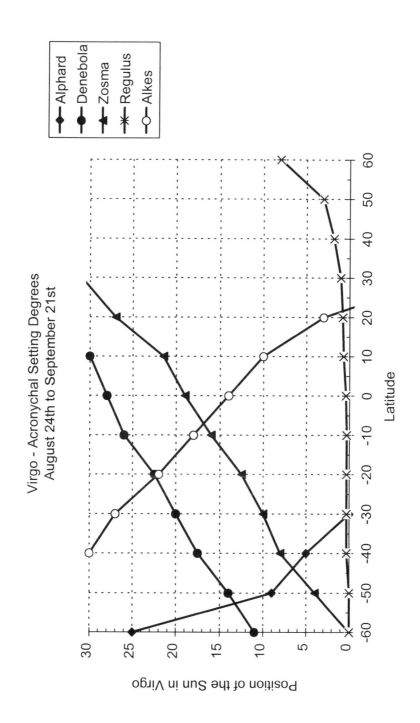

Virgo - Acronychal Setting Degrees
August 24th to September 21st

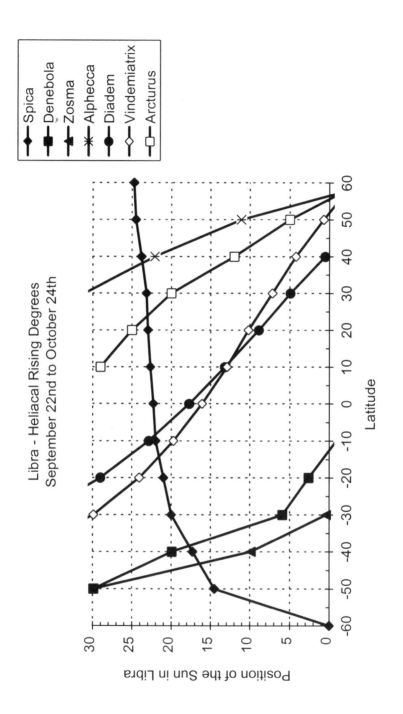

Libra - Heliacal Rising Degrees
September 22nd to October 24th

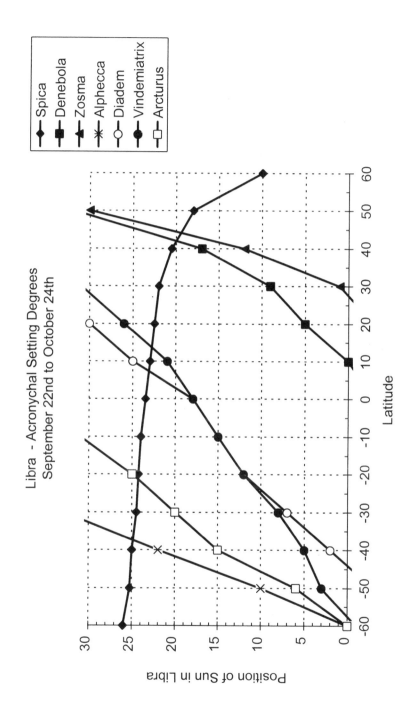

Libra - Acronychal Setting Degrees
September 22nd to October 24th

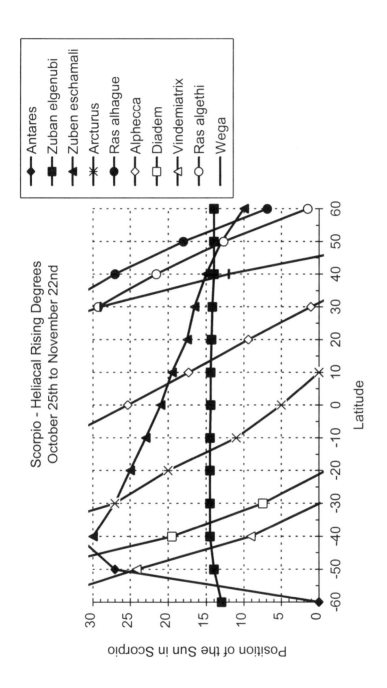

Scorpio - Heliacal Rising Degrees
October 25th to November 22nd

Antares
Zuban elgenubi
Zuben eschamali
Arcturus
Ras alhague
Alphecca
Diadem
Vindemiatrix
Ras algethi
Wega

Position of the Sun in Scorpio

Latitude

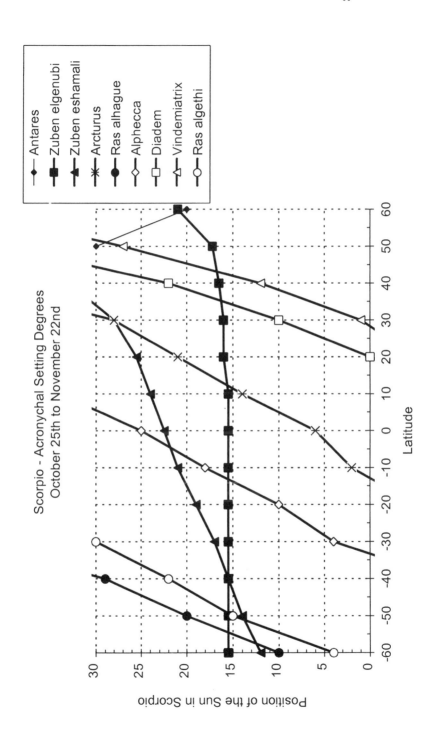

Scorpio - Acronychal Setting Degrees
October 25th to November 22nd

Position of the Sun in Scorpio

Latitude

Legend:
◆— Antares
■— Zuben elgenubi
◀— Zuben eshamali
✳— Arcturus
●— Ras alhague
◇— Alphecca
□— Diadem
△— Vindemiatrix
○— Ras algethi

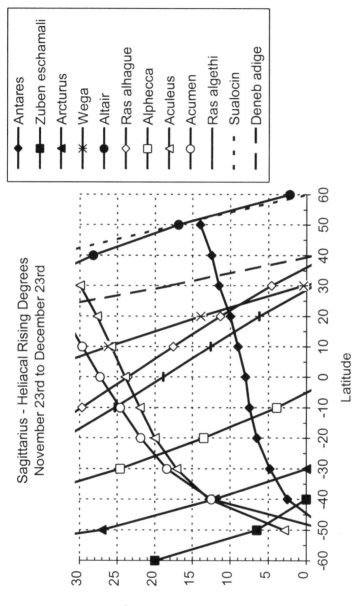

Sagittarius - Heliacal Rising Degrees
November 23rd to December 23rd

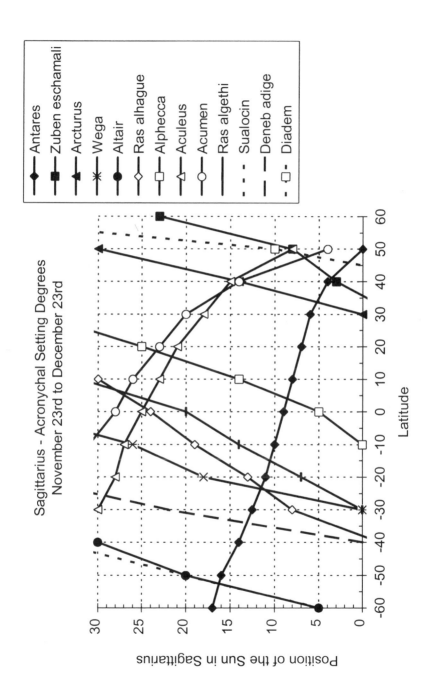

Sagittarius - Acronychal Setting Degrees
November 23rd to December 23rd

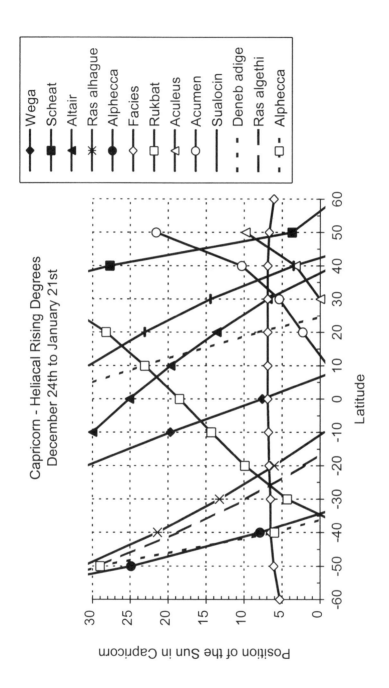

Capricorn - Heliacal Rising Degrees
December 24th to January 21st

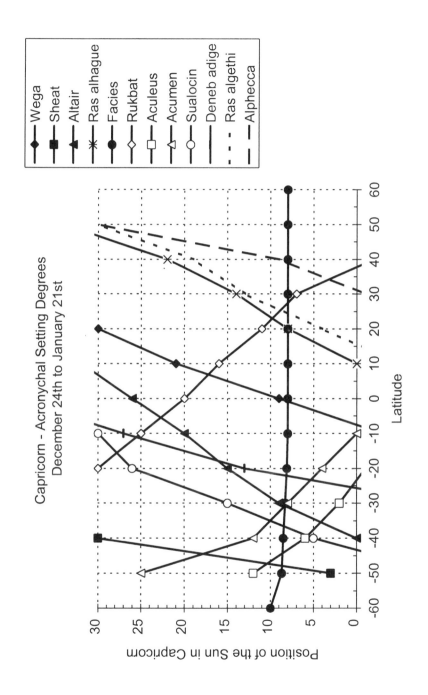

Capricorn - Acronychal Setting Degrees
December 24th to January 21st

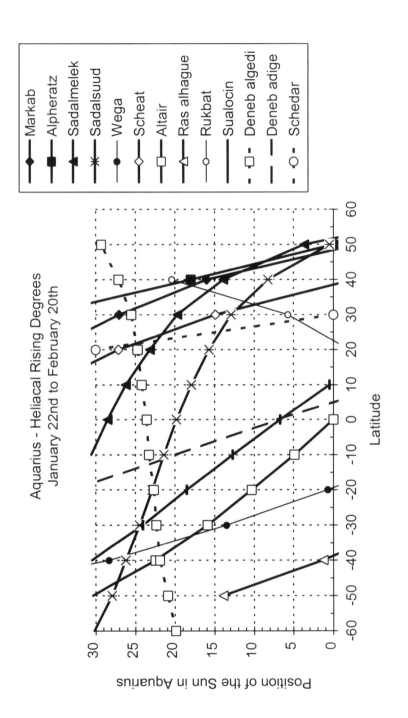

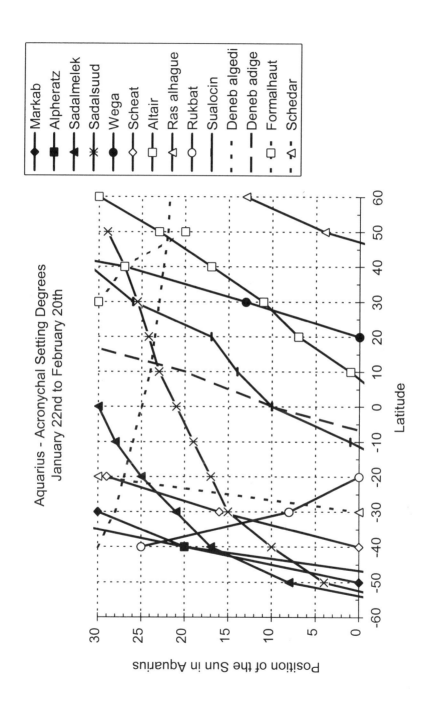

Aquarius - Acronychal Setting Degrees
January 22nd to February 20th

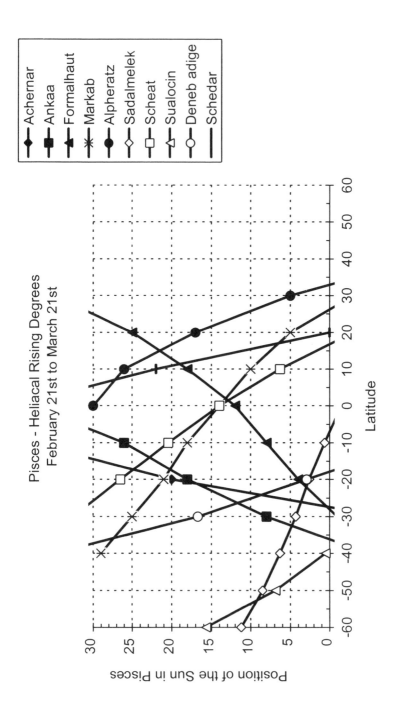

Pisces - Heliacal Rising Degrees
February 21st to March 21st

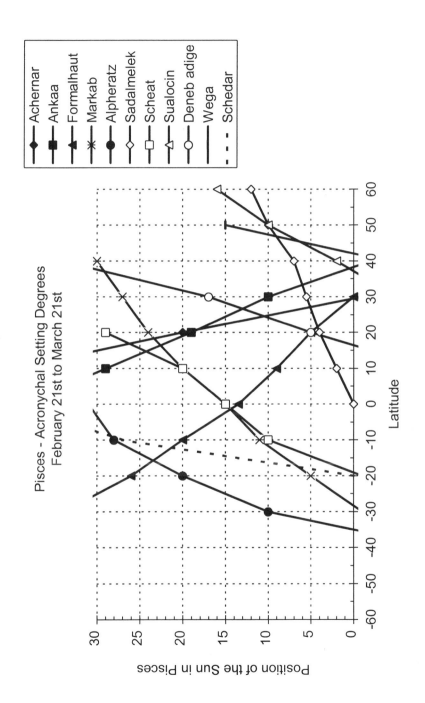

Pisces - Acronychal Setting Degrees
February 21st to March 21st

APPENDIX D:
MUNDANE HELIACAL RISING MAPS

THIS APPENDIX IS MEANT TO ENABLE YOU
to work with first magnitude stars as heliacal rising stars in mundane astrology.
These graphs are very similar to the graphs of Appendix C.[1] However, by only focusing on the first magnitude stars, the full year or 360° of the zodiac can be
placed on one graph. By looking under the appropriate latitude, the true heliacal
rising dates of all of the first magnitude stars for the entire year can be found.
The apparent heliacal rising occurs when the star is about 8° to 10° behind the
zodiac in relationship to the Sun. Thus the apparent heliacal rising date will be
about eight to ten days after the date given on the graph. A star will influence the
period of time from its true or cosmic rising through to its apparent, some ten
days later, unless another star takes its place.

In addition, the heliacal rising of a major star with a transiting planet can
be examined. First of all you need to consider the degree of the zodiac the planet
is transiting. Having found this degree, convert it into the date when the transiting planet will rise with the Sun. For example, if a planet is at 10° Leo, then the
day that the Sun is at 10° Leo (August 2 or 3) will be the date that the planet will
co-rise with the Sun. Once this is found, check the date on the graphs to discover
if the transiting planet will be linked to any heliacal rising star and at what latitude this will occur.

For example, the Neptune ingress into Aquarius occurs in 1998 and will
rise with the Sun on the mornings of January 21 and 22, 1998, in other words,
when the Sun is at 0° Aquarius. In checking the graphs, we see no contacts in
Graph 1 (p. 414), but Graph 2 (p. 415), at 20° South, shows Neptune will rise
and the Sun and Wega. So the Neptune ingress will be involved with Wega in the
southern hemisphere.

In constructing the sunrise charts for the Sun at 0° Aquarius at this latitude[2]
you are then able to find the degree that is culminating as the Sun rises. This is
24° Libra. By referring to the list of culmination degrees given in this appendix,
you can see that Spica (the gift of the goddess) culminates with 25° Libra.

So at a latitude of about 20° South, in late January, 1998, Neptune will rise
with the Sun and Wega, as Spica culminates. This implies breaking away from a
position of powerlessness (Neptune with Wega). Any country in a deprived condition at this latitude could gain greater independence or freedom. Interestingly,

---

[1] Like those in Appendix C, these are calculated for the year 2,000 C.E. See Appendix C for the
implications of precession on these graphs.

[2] The longitude of the location does not affect the actual sunrise chart as sunrise will occur
along the length of a longitude line.

this is the latitude of French Polynesia, a country the UN has requested be given independence from France by the year 2000.

This is simply an introduction to this ancient technique of working with the heliacal rising star when linked to planetary combinations. Further work in this area will increase our understanding of these techniques. Therefore, this appendix has been included for those interested in pursuing this line of research.

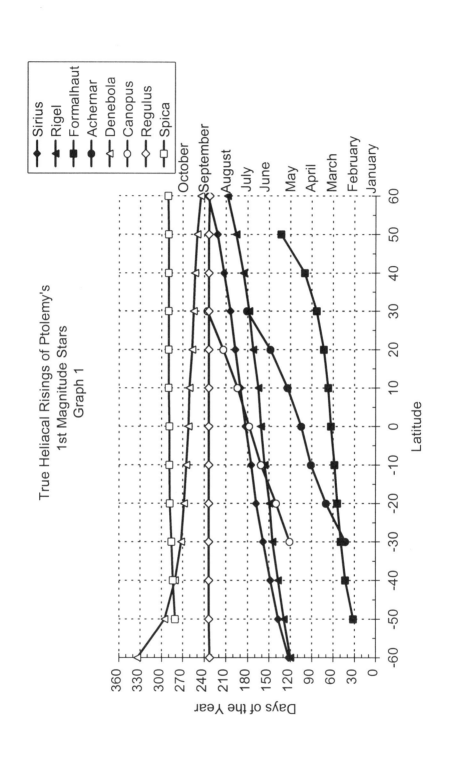

True Heliacal Risings of Ptolemy's
1st Magnitude Stars
Graph 1

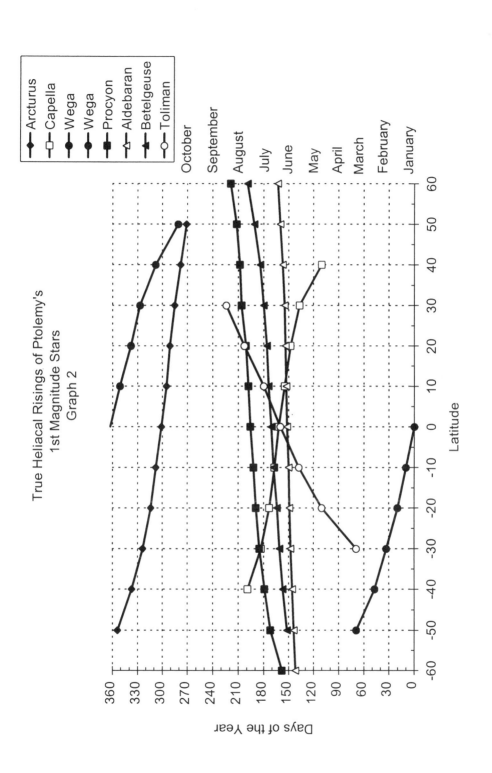

True Heliacal Risings of Ptolemy's
1st Magnitude Stars
Graph 2

Table 1. Degrees of Culmination.

Star	Sign	Star	Sign
Ankaa	7° ♈	Zosma	20° ♍
Schedar	12° ♈	Dubhe	24° ♍
Mirach	17° ♈		
Achernar	26° ♈	Denebola	0° ♎
		Thuban	3° ♎
Al Rescha	3° ♉	Vindemiatrix	17° ♎
Capulus	7° ♉	Diadem	19° ♎
Hamal	12° ♉	Spica	25° ♎
Algol	18° ♉		
Menkar	20° ♉	Arcturus	10° ♏
Acrux	23° ♉	Zuben Elgenubi	15° ♏
Mirfak	24° ♉	Zuben Eschamali	21° ♏
		Alphecca	26° ♏
Alcyone	3° ♊		
Aldebaran	10° ♊	Antares	9° ♐
Agena	14° ♊	Ras Algethi	21° ♐
Capella	18° ♊	Ras Alhague	25° ♐
Rigel	18° ♊	Aculeus	27° ♐
Bellatrix	21° ♊		
El nath	22° ♊	Acumen	0° ♑
Toliman	23° ♊	Facies	15° ♑
Alnilam	25° ♊	Wega	16° ♑
Phact	25° ♊	Rukbat	24° ♑
Betelgeuse	28° ♊	Altair	26° ♑
Canopus	5° ♋	Sualocin	8° ♒
Murzims	6° ♋	Deneb Adige	8° ♒
Alhena	13° ♋	Alderamin	16° ♒
Sirius	14° ♋	Deneb Algedi	25° ♒
Castor	21° ♋	Markab	25° ♒
Pollux	23° ♋	Sadalsuud	26° ♒
Procyon	25° ♋		
		Sadalmelek	5° ♓
Acubens	12° ♌	Formalhaut	13° ♓
Alphard	17° ♌	Scheat	15° ♓
Regulus	28° ♌	Alpheratz	25° ♓
Alkes	15° ♍	Polaris: Always at culmination	

APPENDIX E:
ECLIPTICAL DEGREES:
PTOLEMY'S METHOD VERSUS
THE MODERN SYSTEM

PTOLEMY'S ORIGINAL METHOD OF projecting a star to a position on the ecliptic is no longer used. In order for this method of projection to be reconsidered this appendix takes over 170 stars and gives, firstly, their position according to Ptolemy's original star catalogue; then the position of that star for the year 2000 C.E. using Ptolemy's method of projection from the poles of the ecliptic; and lastly, the position of the star for the year 2000 using the modern methods of projection via the equator.

Ptolemy's modern position is found by adding 25° 49' 23" to the original positions. Ptolemy's positions are all given to the nearest ten minutes. So 25/50 is added to the positions. The numbers after the proper names of the stars come from the *Yale Bright Star Catalogue* (fourth edition, D. Hoffleit and C. Jaschek, Yale University Observatory, 1982). Where Ptolemy's star position varies markedly from the modern position is most likely a scribal error or an actual error by Ptolemy.

Andromeda—Star Map 1 (p. 48)

Name	Location in Constellation	Ptolemy's Position 150 C.E.	Ptolemy's Position 2000 C.E.	Using Poles of Equator 2000 C.E.	Mag.
Almach 603	Above left foot	16° ♈ 50'	12° ♉ 40'	14° ♉ 13'	2.3
Alpheratz* 15	Navel of the horse	17° ♓ 50'	13° ♈ 40'	14° ♈ 18'	2.2
Mirach 337	Above the girdle	3° ♈ 50'	29° ♈ 40'	00° ♉ 24'	2.4

* Ptolemy lists this star as being in Pegasus.

Aquarius—Star Map 26 (p. 306)

Name	Location in Constellation	Ptolemy's Position 150 C.E.	Ptolemy's Position 2000 C.E.	Using Poles of Equator 2000 C.E.	Mag.
Albali 7950	Left hand	14° ♑ 40'	10° ♒ 30'	11° ♒ 42'	3.8
Sadalsuud 8232	Left shoulder	26° ♑ 30'	22° ♒ 20'	23° ♒ 23'	3.1
Sadalmelek 8414	Right shoulder	6° ♒ 20'	3° ♓ 10'	03° ♓ 45'	3.2
Skat 8709	Right shin	11° ♒ 40'	7° ♓ 30'	8° ♓ 51'	3.5
Sadalachbia 8518	Right forearm	9° ♒ 30'	5° ♓ 20'	6° ♓ 42'	4.0

Aquila—Star Map 2 (p. 56)

Name	Location in Constellation	Ptolemy's Position 150 C.E.	Ptolemy's Position 2000 C.E.	Using Poles of Equator 2000 C.E.	Mag.
Alshain 7602	The head	4° ♑ 50'	10° ♒ 40'	2° ♒ 24'	3.9
Altair 7557	The throat	3° ♑ 50'	29° ♑ 40'	1° ♒ 47'	0.9
Deneb Okab 7377	Edge of left wing	26° ♐ 00'	21° ♑ 50'	23° ♑ 37'	3.4
Dheneb 7235	Edge of left wing	22° ♐ 10'	18° ♑ 00'	19° ♑ 47'	3.0
Tarazed 7525	Tail	3° ♑ 10'	29° ♑ 00'	00° ♒ 55'	2.8

Aries—Star Map 17 (p. 224)

Name	Location in Constellation	Ptolemy's Position 150 C.E.	Ptolemy's Position 2000 C.E.	Using Poles of Equator 2000 C.E.	Mag.
Botein 951	Tail	23° ♈ 50'	19° ♉ 40'	20° ♉ 51'	4.5
Hamal 617	The head	10° ♈ 40'	6° ♉ 30'	7° ♉ 39'	2.2
Mesarthim 545	The horn	6° ♈ 40'	2° ♉ 30'	3° ♉ 11'	4.8
Sheratan 553	The horn	7° ♈ 40'	3° ♉ 30'	3° ♉ 58'	2.7

Auriga—Star Map 4 (p. 70)

Name	Location in Constellation	Ptolemy's Position 150 C.E.	Ptolemy's Position 2000 C.E.	Using Poles of Equator 2000 C.E.	Mag.
Capella 1708	Left shoulder	25° ♉ 00'	20° ♊ 50'	21° ♊ 51'	0.2
Menkalinan 2088	Right shoulder	2° ♊ 50'	28° ♊ 40'	29° ♊ 54'	Var

Bootes—Star Map 5 (p. 76)

Name	Location in Constellation	Ptolemy's Position 150 C.E.	Ptolemy's Position 2000 C.E.	Using Poles of Equator 2000 C.E.	Mag.
Arcturus 5340	Left hand	4° ♍ 10'	0° ♎ 00'	24° ♎ 13'	0.2
Izar 5506	Right thigh	0° ♎ 00'	25° ♎ 50'	28° ♎ 06'	2.7
Nekkar 5602	The head	26° ♍ 40'	22° ♎ 30'	24° ♎ 14'	3.6
Princeps 5681	Right shoulder	5° ♎ 40'	1° ♏ 30'	3° ♏ 08'	3.5
Seginus 5435	Left shoulder	19° ♍ 40'	15° ♎ 30'	17° ♎ 39'	3.0

Cancer—Star Map 20 (p. 253)

Name	Location in Constellation	Ptolemy's Position 150 C.E.	Ptolemy's Position 2000 C.E.	Using Poles of Equator 2000 C.E.	Mag.
Acubens 3572	South claw	16° ♋ 30'	12° ♌ 20'	13° ♌ 38'	4.3
Al Tarf 3249	Southern hind foot	7° ♋ 10'	3° ♌ 00'	4° ♌ 15'	3.8
Asellus Austral 3461	Southern Ass	11° ♋ 20'	7° ♌ 10'	8° ♌ 43'	4.2
Asellus Boreali 3449	Northern Ass	10° ♋ 20'	6° ♌ 10'	7° ♌ 32'	4.7

Canis Major—Star Map 6 (p. 80)

Name	Location in Constellation	Ptolemy's Position 150 C.E.	Ptolemy's Position 2000 C.E.	Using Poles of Equator 2000 C.E.	Mag.
Adara 2618	Under the belly	23° ♊ 40'	19° ♋ 30'	20° ♋ 46'	1.6
Aludra 2827	The tail	2° ♋ 10'	28° ♋ 00'	29° ♋ 32'	2.4
Mirzams 2294	The paw	11° ♊ 00'	6° ♋ 50'	7° ♋ 11'	2.0
Muliphein 2657	The neck	23° ♊ 20'	19° ♋ 10'	19° ♋ 36'	4.1
Sirius 2491	The face	17° ♊ 40'	13° ♋ 30'	14° ♋ 05'	-1.4
Wezen 2693	Left thigh	6° ♊ 40'	2° ♋ 30'	23° ♋ 24'	2.0

Canis Minor—Star Map 6 (p. 80)

Name	Location in Constellation	Ptolemy's Position 150 C.E.	Ptolemy's Position 2000 C.E.	Using Poles of Equator 2000 C.E.	Mag.
Gomeisa 2845	The neck	25° ♊ 00'	20° ♋ 50'	22° ♋ 11'	3.1
Procyon 2943	Hinder parts	29° ♊ 10'	25° ♋ 00'	25° ♋ 47'	0.5

Canes Venatici—Star Map 5 (p. 76)

Name	Location in Constellation	Ptolemy's Position 150 C.E.	Ptolemy's Position 2000 C.E.	Using Poles of Equator 2000 C.E.	Mag.
Asterion* 4785	Under the tail of the Great Bear	20° ♌ 10'	16° ♍ 00'	17° ♍ 42'	4.3
Cor Caroli† 4914	Under the tail of the Great Bear	27° ♌ 50'	23° ♍ 40'	24° ♍ 33'	2.9

* Ptolemy lists this star as being in the constellation Ursa Major.
† Ptolemy lists this star as being in the constellation Ursa Major.

Capricorn—Star Map 25 (p. 300)

Name	Location in Constellation	Ptolemy's Position 150 C.E.	Ptolemy's Position 2000 C.E.	Using Poles of Equator 2000 C.E.	Mag.
Armus 8060	The middle of the body	16° ♑ 40'	12° ♒ 30'	12° ♒ 43'	4.9
Bos 7822	The muzzle	8° ♑ 50'	4° ♒ 40'	5° ♒ 09'	5.0
Castra 8260	The horn	23° ♑ 20'	19° ♒ 10'	20° ♒ 11'	4.7
Dabih 7776	The eastern horn	7° ♑ 20'	3° ♒ 10'	4° ♒ 02'	3.2
Deneb Algedi 8322	The tail	26° ♑ 20'	22° ♒ 10'	23° ♒ 32'	3.0
Dorsum 8075	The back	16° ♑ 40'	12° ♒ 20'	13° ♒ 50'	4.2
Oculus 7814	The muzzle	8° ♑ 40'	4° ♒ 30'	4° ♒ 42'	5.2

Carina*—Star Map 3 (p. 63)

Name	Location in Constellation	Ptolemy's Position 150 C.E.	Ptolemy's Position 2000 C.E.	Using Poles of Equator 2000 C.E.	Mag.
Avior 3307	Lower keel	8° ♌ 30'	4° ♍ 20'	23° ♍ 07'	1.7
Canopus 2326	The oar	17° ♊ 10'	13° ♋ 00'	14° ♋ 58'	-0.9

* All stars of Carina were in the constellation Argo.

Cassiopeia—Star Map 1 (p. 48)

Name	Location in Constellation	Ptolemy's Position 150 C.E.	Ptolemy's Position 2000 C.E.	Using Poles of Equator 2000 C.E.	Mag.
Achird 219	The girdle	13° ♈ 00'	8° ♉ 50'	10° ♉ 14'	3.6
Caph 21	The back of the chair	7° ♈ 50'	3° ♉ 40'	5° ♉ 07'	2.4
Rucha 403	The knees	20° ♈ 40'	16° ♉ 30'	17° ♉ 55'	2.8
Schedar 168	The breast	10° ♈ 50'	6° ♉ 40'	7° ♉ 47'	2.5

Centaurus—Star Map 7 (p. 98)

Name	Location in Constellation	Ptolemy's Position 150 C.E.	Ptolemy's Position 2000 C.E.	Using Poles of Equator 2000 C.E.	Mag.
Agena 5267	Left knee	24° ♎ 10'	20° ♏ 00'	23° ♏ 46'	0.9
Menkent 5288	Right shoulder	15° ♎ 40'	11° ♏ 30'	12° ♏ 18'	2.3
Toliman 5459	Right hoof	8° ♏ 20'	4° ♐ 10'	29° ♏ 28'	0.1

Cepheus—Star Map 1 (p. 48)

Name	Location in Constellation	Ptolemy's Position 150 C.E.	Ptolemy's Position 2000 C.E.	Using Poles of Equator 2000 C.E.	Mag.
Alderamin 8162	Right shoulder	16° ♓ 40'	12° ♈ 30'	12° ♈ 46'	2.6
Alphirk 8238	Under the belt	7° ♈ 20'	3° ♈ 10'	5° ♉ 33'	3.3
Alrai 8974	Left foot	3° ♉ 00'	28° ♉ 50'	0° ♊ 06'	3.4

Cetus—Star Map 8 (p. 105)

Name	Location in Constellation	Ptolemy's Position 150 C.E.	Ptolemy's Position 2000 C.E.	Using Poles of Equator 2000 C.E.	Mag.
Deneb Kaitos 188				2° ♈ 34'	2.2
Kaddaljidhma 804	The mouth	12° ♈ 40'	8° ♉ 30'	9° ♉ 25'	3.6
Menkar 911	The jaw	17° ♈ 40'	13° ♉ 30'	14° ♉ 19'	2.8
Mira 681	The body	not listed		1° ♉ 31'	Var

Columba*—Star Map 6 (p. 80)

Name	Location in Constellation	Ptolemy's Position 150 C.E.	Ptolemy's Position 2000 C.E.	Using Poles of Equator 2000 C.E.	Mag.
Phact 1956	Below the hind feet	26° ♉ 00'	21° ♊ 50'	22° ♊ 10'	2.8
Wazn 2040	Below the hind feet	29° ♉ 00'	24° ♊ 50'	26° ♊ 25'	3.2

* Ptolemy listed the two stars of Columba as being in Canis Major.

Corona Borealis—Star Map 11 (p. 143)

Name	Location in Constellation	Ptolemy's Position 150 C.E.	Ptolemy's Position 2000 C.E.	Using Poles of Equator 2000 C.E.	Mag.
Alphecca 5793	In the crown	14° ♎ 40'	10° ♏ 30'	12° ♏ 17'	2.3
Nusakan 5747	Western edge of crown	11° ♎ 40'	7° ♏ 40'	9° ♏ 06'	3.7

Corvus—Star Map 12 (p. 149)

Name	Location in Constellation	Ptolemy's Position 150 C.E.	Ptolemy's Position 2000 C.E.	Using Poles of Equator 2000 C.E.	Mag.
Alchita 4623	In the beak	15° ♍ 20'	11° ♎ 10'	12° ♎ 14'	4.2
Algorab 4757	The wing	16° ♍ 40'	12° ♎ 30'	13° ♎ 26'	3.1
Kraz 4786	The foot	20° ♍ 30'	16° ♎ 20'	17° ♎ 21'	2.8

Crater—Star Map 12 (p. 149)

Name	Location in Constellation	Ptolemy's Position 150 C.E.	Ptolemy's Position 2000 C.E.	Using Poles of Equator 2000 C.E.	Mag.
Alkes 4287	The base of the bowl	26° ♌ 20'	22° ♍ 10'	23° ♍ 41'	4.2
Labrum 4382	Middle of the bowl	0° ♍ 00'	25° ♍ 50'	26° ♍ 41'	3.8

Cygnus—Star Map 2 (p. 56)

Name	Location in Constellation	Ptolemy's Position 150 C.E.	Ptolemy's Position 2000 C.E.	Using Poles of Equator 2000 C.E.	Mag.
Albireo 7417	The beak	4° ♑ 30'	0° ♒ 20'	1° ♒ 14'	3.2
Deneb Adige 7924	The tail	9° ♒ 10'	5° ♓ 00'	5° ♓ 19'	1.3
Gienah 7949	Left wing	0° ♒ 50'	26° ♒ 40'	27° ♒ 44'	2.6
Sador 7796	The breast	28° ♑ 30'	24° ♒ 20'	24° ♒ 49'	2.3

Delphinus—Star Map 2 (p. 56)

Name	Location in Constellation	Ptolemy's Position 150 C.E.	Ptolemy's Position 2000 C.E.	Using Poles of Equator 2000 C.E.	Mag.
Rotanev 7882	Western side of body	18° ♑ 30'	14° ♒ 20'	16° ♒ 19'	3.7
Sualocin 7906	Western side of body	20° ♑ 10'	16° ♒ 00'	17° ♒ 22'	3.9

Draco—Star Map 9 (p. 134)

Name	Location in Constellation	Ptolemy's Position 150 C.E.	Ptolemy's Position 2000 C.E.	Using Poles of Equator 2000 C.E.	Mag.
Rastaban 6536	The eye	13° ♏ 10'	9° ♐ 00'	11° ♐ 56'	3.0
Dziban 6636	In the fourth coil	13° ♊ 20'	9° ♋ 10'	13° ♋ 51'	4.9
Edasich 5744	In the last coil	12° ♍ 40'	8° ♎ 30'	4° ♎ 56'	3.5
Etamin 6705	Above the head	29° ♏ 40'	25° ♐ 30'	27° ♐ 56'	2.4
Grumium 6688	The jaw	27° ♏ 20'	23° ♐ 10'	24° ♐ 43'	3.9
Kuma 6554	The mouth	11° ♏ 50'	7° ♐ 40'	10° ♐ 17'	5.0
Nodus I 6396	In the fourth coil	8° ♍ 20'	4° ♎ 10'	3° ♎ 23'	3.2
Nodus II 7310	In the first coil	20° ♓ 30'	16° ♈ 20'	17° ♈ 09'	3.2
Thuban 5291	The tail	11° ♌ 10'	7° ♍ 00'	7° ♍ 27'	3.6
Tyl 7582	In the second coil	7° ♈ 40'	3° ♉ 30'	2° ♉ 42'	4.0

Eridanus—Star Map 10 (p. 139)

Name	Location in Constellation	Ptolemy's Position 150 C.E.	Ptolemy's Position 2000 C.E.	Using Poles of Equator 2000 C.E.	Mag.
Acamar 897	The end of the river	0° ♈ 10'	26° ♈ 00'	23° ♈ 16'	3.4
Achernar 472	The modern end of the river	not listed		15° ♓ 18'	0.6
Zaurak 1231	Midway along the river	27° ♈ 00'	22° ♉ 50'	23° ♉ 52'	3.2

Gemini—Star Map 19 (p. 244)

Name	Location in Constellation	Ptolemy's Position 150 C.E.	Ptolemy's Position 2000 C.E.	Using Poles of Equator 2000 C.E.	Mag.
Alhena 2421	Left heel of eastern twin	12° ♊ 00'	7° ♋ 50'	9° ♋ 06'	1.9
Castor 2891	The head of the western twin	23° ♊ 20'	19° ♋ 10'	20° ♋ 14'	1.6
Mebsuta 2473	Left knee of western twin	13° ♊ 00'	8° ♋ 50'	9° ♋ 56'	3.2
Pollux 2990	The head of the eastern twin	26° ♊ 40'	22° ♋ 30'	23° ♋ 13'	1.2
Tejat Posterior 2286	In the foot of the western twin	8° ♊ 30'	4° ♋ 20'	5° ♋ 18'	3.2
Wasat 2777	Left testicle of eastern twin	21° ♊ 40'	17° ♋ 30'	18° ♋ 31'	3.5

Grus*

Name	Location in Constellation	Ptolemy's Position 150 C.E.	Ptolemy's Position 2000 C.E.	Using Poles of Equator 2000 C.E.	Mag.
Alnair 8425	The tail of the Southern Fish	20° ♑ 10'	16° ♒ 00'	15° ♒ 53'	2.2

* Ptolemy allocated the stars of Grus to Piscis Australis.

Hercules—Star Map 11 (p. 143)

Name	Location in Constellation	Ptolemy's Position 150 C.E.	Ptolemy's Position 2000 C.E.	Using Poles of Equator 2000 C.E.	Mag.
Kornephoros 6148	Right shoulder	3° ♏ 40'	29° ♏ 30'	1° ♐ 04'	2.8
Maasym 6526	In the left arm	22° ♏ 00'	17° ♐ 50'	19° ♐ 53'	4.5
Ras Algethi 6406	The head	17° ♏ 40'	13° ♐ 30'	16° ♐ 05'	Var
Sarin 6410	Left shoulder	16° ♏ 40'	12° ♐ 30'	14° ♐ 45'	3.2

Hydra—Star Map 12 (p. 149)

Name	Location in Constellation	Ptolemy's Position 150 C.E.	Ptolemy's Position 2000 C.E.	Using Poles of Equator 2000 C.E.	Mag.
Alphard 3748	The heart of the Serpent	00° ♌ 00'	25° ♌ 50'	27° ♌ 16'	2.2

Leo—Star Map 21 (p. 260)

Name	Location in Constellation	Ptolemy's Position 150 C.E.	Ptolemy's Position 2000 C.E.	Using Poles of Equator 2000 C.E.	Mag.
Adhafera 4031	The throat	0° ♌ 10'	26° ♌ 00'	27° ♌ 33'	3.6
Al Jabhah 3975	The throat	0° ♌ 40'	26° ♌ 30'	27° ♌ 54'	3.6
Algieba 4057	The throat	2° ♌ 10'	28° ♌ 00'	29° ♌ 36'	2.6
Alterf 3773	The mouth	21° ♋ 10'	17° ♌ 00'	17° ♌ 52'	4.5
Denebola 4534	The tip of the tail	24° ♌ 30'	20° ♍ 20'	21° ♍ 36'	2.2
Ras Elased Aust. 3873	The head	24° ♋ 10'	20° ♌ 00'	20° ♌ 42'	3.1
Regulus 3982	The heart of the Lion	2° ♌ 30'	26° ♌ 20'	29° ♌ 42'	1.3
Zosma 4357	The back	14° ♌ 10'	10° ♍ 00'	11° ♍ 18'	2.6

Lepus—Star Map 6 (p. 80)

Name	Location in Constellation	Ptolemy's Position 150 C.E.	Ptolemy's Position 2000 C.E.	Using Poles of Equator 2000 C.E.	Mag.
Arneb 1865	The middle of the body	25° ♉ 50'	21° ♊ 40'	21° ♊ 23'	2.7

Libra*—Star Map 23 (p. 278)

Name	Location in Constellation	Ptolemy's Position 150 C.E.	Ptolemy's Position 2000 C.E.	Using Poles of Equator 2000 C.E.	Mag.
Zuben Elakrab 5787	Middle of northern claw	27° ♎ 50'	23° ♏ 40'	25° ♏ 07'	4.0
Zuben Elgenubi 5531	End of the southern claw	18° ♎ 00'	13° ♏ 50'	15° ♏ 04'	2.9
Zuben Eschamali 5685	End of the northern claw	22° ♎ 10'	18° ♏ 00'	19° ♏ 21'	2.7

* Libra was defined as the Claws of the Scorpion.

Lyra—Star Map 2 (p. 56)

Name	Location in Constellation	Ptolemy's Position 150 C.E.	Ptolemy's Position 2000 C.E.	Using Poles of Equator 2000 C.E.	Mag.
Sheliak 7106	In the crossbar of the Lyre	21° ♐ 00'	16° ♑ 50'	18° ♑ 52'	Var
Wega 7001	In the shell of the Lyre	17° ♐ 20'	13° ♑ 10'	15° ♑ 17'	0.1

Ophiuchus—Star Map 13 (p. 159)

Name	Location in Constellation	Ptolemy's Position 150 C.E.	Ptolemy's Position 2000 C.E.	Using Poles of Equator 2000 C.E.	Mag.
Han 6175	Left knee	12° ♏ 10'	8° ♐ 00'	9° ♐ 13'	2.7
Kelb Alrai 6603	The right shoulder	28° ♏ 00'	23° ♐ 50'	25° ♐ 19'	2.9
Ras Alhague 6556	The head	24° ♏ 50'	20° ♐ 10'	22° ♐ 26'	2.1
Yed Posterior 6075	The left hand	6° ♏ 00'	1° ♐ 50'	3° ♐ 30'	3.3
Yed Prior 6056	The left hand	5° ♏ 00'	0° ♐ 50'	2° ♐ 17'	3.0

Orion—Star Map 14 (p. 164)

Name	Location in Constellation	Ptolemy's Position 150 C.E.	Ptolemy's Position 2000 C.E.	Using Poles of Equator 2000 C.E.	Mag.
Alinlam 1903	In the middle of the belt	27° ♉ 20'	23° ♊ 10'	23° ♊ 27'	1.8
Alnitak 1948	In the belt	28° ♉ 10'	24° ♊ 00'	24° ♊ 41'	2.0
Bellatrix 1790	Left shoulder	24° ♉ 00'	19° ♊ 50'	20° ♊ 56'	1.7
Betelgeuse 1698	Right shoulder	2 ° ♊ 00'	27° ♊ 50'	28° ♊ 45'	Var
Meissa 1879	The head	27° ♉ 00'	22° ♊ 50'	23° ♊ 42'	3.7
Mintaka 1852	In the belt	25° ♉ 20'	21° ♊ 10'	22° ♊ 24'	2.5
Rigel 1713	The left foot	19° ♉ 50'	15° ♊ 40'	16° ♊ 49'	0.3
Saiph 2004	The right knee	0° ♊ 10'	26° ♊ 00'	26° ♊ 24'	2.2

Pegasus—Star Map 15 (p. 178)

Name	Location in Constellation	Ptolemy's Position 150 C.E.	Ptolemy's Position 2000 C.E.	Using Poles of Equator 2000 C.E.	Mag.
Algenib 8739	End of the wing	12° ♓ 10'	8° ♈ 00'	9° ♈ 09'	2.9
Kerb 8880	In the body under the wing	4° ♓ 30'	0°·♈ 20'	1° ♈ 02'	4.6
Markab 8781	Broad of the back	26° ♒ 40'	22° ♓ 30'	23° ♓ 28'	2.6
Matar 8650	Right knee	29° ♒ 00'	24° ♓ 50'	25° ♓ 42'	3.1
Scheat 8775	Right shoulder	2° ♓ 10'	28° ♓ 00'	29° ♓ 22'	2.6

Perseus—Star Map 1 (p. 48)

Name	Location in Constellation	Ptolemy's Position 150 C.E.	Ptolemy's Position 2000 C.E.	Using Poles of Equator 2000 C.E.	Mag.
Algol 936	The Gorgon's head	29° ♈ 40'	25° ♉ 30'	26° ♉ 10'	Var
Capulus*	The right hand	26° ♈ 40'	24° ♉ 00'	24° ♉ 11'	4.4
Miram 834	The right elbow	1° ♉ 10'	27° ♉ 00'	28° ♉ 42'	3.9
Mirfak 1017	The right side of the body	4° ♉ 50'	0° ♊ 40'	2° ♊ 04'	1.9
Misam 941	Left elbow	0° ♉ 30'	26° ♉ 20'	27° ♉ 41'	4.0

* Capulus is a nebula.

Pisces—Star Map 27 (p. 311)

Name	Location in Constellation	Ptolemy's Position 150 C.E.	Ptolemy's Position 2000 C.E.	Using Poles of Equator 2000 C.E.	Mag.
Al Pherg 437	In the north cord	00° ♈ 40'	26° ♈ 30'	26° ♈ 48'	3.7
Al Rescha 596	The knot of the two cords	2° ♈ 30'	28° ♈ 20'	29° ♈ 22'	3.9

Piscis Australis—Star Map 16 (p. 195)

Name	Location in Constellation	Ptolemy's Position 150 C.E.	Ptolemy's Position 2000 C.E.	Using Poles of Equator 2000 C.E.	Mag.
Formalhaut 8728	The mouth	7° ♒ 00'	2° ♓ 50'	6° ♓ 02'	3.5

Sagittarius—Star Map 24 (p. 293)

Name	Location in Constellation	Ptolemy's Position 150 C.E.	Ptolemy's Position 2000 C.E.	Using Poles of Equator 2000 C.E.	Mag.
Albaldah 7264	The head	19° ♐ 10'	15° ♑ 00'	16° ♑ 14'	3.0
Alnasl 6746	Tip of the arrow	4° ♐ 30'	0° ♑ 20'	1° ♑ 15'	3.1
Ascella 7194	In the armpit	16° ♐ 20'	14° ♑ 10'	13° ♑ 37'	2.7
Facies 7116	The eye	15° ♐ 10'	11° ♑ 10'	8° ♑ 17'	5.9
Kaus Australis 6879	Southern part of the bow	8° ♐ 00'	3° ♑ 50'	5° ♑ 04'	2.0
Kaus Borealis 6913	Northern part of the bow	9° ♐ 00'	4° ♑ 50'	6° ♑ 18'	2.9
Kaus Medius 6859	The grip of the left hand	7° ♐ 40'	3° ♑ 30'	4° ♑ 34'	2.8
Rukbat 7348*	Left knee	17° ♐ 00'	12° ♑ 50'	16° ♑ 37'	4.1

* The NASA Ptolemy Star Catalog lists this Yale number to Rukbat as in dispute. Star number 7292 seems a better candidate. Ptolemy located this star at 20° ♐ 00', thus bringing its modern position to 15° ♑ 50'.

Scorpius*—Star Map 23 (p. 278)

Name	Location in Constellation	Ptolemy's Position 150 C.E.	Ptolemy's Position 2000 C.E.	Using Poles of Equator 2000 C.E.	Mag.
Acrab 5984	The forehead	6° ♏ 20'	2° ♐ 10'	3° ♐ 10'	2.9
Antares 6134	The heart of the Scorpion	12° ♏ 40'	8° ♐ 30'	9° ♐ 45'	1.2
Dschubba 5953	The forehead	5° ♏ 40'	1° ♐ 30'	2° ♐ 33'	2.5
Sargas 6553	The 5th joint	28° ♏ 10'	24° ♐ 00'	25° ♐ 35'	2.0
Shaula 6527	The 7th joint	27° ♏ 30'	23° ♐ 20'	24° ♐ 34'	1.7

* Aculeus and Acumen are two clusters in the sting of the Scorpion. Ptolemy does not include them in the constellation and only lists one nebula that the NASA Ptolemy Star Catalog has some doubt in allocating.

Taurus—Star Map 18 (p. 230)

Name	Location in Constellation	Ptolemy's Position 150 C.E.	Ptolemy's Position 2000 C.E.	Using Poles of Equator 2000 C.E.	Mag.
Ain 1409	The northern eye	11° ♉ 50'	7° ♊ 10'	8° ♊ 27'	3.6
Alcyone 1165	In the Pleiades, the shoulder	3° ♉ 40'	29° ♉ 30'	29° ♉ 59'	3.0
Aldebaran 1457	In the Hyades, the southern eye	12° ♉ 40'	8° ♊ 40'	9° ♊ 47'	1.1
El Nath* 1791	Tip of the northern horn	25° ♉ 40'	21° ♊ 30'	22° ♊ 34'	1.8
Hyadum II 1373	In the face	10° ♉ 20'	6° ♊ 10'	6° ♊ 52'	3.9

*El Nath is also the foot of the Charioteer, Auriga.

Ursa Major—Star Map 9 (p. 134)

Name	Location in Constellation	Ptolemy's Position 150 C.E.	Ptolemy's Position 2000 C.E.	Using Poles of Equator 2000 C.E.	Mag.
Alioth 4905	Base of the tail	12° ♌ 10'	8° ♍ 00'	8° ♍ 56'	1.7
Alkaid 5191	Tip of the tail	29° ♌ 50'	25° ♌ 40'	26° ♍ 55'	1.9
Dubhe 4301	On the back of the bear	17° ♋ 40'	13° ♌ 30'	15° ♌ 12'	2.0
Megrez 4660	Beginning of the tail	3° ♌ 10'	29° ♌ 00'	1° ♍ 04'	3.4
Merak 4295	On the flank	22° ♋ 10'	18° ♌ 00'	19° ♌ 26'	2.4
Phecda 4554	The left thigh	3° ♌ 00'	28° ♌ 50'	0° ♍ 28'	2.5
Talitha 3569	Left forepaw	5° ♋ 30'	1° ♌ 10'	2° ♌ 48'	3.1
Tania Borealis 4033	Left hindpaw	22° ♋ 40'	18° ♌ 30'	19° ♌ 33'	3.5

Ursa Minor—Star Map 9 (p. 134)

Name	Location in Constellation	Ptolemy's Position 150 C.E.	Ptolemy's Position 2000 C.E.	Using Poles of Equator 2000 C.E.	Mag.
Kochab 5563	The shoulder	17° ♋ 30'	13° ♌ 20'	13° ♌ 19'	2.2
Pherkad 5735	Right elbow	26° ♋ 10'	22° ♌ 00'	21° ♌ 36'	3.1
Polaris 424	The tip of the tail	0° ♊ 10'	26° ♊ 00'	28° ♊ 34'	2.1
Yildun 6789	In the tail	2° ♊ 30'	28° ♊ 20'	1° ♋ 12'	4.4

Virgo—Star Map 22 (p. 271)

Name	Location in Constellation	Ptolemy's Position 150 C.E.	Ptolemy's Position 2000 C.E.	Using Poles of Equator 2000 C.E.	Mag.
Heze 5107	The right buttock	24° ♍ 50'	20° ♎ 40'	21° ♎ 52'	3.4
Khambalia 5359	The left foot	10° ♎ 00'	5° ♏ 50'	6° ♏ 56'	4.6
Spica 5056	The left hand	26° ♍ 40'	22° ♎ 30'	23° ♎ 50'	1.2
Vindemiatrix 4932	The right wing	12° ♍ 10'	8° ♎ 00'	9° ♎ 56'	3.0
Zavijava 4540	The left wing	29° ♌ 00'	24° ♍ 50'	27° ♍ 09'	3.8

APPENDIX F: BIRTH DATA

WHEN WORKING WITH FIXED STARS, AN astrologer does not need accurate birth data, for most of the paran contacts are potential connections to a chart rather than actual connections occurring at birth. However, the following is a list of the birth data and sources for all of the examples used in the text. The major source of the data is Astrolabe—the Blackwell Data Set that is available through them. This data is simply marked "Blackwell." All birth times use the convention of the twenty-four hour clock.

Addey, John: 15 June, 1920. 8:15 BST. Barnsley, England. 53N33, 1W29. Blackwell.

Ali, Muhammad: 17 January, 1942. 18:30 CST. Louisville, USA. 38N15, 85W46. Blackwell.

Armstrong, Neil: 5 August, 1930. 05:41 EST. Washington Twp. 40N34, 84W15. Blackwell.

Anastasia of Russia: 17 June 1901. 23:00 LMT. Peterhof, Russia. 59N53, 29E54. Lois Rodden Astro Data II AFA 1988. DD.

Blake, William: 28 November, 1757. 19:34 GMT. London, England. 51N32, 00W07. Blackwell.

Blavatsky, Madam: 12 August, 1831. 2:17 LMT. Ekaterionoslav, Russia. 48N27, 35E01. Lois Rodden, Profiles of Women AFA 1979. A.

Campbell, Joseph: 26 March, 1904. 19:25 EST. New York, NY, USA.. 40N45, 73W57. Lois Rodden Astro Data III AFA 1986. A.

Carroll, Lewis: 27 January, 1832. 03:55 GMT. Daresbury, England. 53N21, 02W38. Blackwell.

Castro, Fidel: 13 August, 1926. 13:00 EST. Colonia Biran, Oriente, Cuba. 20N33, 75W55. Lois Rodden Astro Data III AFA 1986. A.

Chamberlain, Azaria: 11 June, 1980. 13:15 AEST. Mount Isa, Australia. 20S44, 139E30. Lois Rodden Astro Data V AFA 1992. A.

Chaplin, Charlie: 16 April, 1889. 20:00 GMT. London, England. 51N31, 00W06. Lois Rodden Astro Data II. AFA 1988. AA.

Charles, Prince: 14 November, 1948. 21:14 GMT. London, England. 51N30, 00W07. Blackwell.

Christie, Agatha: 15 September, 1890. 4:00 GMT. Torquay, England. 50N28, 3W30. Blackwell.

Cook, Captain James: 27 October, 1728. Marton-in-Cleveland, Yorkshire, England. No time. Encyclopaedia Britannica.

Coward, Noel: 16 December, 1899. 02:30 GMT. Teddington, England. 51N25, 00W20. Blackwell.

Cromwell, Oliver: 5 May, 1599. 03:00 LMT. Huntingdon, England. 51N51, 00W12. Blackwell.

da Vinci, Leonardo: 14 April, 1452. 21:03 GMT. Anchiano, Italy. 43N43, 11E00. Blackwell.

Dean, James: 8 Febuary, 1931. 02:00 CST. Marion, IN, USA. 40N32, 85W40. Blackwell.

Diana, Princess: 1 July, 1961. 19:45 BST. Sandringham, England. 52N50, 00E30. Lois Rodden Astro Data III AFA 1986. A.

Dickens, Charles: 2 February, 1812. 00.05 GMT. Landport, England. 50.47N, 1.05W. Blackwell.

Dreyfus, Alfred: 9 October, 1859. 15:00 LMT. Mulhouse, France. 47N45, 7E20. Lois Rodden Astro Data V AFA 1992. AA.

Dunston, Donald: 21 September, 1926. 6:00 NZ. Suva, Fiji. 18S08, 178E25 (my own files).

Earhart, Amelia: 24 July, 1897. 23:30 CST. Atchison, KS,USA. 39N34, 95W07. Blackwell.

Edward VIII of England: 23 June, 1894. 21:55 GMT. Richmond, England. 51N27, 00W18. Blackwell.

Einstein, Albert: 14 March,1879. 10:50 GMT. Ulm, Germany. 48N30, 10E00. Blackwell.

Eliot, George: 22 November, 1819. 05:06 GMT. Chilvers Coton, England. 52N15, 01W35. Blackwell.

Ford, Henry: 30 July, 1863. 19:32 GMT. Dearborn, MI, USA. 42N19, 83W11. Blackwell.

Freud, Sigmund: 6 May, 1856. 17:17 GMT. Freiberg, Moravia. 49N37, 18E08. Blackwell.

Galilei, Galileo: 15 Feburary, 1564. 14:32 GMT. Pisa, Italy. 43N43, 10E24. Blackwell.

Gein, Edward: 27 August,1906. 23:30 CST. N. La Crosse, WI, USA. 43N48, 91W15. Lois Rodden Astro Data V AFA 1992. AA.

Glenn, John: 18 July, 1921. 16:00 CDT. Cambridge, OH, USA. 40N02, 81W35. Blackwell.

Goering, Hermann: 12 January, 1893. 04:00 CET. Rosenheim, Germany. 47N51, 12E06. Blackwell.

Graves, Robert: 24 July, 1895. 17:00 GMT. Wimbledon, England. 51N25, 00W13. Lois Rodden Astro Data II AFA 1988. D.

Hawke, Bob: 9 December, 1929. 3:30 ACST. Bordertown, South Australia. 36S19, 140E47. (His information to Australian astrologers.)

Hearst, Patty: 20 February, 1954. 18:01 PST. San Francisco, USA. 37N47, 122W25. Mackay Data set from Astrolabe.

Henry VIII: 7 July, 1491. 10:40 LMT. Greenwich, England. 51N29, 00W00. Lois Rodden Astro Data II AFA 1988. AA.

Hitler, Adolf: 20 April, 1889. 17:37 GMT. Braunau am Inn, Austria. 48N15, 13E02. Blackwell.

Joan of Arc: 6 January, 1412. 17:11 GMT. Domremy, France. 46N26, 05E40. Blackwell.

John Paul II: 18 May, 1920. 12:00 CET. Wadowice, Poland. 49N53, 19E30. Blackwell.

Jones, Jim: 13 May, 1931. 22:00 CST. Lynn, IN, USA. 40N03, 84W56. Lois Rodden Astro Data II AFA 1988. A.

Jung, Carl: 26 July, 1875. 19:26 GMT. Kesswil, Switzerland. 47N36, 9E20. Lois Rodden Astro Data II AFA 1988. DD.

Kant, Immanuel: 22 April, 1724. 02:16. GMT. Konigsberg, Germany. 50N05, 10E34. Blackwell.

Kelly, Grace: 12 November, 1929. 05:31 EST. Philadelphia, PA, USA. 39N57, 75W10. Lois Rodden Profiles of Women. AFA 1979.

Kennedy, Jackie: 28 July,1929. 14:30 EDT. Southhampton, NY, USA. 40N53, 72W23. Lois Rodden Profiles of Women. AFA 1979.

Kennedy, John F.: 29 May, 1917. 15:00 EST Brookline, MA, USA. 42N19, 71W08. Blackwell.

Kepler, Johannes: 27 December, 1571. 14:01 GMT. Weil der Stadt, Germany. 48N44. 08E53. Blackwell.

King , Martin Luther: 15 January, 1929. 12:00 CST. Atlanta, GA, USA. 33N45, 84W23. Blackwell.

King, Stephen: 21 September, 1947. 01:30 EDT. Portland, ME, USA. 43N39, 70W16. Lois Rodden Astro Data III. A.

Kissinger, Henry: 27 May, 1923. 5:30 CET. Fuerth, Germany. 49N29, 11E00. Blackwell.

Lennon, John: 9 October, 1940. 18:30 BST. Liverpool, England. 53N25, 02W58. Blackwell.

Lincoln, Abraham: 12 Febuary, 1809. 12:40 GMT near Hodgenville, KY, USA. 37N35, 85W45. Blackwell.

Machiavelli, Niccolo: 2 May, 1469. 22:23:07 GMT. Florence, Italy. 43N46, 11E15. Blackwell.

Mandela, Nelson: 18 July, 1918. 14:54 EET. Umtata, South Africa. 31S35, 28E47. Considerations Vol. X no. 2. April 1995.

Marx, Karl: 5 May, 1818. 01:33:24 GMT. Trier, Germany. 49N46, 6E39. Blackwell.

Michelangelo: 6 March, 1475. 01:00:30 GMT. Caprese, Italy. 43N39 11E59. Blackwell.

Monroe, Marilyn: 1st June, 1926. 09:30 PST. Hollywood, CA, USA. 34N06, 118W21. Blackwell.

Mother Teresa: 27 August, 1910. 14:25 CEST. Skopje, Yugoslavia. 41N59, 21E26. Lois Rodden Astro Data III AFA 1986. C.

Mozart, Wolfgang Amadeus: 27 January, 1756. 19:21 GMT. Salzburg, Austria. 47N48, 13E03. Blackwell.

Mussolini, Benito: 29 July, 1883. 13:10:25 GMT. Dovia, Italy. 44N15, 12E12. Blackwell.

Newton, Sir Isaac: 4 January, 1643. 01:38 GMT. Woolsthorpe, England. 52N48, 00W37. Blackwell.

Nicholson, Jack: 22 April, 1937. 11:00 EST. Neptune, NJ, USA. 40N13, 74W01. Lois Rodden Astro Data II AFA 1988. A.

Olivier, Laurence: 22 May, 1907. 05.00 GMT. Dorking, England. 51N14, 00W20. Blackwell.

Picasso, Pablo: 25 October, 1881. 23:15 LMT. Malaga, Spain. 36N43, 04W25. Lois Rodden Astro Data II AFA 1988. DD.

Rajneesh, Bhagwan Shree: 11 December, 1931. 17:13 IST. Gadarwara, India. 22N55, 78E47. Unsourced. Time not used.

Reeve, Christopher: 25 September, 1952. 03:30 EDT New York, NY, USA. 40N45, 73W57. Lois Rodden Astro Data II AFA 1988. A.

Shatner, William: 22 March, 1931. 04:00 EST. Montreal, Canada. 45N31, 73W34. Lois Rodden Astro Data III AFA 1986. A.

Shaw, George Bernard: 26 July, 1856. 01:05 GMT. Dublin, Ireland. 53N20, 06W15. Blackwell.

Shelley, Mary: 30 August, 1797. 23:20 GMT. London, England. 51N31, 00W06. Blackwell.

Simpson, O. J.: 9 July, 1947. 8:08 PST. San Francisco, CA, USA 37N47, 122W26. Lois Rodden Astro Data II AFA 1988. AA.

Superman: 12 February, 1940. 17:15 EST. New York, NY, USA. 40N45, 73W57 Lois Rodden Astro Data III AFA 1986. A.

Taylor, Elizabeth: 27 Feburary, 1932. 02:00 GMT. London, England. 51N31, 00W06. Blackwell.

Tennyson, Alfred, Lord: 6 August, 1809. 00:06:28 GMT. Somersby, England. 52N55, 0W22. Blackwell.

Thatcher, Margaret: 13 October, 1925. 09:00 GMT. Grantham, England. 52N55, 00W39. Blackwell.

Tse-Tung, Mao: 26 December, 1893. 07:30 LMT. Siangton, China. 27N55, 112E47. Blackwell.

TWA Flight: 17 July, 1996. 20:02 EDT. New York, NY, USA. 40N40, 73W47. From newspapers at the time.

van Gogh, Vincent: 30 March, 1853. 10:41:20 GMT. Zundert, The Netherlands. 51N28, 4E40. Blackwell.

Verne, Jules: 8 Febuary, 1828. 12:20 GMT. Nantes, France. 47N13, 01W33. Blackwell.

Wordsworth, William: 7 April, 1770. 22:15:24. Cockermouth, England. 54N40, 3W21. Blackwell.

APPENDIX G:
STAR GUIDE

THIS STAR GUIDE IS DESIGNED TO ENABLE
you to find any star quickly, and to provide a short definition for each star.

BIBLIOGRAPHY

Al-Biruni. *The Book of Instruction in the Elements of the Art of Astrology.* Ramsey Wright, trans. London: R. Luzac, 1934.

Alexander, H. B. *"North American Mythology"* in *Mythology of All Races,* vol. 10. Boston, 1916.

Allen, Richard Hinckley. *Star Names: Their Lore and Meaning.* New York: Dover, 1963.

Anonymous of 379. *The Treatise on the Bright Fixed Stars.* Robert Schmidt, trans. Berkeley Springs, WV: Golden Hind Press, 1994.

Ashmand, J.M., trans. *Ptolemy's Tetrabiblos.* London: Foulsham, 1917.

Baring, A and Cashford, J. *The Myth of The Goddess.* London: Arkana, 1993.

Beck, Lewis White, ed. *Immanuel Kant Selections.* New York: Macmillan, 1988.

Bierlein, J. F. *Parallel Myths.* New York: Ballantine Books, 1994.

Blake, John F. *Astronomical Myths.* London, 1877.

Branley, Franklin M. *Experiments in Sky Watching.* London: Faber & Faber, 1962.

Brennan, Martin. *The Stars and the Stones.* London: Thames & Hudson, 1983.

Brewer, E. Cobham. *Brewer's Concise Dictionary of Phrase & Fable.* London: Cassell, 1992.

Budge, Wallis E. A., trans. *The Egyptian Book of the Dead.* New York: Dover, 1967.

———. *The Gods of the Egyptians,* 2 vols. New York: Dover, 1969.

Bulfinch, Thomas. *Myths of Greece and Rome.* New York: Penguin, 1979.

Caldecott, Moyra. *Women in Celtic Myth.* Rochester, VT: Destiny, 1992.

Campbell, Joseph. *The Hero with a Thousand Faces.* London: Paladin, 1988.

Chetwynd, Tom. *The Age of Myth.* London: Mandala, 1991.

———. *Dictionary of Sacred Myth.* London: Aquarian/Thorsons, 1994.

Cooper, Jason D. *Mithras.* York Beach, ME: Samuel Weiser, 1996.

Crowley, Aleister. *777 and Other Qabalistic Writings of Aleister Crowley.* York Beach, ME: Samuel Weiser, 1977.

Davidson, Norman. *Astronomy and the Imagination.* New York: Routledge & Kegan Paul, 1985.

Davies, W. V. *Egyptian Hieroglyphs.* London: Berkeley, 1987.

de Santillana, Giorgio, and von Dechend, Hertha. *Hamlet's Mill.* Boston: Nonpareil, 1977.

Dorotheus of Sidon. *Carmen Astrologicum.* David Pingree, trans. Mansfield, England: Ascella, 1993.

Durdin-Robertson, Lawrence. *The Year of the Goddess.* London: Aquarian, 1990.

Ebertin, Reinhold and Hoffman, Georg. *Fixed Stars and their Interpretation.* Tempe, AZ: AFA, 1971.

Ellis, P. B. *Dictionary of Celtic Mythology.* London: Constable, 1993.

Filsinger, Tomas J. *Manual Notes and Tables for the Map of the Universe.* Berkeley, CA: Celestial Arts, 1988.

Gantz, J., trans. *The Mabinogion.* London: Penguin, 1976.

Graves, Robert. *The Greek Myths.* 2 vols. London: Penguin, 1960.

———. *The White Goddess.* London: Faber & Faber, 1988.

Green, Miranda J. *Dictionary of Celtic Myth and Legend.* London: Thames & Hudson, 1992.

Greene, Liz. *The Astrology of Fate.* York Beach, ME: Samuel Weiser, 1984.

Gregory, Lady. *Gods and Fighting Men.* Gerrards Cross, England: Colin Smythe, 1970.

———. *Cuchulain of Muirthemne.* Gerrards Cross, England: Colin Smythe, 1990.

Grimal, Pierre. *The Dictionary of Classical Mythology.* A. R. Maxwell-Huslop, trans. Cambridge: Blackwell Reference, 1986.

Guerber, H. A. *The Myths of Greece and Rome.* London: Harrap, 1991.

Hawking, Stephen W. *A Brief History of Time.* New York: Bantam, 1988.

Hinnells, John R., ed. *The Penguin Dictionary of Religions.* London: Penguin, 1984.

Jackson, K. H. *A Celtic Miscellany.* London: Penguin, 1971.

Jobes, Gertrude and James. *Outer Space: Myths, Name Meanings, Calendars.* New York: Scarecrow, 1964.

Johnson, Robert A. *Owning Your Own Shadow.* San Francisco: HarperSanFrancisco, 1991.

Jones, Steve. *The Language of the Genes.* London: Flamingo, 1994.

Kinsella, Thomas. *The Tain.* Oxford: Oxford University Press, 1989.

Koltuv, Barbara Black. *The Book of Lilith.* York Beach, ME: Nicolas-Hays, 1986.

La Caille, N. Louis de. *A Catalogue of 9766 Stars in the Southern Hemisphere.* London, 1847.

Layard, John. *The Lady of the Hare.* Boston: Shambhala, 1988.

Levi-Strauss, Claude. *Anthropology and Myth.* Oxford: Basil Blackwell, 1984.

Lilly, William. *Christian Astrology.* London: Regulus, 1985.

Lockyer, Norman J. *The Dawn of Astronomy.* Kila, MT: Kessinger, 1992.

Luce, J. V. *An Introduction to Greek Philosophy.* London: Thames & Hudson, 1992.

Mackey, Samson A. *Mythological Astronomy of the Ancients.* Minneapolis: Wizard's Bookshelf, 1922.

Magnusson, Magnus. *BC—The Archaeology of the Bible Lands.* London: British Broadcasting Corporation, 1977.

Mair, A. W. and G. R., trans. *Callimachus, Lycophron, Aratus.* Cambridge: Harvard University Press, 1989.

Malin, Stuart. *The Greenwich Guide to Stars, Galaxies, and Nebulae.* London: George Philip, 1989.

Mann, A. T. *Sacred Architecture*. Shaftesbury, England: Element, 1993.

Mann, Christopher, prod. "The Great Pyramid." Documentary on BBC, 1994.

Ma'sar Abu. *The Abbreviation of the Introduction to Astrology*. K. Ch. Burnett and M. Yano, trans. New York: J. E. Brill, 1994.

Maternus, Firmicus the Mathesis. *Ancient Astrology: Theory and Practice*. Jean Rhys Bram, trans. Park Ridge, NJ: Noyes, 1975.

Mitchell, John. *At the Center of the World*. London: Thames & Hudson, 1994.

Murname, William J. *The Penguin Guide to Ancient Egypt*. London: Penguin, 1983.

New Larousse Encyclopedia of Mythology. London: Hamlyn, 1968.

Plato. *Critias*. Desmond Lee, trans. London: Penguin, 1977.

———. *Laws Book V*. Benjamin Jowett, trans. Electronic publication on internet.

———. *Timaeus*. Desmond Lee, trans. London: Penguin, 1977.

Poynder, Michael. *Pi in the Sky*. London: Rider, 1992.

Ptolemy, Claudius. *The Almagest*. Chicago: Britannica, Great Books of the World, 1985.

———. *The Phases of the Fixed Stars*. Robert Schmidt, trans. Berkeley Springs, WV: Golden Hind Press, 1994.

———. *Tetrabiblos*. Robert Schmidt, trans. Berkeley Springs, WV: Golden Hind Press, 1994.

Ramesey, William. *Astrology Restored*. 1653. Reprint: Adelaide, Australia: Adelaide Publication and Reprints, 1995.

Rigor, Joseph E. *The Power of Fixed Stars*. Hammond, IN: Astrology and Spiritual Center, 1978.

Robson, Vivian E. *The Fixed Stars and Constellations in Astrology*. York Beach, ME: Samuel Weiser, 1984.

Rodden, Lois M. *Profiles of Crime*. Yucaipa, CA: Data News Press, 1982.

———. *Profiles of Women*. Tempe, AZ: AFA, 1979.

Ronan, Colin A. *The Skywatcher's Handbook*. London: Corgi, 1985.

Room, Adrian. *Dictionary of Astronomical Names*. New York: Routledge, 1988.

Sarjeant, W.M.C. Eldon, ed. *The Astrologer's Guide: Anima Astrologiae*. London: Regulus, 1986.

Saulnier, S. *Observations on the Circular Zodiac of Denderah*. London, n.d.

Sellers, J. B. *The Death of the Gods in Ancient Egypt*. London: Penguin, 1992.

Settegast, Mary. *Plato Prehistorian*. New York: Lindisfarne, 1986.

Spence, Lewis. *The Mysteries of Britain*. North Hollywood, CA: Newcastle, 1993.

Stalley, R. F. *An Introduction to Plato's Laws*. Oxford: Basil Blackwell, 1983.

Stewart, R. J. *Celtic Gods, Celtic Goddesses*. London: Blandford, 1990.

Stott, Carole. *Celestial Charts: Antique Maps of the Heavens*. London: Studio Editions, 1991.

Tennant, Catherine. *The Box of Stars*. London: Chatto & Windus, 1993.

Von Hagen, V. W. *Ancient Sun Kingdoms of the Americas*. London: Thames & Hudson, 1962.

Walker, Barbara. *The Woman's Encyclopedia of Myths and Secrets*. San Francisco: HarperSanFrancisco, 1983.

Wilkinson, R. *Reading Egyptian Art*. London: Thames & Hudson, 1992.

INDEX

Bernadette Brady is a Fellow of the Federation of Australian Astrologers and was a member of the FAA Board of Examiners from 1986 to 1998. She is co-principal of Astro Logos, one of Australia's largest astrological schools dedicated to the education and qualification of practicing astrologers. Her previous publications are the astrological software package *Jigsaw* (Astrolabe) and *The Eagle and the Lark: A Textbook of Predictive Astrology* (Weiser, 1992) and various articles in astrological journals. In 1992 Brady was awarded the FAA's inaugural Southern Cross Award for Excellence in the Spoken and Written Word. In 1996 she was awarded the FAA's Southern Cross Award for Research, for her original work on Saros Cycles, Graphic Rectification, and Fixed Stars. She lives and works in Australia but has lectured in New Zealand, England, Ireland, Canada, Europe, and the United States. She has also lectured at the well-known United Astrology Congress held every three years in the United States.